Developments in Health Economics and Public Policy

Volume 13

Series Editors

H. E. Frech, Santa Barbara, CA, USA
Peter Zweifel, Zurich, Switzerland

More information about this series at http://www.springer.com/series/6039

Klaus Schmerler

Medical Tourism in Germany

Determinants of International Patients' Destination Choice

Springer

Klaus Schmerler
Martin Luther University Halle-Wittenberg
Halle (Saale), Sachsen-Anhalt
Germany

ISSN 0927-4987
Developments in Health Economics and Public Policy
ISBN 978-3-030-03987-5 ISBN 978-3-030-03988-2 (eBook)
https://doi.org/10.1007/978-3-030-03988-2

Library of Congress Control Number: 2018961404

This Springer imprint is published by the registered company Springer Nature Switzerland AG
The registered company address is: Gewerbestrasse 11, 6330 Cham, Switzerland

Foreword

This volume is a must-read for everyone who wants to be on top of the ongoing transition in health care, from a service different from all others protected by walls of national regulation to a tradable commodity subject to the forces of international competition. Klaus Schmerler, the author of this study, has a clear understanding of medical tourism as the harbinger of this transition. For decades, patients—to the dismay of the medical profession, social health insurers, and governments—have been migrating between domestic physicians in search of the treatment they prefer (or simply of a prescription or a report testifying their inability to work). Increasingly, however, they cross international borders, lured by both private clinics and public hospitals who seek to balance their accounts, being exposed to the pressures of prospective payment in many countries.

In this situation, viewing medical tourism as a form of interregional and international trade is an extremely helpful starting point for analysis. Its single special aspect is a high degree of product differentiation because persons with their characteristics rather than goods move, resulting in a contact with a service provider and a setting that match their preferences. Far from limiting his research to Germany, the author provides a wide range of international data on medical tourism flows. An overview shows that Asia lies at the center of medical tourism with, e.g., South Korea reporting 267,000 patients in 2014. However, his calculations based on inpatient and medical visa data arrive at similar numbers for Germany with Russia being the most important source country.

According to international trade theory, differences between foreign and domestic price induce arbitrage, with the lower-cost country becoming the exporting one (attracting medical tourists in the present context). As a striking example, the author cites the cost of a gastric bypass, which is between USD 25,000 and 48,000 in the United States (quite a range within the same country) as of 2012. The bypass can be obtained for USD 6000–11,000 in India and USD 15,000–26,000 in Singapore, a location that has built a reputation for quality. Of course, the net cost to the patient depends on the portability of health insurance, about which little is known outside the European Union (where it is subject to conditions). Heterogeneity of consumers, exporting firms (medical clinics in the present context), countries of origin, and impediments to trade are added to the basic model, resulting in a comprehensive relationship between exports (i.e., inbound medical tourism) and a host of determining factors.

In the case of Germany, the available data at the national level do not permit a full implementation of this theoretically appealing approach. In particular, price information is lacking for most source countries. It would have been extremely instructive to compare the estimated impact of price differentials with the well-known finding that domestic medical providers hardly compete on price in western European countries, likely because of almost complete insurance coverage. Still, the author's careful econometric work suggests several insights. First, migrant density in Germany acts as an important facilitating factor across all treatment categories. Second, European Union (EU) membership of the country of origin plays a minor role as soon as country heterogeneity is accounted for, again regardless of whether treatment is elective or not. This is amazing because a patient who wants to obtain a healthcare service in another EU country must present a physician report testifying to urgency and lack of a domestic alternative. Third, elective surgery does stand out in that distance from the country of origin seems to matter more than for the other types of treatment; since covering the distance often is a major component of total cost, this points to the importance of cost differentials noted above.

The author goes on to analyze inflows of patients into the 15 member states of Germany using regional hospital data. Once again, a full implementation of the relationships predicted by trade theory is not possible. Hospitals in West Germany appear to attract more medical tourists than their Eastern counterparts, but the effect vanishes as the definition of medical travel as a choice to travel for treatment is enforced and treatments of acute conditions are removed. A hospital's university affiliation exhibits the strongest positive effect on international patient inflows, while it does not seem much of a difference whether the setting is public or private.

Finally, the analysis is completed by interviews with stakeholders and patient surveys. This information is used not only descriptively but also for modeling individual choices by means of a discrete choice experiment (DCE, also known as conjoint analysis). Through their repeated choices between hypothetical settings that differ in their attributes, respondents reveal their preferences. Not surprisingly, the presence of a physician specializing in the particular treatment demanded turns out to be the most important attribute, followed by the country of provision (location in the Czech Republic and Switzerland is associated with a lowered probability of choice compared to Germany) and whether or not the hospital is certified. Interestingly, cost fails to be a significant predictor; however, this may be due to the fact that it was not possible to measure cost differentials with the country of origin as the benchmark.

In sum, this well-written volume provides the reader with valuable insights into the how, why, and where of medical tourism. Especially readers working in the healthcare sectors of this world will greatly benefit because growth in income is going to enable millions of patients to seek care beyond their national borders. Competition for these patients is bound to intensify—physicians, nurses, hospital managers, and last but not least policy makers, take note!

Emeritus University of Zurich, Zurich Switzerland
August 2018

Peter Zweifel

Contents

List of Abbreviations

ASC	Alternative-Specific Constant
BIC	Bayesian Information Criterion
CCE	Common Correlated Effects
CCR	Conditionally Correlated Random
CEPII	Centre d'Ètudes Prospectives et d'Informations Internationales
CES	Constant Elasticity of Substitution
CIS	Commonwealth of Independent States
CL	Conditional Logit
CNL	Common Native Language
CSL	Common Spoken Language
DCE	Discrete Choice Experiment
DESTATIS	Federal Statistical Office of Germany
DRG	Diagnosis-Related Groups
DV	Dummy Variable
FE	Fixed Effects
FMM	Finite Mixture Model
G-MNL	Generalized Multinomial Logit
GCC	Gulf Cooperation Council
GDP	Gross Domestic Product
GOÄ	German Medical Fee Index
ICD	International Classification of Diseases
IFHP	International Federation of Health Plans
IIA	Independence of Irrelevant Alternatives
IPS	International Passenger Survey
ITU	International Telecommunication Union
LL	Log-Likelihood
ML	Maximum Likelihood
MNL	Multinomial Logit
NEGBIN	Negative Binomial

NHS	National Health Service
OECD	Organisation for Economic Co-operation and Development
OLS	Ordinary Least Squares
RE	Random Effects
SD	Standard Deviation
S-MNL	Scaled Multinomial Logit
TPB	Theory of Planned Behavior
WDI	World Development Indicators
WTO	World Trade Organization

List of Figures

List of Tables

Chapter 1
A Dearth of Empirical Investigations

Medical tourism on a large scale is a recent manifestation of service trade that has grown to considerable economic significance at the international level. Destinations are no longer confined to poster child examples in East Asia that were frequented by American, British and regional residents but now extend to numerous countries worldwide that consider themselves and foster their roles as hubs, such as Dubai and Hungary.

There is ample motivation for protagonists in the health care market to scrutinize medical tourism: Patients may benefit from access to higher-quality care or reduced self-payments; public providers may generate extra-budgetary income; private providers may generate both extra income and build a reputation with medical tourists as they are expanding abroad (Xin 2014; Ying 2015); providers may productively employ a mobile international workforce in an international environment; and insurers may differentiate their services and pursue both quality assurance and cost containment strategies (Klusen et al. 2011; Rosenmöller et al. 2006). At the aggregate level, medical tourism may entail both private and public savings through outbound medical tourism (Baker and Rho 2009; Cohen 2010; Ehrbeck et al. 2008) or provide cross-funding of domestic services and advanced technology via inbound patients. At a time when both demographics and rapid technological progress strain public resources (Davis and Erixon 2008), medical tourism may alleviate some of that pressure. As a sophisticated service export, medical tourism may further serve as an important driver of economic growth. In a survey among insurants, Wagner and Verheyen (2010) found that medical tourism and converging health care markets in the EU are perceived as a chance for patients (60%), as a chance for German providers (18%), as a risk for patients (17%), and as a threat for German providers (13%). After recent regulation acknowledged the fundamental possibility of cross-border provider choice in the European Union (European Union 2011), it became clear that ongoing market unification and open borders continue to create new economic choices whose consequences need yet to be gauged.

The OECD and the NHS have recognized the potential of medical tourism, both in terms of opportunities and threats, and have launched research projects that deal

K. Schmerler, *Medical Tourism in Germany*, Developments in Health Economics and Public Policy 13, https://doi.org/10.1007/978-3-030-03988-2_1

with its various aspects and potential impacts. Lunt et al. (2011) reviewed the available literature and outlined the various policy levels that deal with implications of medical tourism. These implications are mostly of domestic nature, are induced by outbound consumers who seek to benefit from significant savings abroad, and range from public insurance schemes, ethical questions, public health issues and consumer information to legal aspects of medical tourism. While the medical tourism literature explores the legal and ethical issues of medical tourism in considerable detail, there is comparatively scarce literature with an economic focus, which often remains at a speculative or anecdotal level. Economic impacts of medical tourism at large and relevant drivers of the demand for medical treatments abroad thus remain to be investigated in an adequate and comprehensive fashion. With a broader framing, the medical tourism literature can be embedded in the economic trade literature and its recent research of sophisticated service exports as a channel of growth. This research stresses the increasing service export share of world trade as well as the role of relative factor endowments and the sophistication of service exports as drivers of economic growth. However, it provides little information about medical tourism and its impact, specifically.

Well-guided business strategies and public policies require a substantial amount of insight into medical tourism, which we are still lacking. Tradability of medical services as a whole may be beneficial or bode ill for domestic providers as sources of income and employment. Similarly, consumers are expected to gain from a larger choice set but transaction costs and asymmetric information may prevent such gains from being realized. Optimal policies need to consider total welfare, i.e. they must not only be informed about consumers and producers but also consider the public's exposure to financial and public health-related risks resulting from returning patients who may require follow-up care or international patients with infectious diseases, for example. Given the missing empirical groundwork in this field, sound policy advice is a tall order. We are therefore interested in the decision-making process and the drivers underlying medical tourism, which are the foundation of any more comprehensive economic analysis.

Our investigation of medical tourism will focus on inbound medical tourism to Germany for three reasons. First, there is a severe lack of multilateral trade data that allows the identification of international patients. We will discuss this issue in more detail below and describe an approach to overcome this problem for inbound inpatients in Germany. Second, much of the literature focuses on low-cost destinations and most studies—even in Germany—are concerned with outbound patients in search of cost savings. However, a substantial if not larger number of patients flocks to high-cost destinations and their main drivers remain to be unearthed empirically. Third, Germany has recognized, investigated and quantified the overall impact of the health care sector on its economy (Schneider et al. 2015) and inbound medical tourism provides an informative, complementary perspective on the issue.

Our research focus lies on the identification and quantification of drivers of medical tourism in Germany, yet we need to address a number of fundamental issues before we can turn to the various drivers. Previous empirical analyses of medical tourism have been struggling with two key challenges: the measurement of medical tourists and ad hoc, unsystematic approaches to the modelling of demand. Poor data quality, measured against the data requirements that the concept of medical tourism implies, and a lack of data in general compounded these challenges. We thus need to establish a working definition of medical tourism, identify and produce data sets suitable to an empirical investigation and develop a modelling framework within which we can discuss the feasibility of demand modelling. Our modelling framework also allows us to identify conceptual and methodological shortcomings of the few previous empirical investigations systematically. In absence of individual level data and price data, we then propose gravity model approaches that allow us to investigate the role of drivers of medical tourism with appropriate data sets. The analysis is complemented and augmented by additional data sets generated from stakeholder interviews and a patient questionnaire including a discrete choice experiment.

We derive a large set of candidate drivers of destination choice from the literature but our research focuses on a particular set of drivers that can be readily motivated by the market imperfections of health care markets. A complex network of actors gives rise to such imperfections at the national level. At the international level, we suspect a more prominent role of individual monetary outlays and fewer institutional restrictions to destination choice. We hypothesize a refocus on the core patient-physician relationship and a significant role of personal networks and cultural ties to establish trust in a destination—when little to no institutional relations obviate destination choice. Clearly, demand capacity and other aspects also determine the choice of a destination but we suspect that exceptional proximity in the form of personal networks or reputation is required to credibly communicate information about a foreign destination and to instill the trust required to consume a vital and complex credence good such as a medical treatment abroad.

The role of networks has been investigated in the economic literature in the context of goods trade and we surmise it to be critical in the service trade of medical treatments where products are even more heterogeneous. The medical tourism literature has pointed to facilitators and personal information as important drivers (Hanefeld et al. 2013; Lunt et al. 2014), but evidence has often been anecdotal. We attempt to identify networks relevant for inbound medical tourism to Germany and to quantify the importance of cultural ties more systematically using a unique data set. In addition, we attempt to identify and quantify other drivers along the various dimensions of our modelling framework and to answer secondary research questions about real consideration sets of international patients, the role of recreational travel in the context of medical treatments and the appropriate level of supplier modelling. These questions arise naturally in the development of our modelling framework and their answers can guide future modelling.

The remainder of this book is structured as follows: Chap. 2 surveys the medical tourism literature to provide a working definition of medical tourism for our purpose, to describe known patterns of medical tourism flows and their economic magnitude, to present broader implications of medical tourism flows and to identify known and theorized drivers of medical tourism. We then expound our focus on personal networks and measures of cultural proximity and derive appropriate measures thereof. In Chap. 3, we develop a modelling framework that combines and organizes the insights from our literature review with modelling considerations. We identify three feasible empirical investigations and embed them in our framework. Chapter 4 employs a gravity model as an indirect approach to demand modelling that is suitable for the investigation of cultural ties and other drivers at an aggregate level. Chapter 5 zooms in to the district level and investigates the role of cultural ties and selected provider characteristics. Chapter 6 presents the results of interviews with stakeholders in the medical tourism sector and an exploratory survey among international patients in Germany. We identify specific networks and investigate our secondary research questions including consideration sets, the role of recreational travel and supplier aggregation. Chapter 7 summarizes our findings, discusses their relevance for destinations, draws lessons for German and international policy makers, and proposes promising avenues for further research.

References

Baker, D., & Rho, H. J. (2009). *Free trade in health care: The gains from globalized medicare and medicaid.* Washington, DC: Centre for Economic Policy Research.

Cohen, I. G. (2010). Protecting patients with passports: Medical tourism and the patient-protective argument. *Iowa Law Review, 95*, 1467–1567.

Davis, L., & Erixon, F. (2008). *The health of nations: Conceptualizing approaches to trade in health care.* ECIPE Policy Briefs 04/2008. European Centre for International Political Economy.

Ehrbeck, T., Guevara, C., & Mango, P. D. (2008). *Mapping the market for medical travel.* Seattle, WA: The McKinsey Quarterly.

European Union. (2011). Directive 2011/24/EU of the European Parliament and of the Council of 9 March 2011 on the application of patients' rights in cross-border healthcare.

Hanefeld, J., Horsfall, D., Lunt, N., & Smith, R. (2013). Medical tourism: A cost or benefit to the NHS? *PLoS One, 8*, 1–8. https://doi.org/10.1371/journal.pone.0070406.

Klusen, N., Verheyen, F., & Wagner, C. (Eds.). (2011). *England and Germany in Europe: What lessons can we learn from each other?: European health care conference 2011* (Vol. 32, 1st ed. Beiträge zum Gesundheitsmanagement). Baden-Baden: Nomos-Verl.-Ges.

Lunt, N., Smith, R., Exworthy, M., Green, S. T., Horsfall, D., & Mannion, R. (2011). *Medical tourism: Treatments, markets and health system implications: A scoping review.* Paris: OECD.

Lunt, N., Horsfall, D., Smith, R., Exworthy, M., Hanefeld, J., & Mannion, R. (2014). Market size, market share and market strategy: Three myths of medical tourism. *Policy & Politics, 42*, 597–614. https://doi.org/10.1332/030557312X655918.

Rosenmöller, M., McKee, M., & Baeten, R. (2006). *Patient mobility in the European Union: Learning from experience.* Copenhagen: World Health Organization, Regional Office for Europe.

Schneider, M., Krauss, T., Hofmann, U., Köse, A., Ostwald, D. A., Gandjour, A., Gerlach, J., Hofman, S., Karmann, B., Legler, B., Marion, S. C., Karmann, A., Plaul, C., Henke, K.-D., Troppens, S., Braeseke, G., & Richter, T. (2015). *Die Gesundheitswirtschaftliche Gesamtrechnung für Deutschland.* Berlin: Bundesministerium für Wirtschaft und Energie.

Wagner, C., & Verheyen, F. (2010). *TK-Europabefragung 2009: Deutsche Patienten auf dem Weg nach Europa.* Hamburg: Techniker Krankenkasse.

Xin, W. (2014). Taking wellness high-tech in prevention and rehabilitation. *China Daily*, 10.

Ying, G. (2015). Desperation, money drive patients abroad. *China Daily*, 16.

Chapter 2
Traveling for Treatment: Taxonomy, Patient Flows and Candidate Drivers

Medical tourism is a relatively recent phenomenon of international trade that has evolved over the past 10 to 15 years and only gradually received the scrutinous focus of academia. This may be surprising at first as medical tourism can be assigned to the larger field of international trade, which is characterized by the availability of large data sets that stimulate research. Medical tourism, however, often finds itself excluded for four reasons: its uncommon mode of delivery, its inconsistent definition, its lack of data and its poor data quality when available.

This first section will survey the available literature and address four main questions:

- What is an appropriate definition of medical tourists that allows their examination from an economic choice perspective?
- Which flow patterns arise in medical tourism and which data sets are available?
- Which drivers of medical tourism does the medical tourism literature identify?
- What are the broader implications of medical tourism?

2.1 Medical Tourists

Depending on the research perspective, medical tourism is often defined very differently. There are many different types of patients and travelers that intersect in one or multiple dimensions and each of these groups has received various labels, with substantial overlap between groups. Generally, the definition of medical tourism hinges on the following criteria.

K. Schmerler, *Medical Tourism in Germany*, Developments in Health Economics and Public Policy 13, https://doi.org/10.1007/978-3-030-03988-2_2

2.1.1 Mode of Delivery

The globalization of health care occurs on many levels and leads to numerous multidirectional flow phenomena. The most common examples include pharmaceutical arbitrage via reimporting, the migration of the health care labor force to and from developing and developed countries (Cooper et al. 2002; Leng 2006), telemedicine (Wachter 2006) and patient travel. While the two former examples represent traditional goods or input flows, the two latter fall in the category of service exports.

The World Bank distinguishes between four modes of service supply: The first two are characterized by domestic production where the product is either sent abroad or consumed domestically by a visiting consumer. The other two modes are characterized by foreign production, i.e. by a commercial establishment abroad or by sending a natural person abroad to render a service. Medical tourism submits to the somewhat counterintuitive, second mode of delivery, i.e. a service export that is rendered within the exporting country.

Medical tourism is furthermore a curious mix of both a modern and a traditional service. Mishra et al. (2011) describe traditional services as services that "require face-to-face interaction" as opposed to modern services that can be traded digitally and now benefit from "economies of scale, agglomeration, networks, and division of labor". Face-to-face interaction is most certainly a feature of most medical services but the characteristics of modern services can be observed as well.

A quick note on terminology: *source* refers to a place where demand originates and *origin* to a place where supply originates. A *destination* is a place that patients seek to receive treatment and thus an *origin*.

2.1.2 Treatment Focus

Not all patient travel constitutes medical tourism and one noteworthy distinction in the literature is made between health tourism and medical tourism. Early definitions treated both terms interchangeably (García-Altés 2005; Terry 2007) and refer to any kind of treatment abroad that served the improvement of an individual's overall well-being. Such treatments were often incidental and not necessarily the main purpose of a trip. Instead, culture, cuisine and tourism were decisive drivers. Cohen (2008) distinguishes between various degrees of combined medical and touristic intentions behind trips but typically medical tourism is now characterized by a treatment focus that dominates the touristic benefits of a trip and entails a medical procedure (Bookman and Bookman 2007; Carrera and Bridges 2006; Connell 2006). According to Frädrich (2013), medical tourism is induced by a medical condition as opposed to health tourism which focuses more on preventive care and lifestyle treatments. IPK International (2012) makes a similar distinction between healing and prevention. In summary, medical tourism has been defined as a subset of health tourism with the inclusion criteria "purpose of travel" and "type of treatment obtained". These two criteria have considerable non-overlapping regions: A recent study by Wongkit and McKercher (2013) finds a large amount of incidental treatments obtained by visitors to Thailand who travelled for touristic purposes initially. 39.7% of the visitors surveyed decided on a treatment only upon arrival in Thailand. There were differences in treatments obtained between tourists with incidental and planned treatments but both groups obtained treatments that are typically ascribed to medical tourists, e.g. dental care.

There is no obvious guidance as to which medical conditions lead to medical as opposed to health treatments. Bookman and Bookman (2007) distinguish between invasive, diagnostic and lifestyle treatments and often medical tourism categories share an invasive treatment as a common denominator. These treatments can vary substantially by destination. In Germany, non-representative data on outgoing patients shows a focus on wellness retreats and therapies but there is scant information on specific medical treatments aside from dental care (Wagner et al. 2011; Wagner and Verheyen 2010). The survey was administered to German patients that hold a public health insurance so the outcome is conditional on and likely due to the supply side characteristics of the German health care sector that provides most required medical treatments at a good quality, within a reasonable period of time and no co-payments involved. Incoming patients to Germany may seek medical treatments depending on their source country. While patients from neighboring countries predominantly receive treatments in acute care categories, numbers for actual medical tourists from Kuwait, for example, peak in the treatment of diseases of the musculoskeletal system and connective tissue (Lutze et al. 2010).

Internationally, surgical procedures presumably dominate but there is hardly conclusive data on this issue. Patient numbers are often provided for and by hospitals, which may explain the focus on surgical inpatient and outpatient procedures. Such procedures are also more likely to receive press coverage in source countries to bring up deficiencies of the domestic health care system; cosmetic and spa tourism would hardly imply any serious shortcomings of domestic health care provision. Another reason for bias in reporting is the striking absolute price differentials between surgeries in high and low-cost countries which typically serve to demonstrate the benefits of traveling.

Milstein and Smith (2006), Milstein and Smith (2007), Cohen (2010) report surgical procedures as a main focus of medical tourism and Klingenberger (2009), among others, adds dental care as an important sector. Connell (2006) predicts an increasing focus on cosmetic surgery. These three sectors are also reflected by the offers of large medical tourism facilitators such as MedRetreat and by Pollard (2013) who surveyed 404 individuals from organizations in 77 countries who operate in the medical tourism sector. Despite acknowledged sample bias and a dominance of US, European and Indian representatives in the sample, the survey does represent one of the few comprehensive data sets on medical tourism. The sampled representatives of medical providers confirm the focus of medical tourism on dental treatment, cosmetic and plastic surgery, general surgery and orthopaedic surgery. They further anticipate cosmetic, plastic, dental, cancer, and fertility treatments to be the major source of growth (Pollard 2013).

Kher (2006) reports 83% non-cosmetic treatments in Bumrungrad, Thailand in 2005. A survey among travelers to Thailand by Jotikasthira (2010) finds that of 377 patients interviewed 28.1% go to cure an illness, 25.5% want to obtain cosmetic surgery, 24.9% want to receive a medical check-up, and 21.5% intend to generally improve health. A survey by Wongkit and McKercher (2013) ranks dental care, general check-ups, and cosmetic surgery as the most popular treatments of visitors with any medical treatment in Thailand and note plastic, cosmetic and invasive surgery to be the most common procedures obtained by medical tourists with planned treatments. For British patients in private hospitals in Thailand, Noree et al. (2014) report 25.91% cosmetic operations, 13.92% operations on the musculoskeletal system, 11.78% operations on the eyes, and 10.92% operations on the digestive system as the most common treatments.

Dated but official statistics for Singapore list general medicine, ophthalmology, general surgery, gynecology and urology as the most popular day-surgery treatments and general surgery, cardiology, general medicine, gynecology and orthopedic surgery as the most popular inpatient treatments with medical oncology as the runner-up (Khoo 2003). For Malaysia, Musa et al. (2012b) report 41.3% of the surveyed, inbound tourists receiving medical treatment, 20.3% cosmetic procedures and 14.5% medical check-ups. Unfortunately, the categories inquired do not allow a precise allocation to specific treatments and are, as in Jotikasthira (2010), not even mutually exclusive. Alsharif et al. (2010) survey patients in China, India, Jordan, and the United Arab Emirates. These destinations share dental, eye and cosmetic treatments with local foci on alternative medicine in China and India and invasive treatments and oncology at the higher-cost locations Jordan and the United Arab Emirates.

Invasive treatments are explored in Crone (2008) who reports bariatric surgery, cardiac surgery, cosmetic surgery, and joint replacements as typical procedures that result from diseases related to increased life expectancy. According to Lunt et al. (2011), medical tourism focuses on a relatively narrow subset of elective medical procedures including dental care, cosmetic surgery, elective surgery, fertility treatment. These categories are spelled out in more detail in Lunt and Carrera (2010):

- Cosmetic surgery
- Dentistry
- Cardiology/cardiac surgery
- Orthopedic surgery
- Bariatric surgery
- IVF/reproductive system
- Organ and tissue transplantation
- Eye surgery
- Diagnostics and check ups

Mattoo and Rathindran (2006), who do not focus exclusively on procedures at the upper end of the price scale, identify treatments by their tradability. They apply the following six criteria:

- The surgery constitutes treatment for a non-acute condition.
- The patient is able to travel without major pain or inconvenience.
- The surgery requires minimal follow-up treatment on site.
- The surgery generates minimal laboratory and pathology reports.
- The surgery results in minimal post-procedure immobility.
- The surgery is fairly simple and commonly performed with minimal rates of postoperative complications.

The first two points are useful and necessary conditions for medical tourism and point three is increasingly being addressed by follow-up networks. Point four is a non-issue at large international providers and point five is often countered by follow-up rehabilitation or tourism. Point six is at odds with the reported procedures performed by offshore providers (Milstein and Smith 2006).

Even if an exhaustive list of medical tourism treatments or universal inclusion conditions is impossible to compile, the invasive and often curative character of treatments demanded by medical tourists stands out. The need to travel further necessitates a minimal health status. The purpose of travel is a more ambiguous criterion as the evidence presented hints to a substantial amount of vacation stays that were not primarily planned with medical treatments in mind. These treatments differ somewhat from those obtained by tourists with planned medical care but are not restricted to wellness and are generally ascribed to the realm of medical tourism.

On a final note, it can be difficult to identify and to isolate medical tourism empirically since medical procedures may lead to follow-up treatments that can be attributed to the domain of health tourism as is the case with, for example, rehabilitation after a surgical procedure or other extended periods of recovery. In this case, the main purpose of the trip remains the procedure but the follow-up stay needs to be recorded in a different column.

2.1.3 Elective Care

Aside from the treatment type that is often mirrored by the main purpose of a trip, a distinction should be made between acute and elective treatments. Acute treatments are relevant from an accounting and an actuarial perspective as they reflect spatial cost and risk distributions abroad but they are less informative in terms of destination choices for treatments.

To assess the magnitude of its insurants' demand abroad, Wagner and Verheyen (2010) choose acute and elective treatments as their main classification. Terry (2007) disregards patients who fall ill during their stay abroad and choose to be treated there due to acute conditions. Richter and Richter (2012) also subscribe to this view but they cannot and do not need to discriminate between both types empirically. The purpose of their calculations is a net export balance in value terms, which is independent from the reason for demand. Internationally, there are few numbers available on emergency treatments and they are implicitly discarded by focusing on select treatment types. Ehrbeck et al. (2008) provide an estimate of 30–35% emergency treatments among inpatients and Bookman and Bookman (2007) report a total of 8% of all travelers requiring acute treatments.

2.1.4 Cross-Border Operations

Another defining characteristic of medical tourism is the potential institutional framework of cross-border operations. Cross-border operations may either be of a voluntary nature or institutionalized via shared operations or outsourcing.

Voluntary cross-border demand represents demand by individuals as in the state of Brandenburg, Germany, for example (Müller 2006). These patients are consumers that elect themselves into alternative destinations (Carrera and Lunt 2010). Aside from the voluntary treatment elsewhere, Lunt and Carrera (2010) require a willingness-to-pay from medical tourists which is reasonable as patients will face a monetary outlay even if the actual treatment abroad is covered by their insurance. Such an outlay may include the cost of information, travel or accommodation. Patients also exhibit a willingness-to-pay, or lack thereof, if they voluntarily seek care at providers abroad that are contracted by their health care providers in order to reduce their co-pay (Wagner et al. 2011).

Semi-voluntary cross-border patient flows that result from shared operations at borders will inflate and thus distort medical tourism flows. These numbers do not permit any conclusions about real economic choices. Outsourcing reflects economic choices but by institutions rather than by individuals. Rosenmöller et al. (2006) provide numerous examples for Europe such as Estonian insurers selecting providers in Finland and Germany or the NHS contracting Belgian hospitals. Cross-border contracting by insurers in Denmark, Germany, Ireland, the Netherlands, Norway and the UK is also documented by Glinos et al. (2010).

Examples of institutionalized outsourcing are abundant in the U.S. where health plans by employers may contract health care providers overseas as the default option for expensive medical procedures (Cohen 2010; Kher 2006; Milstein and Smith 2006). Texas banned the mandatory use of foreign providers from health plans (Cohen 2010) while West Virginia actually considered this option for its public employees but rejected it in the end (Terry 2007). Employees make an indirect choice at best by selecting their employer and choosing between health plan options if such a choice is available, but the assumption of a voluntary decision to go abroad is far-fetched in such a scenario. The distinction between voluntary, insurer-prompted and employer-sponsored medical tourism as well as between incentivizing and penalizing contracts will be discussed in more detail below.

Interestingly, there is little to no information about global supply chains in medical tourism. Recent trade literature has focused on the trading of tasks that are isolated as a result of the supply-chain fragmentation (Baldwin 2012; Grossman and Rossi-Hansberg 2008). It is unclear, however, if this concept is applicable to medical tourism as to digital services, a fact also recognized by Grossman and Rossi-Hansberg (2008). Limited evidence of intra-provider shifting is documented for specific services in some regions of the world (Levy and Kyoung-Hee 2006; Wibulpolprasert et al. 2004) but the issue has been met by certification requirements and somewhat subsided since. There exist transnational hospital chains such as Apollo Hospitals, Fortis Health care or Wockhardt Hospitals that provide care at multiple destinations but little is known about their internal shifting of capacities. Private conversations with one provider indicated that large private providers set up diagnostic centers in Eastern European countries but it is unknown to the author where follow-up treatments take place. Apollo Hospitals disclosed to us that patient transfers between different locations are uncommon as patients are initially directed to a location that is able to provide all services required. Tertiary care centers that focus on the provision of services to international patients are among these full-service locations. A thorough analysis of this issue would require detailed data from cross-border operating providers or very detailed multilateral trade flow data that allows the disaggregation by treatments.

Similar to shared border operations, business-internal relocation as a result of cross-border resource distribution is not considered medical tourism. On the other hand, voluntary travel as a result of recommendations by primary care providers, for example, does constitute medical tourism and referral networks of large international providers have been reported.

2.1.5 Time Horizon

A final qualification needs to be made in light of a much-cited definition by Arellano (2007) that defines medical tourism as "traveling abroad with the express purpose of obtaining health care, including elective surgery and long-term care." Long-term care is not of interest to our investigation as the intention to a obtain treatment abroad would be conditional on a previous or simultaneous decision about permanent migration. Bookman and Bookman (2007) consider long-term residents a subgroup of patients with incidental treatments but their consumption of inpatient treatments should also be disregarded. Domestic treatments to retirement migrants or long-term nursing may constitute economic choices but they do not constitute acts of travel. Expatriates returning home for a temporary stay are a relevant group that makes an explicit decision to travel in order to obtain a treatment. In order to make this distinction empirically, we need to know a patient's place of residence. Ehrbeck et al. (2008) venture an estimate of 25–30% of all inpatients being expatriates returning home for treatment.

Within short-term term stays, a further distinction can be made between inpatient and outpatient visits. Connell (2013) reports dominating outpatient visits for Bumrungrad, Thailand which matches results in Noree et al. (2014) who further find very different treatments, average costs and median costs for inpatient and outpatient visits. Both groups travel on their own volition and consciously elect into a treatment so both should be included in medical tourism but we suspect drivers for inpatient and outpatient treatments to vary in magnitude.

2.1.6 Summary

There exists a multitude of medical tourism definitions and of characteristics that delimit medical tourism conditional on drivers of demand, recreation, cultural ties, availability at home or circumvention, for example (Hall 2011). Connell (2013) considers intent, procedure and duration of a trip and suggests five groups of patients: elite patients seeking the best quality, middle class patients seeking cosmetic surgery or savings, less affluent diaspora patients returning home for treatment, cross-border patients in Europe, and reluctant tourists that lack availability at home. Lunt and Carrera (2010) define five different groups: short-term tourists with acute treatments, long-term residents such as migrated retirees, outsourced patients as a result of contracted services, patients who seek their cross-border treatments due to proximity, and medical tourists.

Taking the aforementioned aspects and definitions into account, we define medical tourists as persons who

- make a conscious choice to
- travel to a location outside their usual country of residence
- for a limited period of time
- to obtain an elective medical treatment of interventionist, curative character
- and bear some direct or indirect costs.

This excludes the subset of patients with acute treatments and patients using common border cooperation or national outsourcing agreements in absence of a choice. It includes expatriates seeking care at home and patients who voluntarily seek care at contracted providers abroad while holding a financial stake. These patients have undergone an economic decision-making process and their actions thus constitute conscious demand. They also allow a willingness-to-travel, a willingness-to-treat and ultimately a willingness-to-pay framing and the resulting medical tourism flows are the aggregate outcome of individual, welfare-maximizing choices. Treatments are characterized by their interventionist and curative character as opposed to preventive or wellness activities. Although more specific categories for procedures were identified, a narrower definition of treatments is not required at this point.

We define medical travelers as medical tourists with the additional condition that

- the medical treatment is the initial and primary purpose of the trip.

Complementary purposes such as the visiting of friends or family or recreation are also conceivable and suspected. The combination of these purposes and the desire for a medical treatment form a continuous scale of purpose mixes with varying degrees of emphasis on the medical treatment. We will use the term "medical

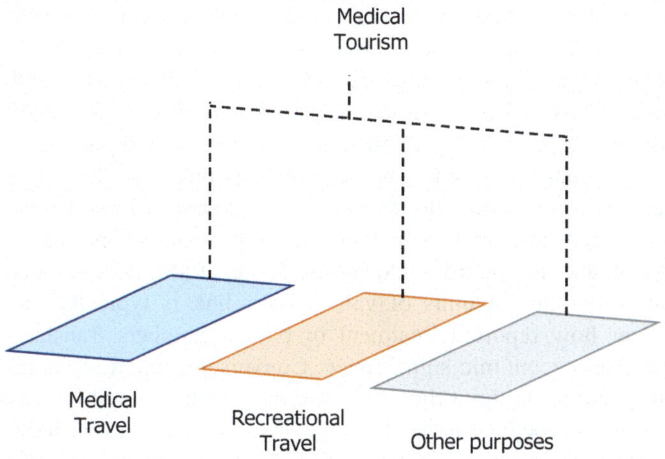

Fig. 2.1 Purpose of travel mix

tourism" throughout this chapter as the reviewed literature commonly refers to it and make the explicit distinction of trips by purpose as depicted in Fig. 2.1 in Chap. 3. Thereafter, "medical tourism" continues to cover trips with any purpose of travel mix while "medical travel" refers to trips made with the main purpose of receiving a medical treatment.

2.2 Medical Tourism Flows

While the literature discussed in the preceding subsection provides guidance to the delineation of medical tourism as an outcome of an economic choice, such guidance is nowhere to be found for the interpretation of most circulating medical tourism figures. Estimating the market size is most difficult as definitions of medical tourism vary. Youngman (2009), for example, argues that the numbers in Ehrbeck et al. (2008) are generally incompatible with nearly all other statistics and blames that partly on the exclusion of outpatients. A similar concern is the often unclear mixture of medical and incidental health care treatments in reported figures. Another problem lies in data reliability as much of the early literature and most of the reports on medical tourism quote and reproduce only a few core sources. The numbers of many reports (Crone 2008; MacReady 2007; Whittaker 2010) can be traced back to a handful of sources such as Ernst and Young (2006) and Keckley and Underwood (2008). Reports such as MacReady (2007) quote specific industry statistics whose reliability is doubtful at a time when medical tourism was celebrated to be a new path to prosperity. Others rely on a substantial amount of newspaper figures (Connell 2006) or search term popularity without accounting for varying search engine popularity or search languages across countries (Hope 2015).

Aside from concerns about the inclusion criteria and reliability of data sources for medical tourism, additional problems arise. First, treatments tend to be confused and compared with patients. Few studies such as Lutze et al. (2010) work with verifiable, official data and acknowledge that discharges, for example, may lead to multiple treatment counts per patient. The confusion of treatments and patients may explain some of the discrepancies in early reported figures but is unlikely to account for much of them. Second, nationality as opposed to country of residence is typically used to identify medical tourists, which erroneously captures expatriates who do not travel for their treatments. Third, trade volume is sometimes denominated in units of quantity and sometimes in units of value. Their link is typically blurred and it remains unclear how reported treatment or patient numbers translate into value terms and thus into economic significance. Conversely, reported values cannot be converted to quantities without the disclosure of price levels and information about the inclusion of non-medical expenditures as well as indirect and induced effects. Fourth, available data sources overlap and cannot be disentangled: official hospital statistics may only record inpatient care for international patients; private clinics may not report any numbers for confidentiality reasons; private facilitators do not reveal their business very often; medical visa statistics only identify patients from select countries and non-exhaustively so as some patients may travel on different types of visas; and trade statistics usually capture tourism-related figures but do not distinguish between the various subsets of tourists—particularly medical tourists.

While the magnitude and therefore the economic significance of trade flows is difficult to capture for the aforementioned reasons, available sources still provide an indicator of the various flow directions. As it turns out, there are few countries that do not or have not made an effort to engage in medical tourism and thus dilute the pool of medical tourism destinations.

2.2.1 World

Early reports of medical tourism flows used to focus on North-South and South-North flows which suggested product differentiation by lower prices and high-end quality, respectively (Crozier and Baylis 2010; Ehrbeck et al. 2008). As predicted trade flows did not materialize and South-South flows emerged, a more sober view revealed that there seem to exist factors that render much of the observed medical tourism regional with hubs of excellence and specialization (Cattaneo 2009; Hopkins et al. 2010; Horowitz et al. 2007; Smith et al. 2011b; Youngman 2014). Another pattern, even if at a smaller scale, can be traced back to the tapping of expatriates as sources of inbound medical tourism group (Bergmark et al. 2010; Connell 2013; Gill et al. 2008; Lee et al. 2010). Finally, Youngman (2012) and Youngman (2014) note that many medical tourists do not appear to seek out the cheapest destination. Instead of price competition, he suggests a shift to quality, niche and luxury differentiation, which leads to the top three European destinations also being the most expensive ones. His views are in line with Pollard (2013) who reports India, Thailand, U.S. and Germany as today's leading destinations with the U.S., Thailand, Singapore and Germany offering the best in quality and range of services. The surveyed representatives of medical tourism companies further expect India, Thailand, Turkey, U.S, Germany, Singapore and Malaysia to attract the most patients in the future. These results suggest at least three very different segments.

Asia can be considered the pioneering region of modern medical tourism and its large-scale medical tourism has long dominated international reporting. Much capacity for international patients was developed in the private sector after the financial crisis in 1997 (Huat 2006; Turner 2007) and resulted in what Lunt et al. (2011) call the first wave of medical tourism even if substantial capacities had already existed before 1998 (Khoo 2003). Destinations of that first wave were India, Malaysia, Singapore and Thailand. The reported numbers of international visitors were quickly extrapolated to a stunning international market potential (Keckley and Underwood 2008). Despite a substantial number of patients from overseas, medical tourism flows turned out to be largely regional with Malaysia serving patients from Indonesia (Manaf et al. 2015; Musa et al. 2012b; Yeoh et al. 2013); Singapore receiving patients from Malaysia and Indonesia (Khoo 2003; Lautier 2008); and Thailand providing care to patients from Japan (Arunanondchai and Fink 2007) and Myanmar (Maung 2014)—to name but a few links. In addition to their regional significance, Huat (2006) and Jotikasthira (2010) note a focus on higher income countries for Thailand and Singapore. A survey of visitors to Thailand by Wongkit and McKercher (2013) finds shares of 30.4%, 25.5% and 29.3% for Europe, Asia, and Oceania, respectively. A similar pattern of medical inflows can be observed for India, which focuses on both medical tourists from the Middle East and on expatriates from the UK (Confederation of Indian Industry and McKinsey and Company 2002; Hazarika 2010; Johnston et al. 2010; Neelakantan 2003).

Lunt et al. (2011) consider Japan and South Korea to be the second wave of Asian countries trying to establish themselves as medical tourism destinations and, indeed, both the Japanese and the Korean governments have announced such plans and taken steps towards that goal (Japanese Cabinet 2010; Korea Global Healthcare Association). In fact, South Korea has been reporting considerable growth and data from the Ministry of Health and Welfare lists China (29.8%), the U.S. (13.3%), Russia (11.9%), Japan (5.4%), Mongolia (4.8%) and a large and diverse share of other countries (34.8%) as the main source countries in 2014 (Visit Medical Korea 2016). The Philippines as a minor player have also expressed interest in becoming a medical tourism destination (Connell 2006).

The Middle East is another region that has been both source and destination of medical tourism for a long time. Its regional character is documented in the nationality distribution of visitors to Jordan and the United Arab Emirates in Alsharif et al. (2010). Siddiqi et al. (2010) report the involvement of Egypt, Jordan, Lebanon, Morocco, Oman, Pakistan, Sudan, Syria, and Tunisia in health care trade. They attribute most trade to mode 4 delivery of services, i.e. the cross-border flows of personnel, and rank medical tourism second. Both Kangas (2007) and Siddiqi et al.

(2010) discuss Yemen as a source of medical tourists with about 40,000 outgoing patients in 2003. Destinations were India (Kangas 2007) and Jordan as one of the main destinations in the Middle East (Connell 2006). Siddiqi et al. (2010) report about 120,000 inbound patients to Jordan in 2002. Iran has also been documented as a destination for fertility treatments to patients from neighboring countries (Goodarzi et al. 2014; Moghimehfar and Nasr-Esfahani 2011).

The United Arab Emirates and Dubai in particular are the other major medical tourism destination in the Middle East. Crone (2008), Paffhausen et al. (2010) and various other authors describe the measures taken by the government to set up Dubai HealthCare City as a large free-trade zone that caters to medical tourists from the entire Middle East. The infrastructure includes various hospitals, on-site training facilities for physician training, a campus, and a center of excellence that culminated in a co-operation with Harvard Medical School. Other noteworthy destinations in the Mediterranean region are Tunesia with 40,000–45,000 patients in 2004 (Lautier 2008) and Israel as a destination for fertility treatments (Connell 2006).

North and South America constitute another area of regional medical tourism. There are ample reports of medical tourists from the U.S. and Canada that seek affordable treatments in Asia (Crozier and Baylis 2010; Milstein and Smith 2007) but regional destinations are in fact no less popular. Mexico attracts a large diaspora with cheaper treatments (Bergmark et al. 2010; Bookman and Bookman 2007; Horton and Cole 2011; Terry 2007); the Caribbean with Barbados, Jamaica and Puerto Rico focuses on U.S. patients often in search of cosmetic treatments (Connell 2006; Paffhausen et al. 2010; Ramírez de Arellano 2011); and Cuba serves mostly patients from other countries in Latin America (Drager and Vieira 2002; The World Bank 1996). Flows to and within South America can also be observed. Argentina (Connell 2006) and Brazil (Paffhausen et al. 2010) are known to be destinations for cosmetic and plastic surgery; Colombia has attempted to establish itself as a destination (Johnson 2002); and Chile as a South-South destination attracts high income medical tourists from Bolivia, Ecuador and Peru (León 2002). The U.S. experience both outbound and inbound medical tourism. Hudson (2011) notes the potential role of inbound tourism; Bookman and Bookman (2007) observe many of the U.S. inflows to strong hospital brands; Ying (2015) provides a recent account of inflows from China; and Youngman (2012) counts as many inbound as outbound medical tourists to the U.S. In a similar vein, Ehrbeck et al. (2008) suspect as many as 40% of all medical tourists to be in search of the most advanced technology and sees the U.S. as their most important destination.

The proximity of countries in Europe invites medical tourism at a regional level and, indeed, significant cross-border mobility can be observed (Rosenmöller et al. 2006). IPK International (2012) reports Hungary, Germany, and Czech Republic as the main destinations in Europe but Poland has been developing its capacities as well. In a survey among UK patients, Belgium, Hungary, Poland, Czech Republic, Turkey and Spain turned out to be the most popular destinations (Pollard 2012). Hungary is particularly known for its dental tourism (Connell 2006; Hanefeld et al. 2013; Terry 2007) and Pollard (2012) confirms that finding with 38% of all surveyed UK travelers going to Hungary to obtain dental treatment. The second-most important treatment category is cosmetic surgery with Belgium being the most popular destination. Turkey is a known exporter of medical services but the magnitude of its exports is very difficult to assess due to different numbers from multiple official sources (International Medical Travel Journal 2015; Pollard 2017). Reports in Rosenmöller et al. (2006) and Glinos et al. (2010) suggest that waiting lists in source countries lead to much regional cross-border care but overseas travel is also significant (Noree et al. 2014). Smaller destinations in Europe such as Belarus, Latvia and Lithuania have also been reported to develop medical tourism (Connell 2006).

There are more destinations worldwide that have been associated with medical tourism such as China, Iran, and the Philippines (Gill et al. 2008); South Africa (Connell 2006; Terry 2007); and various others. IPK International (2012) reports a survey, which estimates that 3–4% of the world population already travels to foreign countries for medical treatment: "Health and medical travel accounted for a total of 9.4 million trips in 2011, or 2.4% of all European outbound travel. Over the past 5 years, health vacations by Europeans have increased by 38% while medical tourism has gone up by 24%." The reported annual market size growth estimates of 20% are somewhat dubious, however, as the underlying definition of medical tourism probably includes health tourism and possibly other types of tourism with incidental wellness treatments as well.

Table 2.1 summarizes the number of medical tourism patients and medical tourism market values (in parentheses) suggested by some of the available literature. It is not meant to provide a complete account of all numbers ever reported and many redundant reports were reduced to the initial source, if identifiable. As mentioned above, there is not much use in consolidating the various sources as nothing is usually known about the inclusion criteria (inpatients/outpatients, treatments/patients, acute/planned, general tourism/treatment focus). The table provides an account of country coverage rather than actual patient volume: Some numbers have been revised considerably once subjected to a tenable definition of medical tourism: NaRanong and NaRanong (2011) reduced international patients from 1,400,000 to 420,000 in 2007 when accounting for tourists and foreign residents and Noree et al. (2016) arrive at 167,000 patients in 2010 using actual hospital data.

Due to the uncertainty about patient volumes, few attempts have been made to estimate economic impacts of medical tourism. Carrera and Bridges (2006) venture early estimates of health tourism in 2005 based on WTO data and arrive at exports of US$513 billion with Europe, the Americas, Asia-Pacific, Africa and the Middle East accounting for 53.1%, 20.3%, 19.5%, 4.8% and 4.7% respectively. Revenues of medical tourism are guessed at 25–50% of the health tourism value.

Johnson and Garman (2010) use data from the Bureau of Economic Analysis, the Survey of International Air Travelers, and provider interviews to estimate the value of inbound medical tourism to the US between US$491 million and US$1.2 billion. These numbers represent treatment costs and do not include accommodation, other expenses or accompanying persons. Hanefeld et al. (2013) analyzed the contribution of international patients to hospitals in the UK. Patient volumes are based on similar sources, i.e. data from the International Passenger Survey, which includes "medical treatment" as an option for the self-reported main purpose of travel. Costs and

Table 2.1 Selected inbound medical tourism flows worldwide, by country and year

	World											
		Asia						Rest of the world				
			Thailand	Singapore	Malaysia	India	South Korea	Jordan	Poland	Costa Rica	Cuba	U.S. (outbound)
1995											25,000[a]	
2000				150,000[g]								
2001			470,000[e] 550,161[p]									
2002			630,000[e] 630,973[p]	210,000[e] ($420mil)[e]		150,000[b]		120,000[q]				
2003			974,000[e] ($482mil)[e] 973,532[p] 500,000[k,w]		>100,000[e] ($40mil)[e]							
2004			1,103,095[p] 1,000,000[l] 520,000[d] 640,000[s] ($500mil)[l]	320,000[d]	177,000[d]	150,000[d] 100,000[n]						
2005	($128–256bn)[c]		1,249,984[p] 1,000,000[h] 1,200,000[o]	374,000[g] 250,000[h]		500,000[h]						
2006	($60bn)[f]		1,280,000[n] 430,000[r,x] 93,000[f,y]	410,000[n] 555,000[s]	300,000[n]	200,000–500,000[n] 500,000[f]						

2007			1,400,000[t]							150,000[o]	200,000[o]	750,000[j] 50,000–121,000[r]
2008	5,000,000[n] 60,000–85,000[i]	3,000,000[n]		646,000[s]					>500,000[n]			1,500,000[j,z]
2009	4,000,000[m] ($20–40bn)[m]						60,201[w]					3,000,000[j,z]
2010	($78.5bn)[r]	4,300,000[r] ($6.7bn)[r]	1,500,000[s] 167,000[v]				81,789[w]					6,000,000[j,z]
2011	>3,000,000[r]						122,297[w]					7,500,000[j,z]
2012	($40–60bn)[u] ($100bn)[o]	5,600,000[r] ($9.1bn)[r] ($2bn)[n] ($4bn)[o]				(2.2bn)[o]	159,464[w]					9,380,000[j,z]
2013							211,218[w]					10,780,000[j,z]
2014							266,501[w]					12,930,000[j,z]

[a]Chandra (2002), [b]Neelakantan (2003), [c]Carrera and Bridges (2006), [d]Huat (2006), [e]Arunanondchai and Fink (2007), [f]Herrick (2007), MacReady (2007) [g]Turner (2007), [h]Carabello (2008), Herrick (2007) [i]Ehrbeck et al. (2008), [j]Keckley and Underwood (2008), [k]McClean (2008), [l]Lautier (2008), [m]Smith et al. (2009), [n] Youngman (2009), [o]Crozier and Baylis (2010), [p]Jotikasthira (2010), [q]Siddiqi et al. (2010), [r]Johnson and Garman (2010), [s]KPMG (2011), [t]NaRanong and NaRanong (2011), [u]IPK International (2012), [v]Noree et al. (2016), [w]Visit Medical Korea (2016), [x]Bumrungrad Hospital only [y]Arab patients admitted to Bumrungrad Hospital only [z]Predictions

durations of stay were identified via NHS data and supplementary patient interviews. Based on the crude IPS data, this study provides an estimate of £219 million per year that is spent in the UK by incoming patients and their company. This number does take into account a limited degree of tourist activities. However, Noree et al. (2014) highlight the problems of traveler surveys and self-reported purpose of a trip in terms of sampling: they show that IPS data are, at the very best, crude and highlight significant incongruencies between IPS data and hospital data from Thailand on UK citizens.

NaRanong and NaRanong (2011) provide an analysis of inbound medical tourism to Thailand and find that an estimated 1.4 million international patients in 2007 account for US$1.23–1.39 billion which corresponds to 0.4% of GDP. This analysis includes treatments of tourists and foreign residents, however, and a more recent estimate by Noree et al. (2016) arrives at approximately 167,000 non-acute patients that travel to Thailand in 2010 which translates into medical and non-medical expenditures of US$900 million for both patients and accompanying travelers. Klijs et al. (2016) calculate direct and indirect effects of medical tourism based on input-output data for Malaysia. 341,288 patients in 2007 produced US$276.8 million in direct effects and US$95.4 million in indirect effects. Outpatients are explicitly included in the analysis but it rests on many assumptions required for I-O analyses and, more problematically, it suffers from the severe shortcomings in NaRanong and NaRanong (2011) in that the data includes resident retirees, foreign students, resident expatriates, institutionalized cross-border patients and acute treatments of tourists.

Various economic estimates circulate for a number of other countries but they are often unreliable and often contradictory even when from official sources. Boosterism appears to afflict the political arena as much as the commercial sector: Turkish health tourism, for example, has been estimated at US$2.5 billion, which is at odds with a number of other official Turkish sources (International Medical Travel Journal 2015). On the other hand, South Korea publishes fairly detailed and consistent statistics (Korea Global Healthcare Association; Visit Medical Korea 2016). Based on annual KRW-USD exchange rates, revenues from international patients rose from US$43.3 million in 2009 to US$359.4 million in 2013 (Limb 2014) but are once again based on all patients of foreign nationality.

Finally, Loh (2014) and Loh (2015) use balance of payment data of the IMF. It records spending on health-related travel, which is based on a household survey in Germany but may be drawn from other sources elsewhere. Loh (2015) reports spending in the hundreds of millions for single countries but this data is once again difficult to compare to other sources as it is partly self-reported and includes wellness, accommodation and tourism expenses.

2.2.2 *Germany*

Germany exemplifies the multidirectional nature of medical tourism. While survey participants in Pollard (2013) describe Germany as a successful medical tourism destination both today and in the predicted future, it is also listed among the top source countries of medical tourists—along with the UK, U.S., Russia, Australia and the UAE.

IPK International (2012) cite a much-reported result of a representative survey by the International University of Applied Sciences Bad Honnef-Bonn which reports that 52% of German adults can see themselves traveling abroad for medical treatment, including dental treatment and surgery. Actual numbers on outbound medical tourism in Germany are rare as outbound travel is dominated by the broader category of health tourism. Among medical treatments demanded, dental tourism and cosmetic procedures play a prominent role. Surveys by the Techniker Krankenkasse, a statutory health insurance, provide the most comprehensive overview over outbound medical and health tourism. Wagner and Verheyen (2010) surveyed all of their 47,038 insurants who had received acute or elective treatments within the European Union and analyzed the responses of 15,540 patients who represented 29,884 treatments.

Oberhauser-Aslan (2013) reports a Euromedic estimate of 300,000 German patients who seek dental treatment or hair implants abroad every year. Even if the study by Wagner and Verheyen (2010) is not representative, the TK study yields about 3010 out of 4,280,854 million TK insurants in 2008 with planned dental treatments or treatment categories that may comprise hair implants. Further extrapolation to 90% out of 82 million Germans who are insured under the statutory regime yields 51,898 patients. Clearly, this back-of-the-envelope calculation disregards potential underreporting of cosmetic procedures and neglects 10% of the population who are privately insured but under the assumption that privately insured patients have less of a reason to go abroad due to extensive domestic coverage, the estimates by Euromedic are difficult to reconcile with the numbers reported in Wagner and Verheyen (2010).

While data on outbound medical tourism is diluted by health and wellness treatments, data on inbound medical tourism suffers from other deficiencies, most notably the possibility to distinguish between planned and acute treatments and missing information on outpatient treatments. Consequently, these essential data qualifiers are typically not reported. According to Oberhauser-Aslan (2013), the treatment focus of inbound medical tourists varies by source country. Patients from more distant countries seek treatments in more complex cases and the anecdotal visit for a quick check-up is waning. Furthermore, the treatment of children becomes increasingly important.

IPK International (2012) reports 70,000 patients in 2011, mainly from Austria, Belgium, France, Luxemburg and the Netherlands. In light of the preceding discussion, there is good reason to remain skeptical about how many of these patients are medical tourists according to the above definition and how many make use of regional cross-border co-operations. Arab patients are acknowledged as a lucrative niche (IPK International 2012) with a very specific destination focus on Bavaria and Hesse (Frädrich 2013; Lutze et al. 2010). More specifically, Juszczak (2008) suggests a destination focus on specific hospitals such as Hamburg-Eppendorf, Aachen, Kiel, Freiburg, and Kaiser-Karl Clinic Bonn regardless of the patients' source countries. Juszczak was one of the first to follow medical tourism in Germany and his numbers are circulated on numerous occasions. Oberhauser-Aslan (2013) reports Juszczak to estimate annual visitors at 80,000 inpatients and 130,000 to 140,000 outpatients.

Nagel and Neller (2013a) report more than 200,000 patients to Germany in 2012 with approximately 1 billion Euros in revenues to hospitals and another billion Euros in revenues to medical centers, private practices and chief physicians. They estimate a share of Arabic-speaking patients of nearly 10% and dedicate a series of articles to patients from Libya (Nagel and Neller 2013a, b, 2014). However, the current focus is reported to lie on medical tourists from Russia (Nagel and Neller 2013a; Oberhauser-Aslan 2013). The state of Saxony is one particular region that benefits from a growing number of Russian medical tourists (Frädrich 2013). These numbers go along with a rise in overall tourism (Münch 2014). But other hospitals are experiencing an increased demand from Russia as well. Oberhauser-Aslan (2013) once again cites Juszczak (2008) with approximately 5000 Russians per year or just above 6% of all medical tourists.

Several of the numbers reported above are estimates in media reports. In contrast, official figures or surveys are quite rare. Lutze et al. (2010) provide an overview over the source countries, flows as well as treatment types and characteristics of inbound medical tourists in Germany between 1999 and 2006. They make use of the official hospital statistics, which report only inpatient treatments. A treatment ends with the discharge of a patient so the changing of wards initiates a new treatment of the same patient. The official records identify a patient's place of residence but not his nationality, so an unidentified share of the treatments could be rendered to expatriates.

A share of about 0.3% of all patients was of foreign residency and their absolute number increased from 40,501 in 1999 to 53,505 in 2006. The majority of these patients stemmed from core EU countries and much of this medical tourism is characterized by regional cross-border care delivered to residents of neighboring countries. The analysis by state confirms significant cross-border tourism in the regions of Poland/Brandenburg and France/Saarland that is dominated by treatments of acute conditions. At the same time, other regions seem to have focused on patients from selected countries as the concentration of patients from Kuwait in southwestern Germany and Berlin highlights (Lutze et al. 2010). Growth rates for patients from Kuwait, Russia, Romania and the United Arab Emirates stand out with 24, 22, 20 and 18%, respectively, but these countries started at relatively low levels. Other locations displayed very location-specific effects: the drop of Turkish patients may simply be due to a change in residency statuses.

Richter and Richter (2012) choose a rather unusual regional focus and provide an analysis of the export balance of a single German state. Specifically, they calculate the export balance of inpatient services rendered to Saxons by hospitals between 1995 and 2009. In addition to the aggregate net export perspective, they make a distinction between imports from the rest of Germany and the rest of the world. They provide one of the few studies that work with official data but are bound by the typical limitations of their data set: they cannot distinguish between acute and elective treatments and have no information about outpatient treatments as they are not recorded in the official hospital statistics, which the authors use. Richter and Richter (2012) thus choose to extrapolate estimates from Wagner and Verheyen (2010) to calculate Saxony's export balance.

Selected key findings of the study are that 3% of all patients are out-of-state and 2% are out-of-country. The majority of the former are from neighboring states (84.1%) and many of the latter are from neighboring countries (24.3%). These numbers demonstrate that the group of international recruits is more heterogeneous. The authors also compare average costs of hospital stay and average length of hospital stay for domestic and international importing and exporting subgroups but do not control for treatments. They attribute longer stays and higher costs for mobile patients to the potential severity of their conditions and their respective search for specialists elsewhere. Despite the limitations of their data, Richter and Richter (2012) provide a rare analysis of actual health care trade values. Remarkable yet unaddressed is the nearly 60% plunge of inflowing patients in 1998 after consistently high levels from 1995 through 1997. It may have been the reduction of a backlog but the origin cannot be identified due to the starting point of the time series.

2.2.2.1 Inbound Inpatient Statistics

This section provides an overview of the aforementioned hospital statistics provided by the Research Data Centres of the Federal Statistical Office of Germany (RDC 2007–2012). These statistics record inpatient treatments along with a number of patient characteristics. Treatments cannot be aggregated by patient but a treatment can and must reasonably be assumed to correspond to a patient even if a small number of patients may be readmitted after discharge. Self-reported treatments of outgoing patients typically exceed the number of patients as outgoing patients report multiple massages or baths as multiple treatments (Wagner et al. 2011; Wagner and Verheyen 2010) but for inpatients a treatment covers a longer episode that is recorded by the main diagnosis. Access to hospital data is highly restricted and full population data is only accessible via controlled remote data access. Outputs are censored depending on their level of aggregation, the number of outputs and previously disclosed outputs in order to ensure cross-table anonymity. Consequently, joint distributions across all recorded attributes and units of interest are impossible to obtain and the analysis is restricted to selected multivariate distributions and aggregated data. Specifically, we focus on various measures of treatment volumes, duration of stay, treatment types as classified by ICD 10, and age groups.

In the period from 2007 to 2012, 459,224 inpatient treatments of international patients are identified and 43% of the treatments were rendered to women. Over the entire timespan, 69 treatments were encoded to Germany and removed from the analysis. For another 30,622 treatments, countries were encoded as open/not specified, which is driven by 10,382 such encodings in 2007. The following years display more modest shares of unassigned treatments. Table 2.2 depicts the unassigned treatment, inpatient day and export volume shares of total values available. These total values neglect censored cells and refer to computable totals only. There is only a minimal discrepancy between computable total treatments and total treatments reported by the Federal Statistical Office.

Our data set allows us to assign treatments of patients from unassigned countries to treatment categories in order to check for systematic patterns. To ensure privacy, 4-digit ICD codes were aggregated to 22 ICD chapters, which led to the removal of ICD chapters 20 and 22 with 0 and 2 observations, respectively. The remaining 20 ICD chapters were used in the subsequent analysis.

Figure 2.2 depicts the treatment shares by ICD chapter that were rendered to patients with unassigned or missing country codes. High percentages for ICD 1 (infectious and parasitic diseases), ICD 5 (mental and behavioral disorders), ICD 15 (pregnancy and childbirth), ICD 16 (conditions originating in the perinatal period) and ICD 14 (diseases of the genitourinary system) hint to privacy as a suspected driver of both seeking a treatment and concealing one's identity in Germany. However, these ICD chapters also cover a large number of acute conditions so some of these treatments in Germany may just be incidental. Figure 2.2 further shows that the share of unassigned treatments is uncorrelated with the share of total unassigned treatments. It is possible to assign treatments of patients with unassigned/missing source countries to countries based on the observed country

Table 2.2 Unassigned/Missing Country Shares, by inpatient measure and year

	2007	2008	2009	2010	2011	2012
Treatments (%)	14.7	7.0	5.1	6.8	4.4	3.3
Treatment days (%)	13.0	7.8	5.5	8.1	4.1	4.3
Export volume (%)	14.4	6.6	5.8	7.2	3.7	3.5

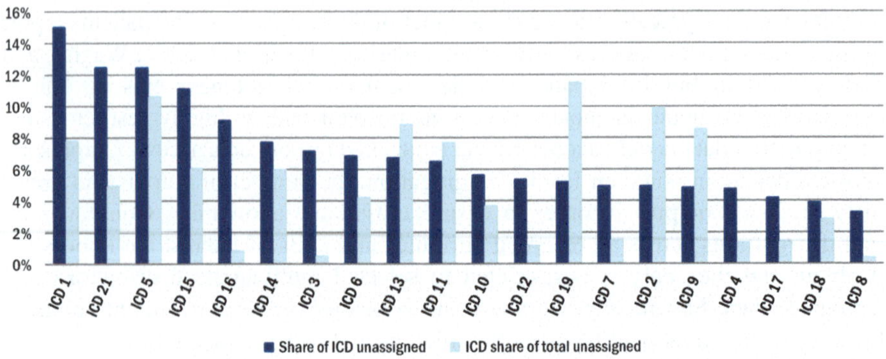

Fig. 2.2 Treatment share with unassigned/missing country, by ICD chapter

shares within ICD chapters but we prefer to discard unassigned treatments as any cultural predispositions for privacy or any other heterogeneous reasons for undisclosed residency across countries would render the ex-post assignment invalid.

Figure 2.3 displays treatment type composition for each year and highlights the magnitude of ICD 19 (injuries), ICD 2 (neoplasms) and ICD 9 (diseases of the circulatory system) followed by ICD 13 (diseases of the musculoskeletal system and connective tissue), ICD 11 (diseases of the digestive system), ICD 5 (mental and behavioral disorders) and ICD 14 (diseases of the genitourinary system). Total inpatient treatments increased from 70,551 in 2007 to 90,481 in 2012. The drop in 2008 coincides with the financial crisis but treatment totals recover quickly and grow rapidly thereafter.

While total inpatient treatments sought in Germany are visibly affected by a global economic downturn, the effect on the various treatment types is very heterogeneous. Figures 2.4 and 2.6 index each ICD to 100 in 2007 and display the relative growth in the following periods. Figure 2.4 contains all ICD chapters that did not fall below 100 and that exhibit growth throughout the period under consideration in orange. Most notably, these ICD chapters include ICD 17 (congenital malformations, deformations and chromosomal abnormalities); ICD 2 (neoplasms); ICD 4 (endocrine, nutritional and metabolic diseases); and ICD 8 (diseases of the ear and mastoid process). Figure 2.4 further includes ICD chapters that fell below their index in 2008 and recovered in subsequent years in blue. Most of these ICD chapters exhibit

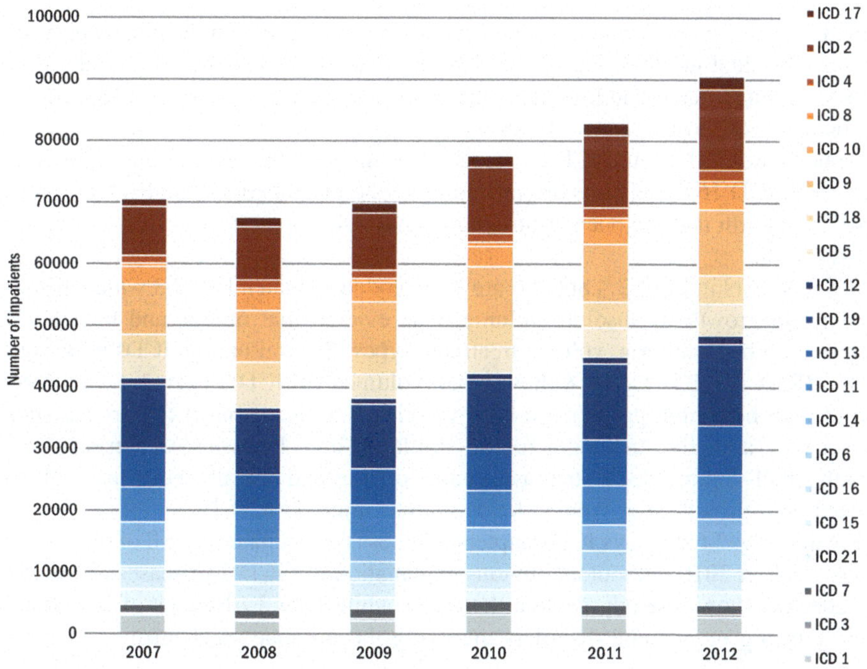

Fig. 2.3 Total treatments and ICD composition, by year

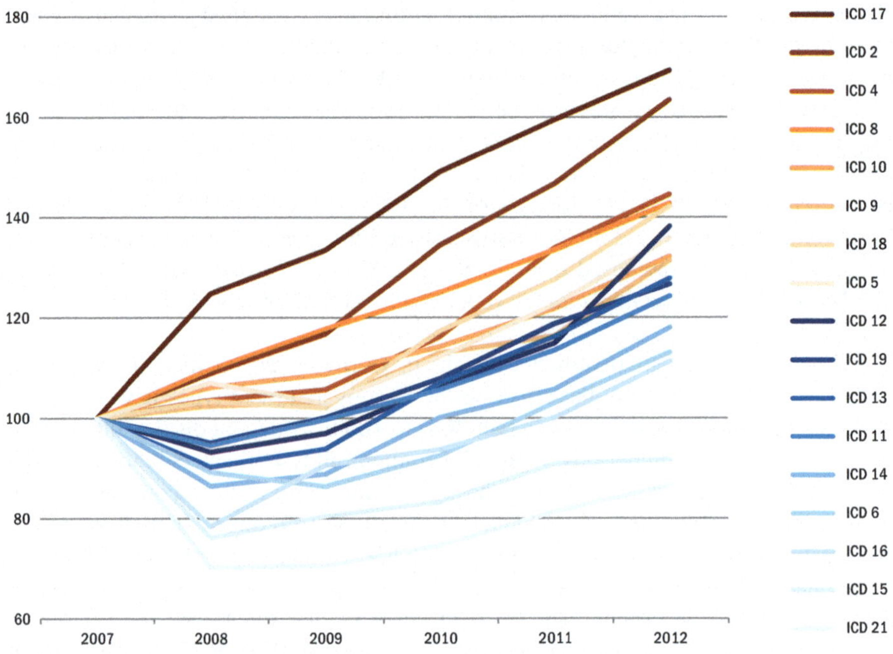

Fig. 2.4 ICD chapter growth, by year

growth over the entire period but somewhat less pronounced than the treatment types that have no dent in 2008. Figure 2.5 depicts the recovery patterns of the blue ICD chapters in more detail and highlights the years with indices below 100. This shows that demand for most treatment types with a dent in 2008 recovered within 3 years. Exceptions are ICD 15 and ICD 21 which remain below the level of 2007. Interestingly, both ICD 16 (conditions originating in the perinatal period) and ICD 15 (pregnancy, childbirth and the puerperium) were among the slowest to recover or did not recover at all.

ICD chapters in Figs. 2.4 and 2.6 are color coded to match Fig. 2.3 which allows us to relate growth to absolute volume. It is evident that orange and blue ICDs capture both high and low volume treatment types. Several orange ICDs with high growth (ICD 17, ICD 4, ICD 8) have small volumes but ICD 2 provides a counterweight with both high growth and high volume. The treatment of tumors has thus been a very attractive treatment focus. Similarly, blue ICDs also represent high-growth small-volume fields such as diseases of skin and subcutaneous tissue (ICD 12) and high-growth high-volume fields such as injuries (ICD 19).

Finally, Fig. 2.6 displays ICD chapters with less typical patterns. All of them have a local peak in 2010 without an obvious explanation but ICD 7 (diseases of the eye and adnexa) show a steady decline thereafter while ICD 3 (diseases of blood and blood-forming organs and disorders involving the immune mechanism) follows a

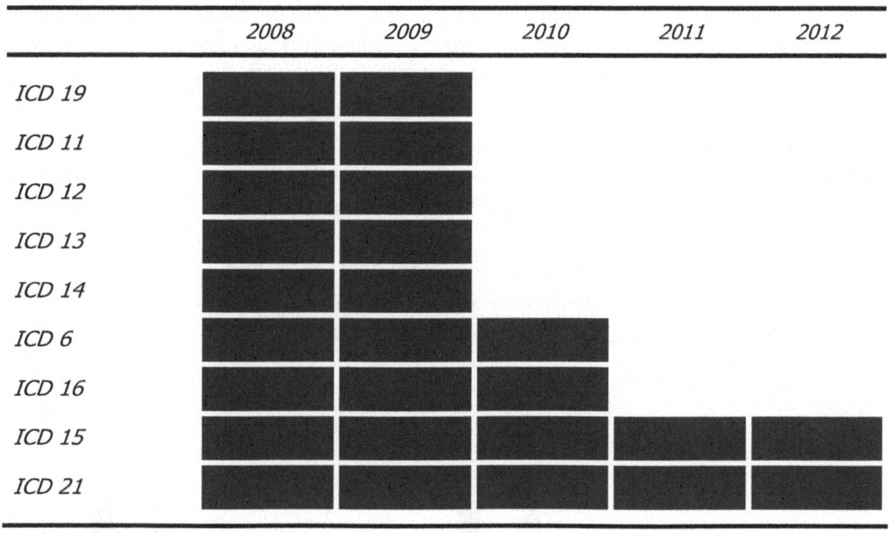

Fig. 2.5 Recovery patterns, by ICD chapter

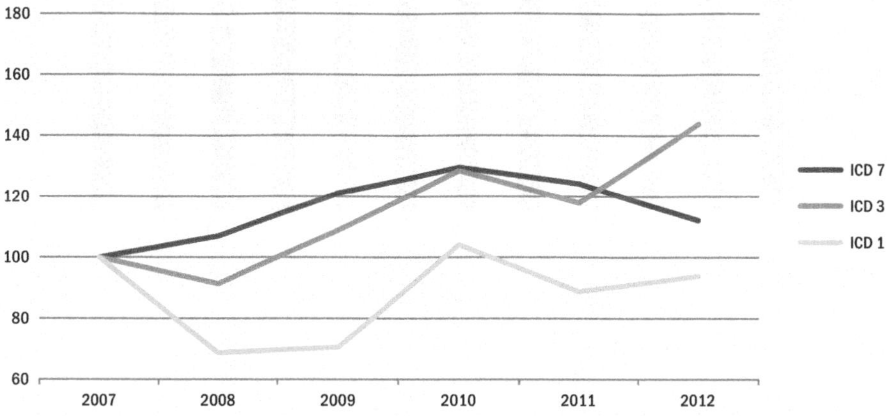

Fig. 2.6 ICD growth, by year

general growth pattern with some setbacks and ICD 1 (infectious and parasitic diseases) oscillates below its index of 2007.

In addition to the development of ICD chapters per year, we are interested in the exports associated with the various regions and countries per year. We measure exports in three different ways: number of patients, number of inpatient days and export volumes. Number of patients is the crudest measure and assumes similarity of the average patient for each country along several dimensions. The number of inpatient days is a more elaborate approximation of export volume that takes into account the complexity, duration and, implicitly, treatment costs for citizens of an importing country. To arrive at export values, inpatient days need to be augmented by prices. We follow Richter and Richter (2012) in approximating these prices by explicit hospital costs, but do not use the annual, adjusted average hospital costs across all hospitals to calculate the export volume. We employ annual, hospital-specific average costs instead which allows for a better approximation of the true export value in the presence of significant treatment clustering as a result of a hospital focus, for example.

Figures 2.7 and 2.8 show treatments, inpatient days and growth patterns by region. It is evident that the majority of treatments are provided to patients from Europe followed by Asia, the Americas, Africa and Oceania. Inpatient days mea-

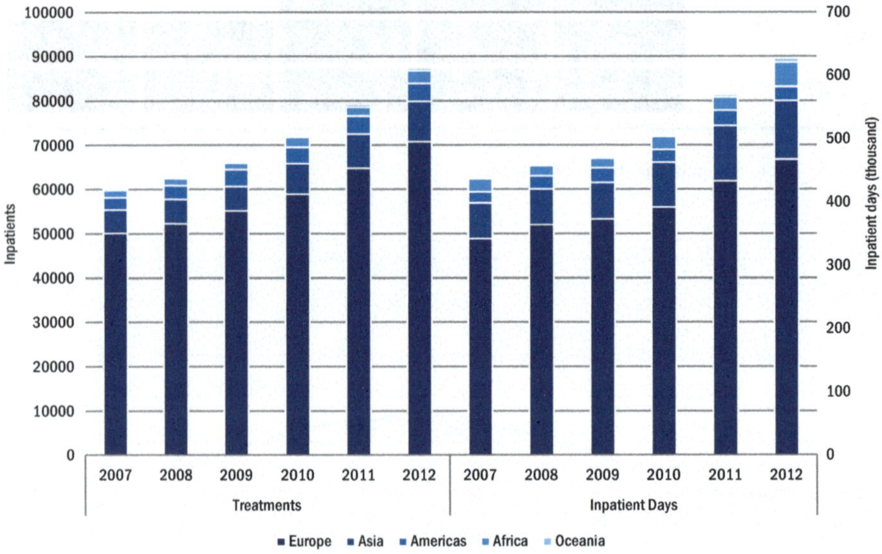

Fig. 2.7 Treatments and inpatient days, by region and year

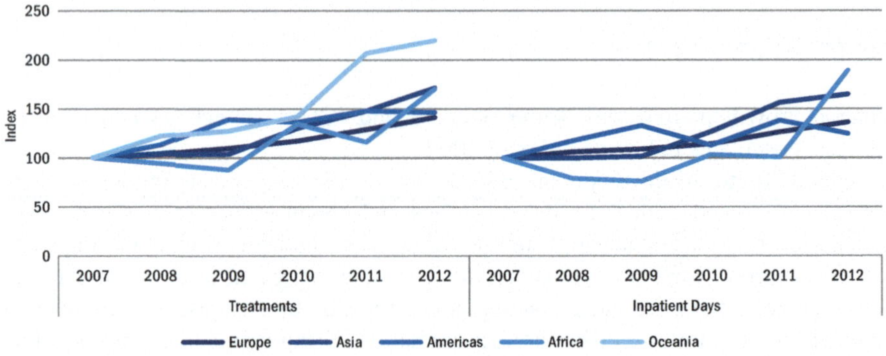

Fig. 2.8 Treatment and inpatient day growth, by region and year

sured on the right axis paint a similar picture but here Asia and Africa capture a larger share, which hints to longer durations of stay. Growth over the entire period is positive for all regions with only Europe and Asia exhibiting a stable growth pattern. The pattern for Africa, on the other hand, is quite volatile and will be explained as we look at single countries below. Finally, note that treatments and the corresponding inpatient days necessarily exclude patients with unassigned residency so treatment totals do not correspond to Fig. 2.3.

Before we disaggregate regions into countries, we take a look at the discrepancy between treatment and inpatient day shares of the regions in Fig. 2.7. This discrepancy highlights the motivation to use inpatient days as opposed to treatments along with hospital-specific average costs to calculate export volumes. Figure 2.9 displays export volume calculations based on inpatient days and hospital-specific average costs (base 1) against calculations based on the number of treatments and hospital-averaged treatment costs (base 2). In addition to the volume deviations, export shares of Asia are underestimated, Europe is severely overestimated and the Americas are slightly overestimated for base 2. Failure to take length of stay and hospital-specific average costs into account denies heterogeneity in treatment types/durations of stay across countries and heterogeneity in specialization/pricing across hospitals and will thus result in questionable export volumes.

We do not have average costs per inpatient day to deconstruct the export volume bias into inpatient day and hospital-specific average cost components but our data set allows us to calculate average durations of stay per region and year and Table 2.3 confirms the anticipated heterogeneity in average duration of stay across regions.

Moving from regions to countries, we can identify the main source countries of each region in Fig. 2.7 by every export measure for every year. We will briefly

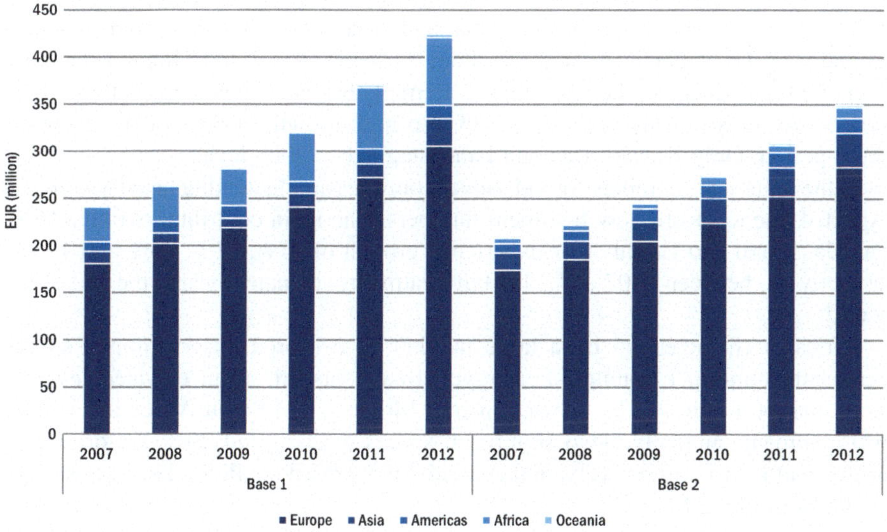

Fig. 2.9 Export volume sensitivity, by region and year

Table 2.3 Average inpatient days per treatment, by region and year

	2007	2008	2009	2010	2011	2012
Europe	6.83	6.96	6.77	6.65	6.69	6.60
Asia	10.64	10.27	10.39	10.34	11.25	10.23
Americas	6.48	6.73	6.19	5.36	6.05	5.52
Africa	11.99	10.09	10.40	9.20	10.40	13.33
Oceania	5.88	6.05	6.87	6.59	7.20	9.61

highlight broad trends here and any numbers cited refer to treatments observed in 2012.

A close look at Europe immediately reveals the elephant in the room: More than 8000 treatments are rendered to Russian patients, which make Russia the largest source country that also boasts an impressive growth of 187% over the timespan under consideration. Aside from Russia, most patients in Europe are from countries neighboring Germany. Numbers range from 1186 for Czech Republic to 7624 for the Netherlands, but most countries i.e. France, Poland, Austria, Switzerland and Belgium can be found at the upper end of the range with 4000 or more patients. With the exception of Denmark, patient volumes from these countries grew up to 30%, with Poland, Czech Republic and Switzerland achieving higher growth at 40%, 71% and 80%, respectively. Countries with the highest growth rates are largely located in Eastern Europe. These include Serbia, Slovenia, Cyprus, Moldova, Latvia, Romania, Bulgaria and Ukraine. While Serbia and Moldova represent relatively few treatments, Romania and Bulgaria rival Germany's neighboring countries Italy and Czech Republic with 2771 and 1132 treatments, respectively.

Most Asian countries display positive growth across the period under consideration but several countries stand out. The United Arab Emirates and Saudi Arabia with more than 2500 and 1200 treatments, respectively, take the top tier in Asia followed by Kuwait, Kazakhstan, Qatar and Iraq with 350–750 treatments in a second tier. Third tier is Azerbaijan, Iran, Armenia, Israel and Oman with more than 200 treatments and the rest follows. Remarkably, most countries in these three tiers do not only display high levels but also high growth of 60% or more for the entire period. Only Kuwait, Iran and Israel stagnate at 2007 levels.

In the Americas, numbers for individual countries are fluctuating heavily which is expected due to mostly low treatment numbers. The main contributors in the U.S., Canada, Brazil and El Salvador experience growth of 47%, 41%, 36% and 136%, respectively, between 2007 and 2012 but treatments stagnate towards the end of the period.

Africa is characterized by a large number of censored observations, i.e. low treatment counts per country. For Egypt, treatments are at an elevated level of more than 600 followed by Libya, Nigeria, Morocco and South Africa at a distant 100 treatments annually. Two significant spikes in 2010 and 2012 are driven by Eritrea and Libya, respectively, and coincide with armed conflicts. These spikes are the kinks in Fig. 2.8.

Oceania contributes less than 1% to treatments and inpatient days and is mostly driven by New Zealand and Australia. For both countries, treatments approximately doubled between 2007 and 2012 but while inpatient days doubled for New Zealand as well, inpatient days for Australia quadrupled. To avoid rescaling of the inpatient chart and in light of its modest relevance in absolute numbers, Oceania is omitted from the growth pattern charts.

Table 2.4 presents a treatment summary for the top five source countries by year and region, sorted by treatments in 2012. Figures 2.10 and 2.11 visualize total treatments and total export volumes in Euros from 2007 to 2012 for each country and underline the regional particularities discussed above.

In addition to clustering countries by treatments and export volumes, we can also analyze their ICD patterns. For this analysis, we must give up the time dimension for privacy reasons so ICD chapters per country are aggregated across 6 years. Unfortunately, this approach still yields a considerable number of censored cells that need to be filled for clustering procedures to calculate their required distance measures. The removal of countries with only censored cells reduces our data set to 146 countries but not to a level of missing cells that allows imputation. Imputation of so many missing values renders clustering meaningless since standard imputation is column-based and we exploit this information when clustering. Standard imputation methods further neglect our uncommon knowledge of the actual row sums, i.e. we can compute the share of missing treatments per row. We use this information to remove all countries whose share of missing treatments exceeds 10% of the row sum. This

Table 2.4 Inpatient treatments for selected countries, by region and year

		2007	2008	2009	2010	2011	2012
Europe	Russia	2887	3833	4117	4873	6193	8280
	Netherlands	6787	6833	7241	7379	7413	7624
	France	5676	5791	6126	6412	6494	6929
	Poland	4801	4710	4628	5173	5992	6714
	Austria	4838	5186	5345	5828	5916	6285
Asia	UAE	1027	1058	1330	1754	2086	2621
	Saudi-Arabia	609	820	462	712	1002	1260
	Kuwait	778	560	713	967	815	749
	Kazakhstan	300	305	318	321	486	606
	Qatar	299	263	322	418	393	479
Americas	USA	2007	2252	2863	2807	2914	2947
	Canada	290	328	395	399	381	409
	Brazil	129	155	140	144	193	176
	El Salvador	42	31	68	98	102	99
	Mexico	48	60	52	46	82	79
Africa	Libya	197	223	299	346	435	1348
	Egypt	697	672	597	653	700	648
	Nigeria	116	110	103	114	122	148
	Morocco	100	107	76	80	102	107
	South Africa	88	74	52	94	100	101
Oceania	Australia	227	285	310	338	512	523
	New Zealand	43	45	41	53	59	87

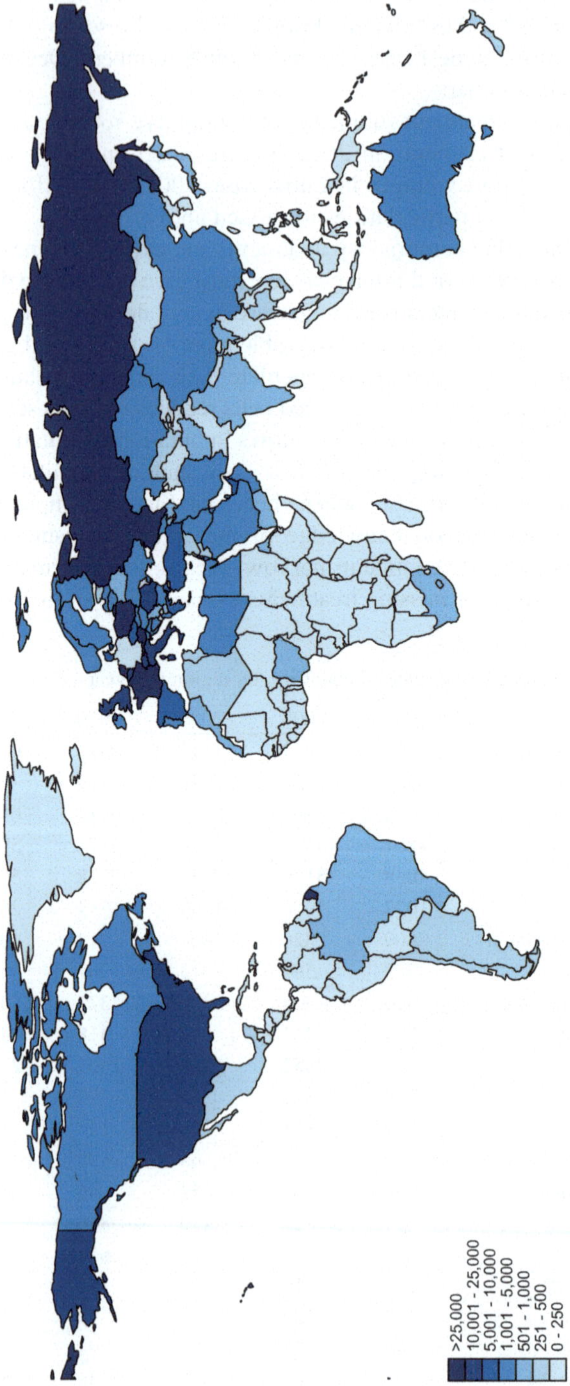

Fig. 2.10 World map of total treatments per country

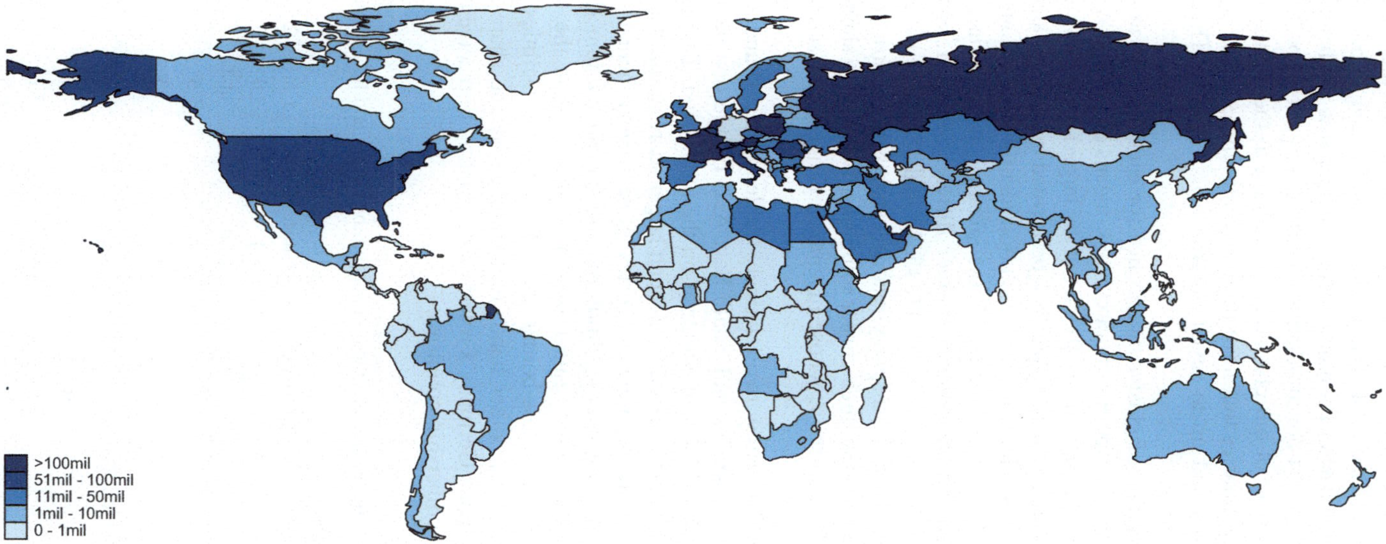

Fig. 2.11 World map of export volume per country

step reduces countries to 99, on which we run our imputation algorithm that simply allocates equal shares of the total treatments missing to each empty cell for a given row. Given the small shares of missing values of their row totals and their mostly single-digit size, we expect our imputation to have negligible impact. Nevertheless, to analyze the sensitivity of our clustering procedures to the imputation, we create three data sets with countries that have up to two missing cells per row, up to four missing cells per row and up to seven missing cells per row. The third data set includes all 99 countries.

We run a broad range of cluster diagnostics for each data set to determine the optimal number of clusters for non-hierarchical k-means clustering. A choice of two clusters was the overwhelming result for all but the largest data set which produced a tie between two and three clusters. We thus performed both a two and three cluster analysis on all data sets. The two-cluster solution identifies two groups that display stark differences in ICD shares for ICD 2 (neoplasms), ICD 19 (injuries) and ICD 5 (mental and behavioral disorders). Further differences of at least single-digit magnitude occur in ICD chapters 1, 10, 11, 15, 17 and 18. These patterns are robust across all samples and Table 2.5 displays treatment shares for countries in both clusters averaged across data sets. The three-cluster solution arrives at very similar results with the exception of ICD chapter 17, whose magnitude is not robust across all data sets given our cut-off.

Figures 2.12 and 2.13 show two relatively stable clusters 0 and 2 consisting of most of Europe, the Americas and South-East Asia on the one hand and Russia, Central Asia and selected African countries on the other hand. Taking into account Table 2.5, cluster 0 is characterized by a much larger share of injuries (ICD 19) and larger shares in most other reported categories, most notably mental and behavioral disorders (ICD 5) and pregnancy, childbirth and the puerperium (ICD 15). The former hint to incidental treatments related to tourism while the latter seem to confirm the considerable cross-border use of childbirth facilities discussed in Chap. 2. Cluster 2, on the other hand, is dominated by the share of neoplasms (ICD 2) which highlights Germany's role as a destination to receive tumor patients from the cluster's membership countries.

Table 2.5 Selected average treatment shares in percent, by cluster and ICD chapter

	Two clusters		Three clusters		
	Cluster 0	Cluster 2	Cluster 0	Cluster 2	Cluster 1
ICD 1	4.1	2.7	4.4	2.9	–
ICD 2	11.3	30.3	10.0	34.4	18.5
ICD 5	5.6	1.3	6.4	1.5	–
ICD 10	4.6	3.2	4.9	3.3	–
ICD 11	8.9	6.2	9.1	5.9	–
ICD 15	3.8	1.5	3.9	1.4	–
ICD 17	2.5	3.9	–	–	–
ICD 18	5.3	3.1	5.7	3.1	–
ICD 19	15.0	6.8	16.3	6.6	–

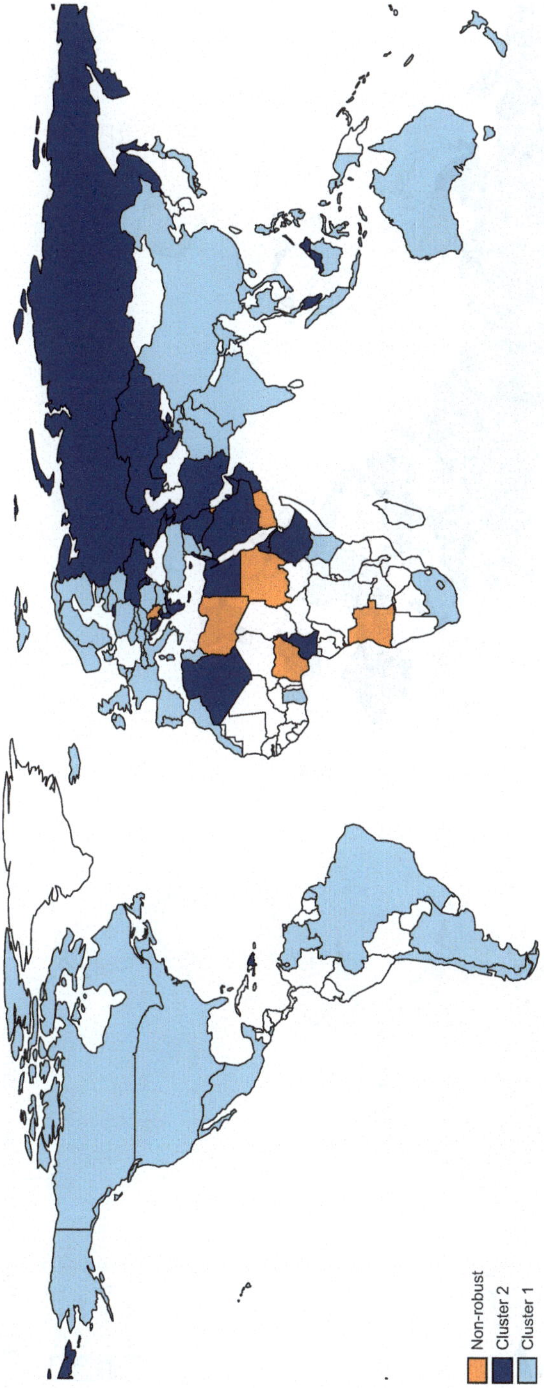

Fig. 2.12 Two-cluster country solution

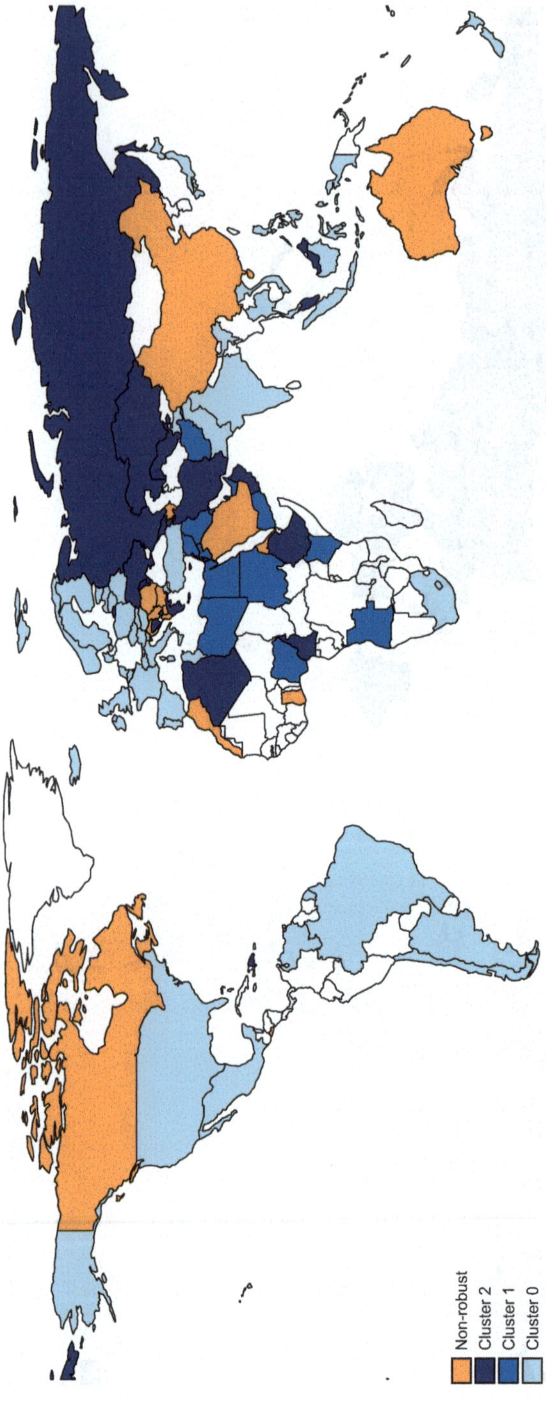

Fig. 2.13 Three-cluster country solution

The effect of introducing a third cluster is very heterogeneous across data sets as cluster 1 feeds from cluster 0, cluster 2 or both, depending on the data set. The only robust effect across all data sets was another increase in the ICD 2 share of the cluster 2 countries shown in Table 2.5. Given that the three-cluster solution in Fig. 2.13 moves most Middle Eastern and African countries from cluster 2 to 1, it also reveals Russia, Central Asia and the other cluster 2 countries as the dominating source of neoplasm patients. However, Table 2.5 reports that countries in cluster 1 still have a significantly higher share of ICD 2 treatments than in cluster 0. Two data sets further suggest that cluster 1 also captures countries with high shares of congenital malformations, deformations and chromosomal abnormalities (ICD 17) and very high shares of diseases of the musculoskeletal system and connective tissue (ICD 13). Finally, the introduction of a third cluster further increases the share of mental and behavioral disorders among cluster 0 countries but the effect is not very pronounced.

The two- and three-cluster solutions only share Serbia as a non-robust country while the remaining countries differ. Serbia is a very special case due to political turmoil and multiple changes in boundaries throughout the period under consideration that continued to reassign treatments to new states or territories. Consequently, the entire region turns non-robust as we move to three clusters and needs to be considered separately if interest lies therein. The other major non-robust results are Australia, Canada and China, which the larger samples assign to cluster 0, and Saudi-Arabia, which the larger samples assign to cluster 1 like most of the region. However, the smallest and most restrictive sample proposes clusters 1 and 2, respectively.

Another informative distribution in the data set covers the age of international inpatients. Patients were aggregated to nine age groups and Fig. 2.14 shows that patients are distributed quite evenly across these groups. We suspected a larger share of patients groups 41–70 than in 0–40 due to an increasing disease burden and a higher ability to pay but this hypothesis is not confirmed. Treatments are unfiltered, however, and treatment types between these segments may vary. Younger cohorts may travel more and be afflicted by incidental conditions while older cohorts may indeed travel more for planned care. The second graph in Fig. 2.14 shows that

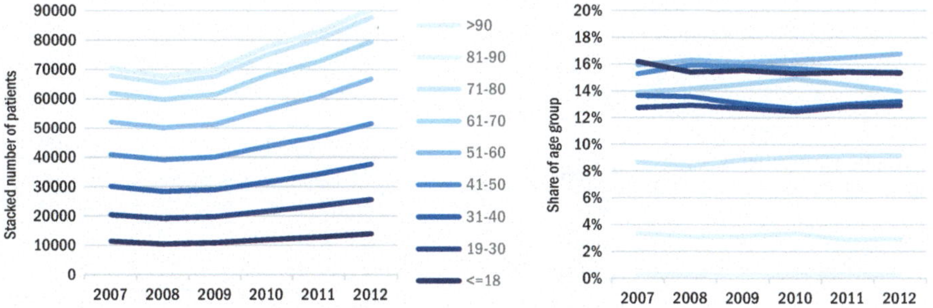

Fig. 2.14 Number of patients and share of age groups, by year

inpatient growth is evenly distributed across age groups as their shares are essentially constant over time.

Finally, we calculated the average age of an international patient by country and aggregated across years. We removed countries with all years censored and with less than three annual values to support the reported average, so the average is based on a reasonable number of observations. We further removed countries with censored treatment totals across all years, which were used to weigh the age data. The average international patient is 43.8 years old with relatively small deviations from the average and no discernible country pattern. There are, however, regional differences as displayed in Table 2.6. Bartlett's test rejects equal variances at $\alpha = 5\%$ and the subsequent Bonferroni test rejects equal means of Europe, the Americas and Oceania in pairwise comparison with Asia. Asian patients are thus significantly younger on average than patients from Europe, the Americas and Oceania. Equal means cannot be rejected for all other pairwise comparisons. Note that average age of Oceania is once again driven by Australia with a dominating treatment count and few other countries entering the grand average of Oceania.

We have come full circle and examined the multivariate distributions of treatment types per year, export measures by country and year, treatment types by country and age by year, country and region. In summary, we have identified injuries (ICD 19), neoplasms (ICD 2), diseases of the circulatory system (ICD 9), diseases of the musculoskeletal system and connective tissue (ICD 13) and diseases of the digestive system (ICD 11) to be the most common treatment types among international inpatients in Germany but found that ICD chapter growth is not related to ICD chapter volume. Europe and Asia dominate all export measures while a temporary surge of African patients towards the end of the period is apparently driven by armed conflicts. Europe and Asia further draw from a mix of source countries while flows from other regions are dominated by relatively few countries. Source countries can further be clustered across the regions used above which yields clusters that can be distinguished by their shares of injuries (ICD 19), neoplasms (ICD 2), diseases of the musculoskeletal system and connective tissue (ICD 13) and congenital malformations, deformations and chromosomal abnormalities (ICD17). Finally, average age across regions is significantly lower for Asian patients and patient shares by age group are of similar magnitude but for the oldest cohorts and stable over time.

Table 2.6 Average age of international inpatients, by region

	Average age	Countries
Europe	44.17	45
Asia	40.67	39
Americas	43.58	22
Africa	42.63	33
Oceania	47.56	4

2.2.2.2 Medical Visas

A data source that has not previously been investigated but provides quite recent information for Germany is medical visas. Medical visas are a subcategory of Schengen visas that enable foreigners to stay in Germany for up to 90 days, which allows for both outpatient and inpatient treatments. Medical visas thus overlap with official hospital statistics, which only include inpatient stays recorded at German hospitals.

The data set at hand contains data on 141 countries or territories for the years 2006 through 2013. Multiple locations within countries were aggregated for the analysis. Summation across countries revealed a minor inconsistency in the data for 2012 where the sum of medical visa reported deviates from the calculated sum by −0.4% or 145 medical visas issued. The calculated totals are used in the analysis.

A second deficiency in the raw data was identified for Belarus, where medical visas issued display an inexplicable increase in 2009 that fades out in 2010 and returns to pre-2009 levels afterwards. This increase by one order of magnitude is so large that it causes the kink in Fig. 2.15. Further examination found a possible explanation in the multiple thousand visas issued to children from Chernobyl fallout regions that may have accidentally been recorded as medical visas in 2009. In 2010, however, the number of medical visas was still 3 times higher than in 2008 before returning to very low levels in the following years. Two ways to deal with this deficiency lie in the removal of an order of magnitude for both 2009 and 2010 or in removing the observations for both years altogether. Both methods produce similar results in aggregated totals but the former yields medical visa numbers that are well in line with the country trend so we opted for that method. Removing the order of

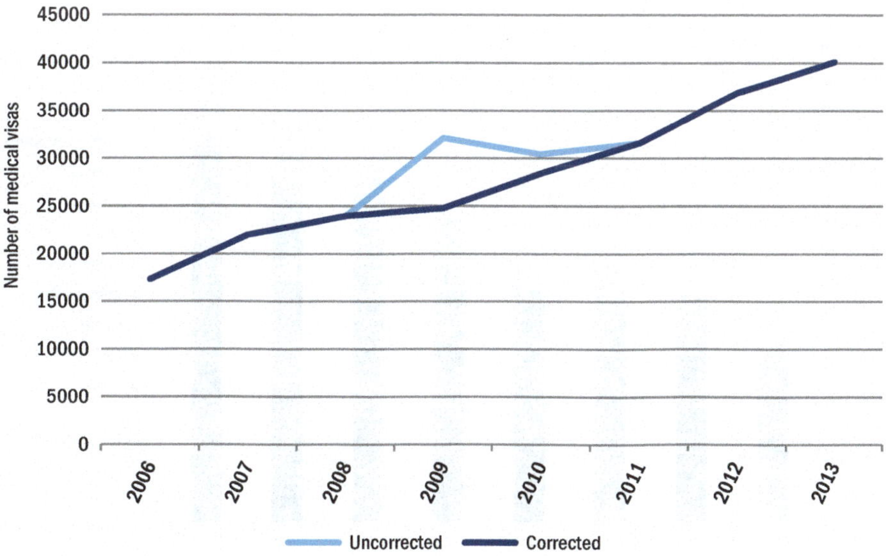

Fig. 2.15 Total medical visas issued, by year

magnitude increases in both 2009 and 2010 leads to the totals reported as "corrected". These totals are more plausible as they reflect the expected, moderating effect of the financial crisis in 2008 and its aftermath.

91 of the 141 countries included in the medical visa statistics issued minimal numbers of medical visas not exceeding 50 in any of the years reported. These countries are excluded from further analysis to avoid clutter in the exposition. The remaining 50 countries represent a minimum of 97.9% of all annual visas issued in any year of the reported period.

About one-third of all medical visas issued by German embassies and consulates are issued in Russia, which warrants a separate category for this country. A vast majority of the countries is located in Western Asia and its bordering regions. These geographic regions are relatively homogeneous clusters in both the number of medical visas issued and dynamics within clusters but heterogeneous between clusters. A classification by political entities gives a more heterogeneous picture for CIS states and suggests a separate cluster for the four strongest GCC economies whose medical visa levels far exceed those of the other countries in the region. We chose to group countries as follows: Africa, Asia, Central Asia, Europe, GCC, the Mediterranean area, Western Asia, Russia and a mix of various heterogeneous countries that is discussed below. The countries included in each group can be found in Figs. 2.17 and 2.18.

Figure 2.16 shows that total medical visas issued increased from 17,326 in 2006 to 40,141 in 2013 with positive growth throughout the entire period. In line with the hospital statistics on inpatients, Russia is the most important source country with a share of 34% medical visas issued in 2013 followed by the GCC. Notably, the GCC

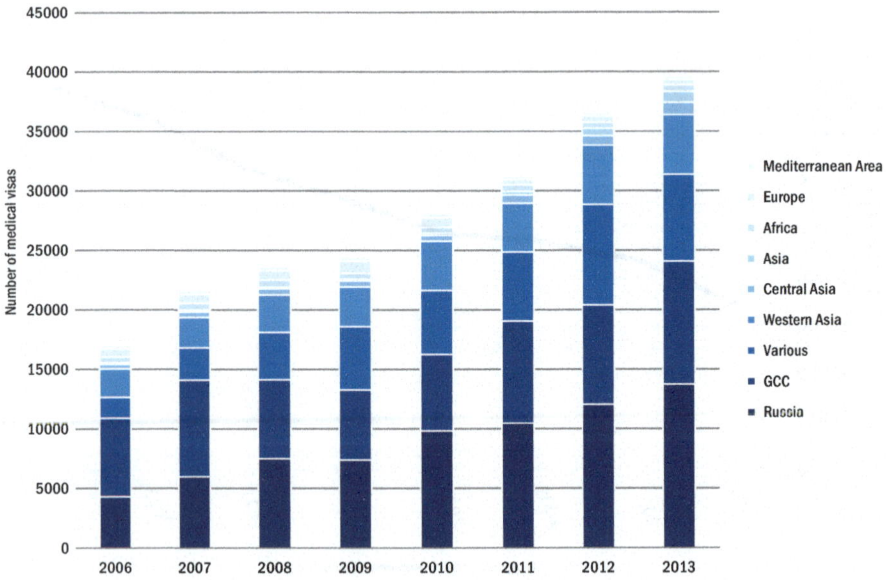

Fig. 2.16 Medical visas issued, by region and year

started with the largest share of 38% in 2006 but took a hit of 9% in 2008 and did not recover thereafter.

Given the dominance of medical visas issued in Russia, the country merits a closer look and we will turn to the other groups in Figs. 2.17 and 2.18 first. GCC countries, Western Asia, Central Asia and remaining Asia—which represents more Eastern Asian countries—are the four regions with upward trend in total medical visas issued but at very different levels. Among the four GCC countries, most medical visas are issued in UAE but Qatar and Kuwait drive the trend while Saudi Arabia has been hovering at a constant level. The upward trend in Western Asia is driven by multiple countries except for Bahrain and Iran where numbers have been falling since 2010 and 2011, respectively. In Central Asia, both Afghanistan with its peak in 2008 and Uzbekistan with its strong upward trend stand out. Finally, the rest of Asia also exhibits an upward trend but at a significantly lower level. Here, the Philippines with a sharp increase in 2012 are ahead of the curve possibly due to a chain of natural disasters.

A stagnating trend can be found for both Africa and the Mediterranean area. In Africa, Nigeria has seen an increase in medical visas issued since 2011, possibly due to post-election violence. Other countries have experienced some fluctuations but the overall trend is flat. The Mediterranean area demonstrates the effects of closed and opened offices. As the German representation in Syria was closed from 24.07.2011 until 31.08.2011 and after 09.12.2011, medical visa issuance drops and effectively comes to a halt. The other two curves that mark the distinct intersection between 2011 and 2012 are those of Israel and Palestine. The intersection highlights the shift in locations documented in Table 2.7, i.e. medical visa issuance in Israel stopped once an office in Ramallah opened.

In Europe, medical visas follow a downward trend and the peaks in 2008 and 2009 mark political unrest in Serbia and Albania. Countries in the "selected" group are characterized by levels that are very different from the rest of their geographic regions and often display substantial volatility. These levels are often very high so the group of various countries contributes a significant share to the total of medical visas in Fig. 2.16. Libya and Tunisia demonstrate the problem of truncated medical visa statistics as embassies or consulates remain closed. In Libya, offices remained closed from 03.03.2011 until 24.09.2011 and from the end of April 2013 until 15.09.2013, so no medical visas were issued during those periods. The political turmoil is likely bypassed via neighboring countries as Table 2.8 demonstrates for Libya from 2011–2013.

Medical visas issued were at a high level before the conflict in Libya escalated and peaked in 2012 when the German embassy was open. In 2011 and 2013 when the embassy was closed, medical visas issued in the neighboring Tunisia increased sharply. The link between medical visas issued in Tunisia and Libya is only moderately convincing for 2011 due to the Arab spring in Tunisia but the negative correlation in both 2012 and 2013 strengthens the tie. Pre- and post-conflict patients need not be the same, however, as a substantial number of Libyan patients was government-sponsored (Nagel and Neller 2013a).

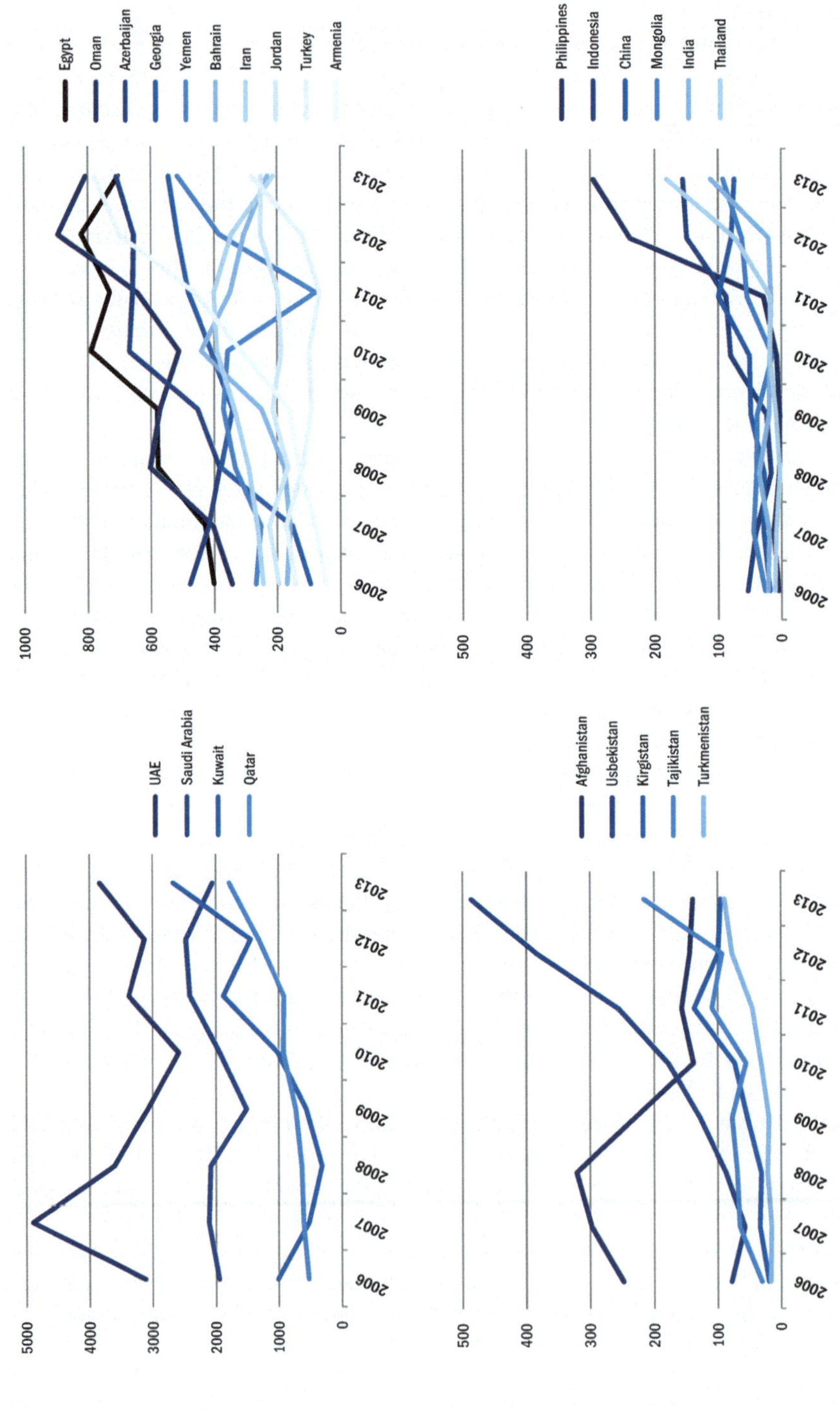

Fig. 2.17 Number of medical visas issued, by country and year, part I

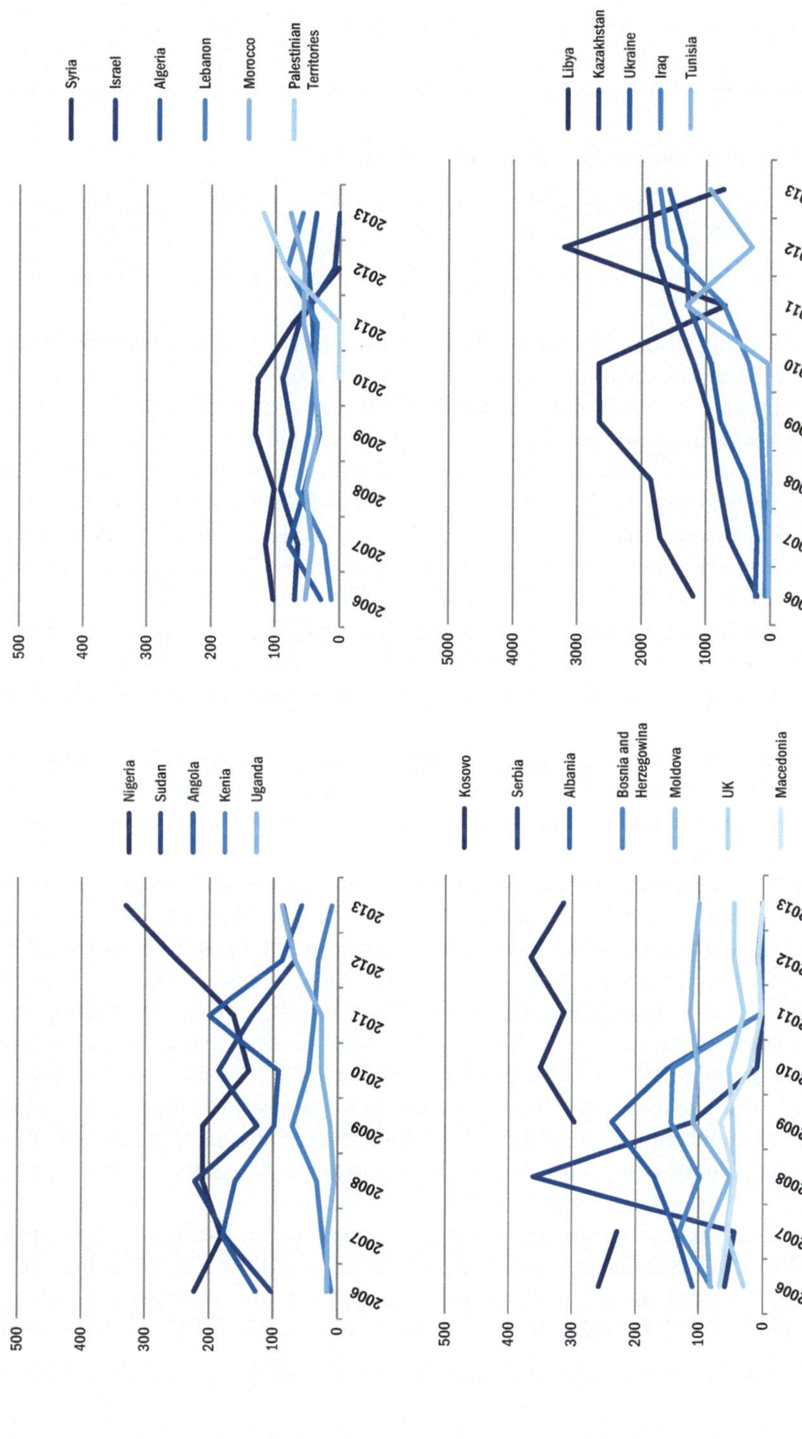

Fig. 2.18 Number of medical visas issued, by country and year, part II

Table 2.7 Medical visas issued in Israel and the Palestinian territories, by year

	2006	2007	2008	2009	2010	2011	2012	2013
Israel	69	64	91	73	88	63	8	0
Palestinian territories	0	0	0	0	0	0	83	118

Table 2.8 Medical visas issued in Libya and Tunisia, by year

	2006	2007	2008	2009	2010	2011	2012	2013
Libya	1188	1712	1859	2651	2657	704	3200	730
Tunisia	20	22	14	20	39	1300	287	933

The preceding discussion across all regions suggests political instability as one driver of inbound medical tourism to Germany and likely to other destinations. At the same time, the degree of political stability truncates visa observations from above as embassies and consulates will close above a certain threshold of unrest and demand for medical visas can no longer be observed. This is evident in the data for Libya in 2011 and 2013, for Syria after 2011, and for Yemen in 2011.

In Russia, medical visas are issued in five locations: Kaliningrad, St. Petersburg, Moscow, Yekaterinburg and Novosibirsk. Kaliningrad and Yekaterinburg were only opened in 2004 and 2005, respectively. Figure 2.19 shows that total medical visas issued in Russia more than tripled between 2006 and 2013. The financial crisis in 2008/2009 lead to a −1.32% stagnation of medical visas issued in 2009 but the subsequent growth of 32.73% in 2010 took the numbers back to their original growth trajectory.

At a first glance, the exchange rate change in Table 2.9 suggest that diminished real purchasing power during the financial crisis might have played a key role in the 2009 stagnation but the exchange rate continues to rise and medical visa growth continues unabated.

Table 2.10 presents information on medical visa growth and distance measures for the five locations that issue medical visas in Russia. High average growth in Kaliningrad is an artifact of its initial growth between 2007 and 2008 and absolute numbers stagnate at a low level. Without 2007/2008, average growth of medical visas issued in Kaliningrad hovers at 4.97%. Growth in St. Petersburg has been moderate and average growth is also driven by the first 2 years in the data set. From 2008 through 2013, average growth amounted to 2.13% with—consequently—stagnating, absolute numbers. Moscow accounted for nearly 90% of all medical visas issued in 2006 and remains at a dominatingly high level of around 75% throughout the entire period. Numbers for Moscow have been growing consistently and it is the only location that managed to not only maintain but to increase the number of visas issued throughout the financial crisis. Interestingly, the most distant locations of Yekaterinburg and Novosibirsk managed to capture a share of nearly 20% of all medical visas issued and achieved rapid growth over the span of 7 years—where Yekaterinburg benefits from 2007/2008 much like Kaliningrad but remains at 14.6% even without that year.

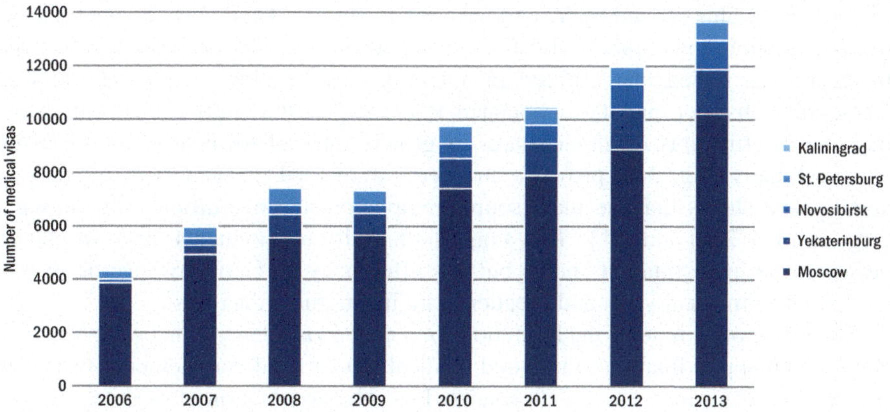

Fig. 2.19 Medical visas issued in Russia, by city and year

Table 2.9 Average RB/EUR exchange rate, by year

	2006	2007	2008	2009	2010	2011	2012	2013
RB/EUR	34	35	36	44	40	41	40	42

Table 2.10 Medical visa issuers in Russia, by embassy

	Distance to Berlin	Flight to Berlin	Average share (%)	Average growth (%)	Growth in 2009 (%)
Kaliningrad	528 km	1:20 h	0.65	27.80	−9.33
St. Petersburg	1321 km	2:05 h	6.56	15.06	−17.28
Moscow	1608 km	2:25 h	77.71	15.32	1.91
Yekaterinburg	3012 km	6:40 h	9.50	38.01	−7.03
Novosibirsk	4389 km	8:20 h	5.58	36.15	−7.10

There are several competing explanations for this observation: From a comparative point of view, the more dynamic growth compared to closer destinations such as Kaliningrad or St. Petersburg may reflect a poorer availability of medical services in more remote regions and thus greater excess demand. Alternatively, stronger social or economic ties between closer destinations and Germany may have led to the use of different visas and medical visas thus understate true medical tourism flows. Unfortunately, the available data set does not include information on other visa types.

Airfares to Novosibirsk have remained relatively stable in EUR terms with 18% and 16% average price increases over 7 years but increased by over 40% in RB terms, so these costs appear to be a poor explanation for increased demand. However, the amount of connections has increased as additional carriers such as Aeroflot, Astana-Air, Rossiya, Transaero, Ural-Airlines and UT-Air added connecting flights to the direct flights offered by S7 and formerly Lufthansa. On the whole, the broader macroeconomic development did have a noticeable but non-permanent effect on medical visas issued that differed in magnitude by location within the country. Geographic distance and the associated travel expenditures do not appear to be decisive determinants of either shares or growth rates of medical visas issued in Russia. Finally, Fig. 2.20 provides an overview of total medical visas issued per country and shows that the main source regions outside of Europe coincide with those in Figs. 2.10 and 2.11. This suggests that visa requirements may not play a decisive role in destination choice but this effect may be Germany-specific or not hold at all as medical visas and inpatients are incongruent data sets.

There is another note on the limitations of medical visa statistics in order: Medical visas are an approximation to inbound medical tourism and complement other data sources but suffer from some deficiencies: First, the observation of medical visas is of course conditional on the existence of a visa requirement which is only true for a subpopulation of all source countries of medical tourism. The universal relevance of drivers of medical tourism based on this subpopulation thus depends on whether or not these drivers also determine a membership of the subpopulation, i.e. whether or not the existence of a visa requirement is in fact exogenous. If members of higher-income strata travel on preexisting multiple-entry business visas, for example, the sample of medical visas will be biased. Second and related, visitors may not necessarily select medical travel as their main purpose. Medical, visitor and business visas from the Schengen category require invitations from a medical provider, relatives or business partner so the type of visa being used may just be the one that is easiest to obtain. Providers that focus on medical tourists offer assistance with the required documents but the share of patients that enter on other visas is unknown. Third, the purpose of medical travel is not evaluated for multi-annual visas so they are excluded from the data set. Fourth, visas are recorded by place of application and not by nationality so applicants can use neighboring countries' embassies or embassies in their current place of residence as their closest points of contact. This produces spatial correlation and leads to small application numbers in countries whose citizens do not require a visa to enter Germany. While medical visas are an imperfect estimate of total medical tourism and overlap with other sources, there is no dominant alternative so their analysis is still informative. Official hospital statistics, for example, cover more source countries but do not include outpatients and are thus restrictive in terms of treatment types observed.

2.2.2.3 Summary

The analysis of the inpatient and medical visa data sets has provided profound insights into the source countries and regions of inbound medical tourism to Germany and allowed us to identify export destinations by a number of characteristics such as treatment composition, average patient age or the presence of conflicts. It has highlighted a treatment heterogeneity across source countries as well as the importance of broader global phenomena such as the financial crisis in 2008 that

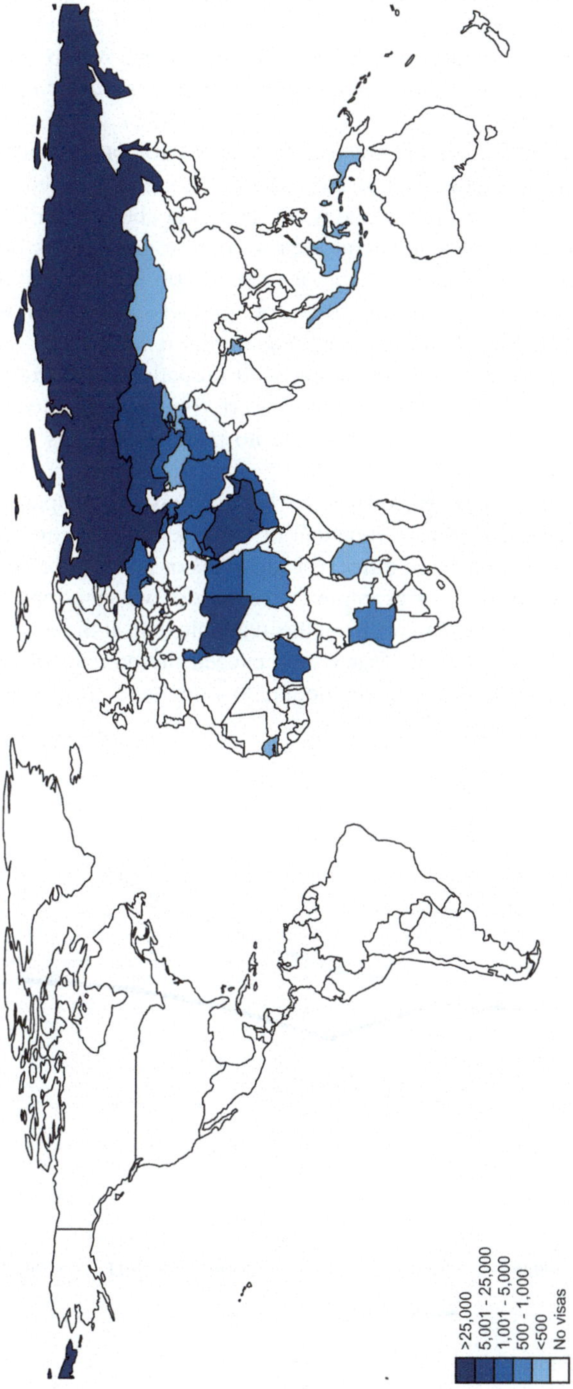

Fig. 2.20 World map of medical visas issued

influenced our measures of international patients. Relating our data to the figures in the introductory part of this section, they confirm Russia as the main source country but do not support an increase in children seeking treatment. We do not cover dental treatments, plastic surgery or other outpatient treatments so other circulating estimates are difficult to verify.

Overall, international inpatient treatments account for only about 0.5% of all inpatient treatments in Germany but the export volume associated with medical expenditures for inpatient exports alone is substantial at about 250 million Euros in 2012. Figure 2.21 shows that inpatient export volume growth has outpaced total export volume growth with each volume indexed at 100 in 2007 and that excludes substantial non-medical expenditures that are typically associated with medical tourism, including travel, accommodation, rehabilitation, leisure and accompanying family members. These expenditures along with outpatients and their expenditure structure (Musa et al. 2012b) may put total export volume associated with medical tourism close to 2 billion Euros but there are no reliable numbers for Germany to make a definitive claim.

It is difficult to check for even consistency between visas and inpatient treatments as the former can be used towards inpatient or outpatient treatments and additional patients may enter the country on other types of visas or not require any visas at all, as is the case for expatriates, for example. Nevertheless, we can draw some conservative conclusions about outpatients from the available data at the country level as is outlined in Fig. 2.22: If medical visas issued exceed the number of inpatients, the difference can be considered a lower bound to outpatient treatments. There are

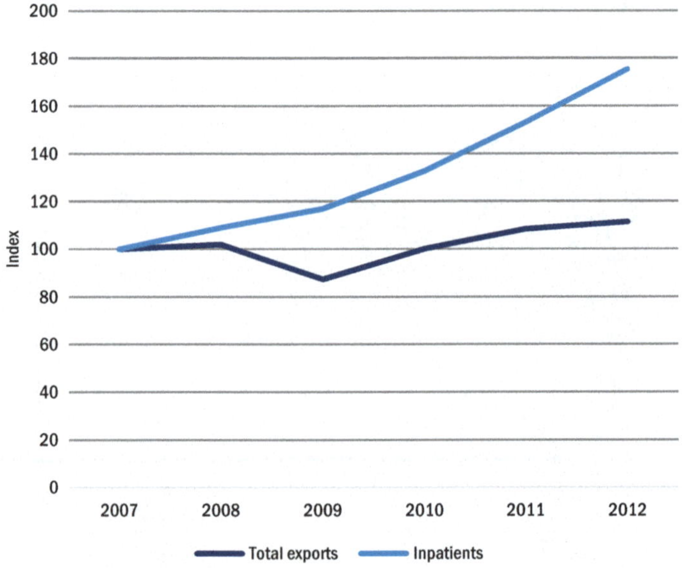

Fig. 2.21 Export volume growth

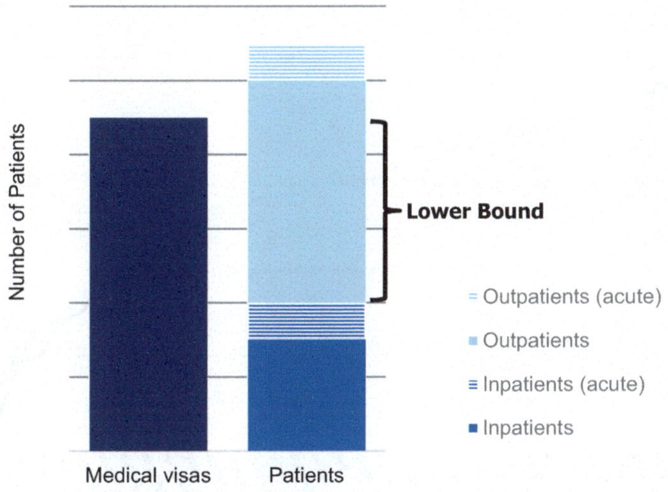

Fig. 2.22 Lower bound of outpatients schematic

potentially more outpatients that did not use or require medical visas or that used medical visas if none of the inpatients used any, but total outpatients cannot fall below our lower bound. This argument rests on the assumption that inpatient treatments are recorded very thoroughly and that no additional inpatient treatments occur. In reality, outpatients are very likely to exceed our lower bound as our inpatient treatments include treatments of acute conditions and these patients are not expected to travel on medical visas. Their medical visas would then have to be assigned to outpatients as well. Finally, if inpatients exceed medical visas issued, nothing can be said about outpatients.

For this analysis, we removed countries without visa requirements or insufficient data, Belarus due to its visa outliers, and countries with negative visa-inpatient balances which are largely in Africa and South America. Of the remaining 35 countries, Egypt was removed due to a negative aggregate visa-inpatient balance. Figure 2.23 depicts the calculated lower bounds of outpatients and shares of outpatients per country across all periods observed. The assumption that no unrecorded inpatient treatments are rendered in Germany is potentially problematic given a significant share of unassigned treatments particularly in 2007, so Fig. 2.23 also includes a lower bound for the share of outpatients excluding 2007. The original bound turns out to be quite robust to this modification. Across all countries included, a lower bound of outpatients in the 40–80% band is evident and substantial in magnitude. We did not proceed to investigate determinants of the calculated outpatient shares in detail but there is no obvious pattern discernable.

Our results imply that 52% of the medical visas issued in the included countries from 2007 to 2012 were used on outpatient treatments. If this percentage extends beyond countries with medical visa requirements, our minimum estimate of outpatient treatments in 2012 is approximately 190,000 and thus ranks at the upper end of

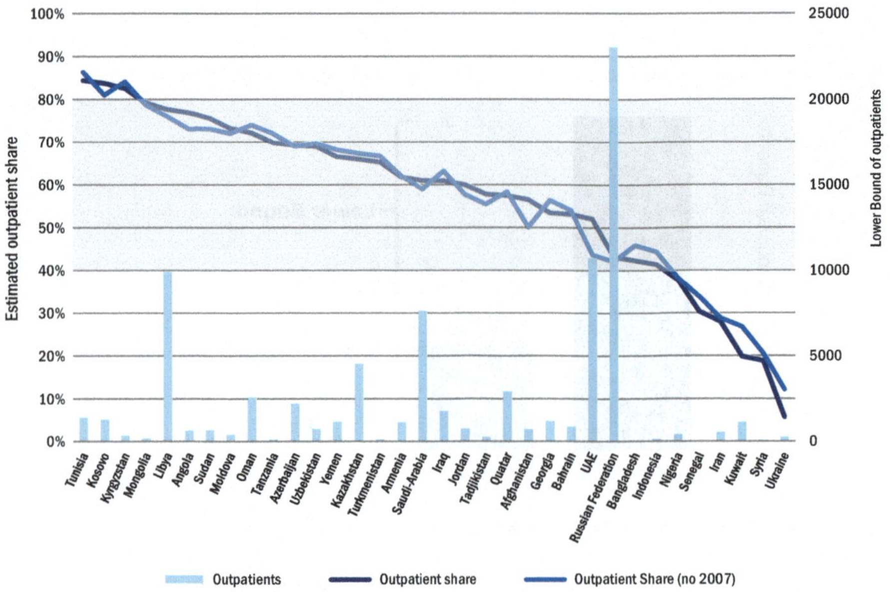

Fig. 2.23 Lower bound of outpatients and outpatient shares, by country

the circulating estimates. Whether or not the outpatient share actually extends beyond our country sample cannot be verified with our data. Finally, outpatient shares based on our calculations need not be stable across years. A case in point is Kuwait whose medical visas in Fig. 2.17 grow while inpatient treatments in Table 2.4 stagnate.

2.3 Drivers of Medical Tourism

A natural extension to the questions of what medical tourism is and where medical tourists travel is the identification of what drives them. The previous section has already touched on this topic and foreshadowed some of the patients' potential drivers. We will now explore these drivers in more detail.

2.3.1 Domestic Availability

Generally, individuals exhibit local preferences for the consumption of a service (White and Morrisey 1998). Many authors such as Glinos and Baeten (2006) and Keckley and Eselius (2009) thus name dissatisfaction with the domestic system as main drivers of medical tourism. A lack of availability may be due to various reasons such as armed conflicts in the source region (Nagel and Neller 2013a) or elevated demand as a result of demographic shifts that lead to large populations with chronic diseases and financial means to consume life-transforming procedures (Crone 2008). Failure to meet excess demand often stems from domestic cost containment strategies or the inability to provide sufficient domestic supply because of unavailable inputs. The resulting waiting lists may encourage medical tourism (Connell 2006; Crone 2008; Crozier and Baylis 2010; Frädrich 2013; IPK International 2012; Johnston et al. 2012; Jotikasthira 2010; Müller 2006; Oberhauser-Aslan 2013; Richter and Richter 2012; The Gallup Organization 2007). Glinos et al. (2010) give examples of how waiting lists in statutory systems lead to contracting with both domestic and foreign private providers and Glinos and Baeten (2006) surmise that unsatisfied domestic demand is likely to be met by foreign providers inside the source country. That may not be the case, however, if affordable excess capacities exist elsewhere; if there are reasons to refrain from investment in the source country; or if there exists a global shortage and thus competition over inputs (Crone 2008; Hopkins et al. 2010).

Another reason for domestically unavailable treatments can be their legal status. Circumvention tourism is very attractive from a patient's point of view. Wachter (2006) and Herrick (2007) report efforts of mode 1 outsourcing of medical services via telemedicine but the topic has almost subsided due to certification and licensing countermeasures. Travel, on the other hand, is more difficult to stop. IPK International (2012) report legal restrictions on treatments as a driver; Ye et al. (2011) document medical tourism to Hong Kong as a way to circumvent China's one-child policy and to obtain residency status for their children; and Müller (2006) discusses cross-border medical tourism to the state of Brandenburg, Germany that also includes abortions which were illegalized in Poland in 1993. The importance of bioethical regulations is further confirmed by Smith et al. (2009) and Whittaker (2010) who find cross-border reproductive travel in Asia and stem cell therapy in Singapore. Particular treatments such as fertility treatments are often associated with legal arbitrage but they also occur in absence of restrictive regulations (Culley et al. 2011).

Lack of domestic availability is often observed in countries that deliberately ration supply or do not attract a private sector to meet excess demand. The existence of a private sector to meet excess demand is no indication for the absence of medical tourism flows, however. Domestic providers of private or public nature may simply not be able to provide the desired product varieties where a variety is a bundle of characteristics that defines a destination. The following differences in destination characteristics are usually offered to explain medical tourism flows.

2.3.2 *Price*

Savings on out-of-pocket expenditures are the most-cited driver in the medical tourism literature (Arunanondchai and Fink 2007; Connell 2006; Crone 2008;

Crozier and Baylis 2010; Frädrich 2013; Froelich 2012; Glinos and Baeten 2006; Herrick 2007; Heung et al. 2011; Johnston et al. 2012; Jotikasthira 2010; Keckley and Eselius 2009; Klingenberger 2009; Müller 2006; Pollard 2013; Smith et al. 2009; The Gallup Organization 2007). For Germany, IPK International (2012) reports that 52% of German adults could imagine traveling abroad for a medical treatment, including dental treatment and surgery, to save money or to obtain a treatment that is not available in Germany.

Price differentials are reported to be large both within (Connell 2006) and between regions. As an example, the prices in Thailand depicted in Table 2.11 are a fraction of those in the U.S. but cannot compete with those in India. Milstein and Smith (2007) report fees by large accredited international providers of less than 40% of the Californian average and note that costly procedures account for less than 2% of commercial insurance spending, which still amounts to a large amount in light of the U.S. market size. Large facilitators claim typical savings of 50–80% when opting for treatment abroad.

The average procedure costs reported in Table 2.11 are taken from the Polish Association of Medical Tourism (2012) (first row), Carabello (2008) (second row), and Kher (2006) (third row). The third source lists cost ranges for the U.S. and the lower bound is reported here. The upper bounds add between 40% and 50% to the average costs. In this framing, Mexico, Costa Rica, Israel and Singapore are mid-tier locations. Thailand, Jordan and Poland present themselves as low-cost destinations and India is the cost leader. These numbers need to be considered with care, however, as self-reported figures by the Polish Association of Medical Tourism are likely strategic. They rank Poland as the most cost-attractive destination after India. Nevertheless, all three sources combined highlight a global cost structure that demonstrates the different tiers in pricing and the substantial savings associated with alternative destination choices.

Figures 2.24 and 2.25 depict data from the International Federation of Health Plans. It is compiled by an industry network that attempts to provide an international price comparison despite numerous incompatibilities across health care systems such as treatment definitions, inclusions and reimbursement schemes. Specifically, prices are sometimes taken from single plans, snapshots or averages over select periods. Depending on year and country, prices are from public plans, private plans, or an averaged mix.

The data set covers 2010, 2011 and 2012. Prices for Australia, Chile, India, Germany Spain and South Africa are based on private plans and prices for New Zealand stem from the public sector. For Switzerland, data from 2010 understates true costs by excluding state level expenditures, which are included in 2011 and substantially increase prices. 2012 is then based solely on public sector prices while previous years took inpatient prices from private plans. Prices for France represent a mix of public and private plans and prices for the Netherlands are estimates based on bundles in 2010 and based on DRGs in 2012. Data on the UK and Argentina are very consistent again and reflect the NHS payment schedule and a weighted average of three health sub sectors in Argentina, respectively. Data for Canada is based on the province of Nova Scotia for 2011 and 2012 and on a Canadian discharge database in 2010. Finally, U.S. data is based on claims data with low and high representing the 25% and 95% percentiles, respectively. Due to

Table 2.11 Average cost of procedures in US$

	U.S.	Costa Rica	Mexico	Israel	Singapore	Thailand	Colombia	Jordan	Poland	India
Heart bypass	145,000	25,500	28,000	27,000	–	15,500	14,650	14,500	14,000	5500
	113,000	–	–	–	18,500	11,000	–	–	–	10,000
	122,424	–	–	–	20,000	12,000	–	–	–	10,000
Heart valve replacement	170,000	30,000	19,000	28,500	–	22,000	17,500	14,000	19,000	6000
	150,000	–	–	–	12,500	10,000	–	–	–	9000
	159,326	–	–	–	13,000	10,500	–	–	–	9500
Angioplasty	57,000	13,000	13,000	7500	–	5000	5500	5000	5300	5000
	47,000	–	–	–	13,000	13,000	–	–	–	9000
	57,262	–	–	–	13,000	13,000	–	–	–	11,000
Hip replacement	50,000	12,500	13,500	25,100	–	9000	7000	8000	6900	8000
	47,000	–	–	–	12,000	12,000	–	–	–	8500
	43,780	–	–	–	12,000	12,000	–	–	–	9000
Gastric bypass	–	–	–	–	–	–	–	–	–	–
	25,000	–	–	–	26,000	–	–	–	–	6000
	47,988	–	–	–	15,000	15,000	–	–	–	11,000

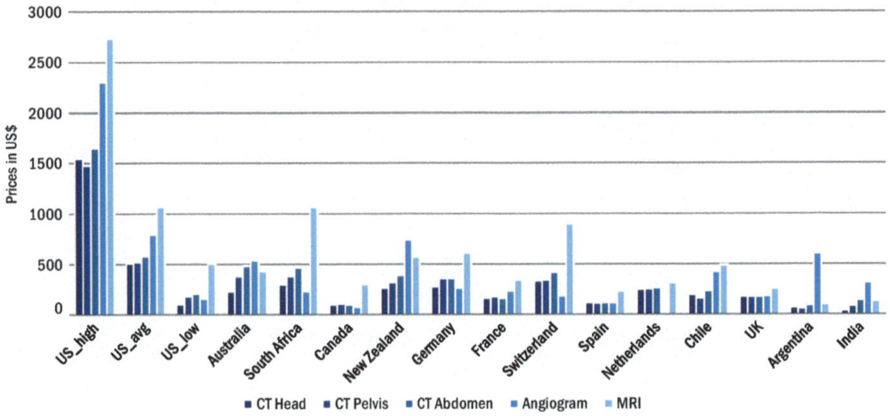

Fig. 2.24 Prices of selected procedures based on IFHP data in US$, by country

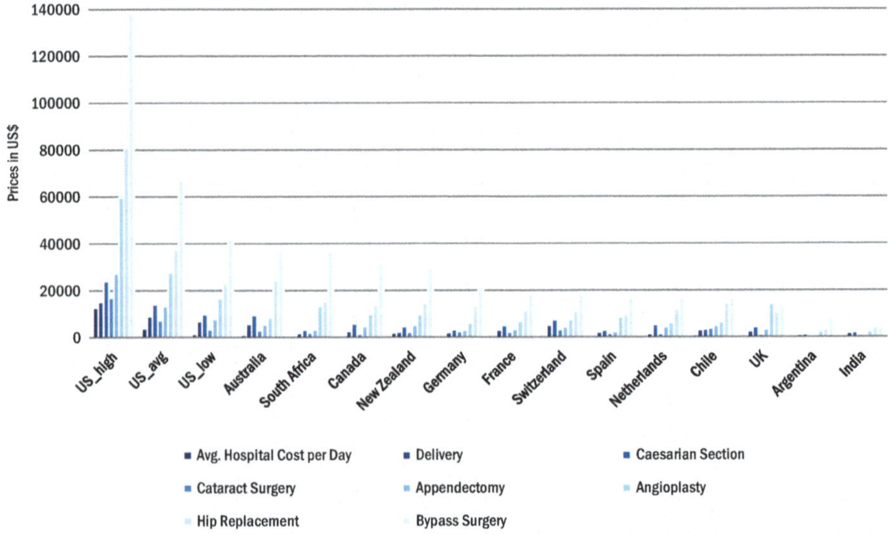

Fig. 2.25 Prices of selected treatments based on IFHP data in US$, by country

missing years for some countries and methodological changes over time, which is a likely source of considerable within-country coefficients of variation, we averaged prices over 3 years.

Figures 2.24 and 2.25 display the costs of selected procedures and treatments in 14 countries. It stands out that the 25th percentile in the U.S. is still competitive for procedures in terms of pricing. The 95th percentile and the average, however, expose the U.S. as an exceptionally high-cost location for both procedures and treatments. Cost patterns for other destinations do not differ substantially between procedures and treatments. Only in Switzerland do relatively high procedure costs meet comparatively moderate total treatment costs. In terms of treatments, Argentina, Chile, France, UK, Spain, and India are the most cost-attractive destinations. Argentina and Chile are in fact medical tourism destinations of some extent, Spain is a regional destination in Europe and India is a major player in global medical tourism. In both France and the UK the domestic health care systems are of predominantly public nature, but while France is known for comprehensive health care coverage, the UK is actually one of the main source countries of medical tourists in Europe. A competitive cost structure that results in rationing can thus represent a push rather than a pull factor.

Leaving out procedures and birth-related treatments, Fig. 2.26 reports potential savings in comparison to U.S. average costs. The dispersion of procedure costs across countries is larger than that of treatment costs but low absolute levels for procedures imply relatively small individual savings from destination hopping. The depicted treatments, on the other hand, promise substantial savings from between-destination choice outside the U.S., ranging from $3361 for a cataract surgery to $37,905 for a bypass surgery.

Lunt et al. (2013) compare UK prices to alternative destinations based on data from an online platform that operates as a facilitator. Depending on the treatment and destination country, they find most savings to lie in the 50–70% range and consider only treatment costs. At a more aggregate level, Smith et al. (2011a) investigate the potential of bilateral trade relations between India and the UK. Using data from 2007–2008, they identify cost savings between £121 million and £206 million.

Mattoo and Rathindran (2006) focus on smaller procedures that are performed more often and that lend themselves to being performed elsewhere according to the authors' criteria. They select foreign countries without explicit regard for distance or

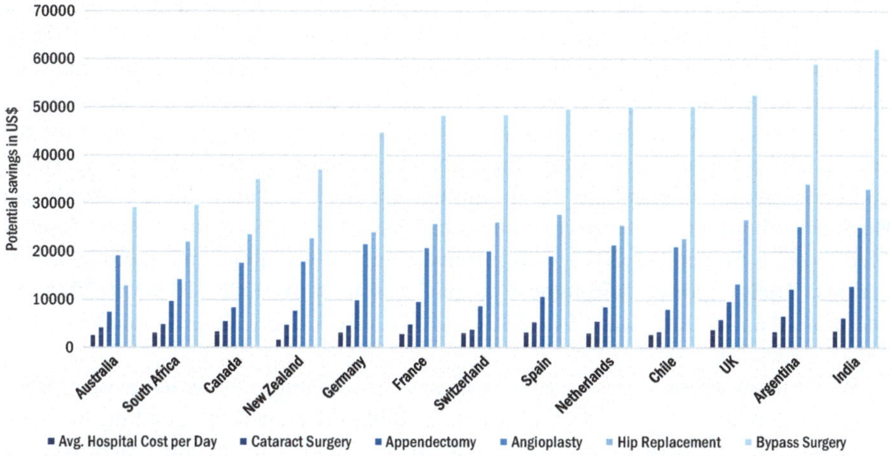

Fig. 2.26 Potential savings in US$, by country

Table 2.12 Savings potential for select treatments in the U.S. in US$, by treatment

	U.S. inpatient price	U.S. outpatient price	Foreign price including travel
Knee surgery	10,335	4142	1321
Shoulder arthroplasty	5940	7931	2217
Hysterectomy	5783	5420	1987
Rhinoplasty	5050	3417	1936
Varicose vein surgery	7065	2373	1411
Hernia repair	4753	3450	1651

any criteria other than price, so the results in Table 2.12 are mostly an exercise at calculating a maximum savings potential for treatment and travel costs.

Treatment costs may dominate medical tourism expenditures for certain treatments, but affordable treatment prices do not ensure an affordable package price. Travel, accommodation, and other expenditures in addition to treatment costs may add up to around 40% of the total costs excluding leisure activities (Musa et al. 2012b). This also raises the issue of using medical services abroad as an individual choice. Savings on a cheaper treatment may become negligible at the individual level after figuring in all travel expenses, even if the potential of total savings is substantial due to a large total quantity of treatments demanded. Finally, some items on the bill such as air travel have made medical tourism more affordable but others such as unfavorable exchange rates may put a halt to inbound tourists (Connell 2006).

Milstein and Smith (2007) provide a rare willingness-to-pay analysis for medical tourists and find different thresholds for individuals in self-reported, stressed or uninsured spending situations and individuals with insurance. The representative sample of American households indicates that about 25% of the household with self-reported "stressed spending" or no insurance and 10% of the households with insurance would travel for savings of U.S. $1000–$2400. Of the same groups, 38% and 25% indicated their willingness to travel for savings in excess of U.S. $10,000, respectively. An upward bias of these numbers in terms of savings required is very likely, as no actual outlay was required and no base price was given. Klingenberger (2009) observes a willingness-to-pay between 50 and 70% of the domestic price for crowns and implants in his study on outbound dental tourism in Germany. These numbers suggest a threshold for minimum required savings. Another study on Russian outbound tourists surveyed the total budgets of 428 visitors to the Moscow MedShow in September 2015 who informed themselves about international destinations. Their reported willingness to pay less than 10,000€, 10,000€–25,000€, and more than 25,000€ was 39%, 58% and 3%, respectively (International Medical Travel Journal 2016).

While many reports focus on potential savings, literature on actual expenditures is scarce. Noree et al. (2014) find a considerable difference in spending between inpatients and outpatients from the UK in Thailand. The average and median expenditures for inpatients were $14,955 and $7522, respectively. Outpatients, on the other hand, indicated average and median expenditures of only \$467 and \$160. Treatments obtained at one destination may thus vary widely both in scope and price. The large relative differences between average and median expenditures further imply few patients with very high expenditures. Another survey among outgoing UK patients draws a similar picture but the open expenditure category at the upper end does not allow a more thorough analysis either (Pollard 2012). Musa et al. (2012b) report detailed average expenditures for medical tourists in Malaysia. Medical expenditures range from US\$44 to US\$31,245 with a mean of US\$3580. Non-medical expenditures are divided into a number of items ranging from travel over accommodation to tourism and account for 60% of total expenditures. For South Korea, Lunt et al. (2014b) report stable average expenditures on inpatient treatments but growing expenditures on outpatient treatments, with the exception of check-ups due to strong competition in this field.

Overall, the role of prices in medical tourism appears to be more nuanced than initial reports on medical tourism suggested. First, non-medical expenses often account for a considerable share of total cost. Second, the importance of price is treatment-dependent in many regards. Cross et al. (2000) note that the price of surgical procedures at home is higher for many than their individual willingness-to-pay, but the exact difference is crucial and depends on the treatment received—which in turn interacts with other drivers. The treatment type and its associated medical condition prior to the treatment determine both price of the treatment at home and the willingness-to-pay. Pain relief, for example, will increase willingness-to-pay and thus increase the demand share of presumably more expensive domestic treatments. Milstein and Smith (2006) point to middle class citizens who are driven by out-of-pocket spending and who seek necessary treatments that are still of elective character.

A price focus is also reported for less complicated and cheaper procedures but demand for these procedures can be governed by additional drivers and considerations. Wagner et al. (2011) find a price focus for elderly, outbound German tourists who receive preventive and wellness treatments throughout their 2–3 weeks of vacation. Wongkit and McKercher (2013) identify a large group of medical tourists to Thailand who focus on holidays and decide to receive a treatment in a rather incidental manner. Tourists with a medical treatment as their primary purpose of travel often obtain invasive treatments while holidaying and opportunistic tourists receive dental care and general check-ups. Unfortunately, Wongkit and McKercher (2013) do not report individual spending even if different treatment categories imply different expenditures.

Another important aspect of price is the presence of a health insurance and its lack of portability (Bookman and Bookman 2007; Smith et al. 2009). One would expect the enrollment in a domestic health insurance to greatly influence destination choice and, indeed, Mattoo and Rathindran (2006) lament a local market distortion as potential savings are not completely passed on to patients when health insurances do not reimburse travel expenses. Cohen (2010) thus points to medical tourism as a market for the uninsured and underinsured. Attempts to establish insurance portability in developing countries are reported by Wibulpolprasert et al. (2004).

While an inhibitory role of an existing health insurance is plausible, its practical relevance for observed medical tourism appears to be limited. For domestic hospital choice, Bin Saeed (1998) and McGuckin (2006) report insurance coverage to be important but McGuckin (2006) also finds insurance coverage to be a much weaker exclusion criterion if a hospital has a very good reputation. On the international stage, Jotikasthira (2010) reports that about 50% the surveyed medical tourists in Thailand expect some level of reimbursement from their health plans. For a different sample of medical tourists in Thailand, Wongkit and McKercher (2013) report 67.8% of the visitors with private health insurance and 32.2% with international coverage. There is a difference in the importance assigned to insurance coverage between the tourist types in that hesitant medical tourists who decide about a medical treatment after their arrival appreciate insurance coverage more than other groups, but in general insurance coverage is ranked at the lower end of all destination characteristics inquired. Fisher and Sood (2014) also find a negligible role of insurance coverage but their results are largely based on stated preferences of the wider public. In Wagner and Verheyen (2010), on the other hand, 75% of outgoing Germans receiving mostly preventive treatments report full or partial reimbursement from their public health insurance, 72% from their private health insurance and only 7% full out-of-pocket payment, with an unknown overlap between the two former groups. These findings once again suggest that the importance of destination characteristics such as the presence of a health insurance vary by treatment or other individual-specific characteristics such as income—which turns out to be the case for the sample in Wagner and Verheyen (2010). In fact, many early surveys in the medical tourism literature suffer from such omitted controls that potentially introduce serious bias to the generalizability of reported results.

In addition to public and private health insurance plans, there exist other sources of reimbursement that tend to be neglected. Cattaneo (2009) names Oman as an importer of medical services that reimburses treatments abroad which are not available at home and there are ample accounts of government-sponsored medical tourism from Libya (Nagel and Neller 2013a), Yemen (Siddiqi et al. 2010), Europe (Rosenmöller et al. 2006) as well as Egypt, Jordan and Costa Rica (Drager and Vieira 2002). Such sponsoring mainly occurs in the Middle East and may not necessarily represent voluntary travel in its original meaning (Whittaker 2015). One source estimates 80–90% of all Kuwaiti medical tourists to be government-sponsored with average costs of $150,000–$200,000 per patient (International Medical Travel Journal 2012). These patients may make a conscious choice in selecting their destination but economic constraints are be largely removed from the decision-making process. That needs to be accounted for and is quite different from the observation in Musa et al. (2012b) where visitors to Malaysia indicated “value for money” as the most importance destination characteristic. This suggests a compensatory region in the relationship between the price and other characteristics of a treatment such as the quality of medical services.

2.3.3 *Quality*

While pricing is certainly relevant, it cannot explain the significant inflows to high-cost destinations that command high prices such as (Monaco Cardio-Thoracic Center 2016). Consequently, many authors point out the role of high-quality and -high-technology branding as one of the most sought-after characteristics of a destination characteristic (García-Altés 2005; Glinos and Baeten 2006; Smith et al. 2009; The Gallup Organization 2007).

In their study of medical tourists in Malaysia, Musa et al. (2012b) find quality items such as cleanliness, reputation, track record, and good doctors to be the most important destination characteristics, ranking just ahead of pricing. Visitors to Thailand surveyed in Wongkit and McKercher (2013) and Jotikasthira (2010) also rank quality of treatment related items at the top with explicit mention of hygiene, equipment, standards and doctors in Jotikasthira (2010). Jotikasthira (2010) further attempts to investigate the compensatory or non-compensatory nature of quality and price as well as hygiene and safety. He finds quality to be non-compensatory and price or savings to be compensatory but the analysis is methodologically weak as no joint correlations are considered. Correlations between the self-reported assessment of a characteristic's relevance and the intention to visit a country does reveal something about perceived country images but does not require any trade-offs.

Pollard (2012) reports results of an online survey that included 1045 patients from 74 countries going to 78 countries and receiving more than 100 types of different treatments. The sample is heavily biased with 55% of the survey participants being from the UK and 74% being from English-speaking countries. For UK patients, who received typical out-of-pocket payment treatments in cosmetic, dental, obesity, fertility and orthopedic procedures, physician and facility quality were stated to be the most important criteria of destination choice with 89% and 85%, respectively—with price trailing only slightly behind at 81%. Johnson et al. (2015) investigate a number of health and health system indicators that capture domestic quality in an observational study and find health indicators, i.e. life expectancy and child mortality, to be significant determinants of outbound medical travel to the U.S. while health system indicators, i.e. expenditures and resources, remain insignificant.

For outgoing, German medical tourists to the European Union, 33% and 24% state savings on non-refundable treatments and copay as their main motivations while only 11% seek better quality, 10% more comfort, 6% a doctor of their trust, and 6% a particular specialist (Wagner and Verheyen 2010). Once again a differentiation between health and medical tourists is reasonable. Patients who stayed two to three weeks, i.e. a typical German vacation period, received mostly spa treatments and focused on cost savings whereas patients who stayed up to one week received dental, orthodontic, specialist and inpatient treatments and indicated treatment and physician quality as well as comfort as their most important criteria (Wagner et al. 2011).

Ehrbeck et al. (2008) attribute as much as 72% of medical tourism to the search of advanced technology and quality of care while only 15% aim to reduce waiting times and 13% to reduce costs. These numbers may not be representative but they confirm other findings qualitatively. Milstein and Smith (2007) point out internationally-trained and English-speaking surgeons at large offshore providers that received international accreditations. Mattoo and Rathindran (2006) mention accreditations from source countries as a requirement for more medical tourism and Herrick (2007) also sees a need for providers to communicate their quality via accreditation, provider affiliations, and physician credentials. He provides well-known examples of co-operations between international hospitals and American hospitals and of accreditations by the Joint Commission on the Accreditation of Health Care Organizations. The accreditation business has attracted numerous competing organizations by now and Crone (2008) notes an increasing relevance of accreditations for the medical tourism market in Europe.

Many destinations pursue comprehensive strategies that address the overall quality of their product. Connell (2006) reports such measures taken by providers in India that included the hiring of returning physicians, the import of technology, and the streamlining of administrative procedures. Youngman (2012) and Froelich (2012), however, consider top quality more of a prerequisite and a necessary component of a more comprehensive value proposition. This interesting proposition begs the question about a quality threshold for a destination to be considered but we know of no explicit investigations into such a threshold. Given the studies cited, a threshold is either negligibly low and quality above the threshold compensatory due to the trivial nature of the treatment received (Wagner et al. 2011), so high that it might appear non-compensatory (Musa et al. 2012b), or compensatory but dominant (Ehrbeck et al. 2008).

2.3.4 Tourism

The term “medical tourism” implies a bundling of medical treatments with recreational tourism but the degree of complementarity or substitutability between both services is not obvious. At a first glance, both goods seem to be substitutes separately bidding for consumer expenditures but recent research suggests that this might only be the case for a share of medical tourists.

There is good reason to jointly consume medical treatments and tourism at a distant location due to economies of scope. Travel costs spread over two products and accompanying persons who help deal with perceived treatment risks and provide company are twice as beneficial. Anticipated post-treatment recovery time can also at least partly be used for tourism, but tourist attractions may in fact be a more relevant criterion for healthy chaperones or patients receiving outpatient treatment. Yeoh et al. (2013) report 73.62% of the surveyed visitors to Malaysia traveling with company and Musa et al. (2012b) report an average of two persons accompanying a medical tourist to Malaysia, with expenditures being 12 times higher than those of regular, leisure tourists. According to Pollard (2012), 59% of UK patients travel with relatives and stay up to 2 weeks. Whether that duration reflects actual tourism or merely post-intervention recovery is unknown. IPK International (2012) further mentions Arab patients traveling with extensive company.

The literature draws a somewhat heterogeneous picture of the precise role of tourism for medical tourism. Most surveys find quality and price considerations to dominate destination choice of medical tourists, which suggests a clear treatment focus as opposed to a tourism focus (Jotikasthira 2010; Musa et al. 2012b). This finding for trips with a focus on medical services is in line with the services offered by the Munich Airport Clinic in Germany, for example. On the other hand, Wagner and Verheyen (2010) report the possibility to combine a treatment with a vacation as the main motivation for 45% of the surveyed and outgoing German patients with planned treatments and thus well ahead of anticipated savings on non-refundable treatment costs. This motivation was largely irrelevant for patients who underwent actual procedures as opposed to spa treatments, however (Wagner et al. 2011). Froelich (2012) also reports the significance of combining treatments with vacation for Swedish patients but essentially relies on only one interview. Bookman and Bookman (2007) see a broad range of complementary tourism bundles offered to medical tourists and consider recreation a positive externality to medical travel. Strong links between the medical travel and the tourism sector can be observed worldwide (Connell 2013) and large international providers integrate hotels and other facilities, often at luxurious levels including concierge services (Turner 2007).

In an attempt to develop a medical tourist typology, Wongkit and McKercher (2013) provide the most comprehensive study on the role of tourism for medical tourists in Thailand. They classify medical tourists by their trip purpose and decision horizon which results in 42.3% dedicated medical tourists who indicated the medical purpose to be equally or more important than the touristic purpose and who made a treatment decision prior to their arrival. 15.7% are hesitant medical tourists with similar trip purposes and treatment considerations before departure but a decision after arrival. 18.1% are holidaying medical tourists with vacation as their primary motivation and preplanned treatments and finally 23.1% are considered opportunistic medical tourists with vacation as the main purpose of the trip and on-site treatment decisions. Analysis reveals that long-distance tourists tend to be more opportunistic, and opportunistic as well as holidaying tourists stay in the region for more than 4 weeks on average. The long-distance visitors' focus on tourism is further underlined by the multiple destinations they choose to visit. Regional visitors, on the other hand, represent a larger share of tourists with a medical focus who stay only 2 weeks on average. In terms of treatments received, dedicated and hesitant patients were more likely to receive invasive treatments while holidaying and opportunistic patients received predominantly dental care.

With regards to destination choice, only dedicated medical tourists ranked all or some medical treatment characteristics first for destination choice, all other groups were dominated by destination characteristics (Wongkit and McKercher 2013). Unfortunately, the exact wording of the task is not disclosed, so potentially implied provider characteristics of the used destination characteristics cannot be assessed. Provider characteristics were ranked in a separate task, however, and opportunistic medical tourists stand out as a group that consistently places lower importance on provider characteristics. Significant differences in comparison with dedicated medical tourists can be found in the importance of insurance coverage and the role of recommendations from third parties (Wongkit and McKercher 2013). Overall, the analysis suggests that tourism plays a major if not dominant role for a large segment of medical tourists in Thailand who consider destination attractiveness at large, including e.g. climate and tourist attractions, a key characteristic in destination choice. That segment can be characterized by treatments obtained and duration of the stay. Yu and Ko (2012) find a similar segmentation by source country: Korean and Japanese tourists who are interviewed about hypothetical medical treatments state a greater focus on tourism and on serious treatments abroad compared to Chinese interviewees who prefer lighter treatments abroad. These segments also express different attitudes towards destination characteristics.

From an economic perspective, different types of medical tourists suggest different products and different decision-making processes. Dedicated, hesitant and holidaying medical tourists travel with the notion of at least potentially receiving medical care and thus face expenditures for a combination of medical treatments and tourism. The weighting of both components' relevance may differ among these groups but the joint consideration of both components determines an individual's choice and expenditures. Opportunistic medical tourists, on the other hand, make sequential consumption decisions so their destination choice in terms of location is completely unrelated to medical provider characteristics. These tourists are incidentally exposed to a subset of providers at their recreation destination and select a local provider to consume a medical service. Their decision to consume a medical service is subject to a different utility-maximization problem as prices of non-local destinations are different from those who select their tourism destination in a joint decision. Sunk costs for the current trip may tip decision-making towards a foreign option.

2.3.5 *Facilitation*

There exist essentially two types of facilitators that shape the supply of medical tourism. Private facilitators bundle and communicate medical services. They can act as mere travel agents that focus on informing and packaging trips or represent a manifestation of cultural and social ties that establish trust in a destination. Public facilitation, on the other hand, commonly addresses investment conditions.

Private facilitation occurs at formal and informal levels. Professional facilitators often cooperate with large networks to accommodate various budgets and treatment-tourism combinations in order to meet their clients' demands (Herrick 2007; Turner 2007). Pollard (2013) anticipates large tourism companies to engage in medical travel and IPK International (2012) further notes that tour operators such as Med Journeys (U.S.), The Medical Tourist Company (UK) and Dr. Holiday (Germany) have joined the scene even if their focus is often on wellness retreats.

The focus of communication often lies on price, tourism and reliability through accreditation (Connell 2013). Lunt et al. (2016) identify a focus of facilitating websites on the reduction of perceived treatment risks in the literature. At the same time, medical tourism websites themselves are often elusive, of varying quality and the volatility in the market is considerable (Cormany and Baloglu 2011; Lunt et al. 2010). Mohamad et al. (2012) consider medical travel facilitators one-stop solutions but to what extent they actually influence a patient's destination choice, i.e. if other options beyond the offered choice set are considered or to what extent recommendations by facilitators are relied on, is not explored. Gan and Frederick (2011) find a focus of facilitators on the range of destinations, tourism/vacationing, and physicians whereby the latter refers to quality including accreditation as well as pre- and postoperative care. In practice, the impact of professional facilitators on the range of destinations considered and frequented may be limited (Alleman et al. 2011).

The available choice sets are an issue that is rarely discussed in the literature. Surveys are typically conducted at single destinations and considerations of other potential destinations are rarely inquired. One example is found in Wongkit and McKercher (2013) who note the majority of the medical tourists to be frequent visitors to Thailand with 85% not having considered any other destination. Their sample ranked recommendations from various sources relatively low, which suggests a limited influence of physician referrals and travel agents. The latter is in line with findings on inbound medical tourism to South Korea while the former is at odds with inbound medical tourism to the UK (Lunt et al. 2014b).

In a survey of medical tourists in Malaysia, 44.47% of the interviewees indicated friends, 37.66% family or relatives, 24.47% referring doctors, 10.43% media, 7.66% agents and 4.89% websites as their sources of information Yeoh et al. (2013). 91.53% used only one or two sources of information. Musa et al. (2012b) draw a similar picture in another survey among medical tourists in Malaysia. Their main sources of information about health care services were friends and relatives with 60.2% who either have visited or are living in Malaysia. 14.5% indicated the internet and 12.3% travel agents as their main sources. Medical tourists in Malaysia are predominantly regional visitors from Indonesia and information sources may of course vary by source and thus destination countries. Reports from other countries also find an overwhelming, self-reported significance of word-of-mouth information, however.

For Thailand, Jotikasthira (2010) distinguishes between organic (word of mouth, personal doctor), autonomous (media coverage), and induced (agents and provider marketing) information sources and finds a ranking of importance in the order listed (Jotikasthira 2010). Our conversation with the Apollo Hospital Group confirms the empirical relevance of organic sources, which take the shape of a worldwide referral network. For Chinese, Japanese and Korean medical tourists, Yu and Ko (2012) point to a Korean study that examines the significance of personal recommendations by friends, relatives or neighbors as opposed to the role of internet research. Remarkably, 100% of the Koreans interviewed obtained information via word-of-mouth.

Al-Hinai et al. (2011) report friends (73%) and family members (18.9%) as the main information sources for outgoing patients in Oman. For a sample of medical tourists in China, India, Jordan and the United Arab Emirates, Alsharif et al. (2010)

document 45% of the patients relying on friends, colleagues or relatives as the primary source of information and 35% relying on internet research. In terms of actually arranging their travels, helpers appear to differ by country as 52% and 50% of the visitors to UAE and India used facilitators while 97% and 77% of the visitors to China and Jordan relied on family members or themselves. Other studies also suggest the relevance of word-of-mouth for medical tourism (Glinos and Baeten 2006; Johnston et al. 2012; Wagner et al. 2011; Wagner and Verheyen 2010). In Wagner and Verheyen (2010), 48% of the sample of Germans with planned treatments abroad relied on word-of-mouth as a criterion to select their foreign provider. With multiple answers allowed, word-of-mouth ranked well ahead of the next criterion, internet research, with 20%. One specific source of word-of-mouth can be found in expatriates who represent not only cultural ties but enablers of medical tourism. Expatriates returning for treatment are also mentioned as sources of inbound medical tourism (Connell 2013; Hanefeld et al. 2013) but they can also act as facilitators of outbound tourism.

In Germany, private facilitators dominate the scene. Nagel and Neller (2013a) and Frädrich (2013) report 66–80% of German hospitals involved with international patients cooperate with up to 1500 agencies or private agents in Germany who take care of visas, flights, interpreters and appointments. Their size and the quality of services in terms of reliability of appointments and individual cost estimates vary wildly but no detailed information is available for Germany. A non-representative sample of international facilitators in Pollard (2013) confirms the facilitators' service focus on travel arrangements, service personnel, physician profiles, personalized pre-treatment plans and interpreting services. He takes a tally of customer bases of facilitators at less than 100 patients annually for 50% of the facilitators and of more than 1000 patients annually for 11% of the facilitators.

Facilitators may expose both medical tourists and providers to two-sided markets with commissions of up to 15% from both parties. Such commissions were declared immoral by the district court in Kiel (Landgericht Kiel 2011) but providers have few alternatives to private agents. They may only charge international patients standard German rates even if additional services offered incur costs in addition to the treatment. Marketing restrictions for medical services in Germany further limit medical tourism ambitions of providers (Cormany and Baloglu 2011), so they are essentially pigeonholed into the adaptation of internal processes and need to passively foster marketing.

Contrary to other European destinations such as Hungary or Poland, the German government does not pursue a dedicated medical tourism strategy. However, some marketing at the federal, state and municipal level can be observed. Both the German National Tourist Board and the state of Bavaria published a brochure that promoted medical travel (Bavarian State Ministry of the Environment and Public Health; Deutsche Zentrale für Tourismus e. V. 2011); visitBerlin promotes Berlin as a medical destination; Berlin and Brandenburg jointly investigated the potential of medical tourism (Berlin Partner für Wirtschaft und Technologie GmbH 2015); and the German Hospital Federation attended the Saudi Arabia Days in 2006.

Public facilitation of medical tourism is often motivated by broader economic benefits. Bookman and Bookman (2007) relate the potential of medical tourism to the high income elasticity of both medical services and tourism. Medical tourism allows destinations to capture a large share of that income and to engage in more favorable export sectors than typical, low-income elastic agricultural products—provided demand cannot be met domestically and trade barriers do not prevent trade. Bookman and Bookman (2007) specifically point out income generation through foreign currency, taxes, and investment and Turner 2007 explains a reorientation of Asian countries to overseas patients after the financial crisis with their attractiveness after currency depreciation. Even if regional medical tourism eventually picked back up, an increasing number of overseas patients is also documented by Khoo (2003).

Heung et al. (2011) describe a requested supply-side focus of public facilitation and support for Hong Kong. Based on interviews with public and private representatives, they name labor costs, marketing regulations, a lack of capacity and infrastructure and the absence of a relaxing environment the main barriers to medical tourism in Hong Kong and many governments hurry to provide the conditions demanded. National strategies were involved in the development of the medical tourism industry and led to aggressive marketing and government support. Active industrial policies such as dedicated visas, tax breaks to providers, multi-agency public private partnerships, subsidized real estate, special accounting practices, trade fair support or encouragement of international provider accreditation were introduced in several countries.

Crone (2008) points out a green field approach in India that allowed providers to start from scratch with both facilities and information systems in a low wage country. Hazarika (2010) and Johnston et al. (2010) further mention real estate subsidies and reduced import duties. Bookman and Bookman (2007) elaborate on strategies adopted for the establishment of the essentially tax-free Dubai HealthCare City with minimum entry barriers and fast-lane visas, direct subsidies through supportive infrastructure and service sectors as well as indirect subsidies through tax breaks and lifted import restrictions. Unsurprisingly, Cuba is another medical tourism destination that relied entirely on public facilitation with its SERVIMED agency, which promotes treatments and tourism packages (Cattaneo 2009; Drager and Vieira 2002). Several other destinations such as Hungary, Korea, Malaysia, Puerto Rico, Singapore and Turkey have also enjoyed extensive government support (García-Altés 2005; Johnston et al. 2010; Lunt et al. 2011; Lunt et al. 2014a; Ramírez de Arellano 2011).

Some governments are still conducting strategic studies on the possibility to develop medical tourism (Firman and Wang 2013) as Youngman (2014) slams down the gavel on governments with successful strategies (Malaysia, South Korea and Thailand) and those falling behind (India). To stay within the picture, the jury is still out on what successful national strategies for the establishment of medical tourism actually are. The literature on service trade provides some hints and it turns out that many issues previously discussed return at the aggregate level. Goswami et al. (2012) investigated several countries in case studies and while establishing solid causal links is difficult, three broad areas of importance are identified: a country's factors of production, general trade policies and targeted trade policies. Human capital, institutional quality and infrastructure turn out to be crucial factors of production. Here, human capital refers to education relative to the skills required: while the workforce in countries like Thailand and Tunisia consists of highly-trained doctors or engineers that of others suffers from a severe mismatch of education and requirements. The authors note Kenya with a large business graduate workforce that "needs substantial postgraduate training [to meet] international standards." The lack of foreign language skills is another common shortcoming of education. The focus of institutional quality is on corruption, a complicated legal system and complex export regulations. Infrastructure in its traditional sense is important for travel and tourism but many modern services are rendered electronically. While meeting the infrastructural needs of the producers is a prerequisite to exporting, the penetration and quality of electronic infrastructure in the destination countries is of even greater significance. The former is often provided in developed, economic centers or special zones.

Two interesting successful general policies deal with migration. First, re-migrating professionals may fragment the value chain of multinational companies who react by restructuring and relocating and may thus provide direct investment. Second, domestic firms can tap migrant demand abroad and thus pave the way to larger scale market entry. On the other hand, preferential trade agreements and trading zones cannot be identified as particularly fruitful trade policies. While general improvements to infrastructure, regulations and export procedures benefit the entire economy, specific policies targeted at service sectors of national interest can also be observed in abundance. They range from tax exemptions, import duty exemptions of supplies and public-private-partnerships to public development agencies. Brand policy of industry associations is considered another important factor. Some policies clearly failed due to a lack of regard for general economic conditions required for a sector such as tourism or due to a lack of dedicated resources. Others are inefficient as they did not receive appropriate sunset clauses.

The most glaring research questions concern the causal link between government policies and successful exporting and how much of an observable success results from a shift of focus from goods exports to service exports, i.e. a mere focus on an already existing competitive advantage. Criticism of government involvement in medical tourism occurs along these lines, i.e. a missing, larger picture. Cattaneo (2009) demands adequate regulations and domestic structure for the full realization of potential of trade in health care but considers missing statistics, potential competition among institutions with health, trade or tourism focus, and an excessive focus on export goods as opposed to services problematic. Lunt et al. (2014a) are equally critical of government involvement and argue that not enough is known about medical tourism to warrant such a measure. They point to excessively optimistic market size predictions and to external factors such as shifting consumer preferences, political instability, and a global recession that render naïve government policies futile if path dependency and the role of network-generated demand in medical tourism is neglected.

One facilitating destination characteristic that is related to national governments is political stability. A number of authors point to the safety and security image as an important aspect (Ehrbeck et al. 2008; Fisher and Sood 2014; Jotikasthira 2010). Hanefeld et al. (2013) and Youngman (2014) also find political turmoil and the resulting lack of safety to change the patterns of medical tourism which is well in line with empirical research of tourism in general (Enright and Newton 2004). Crone (2008) reports up to 50% total profits at American hospitals from 5% of their international self-pay patients until 9/11 brought such travel to a halt.

2.3.6 Proximity

Proximity is a multifaceted concept that extends beyond a simple metric of length. It can be measured in a number of dimensions and arises at both the micro and macro level (Boschma 2005). The medical tourism literature as well as the international trade literature typically refer to distance, which is the counterpart to proximity, but distance is often used interchangeably with geographic distance so we opt for the term proximity.

The geographic dimension of proximity includes distance in units of length as well as measures that qualify distance in terms of accessibility and travel comfort. Depending on the level at which destinations are aggregated, geographic distance in units of length may be an objective but still an inappropriate measure if travel time and comfort do not coincide with it. Münch (2014) mentions a direct flight from Moscow to Dresden as a crucial touristic feature whose perceived importance for medical tourists was confirmed in conversations with the University Hospital Carl Gustav Carus Dresden. Johnson and Garman (2015) also confirm the importance of distance and accessibility in the context of medical tourism. The role of geographic distance and price is likely confounded by tourism. Exworthy and Peckham (2006) point out that distant medical tourism destinations are costlier to reach and that willingness-to-travel for a service generally decreases with geographic distance. At the same time, more distant destinations—in terms of geographic or cultural distance—might be more attractive from a tourist point of view. So medical treatments and tourism should be disentangled if one aims at identifying the effects of price and of proximity.

Dimensions of proximity other than geographic distance are implied by Milstein and Smith (2007) who note that proximity provides an emotional benefit. Glinos and Baeten (2006) see a general attachment to domestic health care due to social and cultural ties such as a common polity or language which is in line with empirical work at the aggregate level of trade by Rauch (1999) and Guiso et al. (2009). Participants of the survey in Wagner and Verheyen (2010) report no language barriers but this may result from a heavy sample bias. Wagner et al. (2011) shed more light on this issue as they analyze a similar sample and 87% of the patients with planned health treatments abroad indicated to have spoken German with their doctors. This is uncommon for medical tourism, which usually draws heavily on interpreters or relies on English-speaking personnel. While the potential importance of a common language in terms of communication and information costs is intuitively clear and documented in the economic trade literature, not much is known about its actual importance in the context of medical tourism. The importance of a shared language to communicate has been documented on various occasions (Jotikasthira 2010; Musa et al. 2012b) but whether doctors or personnel with a high language proficiency are preferred over commonly employed interpreters and if the latter offer additional emotional benefit beyond their interpretation services is not known. Often, accompanying persons take on the role of caregivers and provide emotional comfort (Casey et al. 2013).

Non-accompanying persons may also influence the proximity of a destination—a notion that is motivated by the theory of planned behavior and that underlines the subjective character of proximity. TPB comprises attitudes as an individual evaluation about the consequences of a behavior, subjective norms as the perceived social pressure of the environment, and the perception of behavioral control, which takes into account intervening factors that may preclude the desired path of action. Attitudes capture the perceived benefits or detriments of alternatives, which are enriched by subjective norms and finally evaluated by feasibility. The role of subjective norms in medical tourism can be found in an existing physician-patient relationship or the relaxation of a perceived obligation to receive treatment at home. The enforcement of such a norm may be the reported tapping of expatriates as sources of medical tourism inflows (Bergmark et al. 2010; Gill et al. 2008; Lee et al. 2010). Liu and Chen (2013) discuss the broader role of cultural proximity for medical tourism, Smith et al. (2009) explicitly mention cultural ties with expatriates as an attractive destination criterion, and Lunt et al. (2014a) suspect this network-driven tourism—including professional referrals—to be a main driver of medical tourism. Such behavior would be expected to relax perceived, local obligations.

Martin et al. (2011) resort to TPB modeling to explain the intention to engage in medical tourism and find attitudes and subjective norms to dominate intentions while perceived control is of less importance. Overall, however, the explanatory power of their model is quite weak. Lee et al. (2012) apply TPB to Japanese tourists in Korea and find subjective norms to dominate both attitudes and perceived behavioral control in the estimation of behavioral intentions to receive a health treatment. For the second scenario of a beautification treatment, subjective norms are the least important predictor, which hints to treatment-specific drivers and considerations. In terms of specific characteristics, both health and beautification treatments share costs, information, communication as main criteria but location and convenience were added to beautification treatments so even for geographic distance a differentiation by treatment seems warranted (Lee et al. 2012). A different role of the perception of behavioral control is reported by Jotikasthira (2010) who finds an internal health locus of control, i.e. a belief in one's capacity to control one's own health, for visitors to Thailand. Rajagopal (2011) also points to self-control as important individual-specific characteristic and SFU Medical Tourism Research Group find Canadian medical tourists to be independent decision makers with an inner locus of control.

The identified individual characteristics and cultural proximity both have the potential to increase perceived proximity and may in fact have a similar effect on other destination characteristics as trust is established. Goudge and Gilson (2005) define trust as "a judgement in a situation of risk that the trustee will act in the best interests of the truster". Such risks in medical tourism may include outcome risk, quality risks, risks in continuity of care and income risks. Lukas (2009) points to literature that includes cultural ties, historic ties, religious ties, and previous experience as determinants of trust and draws on the manifestations of trust listed in Goudge and Gilson (2005): technical competence, ability to communicate, confidentiality, anxiety of well-being and fidelity. These items essentially decompose what Klingenberger (2009) calls a general attitude towards a treatment abroad into a quality hypothesis and the risks associated with the hypothesis. Technical competence and the ability to communicate are covered by the aforementioned quality and language criteria. Confidentiality and privacy are often mentioned in the context of cosmetic surgeries or fertility treatments and might in fact lead to increased trust in and thus utility from foreign options (Alsharif et al. 2010). Moghimehfar and Nasr-Esfahani (2011) and Esiyok et al. (2017) find religious ties to be of importance in medical tourism and Fisher and Sood (2014) confirm an important role of previous experience with treatments abroad. Mechinda et al. (2010) report trust to be very important for medical tourists who visit Thailand and highlight attitudinal loyalty, which is generally considered a requirement for behavioral loyalty. Wongkit and McKercher (2013) also find a strong tie between medical tourists and Thailand as a destination. 72.2% of the interviewees had previously visited Thailand and 36% had visited Thailand six or more times in the previous 10 years.

Lukas (2009) uses the overall construct of trust to downgrade services abroad with distrust as "subjective perceived quality". This is not to represent transaction costs or a lack of knowledge about a destination's objective quality but a general attitude towards international patient-provider relationships. His modeling renders foreign options second-best even if they are chosen due to their high-quality or attractive pricing. The theoretical result, however, is determined by the chosen modeling of trust into domestic options and one may argue for international varieties that provide, for example, a degree of confidentially that cannot be attained domestically.

In summary, perceived proximity is the product of objective destination characteristics and their subjective perception that depends on individual characteristics whose joint significance in a medical tourism context is poorly understood. Closely tied to the subjective perception of a destination are the aforementioned facilitators which may reduce perceived risks, and increase trust in a destination and lower costs.

2.3.7 Summary

For Germany as a high-cost destination, quality of care is suspected to be an important driver of inbound medical tourism but we have seen that low-cost destinations also market themselves as high-quality destinations and communicate a range of quality measures including high-tech equipment, physician expertise, international accreditations and clinical outcome measures. We thus hypothesize information channels and personal networks that communicate destination characteristics to be a main determinant of destination choice. We expect networks to increase trust in a destination, to lower perceived risks and to actively usher in patients via personal recommendations. In addition, they may reduce costs and provide local support.

The role of personal networks can be motivated by the core relationship in the health care market between patients and physicians, i.e. consumers and producers. This relationship is characterized by features, which give rise to a network of agents that renders market interactions in this sector particularly complicated. Initially, we observe asymmetric information between two parties: patients seek treatment of a medical condition and consult physicians who have private knowledge about the need and/or type of treatment required. Patients face information costs, transaction costs and difficulties of outcome measurement to overcome this principal-agent relationship. Specifically, they suffer from imperfect information that allows only ex-post treatment evaluation with little possibility to establish causal links between treatments and outcomes; they face significant transaction costs if they were to contract every party involved in their treatments; and they face uncertainty about the outcomes of available treatments and about the measurement of treatment quality. Additionally, risk-averse patients fear medical conditions with calamitous monetary outlays and thus have an incentive to pool risks via insurance.

An insurance provider acts as a substitute consumer that modifies the existing principal-agent relationship. Insurance typically lowers transaction costs by maintaining relations with physicians and by evaluating treatments to assess expected outcomes, which determines both feasible and optimal coverage. However, an insurance provider introduces a second principal-agent relationship: Patients want their true preferences to be reflected in coverage considerations and expect their insurance providers to make efficient use of the entrusted resources while insurance providers expect patients to forgo unnecessary physician visits to not strain pooled resources. While insurance providers can be exposed to competition to achieve greater efficiency, moral hazard and adverse selection on the patient's part can be countered by self-selection into insurance schemes, which increases individual stakes in the use of pooled resources and encourages self-production of health.

Finally, the government intervenes in the health care market in multiple ways to address market power, externalities and other market failures. As an example, health insurance may need to be mandatory if ethical considerations dictate the treatment of acute conditions regardless of insurance status and thus invite free-riding. Externalities also abound in health care and further motivate mandatory insurance. Market power may arise from the presence of upper-tier associations that strive for market power and political influence. Such associations represent patients, physicians/providers, insurance providers and other stakeholders and can be viewed as countervailing powers even if they cannot enter all arenas such as the Federal Joint Committee in Germany. Some stakeholders such as pharmaceutical

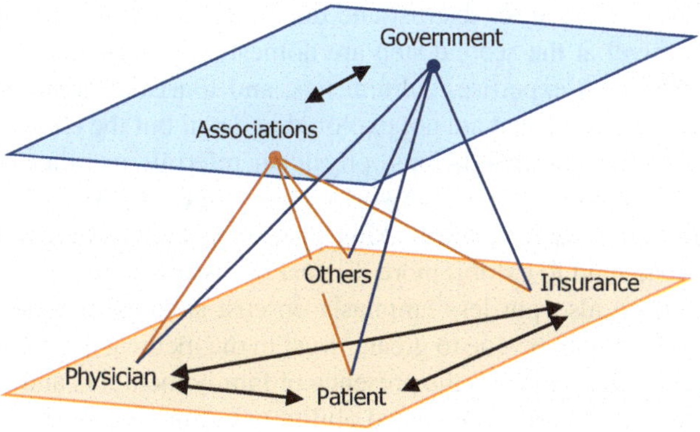

Fig. 2.27 Actors in the health care market

companies or suppliers of medical technology are excluded from the committee but are present in the political domain and entertain asymmetric ties with physicians and insurers, which further complicates the network of actors. Figure 2.27 summarizes the relationships of all parties, omitting direct relationships of other stakeholders in the health care market.

While the national level is fraught with complex relationships between all parties, fewer institutional restrictions obviate destination choice at the international level. Patients must find other ways to deal with the information asymmetry of the core patient-physician relationship when choosing their destination and personal networks are likely to be key, trust-enhancing components of the decision-making process.

In the medical tourism literature, Lunt et al. (2014a) were the first to distinguish between consumer-driven tourism, network tourism, and facilitator-driven tourism. They criticize the price focus of most analyses and a neglect of cultural and individual ties. A subsequent analysis of medical tourists in the UK and South Korea reconfirms the hypotheses that medical tourism markets may be considered networks with long-term relationships and that historic ties, a diaspora, and institutional ties maintained by providers are likely to be important indicators of such networks (Lunt et al. 2014b). A willingness-to-pay framing is still appropriate as price, quality and other destination characteristics remain relevant determinants of destination choice but networks and thus limited consideration sets of medical tourists are likely to play a large role that remains to be scrutinized. Limited consideration sets are a particularly compelling explanation of destination choice as many providers spend relatively little on marketing and consider a lack thereof the main limiting factor to their growth (Pollard 2013).

Hanefeld et al. (2015) were the first to examine the role of cultural and familial ties in more detail. They interviewed 77 medical tourists and propose a four-step decision-making process that starts with the decision to receive private treatment, continues with the decision to travel, and ends with the choice of a destination country and of a provider. The first step is driven by unavailability, non-eligibility, waiting time for a treatment or distrust and dissatisfaction with a particular service. Motivations to travel at the second step are domestic unavailability of a treatment, cost savings, physician expertise, cultural ties, and touristic intentions. Drivers of country choice at the third step are not explored in detail but the choice of a provider was often based on recommendations, physician referrals or other direct connections, i.e. it was driven by personal networks. Hanefeld et al. (2015) find that cultural and familial ties enter the decision-making process at various stages: Patients with cultural ties abroad tend to exhibit more distrust or dissatisfaction with the domestic health system. They also put less emphasis on cost savings generated from treatments abroad, which may be due to greater trust in the medical expertise abroad, due to additional utility derived from the presence of family members and friends, or due to a common language and an enhanced ability to communicate. Similarly, recommendations influence the subjective perception of physician quality abroad and influence final provider choice. This word-of-mouth effect increases as the quality of a treatment becomes more important.

The role of information networks has also been investigated in the international trade literature for goods trade. In his seminal work Rauch (1999) finds an increasing importance of cultural ties as products become more heterogeneous. Such products do not have reference prices as they are complex, i.e. they are differentiated in many dimensions and their quality may be difficult to assess. Consumers thus make use of networks to search for a suitable variety and these networks may be governed and represented by cultural ties. In line with Rauch (1999), we assume that product searches can be conducted in a network of cultural similarity whose existence lowers information costs. Distinct measures of cultural similarity such as linguistic proximity capture direct reductions in costs (e.g. translation costs) and indirect reductions in costs by generating mutual trust (e.g. transaction costs). We argue that network nodes, i.e. personal contacts, do not only lower costs across the board but actively produce trust in select destinations by recommendations. It is, however, difficult to isolate recommendations: Migrants in both the source and in the destination country may act as personal or commercial sources of information which disseminate organic information to their private network of family and friends or induced information to customers. We cannot disentangle private and commercial activities without data on facilitators but will attempt to exploit the non-commercial role of previous patients who return to their source countries with predominantly positive experiences. Recommendations from this group reduce product uncertainty and thus increase the expected utility of a specific destination. The degree of uncertainty reduction depends on the type of information source. In line with Hanefeld et al. (2015), we suspect this organic information to have a significant influence on destination choice.

Specific personal networks are difficult to measure and only observable at the individual level so they are commonly captured by more available, aggregate measures of proximity. One such measure is linguistic proximity, which can capture both ease of communication with and general trust in a destination (Melitz and Toubal 2014). The importance of linguistic proximity increases as products become more differentiated and we suspect an even larger impact of cultural proximity on

Table 2.13 Networks and measures of proximity

	Networks	Measures of proximity	Variables
Micro	Family	Previous patients	Lagged patient flows
	Friends	Migrant stock	Migrants at source
	Support groups		Migrants at destination
	Business networks		–
	Provider networks		–
Macro		Common language	Common spoken language
			Common native language
		Common religion	Common religion
		Common legislation	Common legislation
		Common history	Common colonial past

service trade and medical treatments specifically, a market with highly complex and differentiated products. Other measures of cultural proximity include Hofstede's cultural dimensions, institutional proximity, religious proximity which captures familiarity with values, beliefs and attitudes at a destination and more general measures of affinity (Esiyok et al. 2017; Felbermayr and Toubal 2010; Möhlmann et al. 2010). Finally, migrant stock in both the source and destination country has been employed as measures of cultural proximity and underlying personal networks (Melitz and Toubal 2014).

Table 2.13 summarizes the different networks and measures of cultural proximity that we consider and that may act as drivers of medical tourism. For completeness, we added business networks that arise later in chapter 6 and may also influence destination choice. We make a distinction between the micro and macro level based on Boschma (2005) who defines organizational and social proximity at the micro level and institutional proximity at the macro level. The micro level corresponds to "socially embedded interactions between agents" while the macro level captures more abstract dimensions such as a common language, common beliefs or common habits. The size of networks can be approximated by the bilateral migrant stock and the number of previous patients who engage in word-of-mouth. Measures at the macro level also indicate the presence of networks but they may further capture an underlying trust that can be unrelated to the existence of networks. Common language variables highlight this point: A common spoken language increases the probability of an existing network and social interaction while a common native language and no means of direct communication may not increase this possibility but still reflect familiarity with and thus trust towards another destination.

Finally, we expect medical tourism to be governed by a strong country-of-origin effect. Trust in a destination can be generated via networks and other experiences and the resulting stock of trust, i.e. the reputation of a destination, is expected to greatly influence destination choice aside from with currently available networks. The marketing literature supports this hypothesis of a country-of-origin effect and a role of subjective perception and trust: Weiber and Adler (1995a) define a purchase as a mix of search, experience and credence/trust processes depending on the observability of product characteristics before the purchase. These three processes differ in the degree of scrutiny and effort invested in the investigation of an alternative. Individuals switch from search to experience purchases depending on knowledge, cost and time requirements. The mix of the three processes depends on situational factors, experiences and individual traits (Weiber and Adler 1995a). Weiber and Adler (1995b) find physician visits to be a trust product for which experience matters more than price. Little knowledge about a complex product can then give rise to a pronounced country-of-origin effect (Mai 2011).

2.4 Implications of Medical Tourism

Medical tourism entails a number of wider implications that can translate into drivers. These implications can be usefully divided into implications for source and destination countries. In most of the literature, destination countries lie at the heart of the analysis and these countries often coincide with developing countries as a result of a focus on cost-sensitive patients. Consequently, migration effects and consequences for domestic access dominate the reporting. Concerns about distributive effects on countries with outbound medical tourists are uncommon, as the reaction to waiting times, the search for quality or the circumvention of financial constraints are generally perceived as acceptable drivers to seek care abroad. However, continuity of care and the use of public resources for follow-up care are concerns in source countries (Johnston et al. 2010).

Cohen (2011) presents an instructive argument for medical tourism based on national self-interests. For demonstrative purposes, he assumes that the spillover effects of a developing health care sector in a destination country have the potential to make that country's economy better off as a whole, including improved domestic access to health care. The source country in turn may benefit from a trading partner with increased purchasing power or from lower immigration pressure. Clearly, more empirical work is required as medical tourism does not give rise to obvious winners or losers. Economic effects cannot realistically be captured by simple Ricardian logic and migration flows, including remigration (Mullan 2006), are complex. Bookman and Bookman (2007) list a number of potentially positive impacts of medical tourism on various sectors in developing countries including water and waste management, power, transport, banking and research associated with medical services. They reach no conclusion on dominating positive or negative effects, however. For a normative assessment of medical tourism, Cohen (2011) makes the strong point that many of the implications of medical tourism can in fact be addressed and controlled by the destination countries of medical tourism. This point needs to be kept in mind throughout the following discussion of implications.

2.4.1 Migration and Local Access

Mattoo and Rathindran (2006)—among many other authors—acknowledge the importance of domestic access and suggest destination countries use part of their medical tourism revenues for improved local access. Concerns about local access to health care services are closely tied to the retention of physicians as the latter is a necessary but not a sufficient condition of the former. Labor force migration is usually discussed under the label of brain drain or care drain and refers to the economically attractive conditions that developed countries offer skilled foreign workers. The resulting migration flows occur before or after workers receive their final professional training.

The health care sector is particularly prone to migration as it is very labor intensive and grows in size due to demographic shifts. Examples of migration flows have been documented on various occasions: Crone (2008) discusses a shortage of nursing personnel in the U.S.; Hopkins et al. (2010) report Ghana, Pakistan and South Africa lose about half of their graduates to emigration; Cattaneo (2009) lists shares of African-trained physicians in the U.S. of up to 43% per source country; and Germany attracts doctors from Eastern Europe. Mullan (2006) estimates about 10% of all Indian doctors work in the U.S., Canada, Australia or the UK and Dumont and Zurn (2010) report workforce retention in the health sector to be challenging for both OECD and non-OECD countries.

While migration only occurs at the international level, sectoral shifts within a country may have similar effects on the availability of services. Leng (2006) acknowledges the effect of medical tourism on internal brain drain in Malaysia but argues in favor of keeping doctors inside the country via the private sector. In a second step, the government should then implement policies to ensure broader access to the services available. According to Wibulpolprasert et al. (2004), Thailand has been troubled by external and internal brain drain multiple times, even before medical tourism set in. Hopkins et al. (2010) report thousands of vacant positions for doctors in Thailand's public health care sector in 2005 as a result of competitive salaries in the private sector. Arellano (2007) seconds the analysis and reports a similar drain from the public to the private sector in India.

Part of the private sector's attraction may be due to inbound medical tourism but it is unclear how much of it can be attributed to international patients. A pressing question addresses the counterfactual of inbound medical tourism, i.e. does medical tourism create employment opportunities inside a destination country that the personnel in question would otherwise leave? If so, medical tourism's particular mode of delivery would be a valuable opportunity to retain qualified personnel. In fact, Smith et al. (2009) and Siddiqi et al. (2010) find the moving of health personnel, i.e. mode four of service delivery, to be the most common mode along with medical tourism travel. Cattaneo (2009) considers mode two delivery, i.e. medical tourism, to be the second-best solution for domestic capacity building with mode three, i.e. a foreign commercial presence, being superior. In fact, such investments also lead to mode two delivery as they bring better technology, foreign-trained staff and higher salaries.

Empirically, there are some examples of improved domestic access such as Morocco (Cattaneo 2009) but several accounts indicate the expansion of the private medical tourism sector may come at the cost of the domestic population in developing countries. NaRanong and NaRanong (2011) find that medical tourism puts a strain on health care personnel in Thailand but acknowledge a positive contribution of about 0.4% to Thailand's GDP at the same time. They propose policies to facilitate labor inflows and to redirect some of the additional income to labor force training. The implementation of such measures in Thailand, e.g. a compulsory rural service for domestic medical graduates and financial incentives for working in rural regions, are documented in Cattaneo (2009). However, Noree et al. (2016) find that medical tourism figures for Thailand have been greatly exaggerated and consider the impact of medical tourists on the domestic health system marginal.

Mullan (2006) discusses similar policies for India including investment in public facilities, balancing the private and public education of physicians, keeping tuitions low and providing scholarships. These steps aim at dedicating a larger share of GDP to health care but cost effective measures such as mandatory local residency for graduates for limited periods of time are also feasible. Hazarika (2010) and Sengupta (2011) report a dominating private sector in India and both direct and indirect subsidies of medical tourism. He estimates 75% of the personnel and advanced medical technology, 68% of the hospitals and 37% of the beds to be in the private sector. At the same time, he reports more than 80% out-of-pocket payments in India so the problem lies with the public sector and his suggestions for improvements address exactly that: devise a system of mutually beneficial coexistence. Cattaneo (2009) considers a lack of insurance schemes and inappropriate medical education regulations to be the main problems of the Indian health care sector.

Leng (2006) expresses the fear of segmentation in Malaysia, which could result in a private sector for paying or high-paying individuals and a public sector for the rest. He notes that access is problematic particularly for unregistered migrant users and that there exists no compulsory health insurance, which would alleviate problems and is likely to be introduced in the future. Leng (2006) also acknowledges the role of medical tourists in utilizing local hospital capacities and thus in securing needed income in dire times. In a similar vein, Lutze et al. (2010) find signs of improved capacity usage for hospitals dealing with medical tourists in Germany. Finally, Crone (2008) suggests an indirect effect on public health care providers that he sees in a private sector's focus on lucrative procedures. Whether public providers could perform such procedures at all or of similar quality, given low public investment, or if they should focus on broader primary care, remains unaddressed.

In summary, public investment is necessary regardless of medical tourism and the latter is no means to directly address inequality. It could address it to some extent, however, if private providers had an obligation to treat any patient and if universal coverage existed. In absence of such policies, medical tourism may only address inequality indirectly by providing access to revenue that can be invested in domestic health care. General staff shortage may be a problem to overcome but the counterfactual to employment in the private domestic sector is not necessarily employment in public domestic sector.

2.4.2 Treatment Quality and Continuity of Care

A main concern in source countries of medical tourism is the continuity of care as well as follow-up treatment due to malpractice abroad. Leaving aside concerns about the delivery of potentially unnecessary treatment (Crone 2008) and overconsumption (Mattoo and Rathindran 2006), reports about follow-up treatment due to poor quality are relatively scarce.

The majority of outgoing patients in Germany show a high degree of satisfaction with their treatment abroad (Wagner and Verheyen 2010). 5% of the respondents with planned treatment abroad indicated a need for follow-up treatment at home but an interpretation of this number is nearly impossible as nothing is known about the types of follow-up treatment required and as follow-up treatment cannot be traced to preceding medical or health resort treatment, the latter of which dominate initial treatment received (Wagner and Verheyen 2010). A distinction between health and medical follow-up treatment is made in Wagner et al. (2011): 4% of the patients with inpatient treatment report follow-up treatment mostly due to complications and 4% of the patients who received dental treatment report follow-up treatment—almost of them 50% due to malpractice. Internationally, Alsharif et al. (2010) and Al-Hinai et al. (2011) report very high satisfaction rates for inbound medical tourism to China, India, Jordan and UAE and for outbound medical tourism from Oman. Musa et al. (2012a) find very high satisfaction across five dimensions—doctors, nurses, hospital service, hospital atmosphere and hospital facilities—for inbound medical tourists in Malaysia.

Patients typically possess little expertise to assess the technical aspects of a treatment and official reports about necessary follow-up treatment at home do exist. Cheung and Wilson (2007) present the case of a single patient who received follow-up treatment at home worth $140,000 after a knee arthroscopy in an accredited hospital abroad. The patient paid $8600 for the procedure in the hospital of his choice as opposed to $15,570 in the source country. Hanna et al. (2009) compare 44 patients that underwent surgery in Belgium or the UK and find an increased complication rate. Their main concerns lie with a lack of organized postoperative care arrangements and a lower self-reported quality of life by patients who went abroad. The latter can be traced back to the former, i.e. patients missed a contact person to turn to with their postoperative concerns. Newman et al. (2005) identify a cosmetic surgery center in the Dominican Republic as the common denominator of five Mycobacterium abscessus infections and the same case is discussed in more detail in Furuya et al. (2008). Miyagi et al. (2012) identify and criticize costs to the public health care system in the UK that result from follow-up care to patients who underwent elective cosmetic surgery abroad and Sheppard et al.

(2014) conduct a similar analysis for Canadian patients who seek bariatric surgery abroad.

Gill et al. (2008) document uncommonly severe complications among medical tourists returning for follow-up care. These patients did not choose common medical tourism destinations, however, but 24 out of 33 patients traveled to their home regions China, Iran and the Philippines in order to receive kidney transplants. The motivation and circumstances of such transplant tourism are likely very different from the more typical medical tourism treatments—as is the decision-making process that leads to the destination choice. The decision to go to Iran—as the only country to allow organ sales—can be expected to be driven by the availability of organs rather than by provider quality.

Both Cheung and Wilson (2007) and Gill et al. (2008) point out a potentially problematic doctor-patient relationship of returning medical tourists. While this is plausible for both passed up physicians and uneasy patients, a positive doctor-patient relationship abroad, due to the anticipated proficiency of the attending doctor there, may offset concerns about the relationship with the domestic doctor for quality-seeking patients. More attention should be paid to the doctor-doctor relationship, however, as Wagner et al. (2011) report dissatisfaction with the communication between doctors at home and abroad among 20% of their selective sample.

In summary, small scale reports of complications clash with the minimal complication rates reported by leading international providers (Milstein and Smith 2006). Based on the evidence presented and the very small underlying samples, it is unclear if complication rates are systematically higher than for providers in source countries. Continuity of care is an important issue, however, that concerns patients and causes dissatisfaction (Pollard 2012). In Europe, this topic has implicitly received attention through the creation of a legal framework and universal health care coverage that theoretically ensure follow-up treatment at home. That does not address patient ownership concerns but insurers investigate these issues (Klusen et al. 2011) and establish cross-border partnerships.

2.4.3 *Legal Aspects*

With its very own legal and political features, cross-border care in Europe represents a special case of medical tourism. The European Union, despite the previously discussed instances of cross-border cooperation, generally grants member states considerable autonomy with regards to their provision of health care and aside from universal coverage as a common denominator, they do pursue very different financing and delivery strategies. However, Terry (2007) notes that "the European Court of Justice has taken the position that state health systems cannot act so as to impede federally mandated freedom of movement of persons and services." He goes on to provide an account of well-known ECJ rulings that entitle citizens in the European Union to full domestic reimbursement of treatments obtained abroad if they face unreasonable waiting times at home given their medical condition. Such reimbursement can include expenses for travel but may be limited to the national rate of the source country. European Union 2011 provides a generalization of previous rulings that acknowledges the autonomy of the member states' health care systems in principle, but subjects the provision of cross-border treatments to the freedom to provide services and grants free physician choice. It maintains the option of reimbursement restrictions for "overriding reasons of general interest" such as domestic capacity planning or waste of resources. Other qualifications with regard to, for example, long-term residency to obtain care abroad exist as well. In summary, the European Union has developed a framework for planned treatments that systematically extends the choice set of medical destinations for its member state citizens beyond their national boundaries and several domestic health insurances have contracted selected destination options abroad (Rosenmöller et al. 2006; Wagner and Verheyen 2010).

A rare and interesting treatment of legal concerns about medical tourism from the U.S. perspective is provided by Cohen (2010). The issues and questions raised therein are not entirely specific to only the U.S. and touch on various economic considerations. Cohen (2010) classifies treatments abroad according to their legal classifications in both the source and the destination country and then inquires whether or not there is a case for legal action in the source country to be made (Cohen 2011). The first category includes treatments illegal in both source and destination country. The illegal status of such health care services is not very controversial and the issue of whether or not their use should be penalized at home if lax enforcement abroad is to be expected is not pursued any further.

The second category of treatments that are illegal at home but legal abroad entails more controversy. Such treatments may take the form of fertility tourism, the participation in clinical trials when deemed ineligible at home, or assisted suicide (Cohen 2010). Domestic legislation channels demand to a foreign market or may create a foreign market in the first place. Depending on the economic magnitude of the market in question, the technological relevance attributed to the treatment, and the ethical or legal considerations at hand, resulting circumvention tourism can put substantial pressure on domestic regulation. A prominent example is stem cell legislation as a gatekeeper that effectively determines the players of a market. As opposed to standard goods that can effectively be barred from entry, medical providers can relocate and render their services to patients traveling abroad—a practice that is much more difficult to ban as it is closely tied to the freedom of movement as a human right, which grants "the right to leave any country, including his own, and return to his country." For countries in the European Union, this translates directly into the "primary and individual right to move and reside freely within the territory of the Member States" as a civil right (European Union 2004). Recurring to the previously mentioned example of teleradiology in the U.S. (Wachter 2006), the domestic delivery of services can be barred by licensing but travel is more difficult to stop. From a U.S. point of view, Cohen (2012) discusses if the source country should extend its legal restrictions beyond its territory and deducts a set of rules that justifies the extraterritorial application of criminal law, depending on the involved parties' citizenship and victim protection. Operationally, there is clearly considerable discretion to impair international travel, which requires valid documents from a citizen, for example, but the intention of a trip can hardly be determined beforehand. Overall, this category of treatments is an issue that is anticipated by some to be of increasing importance in the future, especially with regards to reproductive medicine (IPK International 2012).

The third and most interesting category comprises treatments that are legal both in the source and in the destination country. The central question is why a patient's choice of destination should be restricted in the absence of any criminal actions. Cohen (2010) identifies patient protection from poor quality and insufficient or absent malpractice liability as potential prompters for domestic lawmakers to act. Such actions can aim at the regulation of either services or insurers that contract foreign providers. The former may prescribe mandatory information packages or certification of providers while the latter may dictate a purely domestic health plan option or fixed co-pays for domestic and international treatments.

Domestic patient protection in the U.S. is governed by a comprehensive set of regulations stipulating requirements for "accreditation, certification, professional self-regulation of physicians and other health care providers, the medical-malpractice system, the reporting of malpractice suits in the National Malpractice Database, licensure and accreditation of providers, medical staff bylaws, provider privileges regulation, conflict of interest regulation, and anti-kickback statutes" (Cohen 2010). Such regulations do not exist for treatments abroad but there is little empirical evidence that consumers seek destinations of lesser quality than their domestic options. Mandatory licensing abroad is a questionable measure given inter-state regulations that require the licensing of personnel in the state of practice but do not prevent any travel between states. Such travel provides a reasonable analogy to international travel. However, it is of public interest to avoid malpractice liability problems abroad as the public may face the risk of paying for malpractice recovery if no jurisdiction is available for legal actions. While there exist no identical standards between U.S. states either (Cohen 2010), there is a difference between potential immunity and varying levels of recovery in different forums. The need for a working malpractice liability rule is also acknowledged by Mattoo and Rathindran (2006) and can in theory be addressed by a mandatory insurance (Cohen 2010).

On a side note, the settlement of payments faces a similar problem, as it may not be enforceable in a different jurisdiction. While both inbound and outbound medical tourists may benefit from domestic consumer protection (Landgericht Kiel 2011), providers assume full risks for bad debts. Nagel and Neller (2013a, b, 2014) provide accounts of outstanding receivables worth 4.5 million Euros, shares of which account for as much as 7% of some affected hospitals' turnover. These hospitals engaged in treatments of Libyan patients whose payments were settled by a third party, but such problems are reported by other hospitals as well and are often met by advance payment requirements.

Interestingly, Cohen distinguishes between out-of-pocket medical tourists and insurer-prompted medical tourists in his various works. The latter group includes employer-sponsored health care plans. Medical tourism as a health plan component will allow some insurants to switch to more affordable plans and will help a subset of the uninsured obtain health insurance in the first place. The former benefit may be of theoretic nature for several employer-sponsored health plans as the employee's choice set is limited but in theory, he will choose the employer with the most suitable salary/health plan compensation package. Cohen identifies three reasons to regulate insurer-prompted medical tourism. First, insurers face switching behavior and may thus not choose the high-quality provider an insurant would have contracted. Instead the insurer may only focus on minimizing short-term costs (Cohen 2010). Second, Cohen argues that insurers do not internalize all costs of medical malpractice recovery incurred by insurants due to insurer-friendly laws. Third, he points out the insurants' poor understanding of medical plans and the consequences they entail. Cohen recognizes the dominance of employer-sponsored health plans in the U.S. and acknowledges that these may alleviate his concerns about the short-term focus and the internalization of costs, so what remains is a relatively weak third argument to regulate insurer-prompted medical tourism: "[...] it seems less plausible that they [the employees] can adequately assess the benefits and costs of the medical-tourism piece of these plans, especially given the bounded-rationality problems discussed above" (Cohen 2010).

At any rate, any set of regulations would have to address a multitude of questions (Cohen 2010) such as: Is it reasonable to certify providers abroad in light of their good track records? Should certification occur at the state or at the federal level? Are health plans with incentives to receive treatments abroad acceptable? What if these plans are framed with penalties for the use of domestic providers? Who assumes liability if a treatment abroad goes awry—insurer, employer or provider abroad? Cohen (2010) suggests insurers be required to cover domestic emergency follow-up care after treatments abroad in all plans. He furthermore demands an actuarially fair status quo plan that covers exclusively domestic treatment. Employer-sponsored plans shall be subject to the same rules, as it is not clear if employers internalize poor employee choices in their plans.

Essentially, the issue at hand is as much of economic as of legal nature. Laws aim to protect consumers and the public from risks by incurring costs at both the internal and the external margin, i.e. regulations alter the costs for those currently obtaining care at home or abroad and they alter access for those who cannot currently obtain the desired care. Cohen endorses medical tourism at the external margin to give the uninsured and underinsured access to the care they seek but he wants to regulate medical tourism at the internal margin and shifts the focus from access to risk protection. While mandatory domestic emergency and even follow-up treatment coverage are reasonable as domestic providers need to provide emergency facilities at any rate and rolling over follow-up treatments to a mandatory health insurance or the public would result in negative externalities, the status quo plan is problematic. Even if such a plan were actuarially fair, its premium would increase substantially if a large number of patients self-selects out of the purely domestic option and thus drives up unit costs. This results directly from economies of scope in domestic health care provision (Mattoo and Rathindran 2006). Another concern besides the short-term efficient scale and economies of scope arguments is the risk of supplier-induced demand as a result of asymmetric information in the health care market.

A more global perspective is adopted in Cohen (2011) where the author identifies six conditions that he considers potential triggers for action:

- The services consumed would otherwise be available to the poor.
- The services rendered are exclusively available to tourists.
- The supply of physicians in the destination country is inelastic.
- Medical tourism services tie up more resources than they attract to the country.
- Public funds for public support are redirected towards medical tourism.
- The economic benefits of medical tourism do no propagate in the system but serve only few local beneficiaries.

These triggers resemble the issues discussed above and mainly address domestic access in destination countries. Without conclusive evidence of these triggers, Cohen (2011) discusses four approaches to assessing the need for international action provided diminished access did result. These approaches include national self-interest, international distributive justice, distributive justice within national boundaries, and mixed approaches. Cohen arrives at an order in which international intervention in medical tourism might be justified: government-prompted medical tourism, insurer-prompted medical tourism and out-of-pocket medical tourism. He also finds a stronger case to intervene in inessential health treatments as opposed to serious medical treatments. From an economic point of view, the arguments for these results are questionable as they rely on welfare assumptions that are never spelled out. The comparison between insurer-prompted and out-of-pocket medical tourism, for example, rests on the assumption that insurants who gain access to treatments abroad via their insurance merely save money whereas out-of-pocket tourists enjoy the larger benefit of gaining access to new services—which may also be the case for insurants. The analysis also neglects the welfare gains of the previously uninsured who might now benefit from the hypothesized lower insurance premiums and receive access to insurance contracts that not only give them access to outsourced elective care but also to additional domestic services that are part of their new health plan. We do not intend to discuss Global Justice theories in detail but rest on the point that the previous discussion has highlighted how closely intertwined the economic and legal arguments are. Both take individual and public welfare considerations into account and derive a potential need for action. The main difference lies in the more normative criteria that populate the legal arena.

One final legal issue that deserves mentioning is privacy and data protection. Terry (2007) sees a need for transnational patient-protective laws in the long term but finds the addressing of quality concerns to be of minor importance at this point. Instead, privacy and data protection stand out as in need of regulation both domestically and internationally. In practice, privacy can be an important driver of medical tourism and its impact is conditional on the treatment obtained. However, privacy considerations are usually associated with a positive, perceived anonymity as opposed to worries about the proliferation of information (Inhorn and Shrivastav 2010).

2.4.4 Ethics

A thorough discussion of medical tourism's ethical implications lies beyond the scope of this work, but we do want to at least highlight some main concerns that are related to the aforementioned legal concerns. For a detailed treatment of ethics in medical tourism the interested reader is referred to Hall (2013).

Similar to the preceding discussion, Crozier and Baylis (2010) are concerned about the use of unproven or untested methods and about the exploitation of vulnerable third parties abroad. They discuss an example of organ sale in Pakistan and Alsharif et al. (2010) mention organ sales in India and China, but these illegal and unsafe mutations of medical tourism are not very controversial unless the legal status of a treatment actually differs between two countries. The issue shall not be pursued here any further, but it is an interesting, normative question to ask if or when a citizen should be allowed to subscribe to another country's ethic and legal point of view and to consequently receive a treatment abroad that is illegal at home. And if there are no ethical objections to this behavior, what is the fundamental difference to obtaining a treatment that is illegal in both countries as the patient now opted into a smaller, suitable societal unit of like-minded people?

Assuming that a treatment is legal in two countries, there remain at least two questions that are discussed with much fervor: First, is medical care a good like any other and should medical tourism as a manifestation of a willingness-to-pay mechanism be tolerated or fostered? And second, is medical tourism the appropriate answer to address domestic shortcomings?

Innovative sectors such as the biotechnology branch often lament the substitute customer they face in regulators, insurances and employers that act as agents on behalf of individuals and consider them excessively risk averse, politicized or cost-focused. At the same time, doctors and providers of health care are also agents of the patients that they entrust with the selection of appropriate treatments. Emphasis on the first principal-agent relationship leads to the framework that is present in the statutory insurance system in Germany today and allows treatment selection from an approved pool of reimbursable treatments, which is preselected by the insurer in order to contain costs and to minimize treatment risks. Emphasis on the latter principal-agent relationship rests on the claim that risks between medical inputs and outcome risks should be taken on by doctors and providers as they can assume it best. Depending on the concept one subscribes to, the resulting market will be of a more public or private nature. Regardless of the exact mix, however, the resulting system will always be a manifestation of willingness-to-pay considerations.

An entirely private market will allocate treatments to patients based solely on their willingness-to-pay. As revealed willingness-to-pay is a function of ability-to-pay and ability-to-pay is a highly concentrated measure, a completely private health care system is deemed unfair in many societies. On the other hand, public systems also need to determine a maximum willingness-to-pay for a given treatment and the use of a representative willingness-to-pay measure in order to determine the scope and amount of equitably rendered health care services comes with difficulties. First, medical treatments and medicine in general are becoming more personalized—i.e. segmented—and framework setting will become increasingly difficult as it struggles to systematically assess the risks and appropriateness of a treatment for a given individual. It may also struggle with the very motivation of its existence, i.e. the socially acceptable distribution of treatments. While treatments today are often universally authorized or authorized based on a medical condition, authorization based on individual criteria may not be an acceptable distribution mechanism at all. If rationing in public systems based on criteria such as age suffers from limited acceptance, such rationing or authorization based on predicted outcomes that are conditional on individual dispositions will likely be rejected outright.

Not only the scope but also the optimal amount of services rendered is difficult to determine at a representative level. Hall and Jones (2004) find that optimal expenditure shares on health care rise over time due to a diminishing marginal utility of other consumption with rising income levels. If the value of life rises faster than income, there will be a willingness-to-pay for health care even at high levels of income redistribution. If such excess demand due to income or wealth is not met by a private sector domestically, it will manifest itself as medical tourism. If the findings of Hall and Jones (2004) hold, another direct consequence would be an increasing welfare loss among high-income payers into a public system if contributions are uncapped. Initially, the welfare loss may be desired as low-income beneficiaries receive welfare gains from access to services but, depending on the marginal utilities of both groups, deadweight losses may eventually become overwhelming. In practice, contributions to the public health care system in Germany are capped which leaves income that can be directed to excess demand for health care. Determining the appropriate cap thus represents a trade-off between aggregate welfare gains from health care within the public system and aggregate welfare gains from both health care and other consumption outside the public system.

The above-mentioned and lamented difficulty of applying innovative and new technologies in practice is the result of colliding amortization and cost containment strategies. The skimming of individuals' willingness-to-pay arguably allows more innovation, which spills over to common practice in Germany if successful and is included in public reimbursement schemes to eventually benefit society at large. Scale effects and the inflow of international patients can allow innovative providers to reach a critical threshold of patients for the initial delivery of innovative procedures.

In summary, we can observe a coexistence of private and public markets with the latter absorbing demand for innovative and often costly treatments. Willingness-to-pay governs both public and private systems but mirrors preferences either directly or indirectly. While a public system addresses distributional concerns, the private system absorbs excess demand. Such excess demand can be considered a safety valve to distributional, representational and incentivizing shortcomings of a public system and can be met domestically or via medical tourism. There is no obvious reason to restrict excess demand from an economic point of view as the result will be a Pareto improvement—unless the private provision diverts resources that would otherwise be used by public providers. If no private market is desired for distributional reasons domestically, a shift of resources may well occur across borders rather than across domestic sectors. Other public health and system level concerns about medical tourism that are not aligned with individual considerations, such as socialized costs for follow-up care, contagion risks, quality assurance, litigation, brain drain or equity concerns in the destination country, can be in principle be addressed by policies in both source and destination countries (Snyder et al. 2012) or in a bilateral setting (Smith et al. 2011a).

The second question is more empirical than normative: Milstein and Smith (2006) consider medical tourism a symptom of an affordability problem rather than a solution to domestic demand. In the same spirit, Crozier and Baylis (2010) and Frädrich (2013) suggest the domestic system as a first-best solution. Frädrich (2013) coins the term medical tourism 2.0 that refers to a market that sells factors of production as opposed to consumer services. He names Russia and China as examples and refers to factors such as infrastructure, organizational and management knowledge. Whether or not medical tourism 2.0 enjoys a bright future depends on the roles that both quality and domestic availability play. If different degrees of quality-cost-recreation combinations, i.e. product differentiation is demanded or economies of scale for small-scale treatments are to be exploited, medical tourism is likely to persist and differentiated supply across countries will drive intra-industry trade. If a lack of domestic availability is the driving force behind medical tourism, it could be addressed by investments in infrastructure and staff training. However, this strategy crucially depends on the availability of qualified personnel and competitive wages that need to be paid. The second condition is potentially hard to fulfill in light of the previously discussed migration pressure caused by the increased demand for health care services in many aging societies that offer physicians competitive salaries. But even if a country manages to set up the infrastructure, to adopt best practices of the industry and to attract trained personnel to provide the desired health care services of a desired range of quality domestically, there may still remain a small base of medical tourism: Patients who continue to seek specialized care at the technological edge abroad—a manifestation of a high marginal utility of health care spending relative to other consumption.

2.5 Summary

This chapter has provided an overview over the state of research into medical tourism, highlighted the complexity of medical tourism as a concept and hinted at framing and modeling challenges. Not all types of observed treatments represent manifestations of a conscious act of decision-making that determines the destination where a health care service is rendered. Our definition of medical tourism allows an economic-choice framing but is very demanding in terms of data disaggregation as information about types of treatment, purpose of travel and personal expenditures is required.

The scarce availability of high-quality trade flow data complicates the analysis of medical tourism and the reliability of reported figures is questionable for a number of reasons: Industry and ministerial reports are likely influenced by marketing agendas or policy targets and often include extrapolated predictions. Another source of error is the confusion of patients and treatments, both of which may differ. Much of the literature also relies on third-party data that is reproduced until it eventually sticks—its potentially deficient quality notwithstanding. Press reports that proliferate such data turn into sources themselves, reinforce allegedly authoritative numbers and online encyclopedias eventually divulge the data. Finally, some sources provide official data but fail to identify patients that engage in a voluntary act of traveling with the main purpose of obtaining a treatment. As a result, most reported medical tourism flows at the international level should be taken with a grain of salt and merely hint to medical tourism's order of magnitude rather than provide a solid basis for calculation.

Initial analyses found flows from developed to less developed countries that were fueled by low-cost treatments as well as infrastructural developments such as affordable transport and availability of online information. Subsequently, flows from low to high-income countries were reported and recent literature points to a regional focus of medical tourism, which is often treatment-specific and triggered by a domestic lack of availability or lower prices abroad. South-south flows have been a focus of the newest research on equity even if they are often of small scale. Generally, Asia provides services to patients from neighboring countries, Europe, North America, and the Middle East; Central America serves visiting expatriates and U.S. citizens with a focus on low prices; and Europe offers both low-price destinations to regional patients and high-price care to long-distance patients.

Medical tourism flows have important implications for health care systems that we have only touched upon. Several of these implications concerning, e.g. legislation and regulations, reimbursement schemes and privacy may also play a role as drivers of medical tourism. Freyer and Kim (2014) argue that drivers of medical tourism are well researched but that does not turn out to be the case upon closer inspection. There exists a set of common drivers that are repeatedly reproduced in the literature but their applicability and impact across different source countries, destinations, treatments and patients is not very well understood and expected to differ. Commonly mentioned price differences between locations, for example, are plausible drivers but price data reflects potential rather than actual medical tourism flows and thresholds of savings required by individuals have been elicited in but a few contexts. The same holds for domestic availability, quality, proximity with its various dimensions and tourism, which all provide intuitive explanations of medical tourism flows all the while their joint roles are unclear empirically. Upsets of widespread opinions as in Wongkit and McKercher (2013) highlight this point.

Table 2.14 summarizes the hypothesized drivers of demand for medical tourism that we have distilled from the medical tourism literature and that will be embedded in a broader framework in the next chapter. Availability depends on domestic legislation and regulation and supply conditions that determine the quantity supplied such as the competition for global inputs, investment conditions and public infrastructure. Political stability and the absence of armed conflicts can be framed as supply conditions but the latter may also spur demand. The other categories affect

Table 2.14 Drivers of medical tourism in the literature

Availability	Price	Quality of care	Tourism	Proximity	Individual
Legislation/ Regulations	Treatment	Physician expertise	Climate	Geographic distance	Age
Supply conditions	Travel	High-tech equipment	Attractions	Travel time	Income
	Accommodation	Hygiene	Accommodation	Travel comfort	Locus of control
	Visa requirement	Accreditation	Services	Cultural ties	Social norms
	Reimbursement	Reputation		Religious ties	Privacy
				Political ties	Recommendations
				Historic ties	Previous experience

variety rather than quantity: Price depends on treatment, travel and accommodation costs, visa requirements and the availability of a reimbursement scheme or a lack thereof. Travel, accommodation and visa costs include those incurred by accompanying persons. Quality as a destination characteristic has been operationalized by hygiene, high-tech equipment, physician expertise, and reputation. Tourism has been linked to climate, attractions, accommodation and services but the next chapter will draw from the tourism literature to cover recreational aspects more thoroughly. Proximity is a complex construct that may include geographic distance, travel time, travel comfort, cultural ties such as a common polity or language, religious ties, political ties, and historic ties such as a common colonial past. At the individual level, a set of characteristics modifies the perception of a destination and reflects the disposition to engage in medical tourism. This set of characteristics includes age, income, locus of control, perceived social norms such as prestige from going abroad or existing relationships with domestic physicians, a desire for privacy, recommendations from family members, friends or domestic physicians and previous experiences with treatments abroad.

Based on considerations about market imperfections and various strands of literature in Sect. 2.3.7, we have motivated our research focus on proximity as a key determinant of destination choice. In particular, we hypothesized considerable effects of recommendations from returning patients, of migrants as personal network nodes and facilitators, of cultural proximity as a broad measure of trust and of a country-of-origin effect on destination choice in medical tourism. The analysis of these effects is the main focus of our empirical work but we complement them with the investigation of additional drivers whenever the data permits. Before we present our specific empirical approaches, however, we develop a framework that organizes the various dimensions and destination characteristics of medical tourism in the literature. This framework enforces a much-desired acknowledgement of modeling dimensions that are unwittingly or inadvertently excluded from other analyses. It further reveals two additional research questions that we intend to investigate in our subsequent analysis: the relevant level of supplier aggregation in empirical modeling and the composition of real consideration sets.

References

Al-Hinai, S. S., Al-Busaidi, A. S., & Al-Busaidi, I. H. (2011). Medical tourism abroad: A new challenge to Oman's health system. *Sultan Qaboos University Medical Journal, 11*, 477–484.

Alleman, B. W., Luger, T., Reisinger, H. S., Martin, R., Horowitz, M. D., & Cram, P. (2011). Medical tourism services available to residents of the United States. *Journal of General Internal Medicine, 26*, 492–497. https://doi.org/10.1007/s11606-010-1582-8.

Alsharif, M. J., Labonte, R., & Lu, Z. (2010). Patients beyond borders: A study of medical tourists in four countries. *Global Social Policy, 10*, 315–335. https://doi.org/10.1177/1468018110380003.

Arunanondchai, J., & Fink, C. (2007). *Trade in health services in the ASEAN region* (Policy Research Working Paper 4147). The World Bank.

Baldwin, R. (2012). *Global supply chains: Why they emerged, why they matter, and where they are going* (CTEI Working Papers 2012–13). Geneva.

Bergmark, R., Barr, D., & Garcia, R. (2010). Mexican immigrants in the US living far from the border may return to Mexico for health services. *Journal of Immigrant and Minority Health, 12*, 610–614. https://doi.org/10.1007/s10903-008-9213-8.

Berlin Partner für Wirtschaft und Technologie GmbH. (2015). *Potenzialstudie Medizintourismus Berlin-Brandenburg 2015*. Berlin.

Bin Saeed, K. S. (1998). Factors affecting patient's choice of hospitals. *Annals of Saudi Medicine, 18*, 420–424.

Bookman, M. Z., & Bookman, K. R. (2007). *Medical tourism in developing countries*. New York: Palgrave Macmillan.

Boschma, R. (2005). Proximity and innovation: A critical assessment. *Regional Studies, 39*, 61–74. https://doi.org/10.1080/0034340052000320887.

Carabello, L. (2008). A medical tourism primer for U.S. physicians. *The Journal of Medical Practice Management: MPM, 23*, 291–294.

Carrera, P., & Bridges, J. (2006). Globalization and healthcare: Understanding health and medical tourism. *Expert Review of Pharmacoeconomics & Outcomes Research, 6*, 447–454. https://doi.org/10.1586/14737167.6.4.447.

Carrera, P., & Lunt, N. (2010). A European perspective on medical tourism: The need for a knowledge base. *International Journal of Health Services, 40*, 469–484.

Casey, V., Crooks, V. A., Snyder, J., & Turner, L. (2013). Knowledge brokers, companions, and navigators: A qualitative examination of informal caregivers' roles in medical tourism. *International Journal for Equity in Health, 12*, 94. https://doi.org/10.1186/1475-9276-12-94.

Cattaneo, O. (2009). *Trade in health services: What's in it for developing countries?* (Policy Research Working Paper 5115). The World Bank.

Chandra, R. (2002). Trade in health services. *Bulletin of the World Health Organization, 80*, 158–163.

Cheung, I. K., & Wilson, A. (2007). Arthroplasty tourism. *The Medical Journal of Australia, 187*, 666–667.

Cohen, E. (2008). *Explorations in Thai tourism: Collected case studies. Tourism social science series* (Vol. 11, 1st ed.). Bingley: Emerald Group Publ.

Cohen, I. G. (2010). Protecting patients with passports: Medical tourism and the patient-protective argument. *Iowa Law Review, 95*, 1467–1567.

Cohen, I. G. (2011). Medical tourism, access to health care, and global justice. *Virginia Journal of International Law, 52*, 1–56.

Cohen, I. G. (2012). Circumvention tourism. *Cornell Law Review, 97*, 1309–1396.
Confederation of Indian Industry, McKinsey and Company. (2002). *Healthcare in India: The road ahead*. New Delhi: Confederation of Indian Industry McKinsey & Co.
Connell, J. (2006). Medical tourism: Sea, sun, sand and … surgery. *Tourism Management, 27*, 1093–1100. https://doi.org/10.1016/j.tourman.2005.11.005.
Connell, J. (2013). Contemporary medical tourism: Conceptualisation, culture and commodification. *Tourism Management, 34*, 1–13. https://doi.org/10.1016/j.tourman.2012.05.009.
Cooper, R. A., Getzen, T. E., McKee, H. J., & Laud, P. (2002). Economic and demographic trends signal an impending physician shortage. *Health Affairs, 21*, 140–154. https://doi.org/10.1377/hlthaff.21.1.140.
Cormany, D., & Baloglu, S. (2011). Medical travel facilitator websites: An exploratory study of web page contents and services offered to the prospective medical tourist. *Tourism Management, 32*, 709–716. https://doi.org/10.1016/j.tourman.2010.02.008.
Crone, R. K. (2008). Flat medicine? Exploring trends in the globalization of health care. *Academic Medicine, 83*, 117–121. https://doi.org/10.1097/ACM.0b013e318160965c.
Cross, M. J., March, L. M., Lapsley, H. M., Tribe, K. L., Brnabic, A. J. M., Courtenay, B. G., & Brooks, P. M. (2000). Determinants of willingness to pay for hip and knee joint replacement surgery for osteoarthritis. *Rheumatology, 39*, 1242–1248.
Crozier, G. K. D., & Baylis, F. (2010). The ethical physician encounters international medical travel. *Journal of Medical Ethics, 36*, 297–301. https://doi.org/10.1136/jme.2009.032789.
Culley, L., Hudson, N., Rapport, F., Blyth, E., Norton, W., & Pacey, A. A. (2011). Crossing borders for fertility treatment: Motivations, destinations and outcomes of UK fertility travellers. *Human Reproduction, 26*, 2373–2381.
de Arellano, R. (2007). Patients without borders: The emergence of medical tourism. *International Journal of Health Services, 37*, 193–198.
Drager, N., & Vieira, D. (Eds.). (2002). *Trade in health services: Global, regional, and country perspectives*. Washington, DC: Pan American Health Organization, Program on Public Policy and Health, Division of Health and Human Development; World Health Organization, Strategy Unit, Office of the Director-General.
Dumont, J.-C., & Zurn, P. (2010). *International migration of health workers. Policy brief*. Paris: OECD.
Ehrbeck, T., Guevara, C., & Mango, P. D. (2008). *Mapping the market for medical travel*. Seattle, WA: The McKinsey Quarterly.
Enright, M. J., & Newton, J. (2004). Tourism destination competitiveness: A quantitative approach. *Tourism Management, 25*, 777–788. https://doi.org/10.1016/j.tourman.2004.06.008.
Ernst & Young. (2006). *Healthcare*. India Brand Equity Foundation, Accessed April 9, 2013, from http://www.ibef.org/download/Healthcare_sectoral.pdf
Esiyok, B., Çakar, M., & Kurtulmuşoğlu, F. B. (2017). The effect of cultural distance on medical tourism. *Journal of Destination Marketing & Management, 6*, 66–75. https://doi.org/10.1016/j.jdmm.2016.03.001.
European Union. (2004). Directive 2004/38/EC of the European Parliament and of the Council of 29 April 2004 on the right of citizens of the Union and their family members to move and reside freely within the territory of the Member States.
European Union. (2011). Directive 2011/24/EU of the European Parliament and of the Council of 9 March 2011 on the application of patients' rights in cross-border healthcare.
Exworthy, M., & Peckham, S. (2006). Access, choice and travel: Implications for health policy. *Social Policy & Administration, 40*, 267–287.
Felbermayr, G. J., & Toubal, F. (2010). Cultural proximity and trade. *European Economic Review, 54*, 279–293. https://doi.org/10.1016/j.euroecorev.2009.06.009.
Firman, A., & Wang, Y.-Y. (2013). A strategic planning to develop medical travel industry in Indonesia. *World Journal of Social Sciences, 3*, 160–177.
Fisher, C., & Sood, K. (2014). What is driving the growth in medical tourism? *Health Marketing Quarterly, 31*, 246–262. https://doi.org/10.1080/07359683.2014.936293.

Frädrich, A. (2013). Patienten weltweit "auf Achse". *Deutsches Ärzteblatt, 110*, 1426–1428.

Freyer, W., & Kim, B.-S. (2014). Medizintourismus und Medizinreisen – eine inter-disziplinäre Betrachtung. *Gesundheitswesen, 76*, 65–68. https://doi.org/10.1055/s-0033-1343439.

Froelich, N. C. K. (2012). *Medical tourism – A study about motivational factors and the pre-requisites for creating a competitive offer – with a Swedish perspective* (Master's Thesis). Södertörn University.

Furuya, E. Y., Paez, A., Srinivasan, A., Cooksey, R., Augenbraun, M., Baron, M., Brudney, K., Della-Latta, P., Estivariz, C., Fischer, S., Flood, M., Kellner, P., Roman, C., Yakrus, M., Weiss, D., & Granowitz, E. V. (2008). Outbreak of Mycobacterium abscessus wound infections among "Lipotourists" from the United States who underwent Abdominoplasty in the Dominican Republic. *Clinical Infectious Diseases, 46*, 1181–1188. https://doi.org/10.1086/529191.

The Gallup Organization. (2007). Cross border health services in the EU: Analytical report. *Flash Eurobarometer, 210*, 1–42.

Gan, L. L., & Frederick, J. R. (2011). Medical tourism facilitators: Patterns of service differentiation. *Journal of Vacation Marketing, 17*, 165–183. https://doi.org/10.1177/1356766711409181.

García-Altés, A. (2005). The development of health tourism services. *Annals of Tourism Research, 32*, 262–265. https://doi.org/10.1016/j.annals.2004.05.005.

Gill, J., Madhira, B. R., Gjertson, D., Lipshutz, G., Cecka, M. J., Pham, P.-T., Wilkinsons, A., Bunnapradist, S., & Danovitch, G. M. (2008). Transplant tourism in the United States: A single-center experience. *Clinical Journal of the American Society of Nephrology, 3*, 1820–1828.

Glinos, I. A., & Baeten, R. (2006). *A literature review of cross-border patient mobility in the European Union*. Brussels: European Social Observatory.

Glinos, I. A., Baeten, R., & Maarse, H. (2010). Purchasing health services abroad: Practices of cross-border contracting and patient mobility in six European countries. *Health Policy, 95*, 103–112. https://doi.org/10.1016/j.healthpol.2009.11.016.

Goodarzi, M., Taghvaei, M., & Zangiabadi, A. (2014). Factor analysis of effective factors on the improvement of medical tourism in Shiraz Megalopolis. *Environmental Management and Sustainable Development, 3*, 138. https://doi.org/10.5296/emsd.v3i1.4876.

Goswami, A. G., Mattoo, A., & Sáez, S. (Eds.). (2012). *Exporting services: A developing country perspective*. Washington, DC: World Bank.

Goudge, J., & Gilson, L. (2005). How can trust be investigated? Drawing lessons from past experience. *Social Science & Medicine, 61*, 1439–1451. https://doi.org/10.1016/j.socscimed.2004.11.071.

Grossman, G. M., & Rossi-Hansberg, E. (2008). Trading tasks: A simple theory of offshoring. *American Economic Review, 98*, 1978–1997. https://doi.org/10.1257/aer.98.5.1978.

Guiso, L., Sapienza, P., & Zingales, L. (2009). Cultural biases in economic exchange? *Quarterly Journal of Economics, 124*, 1095–1131. https://doi.org/10.1162/qjec.2009.124.3.1095.

Hall, C. M. (2011). Health and medical tourism: A kill or cure for global public health? *Tourism Review, 66*, 4–15. https://doi.org/10.1108/16605371111127198.

Hall, C. M. (Ed.). (2013). *Medical tourism: The ethics, regulation, and marketing of health mobility. Routledge studies in contemporary geographies of leisure, tourism and mobility* (Vol. 33). London: Routledge.

Hall, R. E., & Jones, C. I. (2004). *The value of life and the rise in health spending* (NBER Working Paper Series 10737). National Bureau of Economic Research.

Hanefeld, J., Horsfall, D., Lunt, N., & Smith, R. (2013). Medical tourism: A cost or benefit to the NHS? *PLoS One, 8*, 1–8. https://doi.org/10.1371/journal.pone.0070406.

Hanefeld, J., Lunt, N., Smith, R., & Horsfall, D. (2015). Why do medical tourists travel to where they do? The role of networks in determining medical travel. *Social Science & Medicine, 124*, 356–363. https://doi.org/10.1016/j.socscimed.2014.05.016.

Hanna, S. A., Saksena, J., Legge, S., & Ware, H. E. (2009). Sending NHS patients for operations abroad: Is the holiday over? *The Annals of The Royal College of Surgeons of England, 91*, 128–130. https://doi.org/10.1308/003588409X359411.

Hazarika, I. (2010). Medical tourism: Its potential impact on the health workforce and health systems in India. *Health Policy and Planning, 25*, 248–251. https://doi.org/10.1093/heapol/czp050.

Herrick, D. M. (2007). *Medical tourism: Global competition in health care* (NCPA Policy Report 304). Dallas: National Center for Policy Analysis.

Heung, V. C. S., Kucukusta, D., & Song, H. (2011). Medical tourism development in Hong Kong: An assessment of the barriers. *Tourism Management, 32*, 995–1005. https://doi.org/10.1016/j.tourman.2010.08.012.

Hope. (2015). *Medical tourism*. Brussels: HOPE Publications, European Hospital and Healthcare Federation.

Hopkins, L., Labonté, R., Runnels, V., & Packer, C. (2010). Medical tourism today: What is the state of existing knowledge? *Journal of Public Health Policy, 31*, 185–198.

Horowitz, M. D., Rosensweig, J. A., & Jones, C. A. (2007). Medical tourism: Globalization of the healthcare marketplace. *Medscape General Medicine, 9*, 33.

Horton, S., & Cole, S. (2011). Medical returns: Seeking health care in Mexico. *Social Science & Medicine, 72*, 1846–1852. https://doi.org/10.1016/j.socscimed.2011.03.035.

Huat, J. Y. C. (2006). Medical tourism/medical travel (part one). *SMA News, 38*, 17–21.

Hudson, S. (2011). *Domestic medical tourism: A neglected dimension of medical tourism research*. Accessed April 29, 2014, from http://www.medicaltourismmag.com/domestic-medical-tourism-a-neglected-dimension-of-medical-tourism-research/

Inhorn, M. C., & Shrivastav, P. (2010). Globalization and reproductive tourism in the United Arab Emirates. *Asia-Pacific Journal of Public Health, 22*, 68. https://doi.org/10.1177/1010539510373007.

International Medical Travel Journal. (2012). *The challenges of healthcare investment and provision in the Middle East*. Accessed September 25, 2018, from http://www.imtjonline.com/articles/2012/healthcare-investment-and-provision-in-middle-east-30121/

International Medical Travel Journal. (2015). *Why is every Turkish figure on medical tourism different*? Accessed July 21, 2016, from https://www.imtj.com/news/why-every-turkish-figure-medical-tourism-different/

International Medical Travel Journal. (2016). *Medical tourism from Russia survey*. Accessed July 20, 2016, from https://www.imtj.com/news/medical-tourism-russia-survey/

IPK International. (2012). *ITB world travel trends report 2012/2013*. Berlin: Messe Berlin GmbH.

Japanese Cabinet. (2010). *The new growth strategy: Blueprint for revitalizing Japan*. Tokyo: Japanese Ministry of Economy, Trade and Industry.

Johnson, O. (2002). *Bogotá launches health tourism project*. Accessed April 29, 2014, from http://www.bmj.com/content/325/7354/10.6

Johnson, T. J., & Garman, A. N. (2010). Impact of medical travel on imports and exports of medical services. *Health Policy, 98*, 171–177. https://doi.org/10.1016/j.healthpol.2010.06.006.

Johnson, T. J., & Garman, A. N. (2015). Demand for international medical travel to the USA. *Tourism Economics, 21*, 1061–1077. https://doi.org/10.5367/te.2014.0393.

Johnson, T. J., Youngquist, J. S., Garman, A. N., Hohmann, S., & Cieslak, P. R. (2015). Factors influencing medical travel into the United States. *International Journal of Pharmaceutical and Healthcare Marketing, 9*, 118–135. https://doi.org/10.1108/IJPHM-02-2013-0004.

Johnston, R., Crooks, V. A., Snyder, J., & Kingsbury, P. (2010). What is known about the effects of medical tourism in destination and departure countries? A scoping review. *International Journal for Equity in Health, 9*, 24. https://doi.org/10.1186/1475-9276-9-24.

Johnston, R., Crooks, V. A., & Snyder, J. (2012). "I didn't even know what I was looking for": A qualitative study of the decision-making processes of Canadian medical tourists. *Global Health, 8*, 23. https://doi.org/10.1186/1744-8603-8-23.

Jotikasthira, N. (2010). *Salient factors influencing medical tourism destination choice* (Dissertation). Southern Cross University.

Limb, J.-u. (2014). *Medical tourism figures on the rise*. Accessed June 20, 2016, from http://www.korea.net/NewsFocus/Policies/view?articleId=119579

Juszczak, J. (2008). Dienstleistungen für internationale Patienten: Tagungsband zur Konferenz Medizintourismus; Sankt Augustin 28. September 2007. Schriftenreihe des Fachbereiches Wirtschaft Sankt Augustin, Vol. 21. Sankt Augustin: Fachhochsch. Bonn-Rhein-Sieg.

Kangas, B. (2007). Hope from abroad in the international medical travel of Yemeni patients. *Anthropology & Medicine, 14*, 293–305. https://doi.org/10.1080/13648470701612646.

Keckley, P. H., & Eselius, L. L. (2009). *2009 survey of health care consumers: Key findings, strategic implications*. Washington, DC: Deloitte Center for Health Solutions.

Keckley, P. H., & Underwood, H. R. (2008). *Medical tourism: Consumers in search of value*. Washington, DC: Deloitte Center for Health Solutions.

Kher, U. (2006). *Outsourcing your heart. Time*. 44–47.

Khoo, L. (2003). *Trends in foreign patient admission in Singapore*. Singapore: MOH Information Paper, Ministry of Health.

Landgericht Kiel. (2011) *Sittenwidrigkeit der Provisionsvereinbarung für die Vermittlung von Patienten an eine Klinik*. Accessed September 25, 2018, from http://openjur.de/u/442482.html

Klijs, J., Ormond, M., Mainil, T., Peerlings, J., & Heijman, W. (2016). A state-level analysis of the economic impacts of medical tourism in Malaysia. *Asian-Pacific Economic Literature, 30*, 3–29. https://doi.org/10.1111/apel.12132.

Klingenberger, D. (2009). *Dentaltourismus und Auslandszahnersatz: Empirische Zahlungsbereitschaftsanalysen auf der Grundlage repräsentativer Stichproben im Jahre 2008, Materialienreihe/Institut der Deutschen Zahnärzte* (Vol. 32). Köln: Dt. Zahnärzte-Verlag.

Klusen, N., Verheyen, F., & Wagner, C. (Eds.). (2011). *England and Germany in Europe: What lessons can we learn from each other?: European Health Care Conference 2011, Beiträge zum Gesundheitsmanagement* (Vol. 32, 1st ed.). Baden-Baden: Nomos-Verl.-Ges.

Korea Global Healthcare Association (English). Accessed September 25, 2018, from www.medicalkorea.asia/

Lautier, M. (2008). Export of health services from developing countries: The case of Tunisia. *Social Science & Medicine, 67*, 101–110. https://doi.org/10.1016/j.socscimed.2008.01.057.

Lee, J. Y., Kearns, R. A., & Friesen, W. (2010). Seeking affective health care: Korean immigrants' use of homeland medical services. *Health Place, 16*, 108–115. https://doi.org/10.1016/j.healthplace.2009.09.003.

Lee, M., Han, H., & Lockyer, T. (2012). Medical tourism: Attracting Japanese tourists for medical tourism experience. *Journal of Travel and Tourism Marketing, 29*, 69–86.

Leng, C. H. (2006). *The emergence of a transnational healthcare service industry in Malaysia* (Working Paper Series 76). Asia Research Institute.

Levy, F., & Kyoung-Hee, Y. (2006). *Offshoring radiology services to India* (MIT IPC Working Paper 06–005). MIT Industrial Performance Center.

León, F. (2002). The case of the Chilean health system, 1983–2000. In N. Drager & D. Vieira (Eds.), *Trade in health services: Global, regional, and country perspectives* (pp. 155–183). Washington, DC: Pan American Health Organization, Program on Public Policy and Health, Division of Health and Human Development; World Health Organization, Strategy Unit, Office of the Director-General.

Liu, I.-C., & Chen, C.-c. (2013). Cultural issues in medical tourism. *American Journal of Tourism Research, 2*, 78–83. https://doi.org/10.11634/216837861302318.

Loh, C.-P. A. (2014). Health tourism on the rise? Evidence from the balance of payments statistics. *The European Journal of Health Economics, 15*, 759–766. https://doi.org/10.1007/s10198-013-0521-0.

Loh, C.-P. A. (2015). Trends and structural shifts in health tourism: Evidence from seasonal time-series data on health-related travel spending by Canada during 1970–2010. *Social Science & Medicine, 132*, 173–180. https://doi.org/10.1016/j.socscimed.2015.03.036.

Lukas, D. (2009). *Efficiency effects of cross-border medical demand* (Dresden Discussion Paper Series in Economics 15/09). Technische Universität Dresden.

Lunt, N., & Carrera, P. (2010). Medical tourism: Assessing the evidence on treatment abroad. *Maturitas, 66*, 27–32. https://doi.org/10.1016/j.maturitas.2010.01.017.

Lunt, N., Hardey, M., & Mannion, R. (2010). Nip, tuck and click: Medical tourism and the emergence of web-based health information. *The Open Medical Informatics Journal, 4*, 1–10.

Lunt, N., Smith, R., Exworthy, M., Green, S. T., Horsfall, D., & Mannion, R. (2011). *Medical tourism: Treatments, markets and health system implications: A scoping review*. Paris: OECD.

Lunt, N., Mannion, R., & Exworthy, M. (2013). A framework for exploring the policy implications of UK medical tourism and international patient flows. *Social Policy & Administration, 47*, 1–25. https://doi.org/10.1111/j.1467-9515.2011.00833.x.

Lunt, N., Horsfall, D., Smith, R., Exworthy, M., Hanefeld, J., & Mannion, R. (2014a). Market size, market share and market strategy: Three myths of medical tourism. *Policy & Politics, 42*, 597–614. https://doi.org/10.1332/030557312X655918.

Lunt, N., Jin, K. N., Horsfall, D., & Hanefeld, J. (2014b). Insights on medical tourism: Markets as networks and the role of strong ties. *Korean Social Science Journal, 41*, 19–37. https://doi.org/10.1007/s40483-014-0012-7.

Lunt, N., Horsfall, D., & Hanefeld, J. (2016). Medical tourism: A snapshot of evidence on treatment abroad. *Maturitas, 88*, 37–44.

Lutze, I., Karmann, A., & Schoffer, O. (2010). Empirische Bestandsaufnahme zum Patientenimport im stationären Sektor. *Statistik in Sachsen*, 30–36.

MacReady, N. (2007). Developing countries court medical tourists. *The Lancet, 369*, 1849–1850. https://doi.org/10.1016/S0140-6736(07)60833-2.

Mai, R. (2011). Der Herkunftslandeffekt: Eine kritische Würdigung des State of the Art. *Journal für Betriebswirtschaft, 61*, 91–121. https://doi.org/10.1007/s11301-011-0075-0.

Manaf, N. H. A., Hussin, H., Kassim, P. N. J., Alavi, R., & Dahari, Z. (2015). Medical tourism service quality: Finally some empirical findings. *Total Quality Management & Business Excellence, 26*, 1017–1028. https://doi.org/10.1080/14783363.2015.1068597.

Martin, D. S., Ramamonjiarivelo, Z., & Martin, W. S. (2011). MEDTOUR: A scale for measuring medical tourism intentions. *Tourism Review, 66*, 45–56.

Mattoo, A., & Rathindran, R. (2006). How health insurance inhibits trade in health care. *Health Affairs, 25*, 358–368. https://doi.org/10.1377/hlthaff.25.2.358.

Maung, N. L. Y. (2014). Decision factors in medical tourism: Evidence from Burmese visitors to a hospital in Bangkok. *Journal of Economics and Behavioral Studies, 6*, 84–94.

McGuckin, M. (2006). Consumer attitudes about health care-acquired infections and hand hygiene. *American Journal of Medical Quality, 21*, 342–346. https://doi.org/10.1177/1062860606291328.

Mechinda, P., Serirat, S., Anuwichanont, J., & Gulid, N. (2010). An examination of tourists' loyalty towards medical tourism in Pattaya, Thailand. *International Business & Economics Research Journal, 9*, 55–70.

MedRetreat Treatment Types. Accessed May 21, 2017, from http://www.medretreat.com/procedures/treatment_types.html

Melitz, J., & Toubal, F. (2014). Native language, spoken language, translation and trade. *Journal of International Economics, 93*, 351–363.

Milstein, A., & Smith, M. (2006). America's new refugees – Seeking affordable surgery offshore. *The New England Journal of Medicine, 355*, 1637–1640.

Milstein, A., & Smith, M. (2007). Will the surgical world become flat? *Health Affairs, 26*, 137–141. https://doi.org/10.1377/hlthaff.26.1.137.

Mishra, S., Lundstrom, S., & Anand, R. (2011). *Service export sophistication and economic growth* (Policy Research Working Paper 5606). The World Bank.

Miyagi, K., Auberson, D., Patel, A. J., & Malata, C. M. (2012). The unwritten price of cosmetic tourism: An observational study and cost analysis. *Journal of Plastic, Reconstructive & Aesthetic Surgery, 65*, 22–28. https://doi.org/10.1016/j.bjps.2011.07.027.

Moghimehfar, F., & Nasr-Esfahani, M. H. (2011). Decisive factors in medical tourism destination choice: A case study of Isfahan, Iran and fertility treatments. *Tourism Management, 32*, 1431–1434. https://doi.org/10.1016/j.tourman.2011.01.005.

Mohamad, W. N., Omar, A., & Haron, M. S. (2012). The moderating effect of medical travel facilitators in medical tourism. *Procedia – Social and Behavioral Sciences, 65*, 358–363. https://doi.org/10.1016/j.sbspro.2012.11.134.

Möhlmann, J. L., Ederveen, S., de Groot, H. L. F., & Linders, G.-J. M. (2010). Intangible barriers to international trade: A sectoral approach. In P. A. G. Van Bergeijk & S. Brakman (Eds.), *The gravity model in international trade: Advances and applications* (pp. 224–251). Cambridge: Cambridge Univ. Press.

Monaco Cardio-Thoracic Center. (2016). *CCM prices*. http://www.monaco-cardio.com/pdf/CCM_prices.pdf

Mullan, F. (2006). Doctors for the world: Indian physician emigration. *Health Affairs, 25*, 380–393. https://doi.org/10.1377/hlthaff.25.2.380.

Müller, M. (2006). *Der Gesundheitssektor der Grenzregion Ostbrandenburg-Lubuskie. Strukturen und Optionen in der grenzüberschreitenden Gesundheitsversorgung* (Dissertation). Europa-Universität Viadrina Frankfurt (Oder).

Münch, E. (2014). *Russen fliegen auf Dresden*. SZ Online.

Musa, G., Doshi, D., Wong, K. M., & Thirumoorthy, T. (2012a). How satisfied are inbound medical tourists in Malaysia?: A study on private hospitals in Kuala Lumpur. *Journal of Travel & Tourism Marketing, 29*, 629–646. https://doi.org/10.1080/10548408.2012.720150.

Musa, G., Thirumoorthi, T., & Doshi, D. (2012b). Travel behaviour among inbound medical tourists in Kuala Lumpur. *Current Issues in Tourism, 15*, 525–543. https://doi.org/10.1080/13683500.2011.626847.

Nagel, L.-M., Neller. M. (2013a). Der lybische Patient. *Die Welt*.

Nagel, L.-M., & Neller, M. (2013b). Krumme Geschäfte mit Kranken aus Libyen. *Die Welt*.

Nagel, L.-M., & Neller, M. (2014). Die kranken Seiten des Systems. *Die Welt*.

NaRanong, A., & NaRanong, V. (2011). The effects of medical tourism: Thailand's experience. *Bulletin of the World Health Organization, 89*, 336–344. https://doi.org/10.2471/BLT.09.072249.

Neelakantan, S. (2003). *India's global ambitions*. Accessed June 12, 2014, from www.globalpolicy.org/component/content/article/162-general/28079.html

Newman, M. I., Camberos, A. E., & Ascherman, J. (2005). Mycobacteria abscessus outbreak in US patients linked to offshore surgicenter. *Annals of Plastic Surgery, 55*, 107–110.

Noree, T., Hanefeld, J., & Smith, R. (2014). UK medical tourists in Thailand: They are not who you think they are. *Global Health, 10*, 29. https://doi.org/10.1186/1744-8603-10-29.

Noree, T., Hanefeld, J., & Smith, R. (2016). Medical tourism in Thailand: A cross-sectional study. *Bulletin of the World Health Organization, 94*, 30–36. https://doi.org/10.2471/BLT.14.152165.

Oberhauser-Aslan, H. (2013, January 27). Reiche Russen kommen zunehmend gern in deutsche Kliniken. *Wall Street Journal*.

Paffhausen, A. L., Peguero, C., & Roche-Villareal, L. (2010). *Medical tourism: A survey*. Washington, DC: LC/WAS/L.111, Economic Commission for Latin America and the Caribbean.

Polish Association of Medical Tourism. (2012). *Prices of treatments*. Accessed July 26, 2016, from http://www.pamt.org/patient-pricing.php

Pollard, K. (2012). *The medical tourism survey 2012*. London: Intuition Communication Ltd.

Pollard, K. (2013). *Medical tourism climate survey 2013*. London: Intuition Communication Ltd.

Pollard, K. (2017). *Measuring the ROI from medical tourism promotion*. Accessed December 1, 2017, from https://www.imtj.com/blog/measuring-roi-medical-tourism-promotion/

Rajagopal, S. (2011, July 26–30). *Factors influencing patients' willingness to participate in medical tourism*. The 2nd International Research Symposium in Service Management Yogyakarta, Indonesia. National University of Singapore.

Ramírez de Arellano, A. B. (2011). Medical tourism in the Caribbean. *Signs, 36*, 289–297. https://doi.org/10.1086/655908.

Rauch, J. E. (1999). Networks versus markets in international trade. *Journal of International Economics, 48*, 7–35.

RDC. (2007–2012). *Hospital statistics*. RDC of the Federal Statistial Office of the Länder, Survey years 2007–2012.
Richter, B., & Richter, K. (2012). Export und Import von Krankenhausdienstleistungen in Sachsen 1995–2009. *Statistik in Sachsen*, 27–34.
Rosenmöller, M., McKee, M., & Baeten, R. (2006). *Patient mobility in the European union: Learning from experience*. Copenhagen: World Health Organization, Regional Office for Europe.
Sengupta, A. (2011). Medical tourism: Reverse subsidy for the Elite. *Signs: Journal of Women in Culture and Society, 36*, 312–319. https://doi.org/10.1086/655910.
Sheppard, C. E., Lester, E. L. W., Chuck, A. W., Kim, D. H., Karmali, S., de Gara, C. J., & Birch, D. W. (2014). Medical tourism and bariatric surgery: Who pays? *Surgical Endoscopy, 28*, 3329–3336. https://doi.org/10.1007/s00464-014-3613-8.
Siddiqi, S., Shennawy, A., Mirza, Z., Drager, N., & Sabri, B. (2010). Assessing trade in health services in countries of the Eastern Mediterranean from a public health perspective. *The International Journal of Health Planning and Management, 25*, 231–250. https://doi.org/10.1002/hpm.989.
Smith, R. D., Chanda, R., & Tangcharoensathien, V. (2009). Trade in health-related services. *The Lancet, 373*, 593–601.
Smith, R., Álvarez, M. M., & Chanda, R. (2011a). Medical tourism: A review of the literature and analysis of a role for bi-lateral trade. *Health Policy, 103*, 276–282.
Smith, R., Martínez Álvarez, M., & Chanda, R. (2011b). Medical tourism: A review of the literature and analysis of a role for bi-lateral trade. *Health Policy, 103*, 276–282. https://doi.org/10.1016/j.healthpol.2011.06.009.
Snyder, J., Crooks, V. A., & Johnston, R. (2012). Perceptions of the ethics of medical tourism: Comparing patient and academic perspectives. *Public Health Ethics, 5*, 38–46. https://doi.org/10.1093/phe/phr034.
Terry, N. P. (2007). Under-regulated health care phenomena in a flat world: Medical tourism and outsourcing? *Western New England Law Review, 29*, 421–472.
Turner, L. (2007). 'First World Health Care at Third World Prices': Globalization, bioethics and medical tourism. *BioSocieties, 2*, 303–325. https://doi.org/10.1017/S1745855207005765.
Visit Medical Korea. (2016). *Medical tourism records*. Accessed July 26, 2016, from http://english.visitmedicalkorea.com/eng/medicalTreatments/medicalTreatments01/medicalTreatments01_1.jsp
Wachter, R. M. (2006). The "Dis-location" of U.S. medicine – The implications of medical outsourcing. *The New England Journal of Medicine, 354*, 661–665.
Wagner, C., & Verheyen, F. (2010). *TK-Europabefragung 2009: Deutsche Patienten auf dem Weg nach Europa*. Hamburg: Techniker Krankenkasse.
Wagner, C., Dobrick, K., & Verheyen, F. (2011). *Europabefragung 2010*. Hamburg: WINEG Wissen, Techniker Krankenkasse.
Weiber, R., & Adler, J. (1995a). Informationsökonomisch begründete Typologisierung von Kaufprozessen. *Schmalenbachs Zeitschrift für betriebswirtschaftliche Forschung: Zfbf, 47*, 43–65.
Weiber, R., & Adler, J. (1995b). Positionierung von Kaufprozessen im informationsökonomischen Dreieck: Operationalisierung und verhaltenswissenschaftliche Prüfung. *Schmalenbachs Zeitschrift für betriebswirtschaftliche Forschung: Zfbf, 47*, 99–123.
White, W. D., & Morrisey, M. A. (1998). Are patients traveling further? *International Journal of the Economics of Business, 5*, 203–221. https://doi.org/10.1080/13571519884512.
Whittaker, A. (2010). Challenges of medical travel to global regulation: A case study of reproductive travel in Asia. *Global Social Policy, 10*, 396–415. https://doi.org/10.1177/1468018110379981.
Whittaker, A. (2015). 'Outsourced' patients and their companions: Stories from forced medical travellers. *Global Public Health, 10*, 485–500. https://doi.org/10.1080/17441692.2014.998696.
Wibulpolprasert, S., Pachanee, C.-a., Pitayarangsarit, S., & Hempisut, P. (2004). International service trade and its implications for human resources for health: A case study of Thailand. *Human Resources for Health, 2*, 10. https://doi.org/10.1186/1478-4491-2-10.

Wongkit, M., & McKercher, B. (2013). Toward a typology of medical tourists: A case study of Thailand. *Tourism Management, 38*, 4–12. https://doi.org/10.1016/j.tourman.2013.02.003.

The World Bank. (1996). *Prospects for service exports from the English-speaking Carribbean* (Report 15301-CRG). Washington, DC: The World Bank.

Ye, B. H., Qiu, H. Z., & Yuen, P. P. (2011). Motivations and experiences of Mainland Chinese medical tourists in Hong Kong. *Tourism Management, 32*, 1125–1127. https://doi.org/10.1016/j.tourman.2010.09.018.

Yeoh, E., Othman, K., & Ahmad, H. (2013). Understanding medical tourists: Word-of-mouth and viral marketing as potent marketing tools. *Tourism Management, 34*, 196–201. https://doi.org/10.1016/j.tourman.2012.04.010.

Ying, G. (2015). Desperation, money drive patients abroad. *China Daily*:16.

Youngman, I. (2009). *Medical tourism statistics: Why McKinsey has got it wrong*. Accessed April 9, 2013, from http://www.imtjonline.com/articles/2009/mckinsey-wrong-medical-travel/

Youngman, I. (2012). *Beyond accreditation in medical travel*. Accessed June 17, 2014, from http://www.imtjonline.com/articles/2012/medical-travel-accreditation-30144/

Youngman, I. (2014). *Medical tourism facts and figures 2014*. London: International Medical Travel Journal.

Yu, J. Y., & Ko, T. G. (2012). A cross-cultural study of perceptions of medical tourism among Chinese, Japanese and Korean tourists in Korea. *Tourism Management, 33*, 80–88. https://doi.org/10.1016/j.tourman.2011.02.002.

Chapter 3
The Sum of its Parts: A Structured Approach to the Modeling of Destination Choice

Our survey of the medical tourism and trade literature has revealed multidirectional medical tourism flows to differentiated destinations and a large set of candidate drivers that determines destination choice including destination characteristics, individual characteristics and information sources. Product differentiation with respect to the drivers of medical tourism is a recurrent theme of the medical tourism literature but it is discussed at various levels of supply and consumption. This chapter will disentangle the product, consumer and supplier dimensions of medical tourism and put the many isolated pieces of medical tourism research into a coherent framework that fully captures this field's complexity. A main research question in medical tourism is ultimately one of disaggregation i.e. what differentiated products and competing destinations in medical tourism actually are.

3.1 Product Disaggregation

The previous chapter has provided a useful delineation of medical tourism in various dimensions and has already cast doubt on the combination of different treatments in one construct. The drivers outlined above are usually reported in different contexts, which makes it difficult to attribute them to treatments, destinations, source country conditions or individuals. As an example consider Wagner and Verheyen (2010) who highlight geographic and cultural proximity between East-Germany and Eastern Europe as drivers for traveling and who identify low-income elderly as the main users of the services offered. Juxtaposing this result with, for example, Ehrbeck et al. (2008), who names quality and technology as dominating drivers, and with Crone (2008), who discusses prices as a driver for outflows from a high-quality source country, invites the question whether these different results may be due to the consideration of different income and age groups; due to a negligible effect of geographic and cultural proximity overall; or merely due to the consideration of different treatments types.

K. Schmerler, *Medical Tourism in Germany*, Developments in Health Economics and Public Policy 13, https://doi.org/10.1007/978-3-030-03988-2_3

A plausible aggregation of treatments remains an open question. Disregarding wellness tourism, a common classification of medical treatments is the grouping of dental, general and cosmetic surgery. Such a classification is useful from a data collection point of view as dental treatments are not provided by hospitals, which are a main source of data, and cosmetic treatments are a focus of private clinics and thus not recorded in official hospital statistics either. Dental treatments therefore tend to be disregarded or singled out in analyses (Klingenberger 2009) and cosmetic surgery is only included partially. Even then the question remains how similar the decision-making processes between and within categories such as cosmetic and general surgery are. Is the decision about a varicose vein surgery governed by the same drivers and parameters as the decision about a heart bypass surgery abroad? And if so, is the decision about an outpatient or inpatient treatment governed by these parameters as well even if they imply completely different price ranges (Noree et al. 2014) and are associated with very different degrees of risk? Yu and Ko (2012) suggest that price elasticities differ between treatments for minor and serious conditions and Wagner et al. (2011) find an interesting difference in self-reported drivers between patients who spend 2–3 weeks and patients who spend only 1 week or less abroad. Whereas the former group received mostly treatments at health resorts and indicated cost savings and the combination with tourism as their main drivers, the latter group obtained dental, orthodontic, specialist and inpatient treatments and named quality, comfort, doctor of their choice and proximity to a border as relevant drivers.

Recent work has provided more insight into the role of treatment aggregation and finds that the effects of destination characteristics, individual characteristics and information sources are likely to differ by treatment. The impact of geographic distance, price, and cultural ties has been found to decrease and the importance of quality to increase as the severity of a medical condition increases (Esiyok et al. 2017; Hanefeld et al. 2015; Zhang et al. 2013). However, Hanefeld et al. (2015) note that personal networks and persons with previous experience are increasingly relied upon as the quality of a treatment becomes more important. For an appropriate aggregation of treatments to homogeneous groups, more research into the criteria of homogeneity, which operationalize, e.g. severity via ability to travel, recovery time or required follow-up care, is needed.

Tourism is another confounding factor whose role is suspected to be treatment-dependent (Hanefeld et al. 2015). Tourism can be planned, with e.g. post-care recovery or sightseeing of accompanying caregivers, or can be incidental. The former is difficult to capture empirically if unobserved recreational features of a destination enter consumer choice and the latter is essentially a two-stage process for which there is no reason to assume that it resembles that of a destination choice with a treatment as the main purpose. Wongkit and McKercher (2013) find that inpatients typically travel in a planned fashion whereas outpatient treatments may be either planned or incidental during the consumption of recreational travel. This suggests a very different weighting of destination characteristics in revealed destination choices based on the original purpose of a trip. The purpose is a mixture of recreational or medical intentions, which depends on the treatment type. Inpatient and outpatient

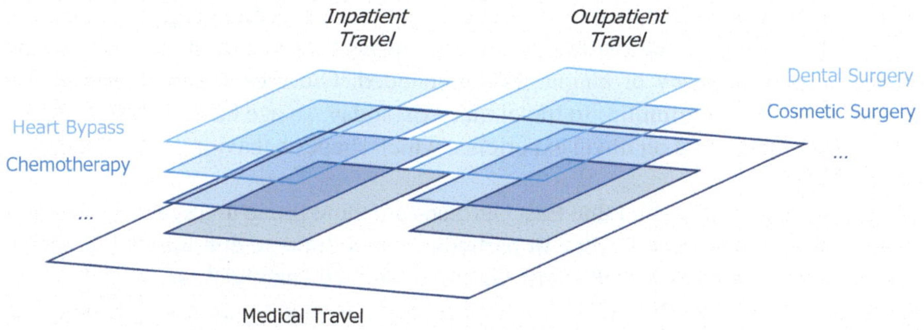

Fig. 3.1 Treatment disaggregation for medical travel

treatments lend themselves to being indicators of the amount of recreational travel involved: Inpatient treatments may be incidental after accidents, for example, but they are unlikely to be demanded in an opportunistic fashion. Figure 3.1 visualizes treatment aggregation for different layers of treatment types within outpatient and inpatient travel embedded in the purpose of travel mix of Fig. 2.1.

Some authors altogether reject the notion of jointly considering recreational travel and medical treatments given the potentially desperate need for a treatment (Kangas 2010; Whittaker 2008) but empirical studies such as Wongkit and McKercher (2013) demonstrated that they may often be combined to some degree. Joint consideration of both types of travel imposes demanding requirements on a suitable data set, which is why the separate consideration of inpatient and outpatient travel is very compelling. If the degree of complementarity between inpatient and recreational travel is very low, then the role of recreational features may be neglected in an empirical investigation of inpatient destination choice.

3.2 Consumer Disaggregation

Total medical tourism flows between countries can be broken down into consumer segments. There may be different reactions to identical stimuli across consumers or segments (Anderson et al. 1992) whose heterogeneity is determined by individual-specific characteristics and the identification of such characteristics has been a major focus of the medical tourism literature. Socio-demographics are typically reported with medical tourism surveys to describe the samples taken. Other individual-specific characteristics such as locus of control, social norms, privacy and previous experience with medical tourism are less commonly reported.

Age appears to be a key factor in the demand of medical treatment abroad. Lee et al. (2012) find age to matter for medical tourism intentions and (Wagner et al. 2011; Wagner and Verheyen 2010) report 79% and 78% of all surveyed insurants with planned treatments outside of Germany to be 60 or older. We cannot assess the representativeness of the sample but the reported shares are disproportionately high in light of only about 24% of all insurants being 60 or older and suggest a positive impact of age on medical tourism. Age is also suspected to have an influence on the number and proficiency of languages commanded. Older generations presumably did not have the opportunities to travel that exist today, so age has a negative impact on the command—and on travel experience which shapes behavioral intentions (Lee et al. 2012).

Wagner et al. (2011) find that East Germans are more prone to travel for treatment in general and to Eastern Europe in particular which hints to cultural and language ties as older generations in Eastern Germany studied mainly Russian and Slavic languages. Consequently, older people in Eastern Germany may just command the right languages to communicate at existing destinations and the overall influence of age on language in the context of destination choice is ambiguous. Age further influences available time to travel so persons of 60 or older may place greater emphasis on recreational features. Indeed, the majority of the persons surveyed named the possibility to combine a treatment with their vacation as a main criterion for their destination choice. At the same time, a higher age implies a poorer health status which potentially renders touristic features less important—even if this was not the case for the sample in (Wagner and Verheyen 2010).

Finally, age affects income. Initially, income increases with increasing duration on the job but retired persons typically have lower incomes than the working population so an excess of time may be offset by a shortage of funds. In Wagner and Verheyen (2010), 76% of the persons with planned treatments reported a monthly gross income of less than 2500€ and 48% a monthly gross income of less than 1500€. Apparently, outbound medical tourists in Germany are predominantly from a lower income bracket, which fits nicely with the narrative of elderly citizens from Eastern Germany, but univariate statistics confound all characteristics. In fact, the previously discussed and overarching theme of treatment types further complicates the analysis: The persons observed mostly received wellness and spa treatments, which limits the insight gained to exactly this treatment type. Is it low income, age, cultural ties, treatment type or all of the above that lead to Czech Republic as a destination choice? And can the result be extrapolated to baby boomers in the U.S. that also dominate the spa market (Bookman and Bookman 2007)?

Extrapolation of medical tourism drivers beyond the observed segments is likely to be wrong. As an example and a juxtaposition to the results in Wagner and Verheyen (2010), The Gallup Organization 2007 assigns a negative effect to age on medical tourism. A survey of medical tourists from the UK Noree et al. (2014) report 80.42% to be between 25 and 64 years of age. Musa et al. (2012) find 79.7% of the interviewed medical tourists to Malaysia 79.7% to be between 21 and 60 years of age and in Wongkit and McKercher (2013) 93.8% of the visitors to Thailand are younger than 60 years. Wongkit and McKercher (2013) also find quite different income brackets for visitors to Thailand with only 18.3% having a monthly household income of less than $2500 and 41.2% having $5000 or more available.

Gender is also typically reported and may impact a person's ability to travel individually (Al-Hinai et al. 2011). Clarke and Griffin (2007, 2008) suggest that gender further plays an important role for the demand of specific treatments that constitute a large share of the medical tourism portfolio. Such treatments include cosmetic treatments as well as fertility treatments. Gender may thus impact destination choice in two ways: First, it clusters women within certain treatments (Noree et al. 2014) whose nature may determine the valuation of destination characteristics such as privacy (Alsharif et al. 2010) and second, gender may influence other individual-specific characteristics such as income and locus of control.

As will be discussed in the next chapter, aggregate trade flow modeling typically assumes a representative CES consumer (Anderson et al. 1992) that does not differ across countries. This assumption turns out to be quite problematic if population characteristics vary across countries and if choice probabilities of destinations depend on individual characteristics as in Boga and Weiermair (2011), for example, who attempt to align branding with personal values of customers—in addition to pricing and other signals. Also note that consumer characteristics do not only determine destination choice but, in general, also total demand for health care in the first place. This has been acknowledged by Grossman (1972) who characterized individuals as producers of health who use health care as an input. If choice of inputs and thus the demand for health care depends on consumer characteristics, then both demand at the first stage and destination choice at the second stage are endogenous.

3.3 Supplier Disaggregation

The previous presentation of medical tourism flows between countries has made the implicit assumption that countries are the appropriate level of aggregation for both supply and for demand of medical treatments. On the other hand, Hwang and Christensen (2008) make a distinction between solution shops and value-adding process businesses with a focus on different consumers and thus imply competition at the provider level based on the underlying complexity of treatments and the associated possibility to compete over the price for such treatments. The appropriate level of competition is in fact unclear and raises the question of what actually lies at the core of a destination. A crucial research question is thus the identification of the relevant levels of supply unit that determine destination choice.

At the lowest tier, doctors deliver medical services that are in demand by patients or consumers. Interviews with hospitals in Germany and international patients in Chap. 6 suggest that several medical tourists visit providers to receive treatments from select specialists but their share is unknown. Such physician focus is plausible for clinics and hospitals that provide facilities to German physicians who practice out-of-residence and has been reported for the domestic physician choice in the U.S. (Tu and Lauer 2008). Bookman and Bookman (2007) describe a general benefit in more patient-doctor interaction at medical tourism destinations. From a physician-centered perspective, the accompanying provider structure and location is of secondary importance but is still very likely to influence destination choice. Doctors cluster within providers, which essentially add amenities, support staff, administrative procedures and a reputation of their own to the treatment. A treatment delivered by a physician is thus enhanced by a provider and the package is often marketed by providers who may be perceived as destinations even if a specialist lies at the heart of the service. At an intermediate level, providers may cooperate in national networks or regions such as the HealthRegion CologneBonn or visitBerlin in Germany and in international networks such as Apollo Hospitals, Fortis HealthCare or Wockhardt Hospitals. Such memberships add a separate layer of reputation and increased visibility. Network membership can be captured by provider-specific characteristics. Finally, providers cluster within countries that may attempt to establish themselves as medical tourism destinations.

In comparison to domestic physician and provider choice, medical tourism conceptually adds countries and their respective characteristics as an extra dimension to the destination characteristics. It expands the choice set by adding options both at the upper tier, i.e. different countries, and at lower tiers, i.e. new providers and physicians. New options may differ in characteristics from one to three levels, i.e. an identical physician who practices at an identical provider in a different country only differs at the country level while another destination may be characterized by different characteristics at all levels.

Succinctly, treatments are rendered by physicians p who cluster within providers pr, which cluster within countries c. The within-cluster correlation structure can conveniently be expressed by a hierarchical model:

$$U_{p,pr,c} = x'_{p,pr,c}\beta_p + u_{p,pr,c} \tag{3.1}$$

The expected utility U of seeing physician p who practices in provider pr in country c depends on the physician's characteristics $x_{p,pr,c}$. The effect of these characteristics varies depending on provider pr in which physician p practices and is explained by provider characteristics $x_{pr,c}$:

$$\beta_p = x'_{pr,c}\gamma_{pr} + u_{pr,c} \tag{3.2}$$

In the same vein, the effect of provider characteristics γ_{pr} depends on the country c in which a provider is located:

$$\gamma_{pr} = x'_c\delta + u_c \tag{3.3}$$

Depending on the fixed- or random nature of the coefficients in the provider and country properties, the model would either retain its hierarchical structure or collapse to a variance components model. This flexible model structure accommodates all types of destinations such as a specialist in Germany who is consulted for specific treatments, the well-known Bumrungrad hospital in Thailand, or Hungary as a prominent destination for dental tourism. Each of these units is complemented by the missing physician/provider/country components whose parameters may be partly empty sets.

3.3.1 Physician Choice

Physician choice is often researched in the context of provider selection but there is some literature on the specific characteristics and channels affecting physician choice. In their study of 493 Iranians, Yassini et al. (2010) find expertise, communication skills and reputation to be the most important criteria of physician choice. Affordability, listening skills and waiting time were considered of lesser importance. Cheng (2004) discusses the previously low impact of provider report cards on consumer choice and interviewed 4015 Taiwanese adults on physician report cards by phone. 73% indicated consulting such a report if available and 76% expressed their willingness to change doctors if their performance results are poor. As performance was a construct of training, specialist qualification and attitude towards their patients, none of these factors can be ranked individually, however.

Rathwell (2013) reports the results of a survey of 1002 Americans on their choice of specialists and treatment facilities. For the choice of specialists, 87% indicated other physicians' referrals, 66% friends' advice and 50% patient rating sites as their most important sources. In terms of *ex-post* value assessment, patients value time spent with a physician, communication skills, and listening skills. These characteristics are confirmed by Haddad et al. (2000).

Tu and Lauer (2008) evaluate data from the 2007 Health Tracking Household Survey in the U.S. and find that there is generally little shopping for quality or price. Word-of-mouth was the decisive factor instead. With multiple answers allowed, the majority indicated relying on recommendations from friends, relatives, doctors and providers in their selection of a primary care physician as reported in Fig. 3.2. 26.9% relied exclusively on friends and relatives. The selection of specialists is guided by primary care referrals and recommendations from friends and relatives as reported in Fig. 3.3. 58.2% relied exclusively on referrals this time. Even if the self-reported use

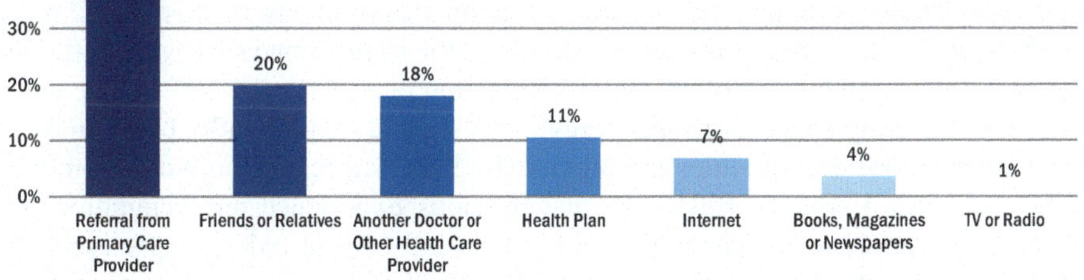

Fig. 3.2 Information sources used in the selection of a primary care physician

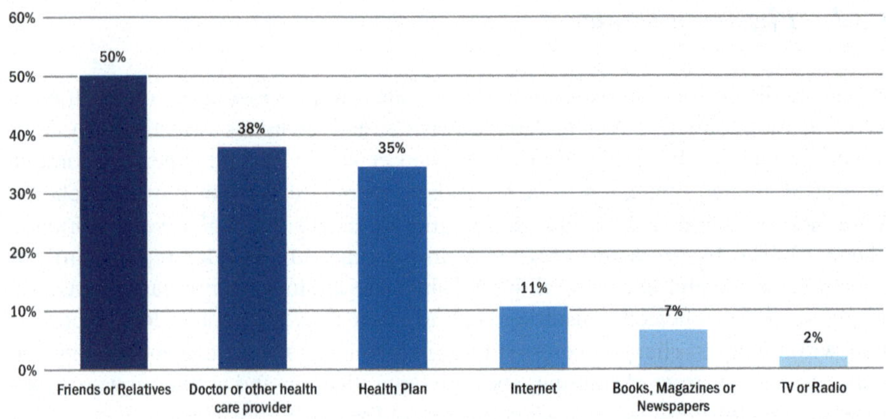

Fig. 3.3 Information sources used in the selection of a specialist

of price and quality information was low and the importance of good communication with a doctor was stressed, the role of price and quality is probably understated if the choice set considered was often within provider networks where no large quality disparities were perceived.

In the context of medical tourism, Johnston et al. (2012) report physician skill to be more important than language barriers and patients in Musa et al. (2012) value personal contact with physicians. Manaf et al. (2015) identify communication skills, language skills, time spent with the physician and friendliness as key items of perceived quality.

3.3.2 *Provider Choice*

Provider and hospital choice has received substantial attention in the academic literature. White and Morrisey (1998) investigate travel distance to providers and finds home market size to lead to shorter travel as expected. Local preferences exist but vary by treatment. Elective serious surgeries, for example, lead to farther travel.

McGuckin (2006) conduct a phone survey among 6360 U.S. citizens and rank cleanliness, low infection rates, hospital reputation, staff friendliness, staff-patient ratio, previous experience and distance as main determinants of hospital choice. Vonberg et al. (2008) report results of essentially the same phone survey in Germany and arrive at a similar order of cleanliness, infection rates, friendly staff, staff-patient ratio, reputation by friends, distance, previous stay, and reputation by public media. McGuckin (2006) also qualifies the previously discussed results on word-of-mouth in Wagner and Verheyen (2010) in that previous experience and reputation are particularly important for persons 55 and older and 65 and older, respectively. In total, clinical quality measures outshine staffing and reputation which in turn dominate previous experience and distance. In an innovative analysis of U.S. data, Jung et al. (2011) find reputation to be a very important contributor to patient utility. Previous experience with a hospital and high clinical scores also contribute to hospital selection.

Raza (2012) provides a descriptive analysis of 369 patients surveyed in India and indicates comprehensive facilities, previous experience with a hospital and the reputation of doctors as the most important determinants of hospital selection. He finds variations by education, i.e. patients with higher education rank the reputation of doctors higher while patients with lower education rank affordability higher. These results are in line with the variation in income that finds a similar pattern of declining importance of doctor reputation and high-tech equipment as income falls. Jannati et al. (2013) investigate the role of referrals, gender, income, costs, and quality on hospital choice after a brief literature review and find costs, income, health insurance and social ties to be particularly important for the two Iranian hospitals investigated. These results are of limited value, however, as they are distorted by the inclusion of emergency treatments. Adaman et al. (2009) focus on the use of private and public hospitals in Turkey and on the role of social ties. For minor health problems, they find that social ties help secure access to local public facilities and thus influence provider choice. Higher income leads to an increased selection of a private provider. Adaman et al. (2009) do not find the same network effects for serious health problems and suspect prohibitively high networking costs to be the reason.

Bin Saeed (1998) investigated the hospital choice between private and public hospitals in Saudi Arabia and analyzed a sample of 541 patients. He finds costs to be the most important factor in the choice of a private hospital, which, in light of a free public option, is taken as an indicator for maximum value seeking. Such value is found in a high quality of services and convenient administrative procedures. In terms of socio-demographic characteristics, health status as a proxy of urgency to avoid waiting times in public hospitals, insurance coverage, employment as a proxy of insurance coverage in private hospitals, age and sex are found to have significant impacts on hospital choice.

Figure 3.4 depicts the sources of information used by patients as reported by Tu and Lauer (2008). They find a dominant 74% of patients using their physician's recommendation for facility choice of which 68.6% indicated to have relied only on the recommendation of their performing doctor. This highlights the focus on physicians as opposed to facilities in the U.S. as most patients seem to simply rely on the specialist they have been referred to—who in turn refers them to a facility. Similarly, Rathwell (2013) reports 70% reputation, 60% specialization on the treatment required, 59% location and 53% waiting time as a ranking of factors for treatment facility selection.

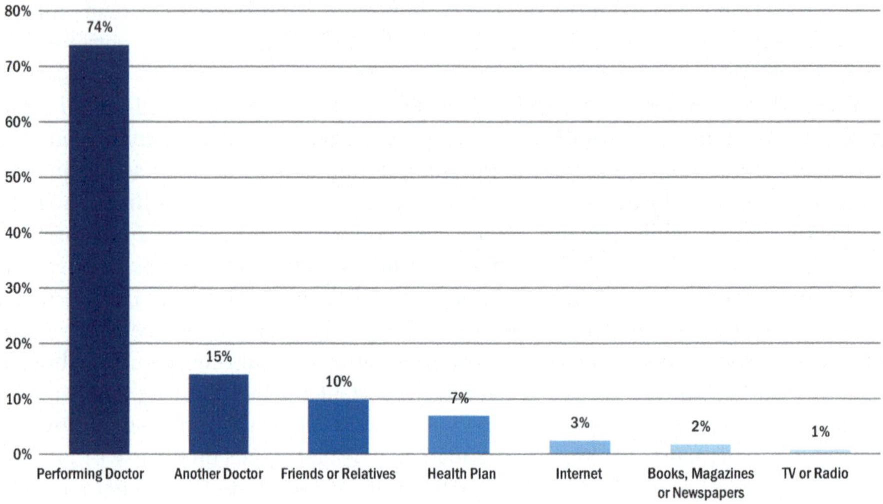

Fig. 3.4 Information sources used in the selection of a facility

3.3.3 *Country Choice*

Countries are not merely an aggregation of the physicians and providers contained therein but convey relevant information about a destination beyond that attributed to doctors and providers. Such information is the specific dimension that medical tourism adds to domestic destination choice and includes the factors discussed in Chap. 2, i.e. political stability, infrastructure for international travel and accessibility, international tourism features, institutional settings such as legislation, public health care coverage, reimbursement schemes, and the reputation associated with a country as a whole.

The latter is also known as the country-of-origin effect in the marketing literature and widely acknowledged to exist but its relevance is very much debated for standard goods. For consumer goods, complex supply chains complicate the country-of-origin concept and studies show a lack of consumer knowledge about the consumption choices' in their source countries (Mai 2011). Both of these issues can be cast aside for medical tourism as the origin of the product is the destination of travel. In fact, the country-of-origin literature very much suggests a prominent role of the country-of-origin effect in destination choice for medical tourism. Mai (2011) surveys the literature and identifies country image, antecedents and moderators as the three main components that influence a country-of-origin effect. Country image comprises cognitive, affective and normative processes. Cognitive processes are typically ruled by heuristics that project a country image onto product characteristics, i.e. irradiation. This is particularly common when there is little knowledge about a complex product—such as medical treatments. Affective and normative processes add emotions such as pride or animosity and expectations of outsiders with regard to morale or politics, for example. Antecedents may include socio-demographics, psychographics and cultural background (Gürhan-Canli and Maheswaran 2000). Finally, moderators are individual-related including direct and indirect, subjective and objective experiences via, e.g. own travel and word-of-mouth; product-related including price and associated risk; situative; and methodological. The country-of-origin construct can thus be considered a subset of alternative-specific, individual-specific and context variables that interact to a reputation effect, which lowers product uncertainty and may thus lead to higher demand in countries with high uncertainty avoidance (Melewar et al. 2007).

3.3.4 Destination Choice

The destination characteristics discussed thus far are usefully augmented by and structured in the literature on tourism destination competitiveness. This strand of literature attempts to cover the many industries involved in tourism, most of which matter for medical tourism also—depending on the amount of actual recreational activities involved in a trip. Tourists directly consume goods and services in the mobility/travel, food, accommodation, culture, shopping, and sightseeing sectors and indirectly create demand for public infrastructure as well as destination management (Fernando and Long 2012).

An updated version of the seminal model in destination competitiveness is that by Ritchie and Crouch (2003). They focus on the supply side and derive destination competitiveness from core resources, such as local climate and culture, and supporting resources, such as infrastructure and accessibility, which are processed by a layer of destination management via marketing and human resource development, for example, and by an additional layer of destination policy and development that defines, for example, the vision and positioning. The output is met by qualifying and amplifying determinants such as safety and security to determine a destination's competitiveness. They trace back comparative advantages to endowed resources and competitive advantages to the efficient deployment of resources. Empirically, Crouch (2008) identifies 10 out of 36 characteristics with above average importance, six of which are core resources: physiography and climate, culture and history, mix of activities, special events, entertainment, and superstructure. The other four include infrastructure, accessibility, awareness/image, and brand/positioning.

A second prominent model of destination competitiveness in tourism is the integrated model by Dwyer and Kim (2003). It is based on the Crouch-Ritchie model but reorganizes its components and makes some additions. The first block includes created resources such as tourism infrastructure, inherited or endowed resources and supporting resources such as general infrastructure or hospitality. The singling out of created resources stresses the room for policy intervention. The second block includes destination management, which aggregates Crouch and Ritchie's two layers into one and includes destination management by both the tourism industry and the government. Dwyer and Kim (2003) also introduce demand factors as an innovation. They represent consumer awareness, perception and preferences and thus add a demand perspective that Dwyer and Kim (2003) felt was underrepresented in the Crouch-Ritchie model. Situational conditions such as trends, regulatory framework or demographic conditions can refer to conditions at sources or at destinations and complete the second block. Interactions between these model components determine destination competitiveness. Subsequent literature that builds on the integrated model occasionally adds components to propose specific hypotheses such as the importance of innovation in experience-oriented, modern tourism (Fernando and Long 2012).

Dwyer and Kim (2003) offer a large set of indicators for their model and suggest a list of 162 items that operationalize their indicators. We will not reproduce that list here as the categories presented in column two of Table 3.1 suffice to demonstrate the substantial conceptual and content overlap between destination characteristics associated with recreational travel and with medical travel. The integrated model is very generic in that it accommodates essentially any type of travel by modifying the destination resources and some other select components. Resources, destination management, demand factors, competitive environment and price competitiveness require a product-specific assessment depending on whether recreation, medical treatment or any other purpose-motivated travel are considered, but the remaining characteristics apply to any type of travel and thus capture many of the components found in the medical tourism literature. These are tourism infrastructure (airports, accommodation), general infrastructure (utilities, communication), quality of service (quality assurance, immigration/customs service), accessibility (travel time, visa requirements), hospitality, market ties (ethnic ties, trade links), destination location (geographic distance), global environment (political stability, regulatory framework), price competitiveness with regards to non-medical and non-recreational items (exchange rate, airfare) and safety/security. Most of these characteristics are reminiscent of the drivers extracted in Chap. 2.

The non-overlapping regions between medical travel and recreational travel are purpose-specific resources (endowed and created), destination management, demand factors, competitive environment and price competitiveness. For medical travel, resources are largely purpose-specific and include physicians and providers who constitute relevant resources. These resources are created (e.g. professional training) and processed into cleanliness, for example, by destination management. Natural resources are less important unless their absence specifically prevents the creation of required resources—as would be the case if certain climatic conditions impede the establishment of tourism infrastructure, for example. Quality of destination management and demand factors vary by product, i.e. the specific purpose of travel or service that is consumed at the travel destination. Demand factors such as preferences for and awareness of a country as a treatment destination may be distinctly different from the preferences for and awareness of the same country as a destination for a recreational trip. The difference in awareness may result from separated destination managements for different purposes even if the latter can be integrated to some degree. Finally, competitive environment and price competitiveness of a destination may also differ by purpose of a trip. An example of purpose-specific

Table 3.1 Destination characteristics in medical tourism

		Destination		
		Country	Provider	Physician
Medical factors	Resources		Facilities	
			Equipment	
			Cleanliness	
			Infection rates	
			Complication rates	
			Certifications	
				Expertise
				Training
				Years of practice
				Communication
	Destination management	Marketing		
			Staffing	
			Administrative procedures	
			Waiting times	
	Demand factors	Reputation		
		Recommendation		
		Previous experience		
	Competitive environment		Rivalry	
			Treatment	
	Price competitiveness		Interpreting services	
			Accommodation	
		Exchange Rate		
Shared factors	Tourism infrastructure		Airport	
			Accommodation	
	General infrastructure		Utilities	
			Communication	
	Quality of service	Immigration/customs		
	Accessibility and location		Geographic distance	
			Travel time	
			Direct flight	
			Connection frequency/capacity	
			Proximity to other stops	
		Visa requirement		
	Hospitality	Friendliness		
		Ease of communication		
	Market ties	Cultural Links		
		Social Links		

(continued)

Table 3.1 (continued)

		Language		
		Religion		
		Food		
	Destination location	Geographic distance		
	Global environment	Legal environment		
		Political stability		
	Price competitiveness (Travel)		Airfare	
			Accommodation	
		Exchange rate		
	Safety/security	Visitor safety		
Recreational factors	Resources		Nature	
			Historic sites	
			Entertainment	
			Marketing	
	Destination management	---		
	Demand factors	---		
	Competitive environment	---		
	Price competitiveness (Tourism)	---		

components of price competitiveness in recreational and medical travel is destination package tour prices and treatment costs. The general structure of the integrated destination competitiveness models and the suggested partitioning of its components into medical travel and recreational travel make the model flexible enough to accommodate the dual-purpose trip that medical tourism constitutes.

Destination characteristics may take effect at a single or at multiple destination levels. Co-lumns three to five in Table 3.1 provide an overview of the characteristics that are associated with physicians, providers and countries at large and integrates Table 2.14. The characteristics are assigned to either treatment-specific, recreation-specific or shared factors of destination competitiveness. The highlighted columns mark the destination level at which a characteristic occurs and is best observed. If a characteristic stretches over multiple columns, each of the destination levels can contribute unique characteristics of the given type. A recommendation, for example, may be given for a specific physician but nothing is known about the provider s/he works for. Alternatively, a recommendation for a provider may exist but nothing is known about the physicians who practice there. The characteristic can occur independently at different levels with different impacts on destination attractiveness. Clearly, characteristics can be aggregated from right to left, i.e. in larger provider or country clusters, but a column is only highlighted if it can add information beyond that of its lower-tier elements to the right.

Medical treatment factors previously identified in this section can be grouped in created resources at the physician and the provider level. While facilities, equipment, cleanliness, infection rates and complication rates are typically reported at the provider level, expertise, training, years of practice and communication skills can only be ascribed to physicians. Certifications and accreditations, on the other hand, exist at both the provider and physician levels. Destination management at the provider level can support a positive treatment experience by ensuring a sufficient staffing level, short waiting times, streamlined administrative procedures and efficient medical treatment marketing. As discussed in Chap. 2, such destination marketing can be observed at the provider, regional and federal level.

Demand factors, i.e. destination awareness, perception and preferences can relate to any of the destination levels. Reputation goes beyond characteristics that can be easily communicated or signaled such as tourist attractiveness or quality via high pricing. It can be approximated by cultural distance, but essentially expresses a leap of faith. Mechinda et al. (2010) finds an attitudinal loyalty to the destination of Thailand at large to be relevant and Wongkit and McKercher (2013) report a large number of frequent visitors among medical tourists to Thailand. In fact, 85% indicated not to have considered another country as their destination but this may well be due to tourism in this particular example. Reputation, recommendations and previous experience can relate to any of the three destination levels.

Competitive environment captures the degree of rivalry or cooperation between domestic competitors at the provider level. Price competitiveness within a country is uniformly affected by the exchange rate while costs for interpreting services and accommodation—for outpatients or company—can differ between domestic locations. Treatment costs, in general, may further vary within providers depending on the seniority and expertise of the physician.

Shared factors were surveyed in Chap. 2 and can also be structured along the three destination levels. The adequacy of tourism and general infrastructure can differ between provider locations and is linked to accessibility and location factors. Visa requirements and immigration/customs aspects are invariant to domestic provider location, however. Hospitality factors such as the ease of communication and religious/social/cultural ties may depend on characteristics of each level again, i.e. the official language determines the general ease of communication with providers in a country. Providers may in turn distinguish themselves by catering to particular cultural or religious needs and physicians can attract patients with their language skills or cultural backgrounds regardless of the provider focus. We omit recreational factors from the exposition, as they will not be of interest in our investigation. Also note that these destination characteristics are viewed through the lens of individual characteristics, which shapes their perception.

In summary, a medical tourism destination serves consumers who seek a combination of medical travel and recreational travel. The attractiveness of a destination is determined by a multitude of characteristics, each of which may be the property of one or multiple columns. For medical travel, we expect medical factors to dominate destination choice. As the focus of a trip shifts from medical procedures to rehabilitation, wellness or recreation, however, recreational factors and its endowed or created resources such as nature and historic sites or entertainment gain importance and increasingly shape overall destination attractiveness (Schalber and Peters 2012).

3.4 Summary

Based on the purpose of travel mix in Fig. 2.1, treatment disaggregation in Fig. 3.1, consumer disaggregation and the identified suppliers with their set of destination characteristics in Table 3.1, we obtain a consolidated scheme to frame our empirical research in Fig. 3.5.

The exemplary inpatient cube isolates inpatient travel with layers representing presumably homogeneous treatment categories. We opt for ICD chapters in the exposition but homogenous treatment categories may also be captured by other criteria as displayed in Fig. 3.1. Within a cube, supplier aggregation at the national level implies monopolistic competition between "nationally" differentiated versions of medical travel. This perspective is reasonable if substitution occurs between countries rather than between providers and if the national version of medical

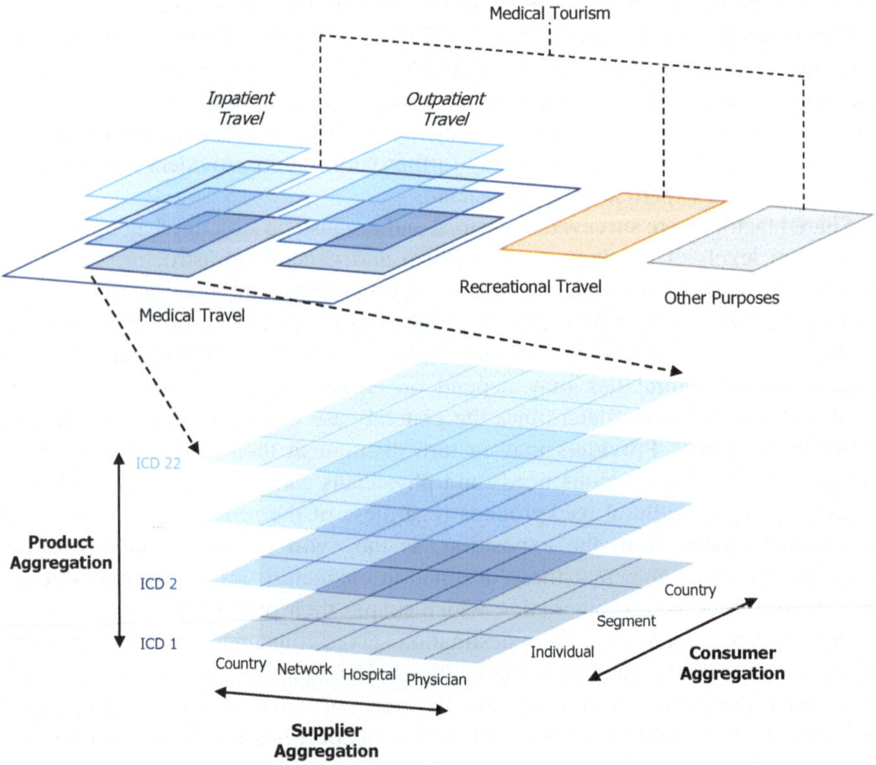

Fig. 3.5 Consolidated modelling framework

tourism is representative of providers within. If countries are representative of the providers within but reflect exclusive treatment foci, i.e. only few countries compete with each other as destinations for a given treatment or treatment category, disaggregation at the product level is appropriate. In this case, lower demand for a destination country may result from exogenously lower demand shares of the treatment categories served. There is some evidence for a particular treatment focus of some countries, e.g. dental treatments in Hungary, but we have no *ex-ante* information that rules out specific countries from aggregate competition in principle. As suppliers are disaggregated, more columns of Table 3.1 can be investigated. Similarly, the aggregation of consumers requires assumptions about population homogeneity across countries. Only the lowest level of aggregation, i.e. consumer-level data on choices of specific physicians for given treatments—with observed physician, provider and country characteristics—would allow the disentangling of every dimension.

Unfortunately, the implied requirements of an ideal data set clash with the quality and quantity of available data. Service exports are typically plagued with little or poor observational data and for medical tourism the situation is particularly grim. To our knowledge, no data set of observed choices with variation at the most disaggregated level across all three dimensions is available and even at the country level there exist no comprehensive statistics on quantities/market shares or prices. The modeling of observed destination choices, i.e. based on revealed preferences, is desirable and destination characteristics of real consideration sets at the individual level could theoretically be recovered in a survey but this approach is troublesome for several reasons: First, the cognitive burden of reproducing a potentially large consideration set of suppliers at the country, provider or even physician level will quickly lead to unreliable and invalid reported destination characteristics. Second, *ex-post* characterizations of *ex-ante* alternatives are likely to be biased based on current experiences. Common satisfaction with the chosen alternative (Wagner and Verheyen 2010) would introduce confirmation bias. Third, varying consideration sets across individuals require an inoperable, open survey format. For these reasons, a large part of medical tourism studies appears to rely on stated preferences (Fisher and Sood 2014; The Gallup Organization 2007; Wagner and Verheyen 2010; Yu and Ko 2012). A stated choice approach offers a number of advantages including identical and known destination characteristics and choice sets whose informational yield can be optimized by experimental design; combinations of characteristics that can go beyond observed production possibility frontiers; consistent description of destination characteristics to minimize individual perception errors; and repeated observations per individual.

To reconcile our desire to model observed choices with the data sets available, we resort to inpatients recorded by the German hospital statistics introduced and described in Sect. 2.2. A restriction to inpatients seems very limiting at first but it turns out to be a key ingredient to the formulation of an estimable model: Medical tourism subsumes a number of travelling phenomena that vary substantially in their decision-making processes and our main interest lies with medical travel, i.e. trips with the initial and primary purpose to obtain a medical treatment. Such trips are driven by the medical and shared factors in Table 3.1. We have seen that decision-making processes may also be sequential, i.e. a decision about a vacation destination followed by an opportunistic decision to receive a treatment, or simultaneous, i.e. a decision to jointly vacation and receive a treatment. The two latter processes are additionally governed by the recreational factors in Table 3.1 which greatly complicates modeling: Observed treatments would have to be assigned to the correct underlying decision-making processes. A simultaneous decision requires a simultaneous model treatment and a sequential decision requires an incorporation of the first stage decision with, for example, sunk costs. Failure to distinguish between these processes leads to a pooled model that attempts to explain all destination choices by one data-generating process with identical driver weights and would be hopelessly biased.

A focus on medical travelers greatly simplifies the problem as it avoids the empirically infeasible assignment of underlying decision-making processes to all treatments and allows us to neglect recreational factors. We propose a three-step process to identify medical travelers: First, our definition of medical travel requires an act of traveling to occur, which we can ensure as the German hospital statistics record international inpatients by their place of residence at the country level. Second, the treatment focus, i.e. a primarily medical purpose of the trip, must be ensured. By assumption, inpatient treatments represent medical conditions that dominate any considerations of tourism. This assumption turns out to be warranted in Chap. 6. Third, inpatient treatments that result from acute conditions of international visitors must be removed. Here, destination choice is not governed by any of the decision-making processes above but merely incidental. Our filtering of inpatient treatments leaves us with observations that qualify as medical travel, which is driven by medical and shared factors. We cannot explicitly control cross-border and institutionalized arrangements as our definition of medical travel prescribes in Sect. 2.1 but we can control for these factors in a panel setting.

With our ability to measure the real phenomenon of interest, we propose three empirical investigations that are both feasible and informative with regard to our research questions. These approaches connect Germany as a destination to source countries at different levels of product, consumer and supplier aggregation. The following vectors will be considered: First and at the very aggregate level, source countries and their bilateral ties to Germany are analyzed to identify drivers that lead to large medical travel outflows to Germany. These outflows will be disaggregated into layers of treatment categories but no disaggregation takes place along the consumer or supplier dimensions. We do have sufficiently detailed data on inpatient inflows only for Germany and will thus have to restrict a model of revealed preferences to unidirectional flows as depicted in Fig. 3.6. With only one destination and no price data, we further need to impose market structure to identify effects of drivers at the aggregate level and focus on recommendations, migrant stock and cultural proximity as drivers of inbound medical travel as outlined in Sect. 2.3.7. Our investigation is in the spirit of Johnson and Garman (2015) and Esiyok et al. (2017) and we argue that their analyses are flawed in a number of ways that our three-step process and focus on medical travelers resolves.

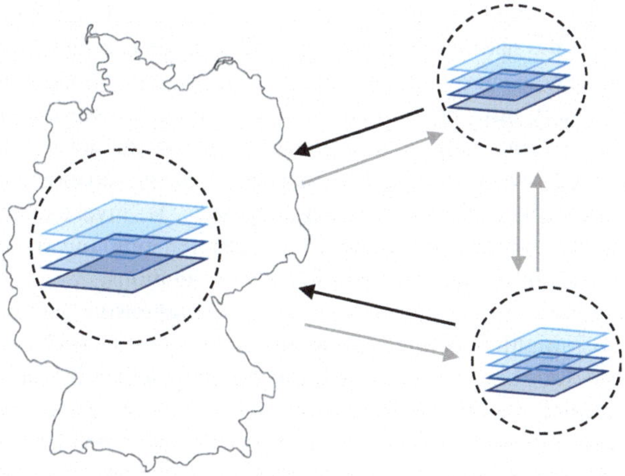

Fig. 3.6 Unidirectional medical travel to Germany

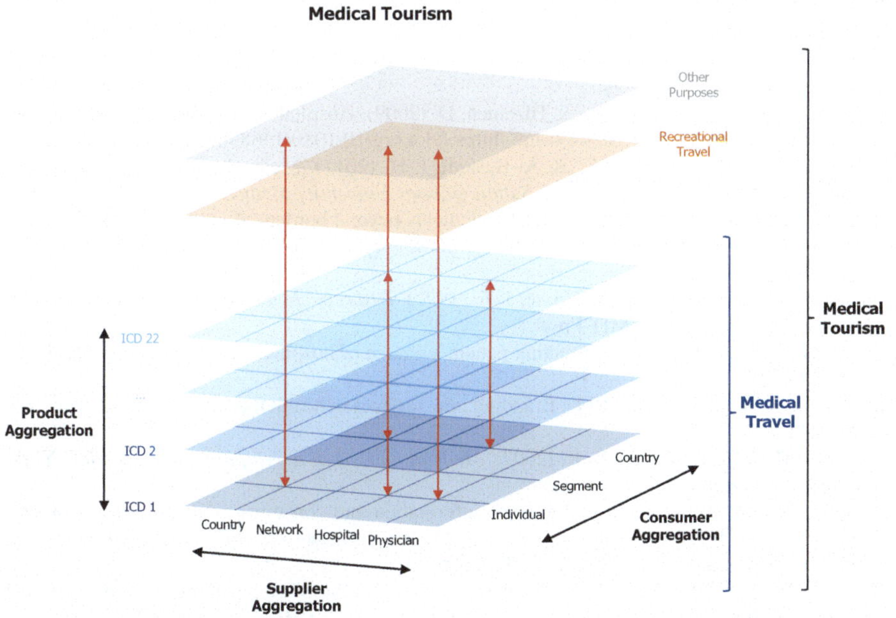

Fig. 3.7 Empirical investigations within the modelling framework

Second, we disaggregate suppliers, which enables the analysis of destination choice in Germany at the hospital level. This data set contains aggregated treatment counts per hospital, selected hospital characteristics and we augment it by a set of district characteristics to investigate the role of migrant stock and hospital characteristics. This approach draws on a rich data set, but requires additional assumptions about the nature of a destination. Third, we conduct expert interviews with stakeholders and a survey among international patients in Germany in order to obtain complementary information that sheds light on our research questions about the networks underlying cultural proximity, real consideration sets of medical travelers, additional drivers of medical tourism such as consumer characteristics and about the relevant level of supplier aggregation. To investigate the latter, we conduct a discrete choice experiment that complements our investigations of revealed preferences in the first two empirical investigations.

Our investigations can be embedded in the comprehensive framework outlined above. Figure 3.7 highlights how our analyses provide a good coverage of the framework space. Our first two investigations are represented by the two arrows in the back and limited to inpatient treatments, which are not driven by recreational factors. The third approach includes both inpatient and outpatient treatments. Its arrows extend beyond medical travel as we inquire into complementary purposes of travel whose drivers may now also influence destination choice.

References

Adaman, F., Ardiç, O. P., Erus, B., & Tüzemen, D. (2009). Hospital choice: Survey evidence from Istanbul. *Turkish Studies, 10*, 443–468. https://doi.org/10.1080/14683840903141780.

Al-Hinai, S. S., Al-Busaidi, A. S., & Al-Busaidi, I. H. (2011). Medical tourism abroad: A new challenge to Oman's health system. *Sultan Qaboos University Medical Journal, 11*, 477–484.

Alsharif, M. J., Labonte, R., & Lu, Z. (2010). Patients beyond borders: A study of medical tourists in four countries. *Global Social Policy, 10*, 315–335. https://doi.org/10.1177/1468018110380003.

Anderson, S. P., de Palma, A., & Thisse, J.-F. (1992). *Discrete choice theory of product differentiation*. Cambridge, MA: MIT Press.

Bin Saeed, K. S. (1998). Factors affecting patient's choice of hospitals. *Annals of Saudi Medicine, 18*, 420–424.

Boga, T. C., & Weiermair, K. (2011). Branding new services in health tourism. *Tourism Review, 66*, 90–106.

Bookman, M. Z., & Bookman, K. R. (2007). *Medical tourism in developing countries*. New York: Palgrave Macmillan.

Cheng, S.-H. (2004). Physician performance information and consumer choice: A survey of subjects with the freedom to choose between doctors. *Quality and Safety in Health Care, 13*, 98–101. https://doi.org/10.1136/qshc.2003.006981.

Clarke, L. H., & Griffin, M. (2007). The body natural and the body unnatural: Beauty work and aging. *Journal of Aging Studies, 21*, 187–201. https://doi.org/10.1016/j.jaging.2006.11.001.

Clarke, L. H., & Griffin, M. (2008). Visible and invisible ageing: Beauty work as a response to ageism. *Ageing and Society, 28*. https://doi.org/10.1017/S0144686X07007003.

Crone, R. K. (2008). Flat medicine? Exploring trends in the globalization of health care. *Academic Medicine, 83*, 117–121. https://doi.org/10.1097/ACM.0b013e318160965c.

Crouch, G. I. (2008). *Modelling destination competitiveness: A survey and analysis of the impact of competitiveness attributes*. Gold Coast, QLD: Sustainable Tourism CRC.

Dwyer, L., & Kim, C. (2003). Destination competitiveness: A model and determinants. *Current Issues in Tourism, 6*, 369–414.

Ehrbeck, T., Guevara, C., & Mango, P. D. (2008). *Mapping the market for medical travel*. Seattle, WA: The McKinsey Quarterly.
Esiyok, B., Çakar, M., & Kurtulmuşoğlu, F. B. (2017). The effect of cultural distance on medical tourism. *Journal of Destination Marketing & Management, 6*, 66–75. https://doi.org/10.1016/j.jdmm.2016.03.001.
Fernando, I. N., & Long, W. (2012). New conceptual model on cluster competitiveness: A new paradigm for tourism? *International Journal of Business and Management, 7*, 75–84. https://doi.org/10.5539/ijbm.v7n9p75.
Fisher, C., & Sood, K. (2014). What is driving the growth in medical tourism? *Health Marketing Quarterly, 31*, 246–262. https://doi.org/10.1080/07359683.2014.936293.
Grossman, M. (1972). On the concept of health capital and the demand for health. *The Journal of Political Economy, 80*, 223–255.
Gürhan-Canli, Z., & Maheswaran, D. (2000). Cultural variations in country of origin effects. *Journal of Marketing Research, 37*, 309–317. https://doi.org/10.1509/jmkr.37.3.309.18778.
Haddad, S., Potvin, L., Roberge, D., Pineault, R., & Remondin, M. (2000). Patient perception of quality following a visit to a doctor in a primary care unit. *Family Practice, 17*, 21–29.
Hanefeld, J., Lunt, N., Smith, R., & Horsfall, D. (2015). Why do medical tourists travel to where they do? The role of networks in determining medical travel. *Social Science & Medicine, 124*, 356–363. https://doi.org/10.1016/j.socscimed.2014.05.016.
Hwang, J., & Christensen, C. M. (2008). Disruptive innovation in health care delivery: A framework for business-model innovation. *Health Affairs (Millwood), 27*, 1329–1335. https://doi.org/10.1377/hlthaff.27.5.1329.
Jannati, A., Bahrami, M. A., Gholizadeh, M.'s., Alizadeh, L., & Khodayari, M. T. (2013). A survey of factors affecting patients' decision in selecting governmental and private hospitals in Tabriz, Iran. *Journal of Tourism Research & Hospitality, 2*, 1–4. https://doi.org/10.4172/2324-8807.1000110.
Johnson, T. J., & Garman, A. N. (2015). Demand for international medical travel to the USA. *Tourism Economics, 21*, 1061–1077. https://doi.org/10.5367/te.2014.0393.
Johnston, R., Crooks, V. A., & Snyder, J. (2012). "I didn't even know what I was looking for": A qualitative study of the decision-making processes of Canadian medical tourists. *Globalization and Health, 8*, 23. https://doi.org/10.1186/1744-8603-8-23.
Jung, K., Feldman, R., & Scanlon, D. (2011). Where would you go for your next hospitalization? *Journal of Health Economics, 30*, 832–841. https://doi.org/10.1016/j.jhealeco.2011.05.006.
Kangas, B. (2010). Traveling for medical care in a global world. *Medical Anthropology, 29*, 344–362.
Klingenberger, D. (2009). Dentaltourismus und Auslandszahnersatz: Empirische Zahlungsbereitschaftsanalysen auf der Grundlage repräsentativer Stichproben im Jahre 2008. Materialienreihe / Institut der Deutschen Zahnärzte, vol 32. Dt. Zahnärzte-Verlag, Köln.
Lee, M., Han, H., & Lockyer, T. (2012). Medical tourism: Attracting Japanese tourists for medical tourism experience. *Journal of Travel & Tourism Marketing, 29*, 69–86.
Mai, R. (2011). Der Herkunftslandeffekt: Eine kritische Würdigung des State of the Art. *Journal Betriebswirtsch, 61*, 91–121. https://doi.org/10.1007/s11301-011-0075-0.
Manaf, N. H. A., Hussin, H., Kassim, P. N. J., Alavi, R., & Dahari, Z. (2015). Medical tourism service quality: Finally some empirical findings. *Total Quality Management & Business Excellence, 26*, 1017–1028. https://doi.org/10.1080/14783363.2015.1068597.
McGuckin, M. (2006). Consumer attitudes about health care-acquired infections and hand hygiene. *American Journal of Medical Quality, 21*, 342–346. https://doi.org/10.1177/1062860606291328.
Mechinda, P., Serirat, S., Anuwichanont, J., & Gulid, N. (2010). An examination of tourists' loyalty towards medical tourism in Pattaya, Thailand. *International Business & Economics Research Journal, 9*, 55–70.

Melewar, T. C., Anne Lee, J., Garbarino, E., & Lerman, D. (2007). How cultural differences in uncertainty avoidance affect product perceptions. *International Marketing Review, 24*, 330–349. https://doi.org/10.1108/02651330710755320.

Musa, G., Thirumoorthi, T., & Doshi, D. (2012). Travel behaviour among inbound medical tourists in Kuala Lumpur. *Current Issues in Tourism, 15*, 525–543. https://doi.org/10.1080/13683500.2011.626847.

Noree, T., Hanefeld, J., & Smith, R. (2014). UK medical tourists in Thailand: They are not who you think they are. *Globalization and Health, 10*, 29. https://doi.org/10.1186/1744-8603-10-29.

Rathwell, S. (2013). *3 factors driving loyalty: Business lessons from the healthcare industry*. Vision Critical. Accessed December 18, 2013, from http://www.visioncritical.com/blog/3-factors-driving-patient-loyalty-in-healthcare-industry

Raza, M. A. (2012). Factors influencing patient's decision of selecting a hospital. *International Journal of Research in Commerce, Economics & Management, 2*, 34–39.

Ritchie, J. R. B., & Crouch, G. I. (2003). *The competitive destination: A sustainable tourism perspective*. Oxon: CABI Pub.

Schalber, C., & Peters, M. (2012). Determinants of health tourism competitiveness: An alpine case study. *Tourism Review, 60*, 307–323.

The Gallup Organization. (2007). Cross border health services in the EU: Analytical report. *Flash Eurobarometer, 210*, 1–42.

Tu, H. T., & Lauer, J. R. (2008). *Word of mouth and physician referrals still drive health care provider choice*. Washington, DC: Research Briefs, Center for Studying Health System Change.

Vonberg, R.-P., Sander, C., & Gastmeier, P. (2008). Consumer attitudes about health care acquired infections: A German survey on factors considered important in the choice of a hospital. *American Journal of Medical Quality, 23*, 56–59. https://doi.org/10.1177/1062860607310915.

Wagner, C., & Verheyen, F. (2010). *TK-Europabefragung 2009: Deutsche Patienten auf dem Weg nach Europa*. Hamburg: Techniker Krankenkasse.

Wagner, C., Dobrick, K., & Verheyen, F. (2011). *Europabefragung 2010*. Hamburg: WINEG Wissen, Techniker Krankenkasse.

White, W. D., & Morrisey, M. A. (1998). Are patients traveling further? *International Journal of the Economics of Business, 5*, 203–221. https://doi.org/10.1080/13571519884512.

Whittaker, A. (2008). Pleasure and pain: Medical travel in Asia. *Global Public Health, 3*, 271–290.

Wongkit, M., & McKercher, B. (2013). Toward a typology of medical tourists: A case study of Thailand. *Tourism Management, 38*, 4–12. https://doi.org/10.1016/j.tourman.2013.02.003.

Yassini, S. M., Harrazi, M. A., & Askari, J. (2010). The study of most important factors influencing physician choice. *Procedia – Social and Behavioral Sciences, 5*, 1945–1949. https://doi.org/10.1016/j.sbspro.2010.07.393.

Yu, J. Y., & Ko, T. G. (2012). A cross-cultural study of perceptions of medical tourism among Chinese, Japanese and Korean tourists in Korea. *Tourism Management, 33*, 80–88. https://doi.org/10.1016/j.tourman.2011.02.002.

Zhang, J., Seo, S., & Lee, H. (2013). The impact of psychological distance on Chinese customers when selecting an international healthcare service country. *Tourism Management, 35*, 32–40. https://doi.org/10.1016/j.tourman.2012.05.007.

Chapter 4
Drivers of Medical Travel at the National Level

The goal of this chapter is the indirect identification and testing of drivers of aggregate inpatient flows to Germany. A natural way to estimate the role of drivers is to resort to applied demand estimation. The literature on industrial organization offers essentially two options: modeling in product or in characteristics space.

Both approaches face similar challenges in that they need to deal with consumer aggregation, depending on the data available, and to address simultaneity biases. To deal with aggregated data, they invoke a representative consumer. Such a construct implies that income redistribution does not alter aggregate demands, i.e. utility formulations that yield parallel Engel curves, which pass through the origin and imply choice probabilities that do not depend on income. Both approaches further share two simultaneity problems: First, expenditures are only exogenous if demand across all sectors is considered. The analysis of sectoral demand requires an exogenously determined expenditure share for a given sector which is usually obtained via two-stage budgeting or the consideration of an outside good. The first stage can be modeled with socio-demographics and income as explanatory variables but the second stage is no less likely to depend on these variables unless taste parameters are assumed identical across all consumer segments. The discussion of heterogeneous consumers in CES and discrete choice settings will shed more light on this issue below. Second, prices are required to be exogenous but are endogenous if suppliers are price-takers. In the presence of unobserved product characteristics, such price endogeneity in the demand equation arises for price setters as well (Berry 1994). Consequently, prices need to be instrumented.

Despite the similarities of both approaches, the discrete choice approach is attractive for three reasons in our context. First, it allows for an easier treatment of differentiated products by defining their characteristics. Second, it reduces parameters by reducing n^2 price parameters for n products to common parameter characteristics while allowing for complex substitution patterns via random coefficients, which rely on distributional assumptions rather than a large number of extra parameters. Third, choice models align well with corner solutions, i.e. medical tourists who

K. Schmerler, *Medical Tourism in Germany*, Developments in Health Economics and Public Policy 13, https://doi.org/10.1007/978-3-030-03988-2_4

seek medical treatments choose one variant and do not buy continuous quantities of their treatment at multiple destinations.

Unfortunately, demand analysis at the international level requires a full set of destination prices and characteristics at the various levels of product aggregation and that information is not available. We therefore opt for a second-best solution that comes at the cost of imposing market structure: a gravity trade flow framework. The gravity framework assumes trade barriers to exist and within this framework, we will test aggregate characteristics of importing countries that are hypothesized to drive medical tourism in that they modify the costs of distance between a source country and Germany as a destination. Economically, high inflows are associated with low trade barriers and these trade barriers are to be inferred. We will first discuss the theoretical underpinnings of the gravity model to establish its appropriateness in the medical tourism context, develop an adequate empirical specification, present our data and estimation methods and finally discuss the results.

4.1 The Gravity Model

The gravity model is arguably the most successful formulation of empirically observed trade flows and offers a promising starting point for the identification of medical travel trade flows. It has been derived from various theoretical foundations and while the general shape of the gravity model and its components of two economic masses and distance remain unchanged, new components have been introduced and measures of distance have evolved significantly.

There exist numerous ah-hoc gravity model specifications that address empirical questions all the while conveniently neglecting the insights and challenges established by the theory. Such specifications are problematic in numerous ways since they do not allow a proper interpretation of the estimated parameters and their lack of theory precludes the recovery of underlying structural parameters. Even if the recovery of structural parameters is not at the heart of this analysis, arriving at an estimable model of adequate functional form with all key components requires careful exploration of the vast literature on gravity modeling and its assessment in a medical tourism context.

4.1.1 Basic Structure

In an attempt to introduce distance to international trade theory Tinbergen (1962) and, shortly after, Pöyhönen (1963) were the first to formulate a model inspired by the gravity theory in physics. The model was originally conceived to explain empirical findings on trade flows and its success laid the foundation for its ongoing popularity.

The basic gravity model relates trade volume X of countries i and j to their sizes and to the distance d_{ij} between them. In its stochastic form, country size is approximated by aggregate income Y while k is the gravity constant and u_{ij} the stochastic error term with $E(u_{ij}) = 1$.

$$X_{ij} = k\left(\frac{(Y_i Y_j)}{d_{ij}}\right)u_{ij} \tag{4.1}$$

The original gravity equation implicitly assumes free trade, i.e. equal prices in all countries—an assumption that is implausible. Medical services are rendered to international patients in the destination country and are affected by both domestic and foreign trade barriers as well as the costs of distance.

Initial attempts to provide a theoretical framework for the gravity model and to introduce prices were made (Leamer and Stern 1970; Linnemann 1966; Savage et al. 1960) but the first comprehensive and sound result was delivered by Anderson (1979) who derived the gravity model from Cobb-Douglas as well as CES preferences for traded goods from different origins, i.e. Armington preferences. Bergstrand (1985) engaged in a similarly rigorous analysis based on Armington preferences which he later reconciled with a monopolistic competition framework in Bergstrand (1989) and in Bergstrand (1990) following Dixit and Stiglitz (1977). The new formulations strayed from the original gravity equation by abandoning free trade and by incorporating complicated price terms for different countries that were most commonly expressed by GDP deflators. Deardorff (1998) showed that the gravity model can also be traced back to a Heckscher-Ohlin framework and argued that the gravity model's empirical robustness should be taken as virtue of its own, but cannot be used to resolve the debate between competing trade theories. Instead, distance and country size, reflecting transport costs and trade potential, should be part of "just about any sensible model". In this spirit, common empirical formulations were based on Eq. (4.1) and took a form along the lines of

$$\ln X_{ij} = \beta_0 + \beta_1 \ln Y_i + \beta_2 \ln Y_j - \beta_3 \ln d_{ij} + \beta_4 D_{ij} + \varepsilon_{ij} \tag{4.2}$$

where D_{ij} was a dummy for two different trade zones, as used in McCallum (1995), for example.

4.1.2 Multilateral Resistance

McCallum's findings of an excessively trade-inhibiting border effect prompted the development of the gravity model's current theoretical foundations by Anderson and van Wincoop (2003). These allow the inference of underlying parameters that go beyond the empirical formulation. Anderson and van Wincoop (2003) realized that the volume of bilateral trade does not only depend on bilateral trade barriers but also on the availability and attractiveness of all other potential trading partners, and thus essentially addressed an omitted-variable problem. They recast the theory and introduced theoretically justified multilateral resistance terms to the gravity equation.

The exposition here will roughly follow Anderson and van Wincoop (2003) and builds on the three assumptions outlined by Anderson and van Wincoop (2004). First, trade separability is required to assure that the aggregate production and expenditure decision of a region is independent of the second-step selection of the supplier. Second, ad valorem trade costs must be independent from the quantity traded and third, the demand structure is identical across countries. Consumers are characterized by CES preferences for substitutable goods within sectors. Utility of consumers in country j increases in both quantity q and varieties N of goods flowing from countries i to j, with $j \in i$. Total consumer utility is the sum of utilities across all varieties, substitutability between products is given by the CES σ, and α is a preference parameter. It is assumed that each variety represents one country.

$$U_j = \left(\sum_i^N \alpha_i^{\frac{(1-\sigma)}{\sigma}} q_{ij}^{\frac{(\sigma-1)}{\sigma}} \right)^{\frac{\sigma}{(\sigma-1)}}. \tag{4.3}$$

Trade costs are introduced in the standard iceberg formulation, so the price of good q_{ij} in country j is its domestic price p_i in country i multiplied by the associated and unknown trade costs τ from i to j.

$$p_{ij} = p_i \tau_{ij} \tag{4.4}$$

Given the budget constraint of balanced trade

$$y_j = \sum_I p_{ij} q_{ij} \tag{4.5}$$

consumers in j maximize their utility by choosing nominal demands x according to

$$x_{ij} = \left(\frac{\alpha_i p_i \tau_{ij}}{P_j} \right)^{(1-\sigma)} y_j \tag{4.6}$$

with consumer price index P_j for country j. Market clearance is achieved by defining exporter income

$$y_i = \sum_j x_{ij} = \sum_j \left(\frac{\alpha_i p_i \tau_{ij}}{P_j} \right)^{(1-\sigma)} y_j \tag{4.7}$$

and by factoring out $\alpha_i p_i$ which can be substituted into x_{ij} and P_j. We obtain

$$x_{ij} = \frac{(y_i y_j)}{y_w}\left(\frac{\tau_{ij}}{P_i P_j}\right)^{1-\sigma} \tag{4.8}$$

$$(P_i)^{1-\sigma} = \sum_j \left(\frac{\tau_{ij}}{P_j}\right)^{1-\sigma}\frac{y_j}{y^w} \tag{4.9}$$

$$(P_j)^{1-\sigma} = \sum_i \left(\frac{\tau_{ij}}{P_i}\right)^{1-\sigma}\frac{y_i}{y^w}. \tag{4.10}$$

with world GDP $y_w = \sum_i y_i$. This solution represents a one sector economy and changes to

$$x_{ij}^h = \frac{\left(y_i^h y_j^h\right)}{y^h}\left(\frac{\tau_{ij}^h}{P_j^h P_i^h}\right)^{1-\sigma_h} \tag{4.11}$$

for sector h. Expenditures no longer equal output within a sector but y_j^h and y_i^h now reflect country *j's* expenditures and country *i's* output in sector h (Anderson and van Wincoop 2004). Trade separability ensures both terms' exogeneity.

Dropping the sectoral subscript h, Eq. (4.8) considers all trade between countries but suffices to make some general observations. Under the assumption that $\sigma > 1$, Eq. (4.8) resembles the original gravity formulation in Eq. (4.1) but now includes inward and outward resistance terms P_j and P_i, which are functions of trade costs and price levels in all other countries.

Empirically, Eq. (4.8) is estimated as

$$\begin{aligned} \ln x_{ij} = & -\beta_0 \ln Y_w + \beta_1 \ln y_i + \beta_2 \ln y_j \\ & + (1-\sigma)\left(\beta_3 \ln \tau_{ij} - \beta_4 \ln P_i - \beta_5 \ln P_j\right) \end{aligned} \tag{4.12}$$

with trade costs depending on border effect B_{ij}, distance d_{ij} and an unobserved error component ε_{ij}:

$$\ln \tau_{ij} = B_{ij} + \alpha_1 d_{ij} + \varepsilon_{ij}. \tag{4.13}$$

From Eq. (4.12) it is clear that y_w is absorbed by a constant as it does not vary across bilateral trade flows.

Multilateral resistance terms are not directly observable and their formulation is essentially a problem of translating a circular theoretical formulation into an estimable model. There exist three strategies to deal with them. First, they can be determined by imposing market structure (Anderson and van Wincoop 2003). Second, they can be solved analytically (Straathof 2008). Third, they can be estimated as dummy variables or fixed effects (Cheng and Wall 2005; Wall 1999).

Attempts to capture multilateral resistance gave rise to various dummy formulations. The basic version for cross-section data uses $N + N$ importer and exporter dummies for $N(N - 1)$ exports and imports between N countries as is depicted in Fig. 4.1. This type of dummies requires a large number of observations of exports and imports activity between all countries. Since P_j and Y_j do not vary for importer j and P_i and Y_i do not vary for exporter i, the use of $N + N$ country dummies also precludes the estimation of country-specific covariates unless imports and exports or multiple observation periods are pooled. Following Baldwin and Taglioni (2007), country dummies capture the multilateral resistance effect well in cross-section data but fail to capture it entirely in panel data. This is obvious as multilateral resistance terms depend on price levels that vary across years and will be averaged out by country dummies. Note that our arrows in Fig. 4.1 represent patient flows, so inbound arrows signify exports and outbound arrows are imports.

Country pair dummies are an alternative that requires panel data. $\frac{N(N-1)}{2}$ country pair dummies can be estimated given a sufficiently long time dimension and coincide with a fixed effect estimator for country pairs. While country pair and time dummies remove some omitted variable bias (Baldwin and Taglioni 2007), they also prevent the estimation of time-invariant bilateral factors such as geographic distance. Another option is the use of time-variant nation dummies in order to address serial correlation in the multilateral resistance. These dummies are substantial in number, $(N + N)T$, and significantly reduce the available degrees of freedom.

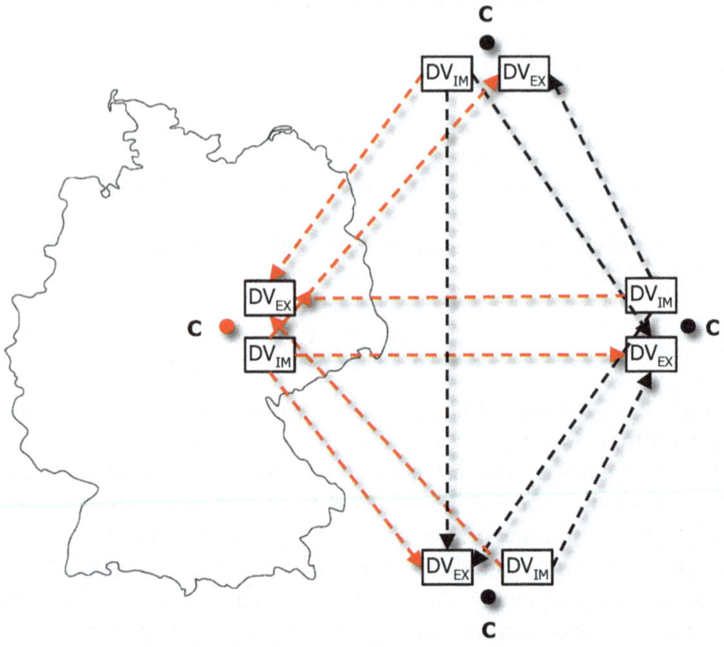

Fig. 4.1 Multilateral resistance: exports and imports—many sources—many destinations

4.1.3 Heterogeneous Firms

The seminal work by Anderson and van Wincoop (2003) and its resulting formulation (4.8) suggests that trade flows between two countries depend positively on the sizes of two economies and negatively on the trade barriers between them. For a plausible elasticity of substitution greater than 1, the CES further amplifies the negative effect of trade barriers on trade flows, i.e. trade barriers will have stronger adverse effects on trade flows in a highly competitive sector with highly substitutable products than in a sector of less substitutable products.

This notion is challenged by Chaney (2008), who introduced heterogeneous firms to the structural modeling of the gravity formulation. He continues to rely on CES consumers with their tractable measure of product substitutability but models the supply side following Melitz (2003), who laid out a tractable formulation of heterogeneous firms at the micro level. These heterogeneous firms self-select into exporting depending on their productivity, which may allow them to overcome the fixed costs associated with exporting. This supply structure enables the decomposition of quantity changes into intensive and extensive margins and Chaney (2008) investigates precisely these margins. Without detailing the entire derivation, he arrives at Eq. (4.14) which resembles Eq. (4.8) but significantly changes the interpretation of the estimated parameters.

$$x_{ij} = k\frac{(l_i l_j)}{l_w}\left(\frac{\tau_{ij}^{v}}{P_j}\right)^{-\gamma}\left(\tau_{ij}^{f}\right)^{-\left(\frac{\gamma}{\sigma-1}-1\right)} \tag{4.14}$$

Trade flows x_{ij} from country i to country j continue to depend on a constant k, the countries' sizes l_i and l_j measured in labor income, and two cost terms. The first includes bilateral variable trade costs τ^{v} and the remoteness parameter P_j and the second adds bilateral fixed costs τ^{f} that are associated with exporting. The estimated exponents now represent different structural parameters. γ captures the homogeneity of producers ($\gamma > \sigma - 1$ and $\gamma > 2$) with larger γ representing increasing homogeneity. Clearly, homogeneity amplifies the negative impact of both fixed and variable trade costs on trade flows. However, the elasticity of substitution σ now dampens the negative effect of fixed costs and no longer exerts an influence on variable trade costs. In contrast, an increasing σ did magnify the negative effect of all trade barriers in the framework of homogeneous firms.

Chaney (2008) essentially identifies two effects. First, in a highly competitive sector, i.e. for products with a high elasticity of substitution, trade barriers have a low impact on trade flows. The reason is that only high productivity firms exist in such sectors, which leads to increased exporting by incumbent firms as trade barriers are removed, but allows few new entrants into the market due to stiff competition. Conversely, sectors with low elasticities of substitution between products benefit more from the removal of trade barriers. The increase of exports by existing firms is lower but the low substitutability allows more market entrants to find their niches. Chaney (2008) shows that for aggregate trade the external margin, i.e. new entrants, dominates the internal margin. Consequently, the impact of trade barriers on trade flows is conditional upon a sector's firm structure and their removal is more beneficial in less competitive markets.

Krautheim (2007) extends Chaney's structural model by including domestic information networks that generate destination-specific spillovers and thus lower the fixed trade costs to be overcome by prospective exporters. The resulting formulation maintains the dampening impact of σ on fixed costs associated with exporting and further extends it to the variable costs.

$$x_{ij} = kL_j\left(\frac{l_i}{l_w}\right)^{(1+\omega)}\left(\frac{\tau_{ij}^{v}}{P_j}\right)^{-\gamma(1+\omega)}\left(\tau_{ij}^{f}\right)^{-\frac{b}{\sigma-1}*\omega} \tag{4.15}$$

With $\omega = f(\sigma,\gamma,b)$, bilateral fixed and variable costs associated with exporting as well as the size of the exporting country now depend on the elasticity of substitution σ, the firm structure γ and the quality b of the domestic information network. Total costs associated with exporting continue to determine the number of exporting firms as is the case in any framework with heterogeneous firms, but variable costs now endogenously determine fixed costs. Lower variable costs lead to more exporters whose information network lowers fixed costs for new exporters—with a decreasing marginal effect. Variable costs are thus also subject to the previously described dampening effect of σ via their impact on fixed costs.

Helpman et al. (2008) suggest an empirically attractive model that generalizes Anderson and van Wincoop (2003) for asymmetric bilateral trade barriers and heterogeneous firms. They derive a two-stage model that models the self-selection of firms into exporting in the first stage and adds the share of exporting firms to the trade flow equation in the second stage. Omitting the share would confound its effect with the estimated trade barrier parameters. The second stage is augmented by the standard Heckman correction to avoid the sample selection bias that is induced by dropping zero trade flow observations. Helpman et al. (2008) consider heterogeneous firms whose exporting profitability from i to j depends on country-specific production costs c_i, bilateral fixed and variable costs of exporting f_{ij} and τ_{ij}, multilateral inward resistance and economic size of j, and firm productivity a. Multiple firms per country produce single products and engage in monopolistic competition, which allows only the most productive firms to export. As in the previously discussed models, consumers are of representative CES type and trade costs τ_{ij} are in iceberg formulation. The derivation of trade flows in this setting yields

$$x_{ij} = \left(\frac{\sigma}{\sigma-1}\frac{c_i\tau_{ij}}{P_j}\right)^{1-\sigma} y_j N_i V_{ij}. \tag{4.16}$$

Trade volume x depends on a country-specific cost factor c_i, bilateral variable trade costs τ_{ij}, country j's price index P_j, N_i number of firms in the exporting country, and the bilateral export volume V_{ij} which depends on a firm-specific cost factor a for each firm. The firm productivity distribution of $1/a$ is identical for every country but the realized draws differ.

Defining market-clearance as in Eq. (4.5) with $y_j = \sum_l y_{ji}$ would yield a similar gravity equation as in (4.8) but the focus here lies on estimating (4.16). Taking logarithms of (4.16) gives

$$\ln x_{ij} = (\sigma - 1)\ln\left(\frac{\sigma - 1}{\sigma}\right) + (\sigma - 1)\ln P_j + \ln y_j - (\sigma - 1)\ln c_i + \ln N_i$$
$$+ (1 - \sigma)\ln \tau_{ij} + \ln V_{ij}. \tag{4.17}$$

Collecting i-specific and j-specific terms in exporter and importer dummy variables, defining a functional form for bilateral trade costs as $(\sigma - 1)\tau_{ij} = \beta_d \ln D_{ij} - u_{ij}$ with bilateral distance D_{ij} and an i.i.d. normally distributed error term u_{ij}, and characterizing export volume $V_{ij} = f(W_{ij})$ which controls for the fraction of firms exporting from i to j, yields

$$\ln x_{ij} = c + DV_j^{(X)} + DV_i^{(X)} - \beta_d \ln D_{ij} + \ln W_{ij} + u_{ij}. \tag{4.18}$$

The only conceptual difference to (4.12) lies in W_{ij} which controls for firm heterogeneity, i.e. the fraction of firms that self-select into exporting in a particular bilateral trade relationship. In a sense, it replaces the exporting country's total size by the more nuanced measure of firms that actually engage in exporting. Self-selection into exporting depends on the exporting firms' productivity draws and is thus expected to be asymmetric. Omission of this variable induces a bias in the estimated distance parameters and additional bias is introduced both by ignoring self-selection altogether and by dropping zero trade flows. Hence, a selection equation is specified that relates the exporting firm share $W_{ij} = f(Z_{ij})$ to an indicator Z_{ij}, which relates total exporting costs and firm productivity to exporting activity.

$$Z_{ij} = \frac{1}{\sigma c_i f_{ij}}\left(\frac{\sigma - 1}{\sigma}\frac{P_j}{c_i \tau_{ij}}\right)^{(\sigma-1)} y_j a_L^{(1-\sigma)} \tag{4.19}$$

This selection condition can be estimated in log-log form

$$\ln Z_{ij} = (1 - \sigma)\ln a_L - \ln \sigma + (\sigma - 1)\ln\left(\frac{\sigma - 1}{\sigma}\right) + \ln yY_j + (\sigma - 1)P_j$$
$$- \ln c_i - (\sigma - 1)\ln c_i - (\sigma - 1)\ln \tau_{ij} - \ln f_{ij} \tag{4.20}$$

by making use of the above definition of bilateral variable costs τ_{ij}, by collecting i-specific and j-specific terms in exporter and importer dummy variables again, and by defining the fixed costs of exporting associated with exporting from i to j as $f_{ij} = \delta_1 C_{ij}^{fix} + \delta_2 C_i^{fix} + \delta_3 C_j^{fix} - v_{ij}$, with C^{fix} being fixed costs of exporting associated with the bilateral relationship *ij*, with exporter *i* regardless of destination and with importer *j* regardless of origin. Error term v_{ij} is i.i.d. normally distributed. This yields the selection equation

$$\ln Z_{ij} = c + DV_j^{(Z)} + DV_i^{(Z)} - \beta_d \ln D_{ij} - \delta_1 C_{ij}^{fix} + \eta_{ij} \tag{4.21}$$

whose error term $\eta_{ij} = u_{ij} + v_{ij}$ is i.i.d. normally distributed. Equation (4.21) can be estimated as a normalized Probit to model the bilateral export decision. Its results will then modify (4.18) in two ways. First, the inverse mills ratio λ_{ij} is added as regressor to the trade flow equation. This is the aforementioned Heckman correction for sample selection that hinges on the joint normality of u_{ij} and η_{ij}, so (4.21) is typically enhanced by an extra identifying variable. Any variable that reflects fixed trade costs and thus affects the export decision but not the export volume is a candidate. Helpman et al. (2008) find common religion, common language and a self-constructed variable that reflects the regulatory costs of establishing business operations between two countries to be appropriate identifiers. Second, W_{ij} is needed as an additional correction unless one was willing to assume that error term in the flow equation is uncorrelated with a firm's decision to export and thus with the share of exporting firms. Helpman et al. (2008) propose three functional forms: a Pareto distribution $W_{ij} = \left(e^{\beta_H\left(\Phi^{-1}\left(P(Z_{ij})+\lambda_{ij}\right)\right)}\right) - 1$, a polynomial approximation of $\Phi^{-1}(P(Z_{ij}) + \lambda_{ij})$ to any distribution, and direct inclusion of the estimated export probabilities $P(Z_{ij})$. All of the variants work equally well, but the first is non-linear in parameter β_H and the third aggregates the share of exporting firms and the sample selection effect in one parameter, so the use of a polynomial indicator is very attractive and allows for OLS trade-flow estimation.

In general, the use of this model is attractive as it relates aggregate destination characteristics to the share of exporting firms without having to explicitly specify the firm productivity distribution even if this precludes the recovery of structural parameters or diagnostics of the multilateral resistances. More problematic are the standard caveats of the Heckman selection procedure in its sensitivity to the identifying variable of the selection equation, in its distributional assumptions and in the presence of heteroscedasticity, which draw the estimation results into question (Santos Silva and Tenreyro 2015).

4.1.4 Heterogeneous Consumers

Most advances in gravity modeling focus on the supply side and comparatively little research has been dedicated to the demand side. CES preferences are a tractable, homothetic utility function and Gorman-aggregatable. This can be seen from the constant elasticity of substitution that all consumers are subject to and that determines the product bundle independent of income. The resulting linear income expansion paths for all consumers allow the defining of demand as a function of aggregate income. Consumers are further assumed to be homogeneous in that they all have identical preferences. Both homogeneity and homotheticity are problematic, however, as they may not properly represent the heterogeneous consumers that are suspected to exist in medical tourism and in most other markets.

CES utility builds on a representative consumer who reflects aggregate preferences for diversity. The underlying population can be considered a group of statistically identical and independent consumers with a draw from a common probability distribution over tastes, or a continuum of consumers with a deterministic taste density function that is identical to the stochastic error distribution of the first group (Anderson et al. 1992). For the stochastic model used in economics, the error term in the utility function stems from missing information: unobservable product characteristics, individual characteristics, measurement errors and functional misspecification. Consequently, a more homogeneous population will improve a choice model (Anderson et al. 1992) and the neglect of heterogeneity will result in misspecification. The close relationship between a choice model formulation and CES demand is worked out below to highlight the problems entailed for heterogeneous consumers.

As in Anderson and van Wincoop (2003), a CES utility function with taste parameters a

$$U = \left(\sum_{i}^{I} a_i^{\frac{(1-\sigma)}{\sigma}} q_i^{\frac{(\sigma-1)}{\sigma}} \right)^{\frac{\sigma}{(\sigma-1)}}. \tag{4.22}$$

and the budget constraint

$$y = \sum_{N} p_i q_i \tag{4.23}$$

yield the expenditure shares in a CES framework

$$s_i = \frac{a_i p_i^{(1-\sigma)}}{\sum_{I} a_i p_i^{(1-\sigma)}} y. \tag{4.24}$$

Similarly, enhancing the choice model formulation in Anderson et al. (1992) by quality parameter b_i gives

$$U_i = \ln(b_i x_i) + \varepsilon_i \tag{4.25}$$

and a budget constraint of

$$y = p_i x_i \tag{4.26}$$

whose joint indirect utility function yields the following MNL formulation

$$P_i = \frac{b_i^{\left(\frac{1}{\mu}\right)} p_i^{-\left(\frac{1}{\mu}\right)}}{\sum_I b_i^{\left(\frac{1}{\mu}\right)} p_i^{-\left(\frac{1}{\mu}\right)}} \tag{4.27}$$

where μ represents the scaling parameter of the MNL model. The expression corresponds to the CES model (4.24) for $\mu = \frac{1}{(\sigma-1)}$ and $a_i = b_i^{(\sigma-1)}$, i.e. the MNL scaling parameter reflects the elasticity of substitution and the taste/quality parameters are a transformation of each other:

$$s_i = \frac{b_i^{(\sigma-1)} p_i^{(1-\sigma)}}{\sum_I b_i^{(\sigma-1)} p_i^{(1-\sigma)}} y = \frac{a_i p_i^{(1-\sigma)}}{\sum_I a_i p_i^{(1-\sigma)}} y. \tag{4.28}$$

Both the CES (4.24) and the MNL (4.28) formulation exhibit the IIA property, i.e. demand ratios of two products are independent of all the other products available. This can be alleviated by a nested specification or the use of random coefficients. Both measures are incorporated by Sheu (2014), which motivates the indexing of both taste parameters a and elasticities of substitution σ by heterogeneous consumer segments r. The nesting adds an upper tier G with substitution elasticity φ, which leads to the augmented model

$$s_i^r = \frac{a_i^r p_i^{(1-\sigma^r)}}{\left(\sum_I a_i^r p_i^{(1-\sigma^r)}\right)^{\frac{\varphi^r-\sigma^r}{1-\sigma^r}} \sum_G \left(\sum_I a_i^r p_i^{(1-\sigma^r)}\right)^{\frac{1-\varphi^r}{1-\sigma^r}}} y^r. \tag{4.29}$$

This construct only collapses to the MNL/CES model for identical a^r, σ^r and φ^r across all consumer segments. The use of random coefficients alone would alter Eq. (4.27) to estimate P_{ki} for individuals k and require the integrating out of the random component in b_i^k given by $X_i(\tilde{\beta} + v_k)$ with fixed parameter vector $\tilde{\beta}$ and random parameter vector $v_k \sim N(0, VCV_{\tilde{\beta}})$ to consequently obtain product and expenditure shares. For discrete segments r as in Sheu (2014), total expenditure shares s_i of product i are represented by

$$s_i = \sum_R y^r s_i^r \tag{4.30}$$

where y^r reflects expenditures by segment r. Note the similarity between (4.6), (4.24), (4.28) and (4.29). Equation (4.6) reflects expenditure shares of country j's total income y_j to spend on I products from single-product countries and Eqs. (4.24) and (4.28) refer to any representative consumer with a total budget y to spend on I products. Trade separability is achieved by assuming income/expenditures to be exogenous in a given tier. Equation (4.29), on the other hand, defines segment-dependent expenditure shares, which preclude the simplification of expenditure shares across all consumers due to segment-specific para-meters. These parameters operate at several levels: First, they may influence tastes for product characteristics a_i^r. Second, they may influence the amount of income y^r that is allocated to expenditures on products I nested in G which varies for different φ^r. Third, they weigh total expenditure shares by segment expenditures y^r as in Eq. (4.30). Heterogeneous consumers thus cause multi-stage budgeting to collapse unless segments are considered separately.

The exposition serves to highlight the roles of consumer heterogeneity and income for a CES consumer as varying expenditure shares or preference parameters across consumers render choice probabilities, market shares and thus conclusions drawn from the simple CES formulation invalid. CES only holds if U_i in Eq. (4.25) is homothetic, of log-linear form, and if choice probabilities in (4.27) are independent of income (Anderson et al. 1992). Augmenting (4.25) by segment-specific characteristics b_i^r, by individual characteristics via random coefficients b_i^k or by fixed interaction terms b_{ki} breaks the CES model and there is no reason to assume that demographics or income would not affect choice probabilities or budget allocations.

This finding is confirmed by the literature on industrial organization. Berry et al. (1995) acknowledge the need to integrate out the distribution of individual characteristics of their choice function that is linear in price and taste parameters but includes random coefficients. They define the distribution of individual characteristics to be the random component v_k of b_j^k which yields

$$U_i^k = b_i^k - p_i + \epsilon_i + \varepsilon_{ki} \tag{4.31}$$

with $b_i^k = X_i\beta_k$, $\beta_k = Z_k\vartheta + v_k$ and ϵ_j as an error that reflects unobserved product heterogeneity of product i. Our formulation generalizes Berry et al. (1995) as their set of Z_i only includes a constant which collapses b_i^k to $X_i(\vartheta + v_k)$. If available, Z_k may hold individual cha-racteristics to define multiple fixed and random parameters or, alternatively, it can accommodate aggregate information on individual characteristics' distributions (Petrin 2002).

If homogeneity of consumers with regard to their characteristics matters for a CES consumer's ability to capture the population and these characteristics differ between countries, then defining identical CES consumers across countries is problematic. Engel (2002) surmises different CES between domestic and international products and Sun 2011 finds evidence for varying substitution patterns, i.e. elasticities, for different income groups by simply interacting quality parameters with income brackets in a choice model. Gohin and Féménia (2009) employ an almost ideal demand system to find evidence against symmetric and some evidence against homothetic CES preferences. Dalgin et al. (2004) also cast doubts on non-homothetic preferences. Head and Mayer (2013) consider within-country consumer heterogeneity in a gravity context but they require an identical heterogeneity distribution across countries.

In summary, preferences are likely to differ among consumer segments both within and between countries. This heterogeneity in preferences is not properly aggregated in the standard CES formulation and may further depend on individual characteristics such as demographics and income levels. The use of identical CES preferences across countries is convenient, however, as it delegates the explanation of trade flows only to the differences in relative consumer prices—and firm structure if heterogeneous firms are considered. In this context, variables enter as trade-cost barriers that alter consumer prices and the variation in trade flows can thus be traced to components of the price term. The major difficulty in implementing domestic and cross-border heterogeneity of consumers lies in identifying trade barriers and in separating the effect from the variation in demand. For Anderson and van Wincoop (2003), this problem arises in Eq. (4.7) which will not simplify Eq. (4.6) if α_i or σ become destination-specific. Finally, note that the heterogeneity discussed here concerns consumers and not products so it can only partly be addressed by further product disaggregation and would then rest on the assumption of increasing consumer homogeneity in more disaggregated product groups.

4.1.5 Heterogeneous Products

French 2011 points to a noteworthy consequence of multilateral resistance that is related to the assumption of trade separability. As noted before, trade separability assumes that domestic production and expenditure decisions are made independently from trade flow decisions. Consequently, price changes of products affect the consumer's allocation within a sector, i.e. the product variety, but not the overall budget allocation to that sector. This assumption allows a stable general market equilibrium and the independent identification of trade costs. For trade separability to work, trade must further be proportional to production costs (Anderson 2011), which iceberg costs clearly are. A different formulation of increasing marginal trade costs, for example, would not be permissible in this context. With trade separability in effect, we can think of the world as one market with fixed production and expenditure shares to which firms export and from which consumers buy. Outward and inward multilateral resistance for a country can then be interpreted as the average trade costs borne when exporting to and average trade costs borne when importing from the world market. Total trade costs are the sum of both exporter *i*'s and importer *j*'s costs.

French 2011 argues that outward resistance, the average trade cost faced when exporting to one world market as a result of trade separability, may vary by a country's output composition. The intuition is that poor, low-exporting countries share common products with a large number of other countries, which leads to exceedingly high estimates of multilateral resistance and thus a misspecified model if output composition is neglected. More explicitly, French shows that poor countries produce products in the same sectors and face heavy competition from other poor countries when exporting. This observation is in line with observable, lower-than-predicted trade of poor countries. Lower trade costs, however, would lead to small gains from trade for low-income countries as they compete within a large pool of other low-income countries that attempt to export similar products. French calculates (and to a large extent imputes) a gravity model at the product level, which suggests that disaggregation is advisable in order to avoid aggregation bias that stems from the pooling of sectors populated by countries with very different industry structures.

Other work by Anderson and Yotov (2010) and by Head and Mayer (2010), who identify product transportability as essential in the estimation of border effects, confirms the appropriateness of sectoral disaggregation. Belenkiy (2008) finds a similar effect in models with firm heterogeneity. He confirms the presence of a selection and firm heterogeneity bias developed in Helpman et al. (2008) but finds different effects for Northern and Southern exporters. The selection effect dominates for southern exporters presumably due to their product homogeneity whereas firm heterogeneity dominates for northern exporters with their presumably heterogeneous products.

4.1.6 Measures of Distance

Trade costs in Eq. (4.12) are the place to insert and test geographic distance as well as other potentially trade cost-invoking or trade cost-dampening factors. The empirical specifications used to estimate distance and other trade-cost related measures are discussed by Bosker and Garretsen (2010) who essentially find exponential and power function specifications of distance to be the most common. They further note a general neglect of country-specific parameters in the estimation of trade cost variables. The estimation of country-specific effects of borders or other impediments would require a time dimension, however, unless one was willing to give up sectoral disaggregation.

Most studies rely on geographic distance and various proxies to indicate borders. As Van Bergeijk and Brakman (2010) point out, there are few studies using actual trading cost data but their results suggest geographic distance to be a potentially inadequate measure. This conclusion is the more discomforting as a meta-study by Disdier and Head (2008) shows that empirical studies find increasingly dispersed and rising effects of distance towards the end of the twentieth century. Head and Mayer (2010) analyze the various measures of distance used such as neighboring countries, areas, and shape and population distributions. They find that overestimated internal distance leads to a substantial upward bias of border effects and suggest a new measure that essentially calls for the disaggregation of economic entities into sub-national, economic centers. The measurement of distances between such centers allows a more sophisticated averaging of distances at the aggregated level. In particular, Head and Mayer (2010) suggest the use of a generalized mean—the mathematical equivalent of a CES formulation—which deemphasizes distances within economic units and indirectly lowers the explanatory power of borders as the strengthened, inverse relationship between distance and trade now absorbs part of the previous border effect.

Numerous other trade cost factors have been suggested and tested: Common candidates are measures of cultural proximity (Felbermayr and Toubal 2010) or membership in a common currency area (Rose et al. 2000). The example of a currency union is very instructive as it demonstrates the effect of misspecification without multilateral resistance. In fact, the reformulation of Rose et al. (2000) in Rose (2001) rendered membership in a currency union insignificant. Cultural differences may also constitute trade barriers as they increase costs of contract enforcement and information (Anderson and van Wincoop 2004). Common language is a commonly used yet crude dummy indicator to indicate communication barriers (Melitz 2003). Melitz and Toubal (2014) refine the concept of linguistic distance by distinguishing between common native language, common spoken language, common official language and linguistic proximity. They show that a common language dummy is too crude a measure, especially for a sector with highly differentiated products. The various combinations of common native language, common spoken language, common official language and linguistic proximity give rise to interpretations of individual measures beyond the ease of communication such as trust, institutionalized support of translation or availability of translators.

In his seminal paper, Rauch (1999) suspects search costs to be a main contributor to the, by then, still poorly understood border effect and investigates the role of networks by approximating them via colonial ties and common languages between trading partners. He found such networks to have a lower impact in sectors with homogeneous products or organized markets than in markets for highly differentiated products. Möhlmann et al. (2010) extend Rauch's analysis by adding an index of Hofstede's dimensions as a proxy of cultural proximity and an index of various governance indicators as a proxy of institutional proximity. Both cultural proximity and cultural barriers are expected to lower information and contract enforcement costs, but it turns out that with a Tobit specification and the inclusion of multilateral resistance, the impact of cultural and institutional proximity is more pronounced for homogeneous goods and less so for heterogeneous goods. The offered explanation suggests that the effect of cultural and institutional distance is dominated by a more negative effect on FDI. The absence of FDI leads to more imports, and more so for heterogeneous products, which can hardly be substituted. For homogeneous products, both FDI and imports cease. Once more, however, this effect appears to be an artifact of product aggregation as total trade flows are dominated by one sector in the data set. Several disaggregated sectors do in fact display the impact of cultural and of institutional distance with the expected negative sign.

Two other channels of cultural proximity that affect trade barriers are suggested by Afman and Maurel (2010) as well as Gould (1994) and Head and Ries (1998). Afman and Maurel (2010) find that official diplomatic and political ties affect trade volumes with transition economies. Gould (1994) and Head and Ries (1998) find that unofficial ambassadors, i.e. the share of migrants, increase both exports and imports with their country of origin. The import elasticity exceeds the export elasticity, however, as the former reflects a network and taste effect while the latter mirrors only networks. Over time, the magnitude of networks' trade enhancing-effect would be expected to decrease as informational barriers are overcome by technology and as international institutions ensure contract enforcement (Rauch 2001). Dunlevy (2006) finds that the effect on trade of migrant stock in a host country is magnified by corruption in the source country. Presumably, networks in corrupt countries are more valuable but the effect is offset by a common language between trading partners. Duanmu and Guney (2013) confirm the positive effect of ethnic networks on trade in their literature review and further refine the effect with regards to the composition of a society. Whereas a culture of strong family ties reinforces the trade-inducing effect of ethnic networks, ethnic diversity lowers it, i.e. ethnic diversity increases the general exposure to and familiarity with diverse products, which reduces transaction costs and the reliance on networks.

4.1.7 Summary

In summary, the theoretical foundations and empirical formulations of the gravity equation still prove challenging even if its main ingredients in country sizes as capacities to supply and demand, distance as transportation costs and multilateral resistance terms as indicators of trade impediments may all be immediately plausible. Much research remains to address the shortcomings of workhorse models such as Anderson and van Wincoop (2003) that are not always seen fit to plausibly explain real data (Balistreri and Hillberry 2006) or that rarely address issues such as volume-varying trade cost elasticities that can explain disproportionate effects of trade barrier removal (Novy 2013).

Recent advances that build on Anderson and van Wincoop (2003) typically rely on the decomposition of existing measures at more disaggregated levels (consumers, firm structure, products, or product characteristics) and on new measures of distance (geographic, cultural and institutional proximity). Such advances sometimes imply modified functional forms and naturally require disaggregated data to bear out their suspected effects. Underlying theories and the structural features they introduced have driven and advanced empirical gravity formulations, yet innovations are usually added to very basic model formulations that neglect advances made on other fronts and are thus justified in an often isolated and outdated setting. Arkolakis et al. (2012) generalize a class of theoretical gravity frameworks that are based on a number of common, underlying assumptions such as trade balance and CES demand. However, there exists no thorough meta-analysis or study that surveys or tests the joint effects of single innovations or even a unifying model. Our goal cannot be the investigation or design of such a model in this context. Instead, we will settle for a model that makes plausible assumptions in a medical travel context and add all extensions suitable to our research focus on cultural proximity and recommendations.

In terms of the gravity framework's general suitability in a medical travel context, its components are very plausible and many of the explanatory variables identified in chapters 2 and 3 reemerged in the literature on gravity modeling. These include economic masses as measures of availability and demand, distance and its various aspects as trade barriers and substitutability as a measure of product heterogeneity. The concept of monopolistic competition as the standard setting of intra-industry trade is further in line with the previously identified multi-directional trade flows.

Trade separability is a strong assumption that translates into expenditures on and production of health care being independent from the subsequent selection of a domestic or foreign provider. It is a reasonable assumption for expenditures if treatments are necessities, i.e. life-saving. This appears to hold for trips with a strong medical focus as those to German hospitals but it may be different for cosmetic treatments. Here, two-stage budgeting probably fails due to diminishing income elasticity. In the case of Germany, production capacity can reasonably be considered exogenous as it is overwhelmingly determined by public capacity planning and public funding in the hospital sector.

CES preferences were demonstrated to be overly simplistic. Keckley and Eselius (2009) suggest that medical travel preferences are heterogeneous within countries but homogeneous preferences for different product varieties within a country are still an innocuous assumption compared to the heroic assumption of homogenous preferences across countries. A common consumer structure across countries is thus a concession to allow the identification of trade barriers but we will attempt to augment it with bilateral preferences.

Various decision-making processes have been proposed for medical tourists (Hanefeld et al. 2015; Heung et al. 2010; Johnston et al. 2012; Klingenberger 2009; Veerasoontorn and Beise-Zee 2010) but the theoretical derivation of the gravity model implies a one-stage decision between consolidated destination alternatives. To operate within theory, we assume a process that is shaped by two different types of information and that allows us to work with a one-stage economic choice: In the presence of a treatment need, an individual consideration set is established, which may include domestic and international destinations. Knowledge about international destinations stems from incidental exposure to marketing activities or personal networks. Jotikasthira (2010) terms this exposure induced and organic, respectively. Patients evaluate their consideration set and attempt to select a utility-maximizing destination based on destination characteristics whose perception is shaped by individual characteristics. Potentially, no acceptable destination can be extracted from the consideration set. This may be due to non-compensatory shortcomings such as waiting lists, compensatory characteristics whose combinations fall short of a value reference point, or infeasibility, i.e. any destinations whose characteristics bundles overcome non-compensatory and value thresholds but violate the budget constraint. If the initial consideration set contains no satisfactory option, individuals will attempt to extend it autonomously. Autonomously researched destinations are met by more distrust while organically recommended destinations are assigned extra utility (Jotikasthira 2010). The expanded consideration set is finally evaluated and a choice will have to be made if the treatment is considered a necessity. Medical tourism is no necessary outcome of the information process: If the final consideration set is entirely domestic and offers an acceptable alternative, then no medical tourism will occur. The expansion of the consideration set can further lead to a reduction in medical tourism if a domestic alternative is established or discovered that is superior to all previously known domestic and international alternatives. This decision-making process serves as a working hypothesis that we will revisit after our empirical investigations in chapter 7.

Another important issue raised in chapter 3 is that of product aggregation, i.e. which level of disaggregation yields homogeneous medical services and homogenous with respect to which criteria. The disaggregation of medical travel flows into treatment groups turns out to be difficult as no expenditures on treatment categories are known, e.g. expenditures on planned procedures. At the same time, the use of aggregate spending on health care or a proxy thereof assumes a time-invariant composition of these expenditures. On the other hand, an aggregated health care sector further assumes available substitutes at all other destinations even if a particular treatment is not offered. This may be less problematic at the national level we investigate but may be a problematic assumption at a more disaggregated level of supply. Finally, a broad set of distance measures has been tested in the gravity framework and there is precedent to modeling information networks via cultural proximity. We expect a particularly pronounced effect of cultural proximity measures in the service trade that is medical travel and will now turn to developing our specification.

4.2 Specification

We follow the idea of Helpman et al. (2008) and Guo (2015) in that a specific bilateral parameter aside from bilateral variable costs characterizes the relationship between two trading partners. The modeling of this parameter often occurs on the supply side where exports are the empirically observed outcome of firm productivity as exporters need to overcome fixed costs of exporting (Helpman et al. 2008) which may be reduced by the presence of exporter networks (Krautheim 2007). We do not follow this approach for two reasons: First, we cannot estimate separate importer and export effects, which are a main feature of these models. Only a bilateral fixed term is identified for the unidirectional trade flows we observe. Second and more importantly, overwhelming anecdotal evidence of the role of word-of-mouth in chapter 2 suggests that medical tourism literature is dominated by consumer search rather than producer outreach. It appears more plausible that information about medical travel options is passed on voluntarily in organic information networks (Jotikasthira 2010). Guo (2015) implements such country-specific consumer heterogeneity, i.e. country-specific preferences for exporters, in the framework of Fitzgerald (2012) but we shall motivate it in the context of Anderson and van Wincoop (2003).

Augmenting Eq. (4.3) by source country-specific preferences a_{ji} of importing country j for exporting country i

$$U_j = \left(\sum_i^N \alpha_{ji}^{\frac{(1-\sigma)}{\sigma}} q_{ij}^{\frac{(\sigma-1)}{\sigma}} \right)^{\frac{\sigma}{(\sigma-1)}} \tag{4.32}$$

the country-pair specific preferences carry through to Eq. (4.8)

$$x_{ij} = \frac{(y_i y_j)}{y_w} \left(\frac{a_{ji} \tau_{ij}}{P_j P_i} \right)^{1-\sigma} \tag{4.33}$$

with multilateral resistances

$$(P_i)^{1-\sigma} = \sum_j \left(\frac{a_{ji} \tau_{ij}}{P_j} \right)^{1-\sigma} \frac{y_j}{y^w} \tag{4.34}$$

$$(P_j)^{1-\sigma} = \sum_i \left(\frac{a_{ji} \tau_{ij}}{P_i} \right)^{1-\sigma} \frac{y_i}{y^w}. \tag{4.35}$$

Consequently, the negative impact of trade barriers may be partly offset by bilateral preferences, and both jointly determine multilateral resistances, i.e. multilateral resistances control for relative prices and preference relationships with all other trading partners.

We estimate Eq. (4.33) as:

$$\ln x_{ij} = -\beta_0 \ln Y_w + \beta_1 \ln y_i + \beta_2 \ln y_j + \beta_3 \ln a_{ji} + \beta_4 \ln \tau_{ij} - \beta_5 \ln P_i - \beta_6 \ln P_j. \tag{4.36}$$

As discussed in chapter 3, there exists no data set to analyze $N(N - 1)T$ multilateral tourism flows over time and it is thus infeasible to estimate a multi-country gravity model. A single country gravity model offers $(2N - 1)T$ observations for imports and exports, respectively, but our data set reports exclusively exports. Despite this limitation, we need to account for trade partner-specific resistances as a crucial ingredient to the unbiased estimation of trade barriers.

The exporter is always Germany so outward resistance is absorbed by the constant. Importer dummies across different source countries cannot be identified with one trade partner in a cross-section but country-pair dummies are identified in a panel setting and correspond to a fixed-effect estimator. Country-pair fixed effect effectively estimate an averaged, time-invariant bilateral resistance between Germany G and its respective trading partners C as depicted in Fig. 4.2. They represent a second-best solution after both time-varying country dummies and time-invariant bilateral dummies as recommended by Baldwin and Taglioni (2007). The first-best solution would fully capture the evolution of both multilateral resistances and unobserved bilateral barriers over time. In a unidirectional context, such evolution is restricted to the identification of year dummies that capture the general economic climate, price trends (Baldwin and Taglioni 2007), ongoing economic integration (Berger and Nitsch 2008), and geopolitical events that may impede aggregate medical tourism flows. They also capture changes in average, unobserved preferences for treatments in Germany across all source countries. Another convenient side effect of year dummies is their control for y_w which is constant within but not across years.

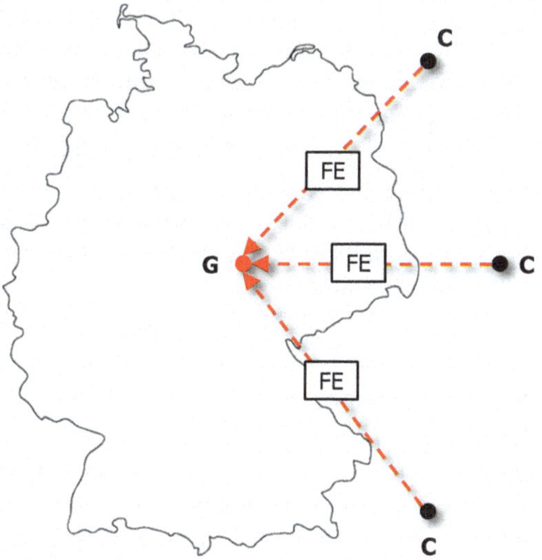

Fig. 4.2 Multilateral resistance: exports—one source—many destinations

Collecting destination-specific characteristics in constant k; setting trade costs $\tau_{ij}^{t} = D^{\gamma} e^{X_{ij}^{t} \beta}$ with D being distance and X_{ij} capturing other bilateral trade barriers; accounting for the panel structure of the data by adding superscripts for periods t; and adding year dummies λ^{t}; we obtain the following formulation for German exports—with some abuse of notation as the betas now reflect a different set of parameters:

$$\ln x_{ij}^{t} = k + \beta_1 \ln Y_j^{t} + \beta_2 \ln a_{ji}^{t} + \beta_3 \ln D_{ij}^{t} + \beta_4 X_{ij}^{t} + FE_{ij} + \lambda^{t}. \tag{4.37}$$

Aside from the unidirectional structure necessitated by our data set, our specification is very similar to (4.12). The key innovation is the bilateral taste parameter a_{ji}^{t}, which—in our setting—would collapse with the year dummy if it were identical for all bilateral relationships or collapse with the constant if it were further constant over time. Based on our discussion of recommendations in chapter 2, we argue that this taste parameter is determined by recommendations from personal networks, which alter tastes rather than costs of distance.

In the gravity framework, information is typically captured by trade costs in their broadest sense, which are defined to "include all costs incurred in getting a good to the final user other than the marginal cost of producing the good itself: transportation costs (both freight costs and time costs), policy barriers (tariffs and nontariff barriers), information costs, contract enforcement costs, costs associated with the use of different currencies, legal and regulatory costs, and local distribution costs (wholesale and retail)" (Anderson and van Wincoop 2004). The measures of distance discussed above have been cast as trade costs as they reduce costs either directly for, e.g. translation or indirectly by creating trust and then requiring, e.g. less legal counseling. We argue that organic information, i.e. recommendations, alter tastes whereas the impact of autonomous and induced information is limited to the reduction of information costs and does little to change preferences (Jotikasthira 2010). Such preferences at the country level can be considered country-of-origin effects that capture reputations and convictions rather than objective destination characteristics. We identify recommendations from organic information sources by means of lagged patient flows. As discussed in chapter 2, there is some evidence for overwhelmingly positive experiences of returning patients and we suspect their recommendations to be a main driver of future patient flows by shaping preferences in the source countries.

From Eq. (4.37) it is clear, that average unobserved bilateral tastes a_{ji}^t are captured by the multilateral resistance term. Similarly to bilateral trade costs, we parameterize bilateral preferences $a_{ji}^t = e^{\vartheta q_{ij}^{t-1}}$, i.e. they are a function of lagged trade flows. Note that a smaller a_{ji} in Eq. (4.32) corresponds to a higher preference for i and thus results in higher trade flows for $\sigma > 1$ in Eq. (4.33). As our data set comprises only 6 years, we have to restrict the analysis to one lag and assume that reputation decay is identical across source countries and captured by λ^t.

For estimation purposes, we reformulate Eq. (4.37) in terms of patients as opposed to trade volume. Trade volume in Eq. (4.33) is defined as $x_{ij} = q_{ij}p_i\tau_{ij}$ which modifies Eq. (4.37) to

$$\ln q_{ij}^t = k + \delta q_{ij}^{t-1} + \beta_1 \ln Y_j^t + \beta_2 \ln D_{ij}^t + \beta_3 X_{ij}^t + FE_{ij} + \lambda^t. \qquad (4.38)$$

With $\delta = (1 - \sigma)\vartheta$, $\beta_2 = -\sigma\gamma$ and $\beta_3 = -\sigma\beta$. Domestic treatment price p_i^t is absorbed by λ^t and we can reasonably assume it to be exogenous as it is largely regulated by German fee schedules. International patients may face additional expenditures for interpreters, for example, but they are related to trade costs τ_{ij}.

Equation (4.38) is a dynamic specification that implies state dependence in medical travel. We motivate this state dependence by recommendations from sources of organic information, which induce changes in tastes for products from various countries. These changes take effect in the following year, which is an appropriate assumption of a decision timeframe for elective treatments of non-trivial medical conditions that our definition of medical travel required.

In addition to the state-dependence term, specification (4.38) includes an economic mass variable Y_j^t of the source country, measures of bilateral distance D_{ij}^t and other bilateral trade barriers X_{ij}^t. Following Anderson and van Wincoop (2004), a sectoral budget is the economic mass variable of choice which suggests total health expenditures as a natural measure in our context. However, we prefer to use GDP as a measure of demand capacity that is highly correlated with total health expenditures in our data set ($\rho = 0.9681$). Our worry is that health care expenditures, when made out-of-pocket abroad or via institutionalized relations, may not be recorded properly so we opt for the broader measure that is GDP. Both GDP and health care expenditures yield very similar results and are exogenous by the assumption of two-stage budgeting. Following Dalgin et al. (2004), we also include population that controls for the per capita dilution of demand capacity and thus challenges homothetic demand. Unfortunately, we cannot include the GINI coefficient to investigate income distribution in more detail. We merged data from a number of sources but there is not nearly enough data available to cover a large enough share of countries in our sample.

We suspect a substantial impact of the domestic health expenditure structure on the propensity to seek treatment abroad and include the share of public health care expenditures as a control variable for the flexibility to allocate expenditures abroad. We expect the share of public health care expenditures to have a negative effect on treatment flows to Germany. The share of public health care expenditures depends on private and, a subgroup thereof, out-of-pocket expenditures. Note that the latter are exogenous by the assumption of two-stage budgeting, i.e. expenditures do not occur because the possibility of medical travel to Germany is discovered. These expenditures would have occurred elsewhere. This assumption is reasonable in the light of our medical travel definition, which includes possibly lifesaving inpatient treatments that patients will fund regardless of destination.

We include another measure to capture the demand propensity in infant mortality. It serves to approximate the quality of health care in a source country and can be assumed to be exogenous—as opposed to the more common measure of life expectancy which is likely to be endogenous to medical travel. Crone (2008) describes medical travel a result of wealth-related diseases and increased life expectancy, which suggests that countries with better health care generate more demand for medical travel. An alternative hypothesis is that countries with lower life expectancy and thus higher infant mortality push patients to seek care abroad.

In addition to geographic distance and shared border as measures of bilateral distance, we include established measures of cultural ties including common legislation, common religion, common spoken language and common native language provided by Melitz and Toubal (2014). We further add internet penetration as a measure of an information channel that conveys both autonomous and induced information in that it enables individuals to both autonomously search treatment destinations abroad and to be exposed to internet-based marketing. We further include source country-specific migrant stock in Germany. This group can engage in both private and commercial activities and provide both organic and induced information to patients in their home countries. Unfortunately, we cannot disentangle this effect. Migrant stock abroad also lends itself to being included as it may play the same role as immigrants and additionally constitute its own source of demand. The problem with emigrant stock is the poor data it is based on: The most comprehensive source of data is the UN International Migration Stock Database, which lists migration stock by source and destination countries. However, it does not cover a substantial number of source countries in our sample and is available only with 5-year gaps. The World Bank's Global Bilateral Migration Database provides migration stock up to the year 2000 and covers, for example, the Middle East, which is missing in the UN data. However, migrant stock in the year 2000 may be a poor approximation of migrant stock in the years 2007–2012 and a comparison of both data sources for the year 2000 reveals substantial discrepancies for German emigrants. Due to the incompatibilities between existing data sources and to avoid selection bias that the use of the UN data set with its 51 missing source countries would introduce, we are forced to forgo the explicit analysis of emigrants.

4.3 Data

This section provides descriptions and sources of the data used in the analysis. All data are aggregated at the country level.

Total medical tourism exports of inpatient treatments are taken from the official hospital statistics in Germany for the years 2007–2012 (RDC 2007–2012). 2012 was the most recent year available as we registered for the use of this data set. It provides the best measure of international inpatients in Germany and records a patient's place of residence. Patients who indicate a domestic address of an agent or a relative can corrupt this statistic, but our interviews with German providers in chapter 6 suggest no such systematic behavior and providers typically require passport copies. Unidirectional flows to Germany limit the analysis of trade barriers to exporting but this is not very restrictive as presumably asymmetric trade barriers would imply a separate estimation of imports and exports even if imports were available.

As every other data set, ours suffers from some imperfections. First, the balanced panel structure of the data is partly destructed by the Statistical Office for the purpose of privacy protection, i.e. they censor annual treatment counts below a certain threshold. In our data set, 121 countries retain their balanced panel structure; 14 countries have reported treatment totals between 10 and 45 across all periods with 2–4 years censored; 13 countries have reported treatments totals between 11 and 21 across all periods with all 6 years censored; and 15 countries have censored treatment totals across all periods and all 6 years individually censored. To avoid selection bias, we impute countries with available row totals by calculating the difference between calculated row sums and given row sums and by assigning random summands of that difference randomly to the missing row cells. Annual treatments for the 15 countries without available row sums were set to zero, which not all of them were but which is a reasonable assumption for most years given that even the row sums were too small to be reported. The resulting data set contains 90 out of 968 zero observations, which corresponds to 9.3%. The distribution of treatment counts per country is depicted in Fig. 4.3 and the summary statistics are presented in Table 4.1.

Second, our analysis considers country clusters that are determined by treatment composition. For privacy reasons, complete treatment compositions are available for only 92 countries, which correspond to 544 observations. As clustering countries with treatment composition vectors of different lengths is misleading, we conduct cluster-related analyses on the reduced sample depicted in Fig. 4.3. The summary statistics of our cluster solution are included in Table 4.1.

Third, our definition of medical tourism in chapter 2 and the discussion in the previous section requires us to enforce a number of requirements: Our data set identifies patients by place of residence as opposed to nationality, which ensures a

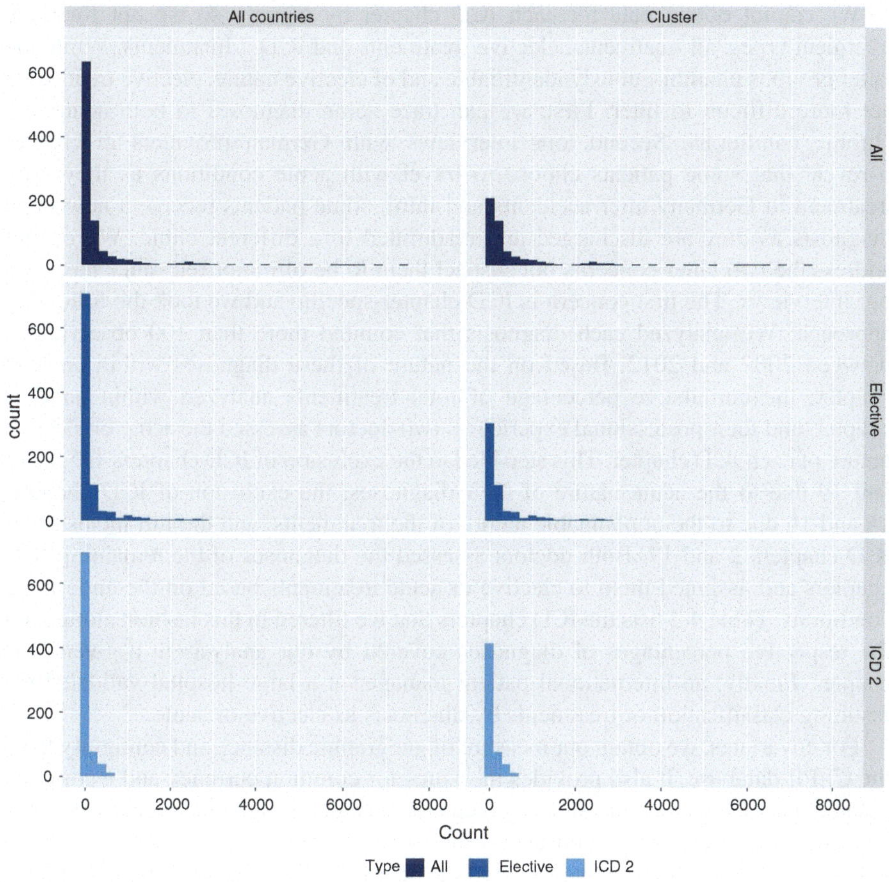

Fig. 4.3 Distribution of treatment counts, by country and type

Table 4.1 Summary statistics of inpatient flows

Countries	Treatments	Observations	Mean	SD
All	All	968	437.20	1171.61
	Electives	944	188.64	498.91
	ICD 2	824	69.61	187.43
Cluster solution	All	544	773.42	1478.48
	Electives	544	325.34	622.96
	ICD 2	544	104.89	222.65

temporary time horizon of travelers. We further limit our analysis to inpatient treatments, which, we argue, implies a treatment focus based on a serious medical condition. To ensure the elective character of a treatment and to remove incidental treatments of acute conditions that may afflict international visitors, we can further filter our data by 4-digit ICD-10-encoded main diagnoses.

We cannot obtain data for each ICD chapter by country so we opt for three treatment types: all treatments, elective treatments and ICD 2 treatments. While the latter group is unambi-guously identifiable and of elective nature, elective treatments are more difficult to filter. First, we can trace some diagnoses to both acute and chronic conditions. Second, our interviews with German providers in chapter 6 reveal that some patients choose to travel with acute conditions as they seek treatment in Germany after accidents and third, some patients receive a new main diagnosis as they are discharged and readmitted to a different clinic. We cannot address the two latter concerns but suspect them to be of minor relevance based on our interviews. The first concern is ICD chapter-specific and we took the following approach: We analyzed each diagnosis that counted more than 100 observations between 2007 and 2012. Based on the nature of these diagnoses within an ICD chapter, the cumulative percentage of total treatments analyzed within an ICD chapter, and their professional experience, two doctors assessed the acute or elective nature of each ICD chapter. This step lead to the exclusion of ICD chapters 1, 5, 8, 18 and 19 due to the acute nature of their diagnoses, the exclusion of ICD chapters 15 and 16 due to the unplannable nature of the treatments, and the full inclusion of ICD chapters 2 and 17. Both doctors assessed the diagnoses of the remaining ICD chapters and assigned them to elective or acute treatments based on the underlying conditions. Table 4.2 lists the ICD chapters that we filtered in this fashion along with the respective percentages of diagnoses covered by our analysis in a given ICD chapter. Finally, an international patient manager at a large hospital validated the resulting classification of treatments by diagnosis as elective or acute.

For covariates, we obtain our measure of geographic distance and contiguity from the CEPII database. It also provides measures for common currency and a common colonial past which we removed as a common currency is potentially endogenous—countries that trade more with each other tend to join a union—and a common colonial past is only driven by Poland in the data set, which renders it unidentifiable.

Table 4.2 Percentage of diagnoses included, by ICD chapter

ICD chapter	Percentage of diagnoses included
2	24
3	44
4	73
6	76
7	69
9	89
10	80
11	65
12	65
13	81
14	79
17	44
21	85

Nominal GDP in US$, population, share of public health care expenditures of total health care expenditures in percent and infant mortality as the number of infants dying before reaching 1 year of age, per 1000 live births in a given year, are taken from the World Development Indicators. Internet penetration as the percentage of internet users is based on data from the International Telecommunications Union.

Measures of linguistic proximity as well as common religion and common legal systems are taken from Melitz and Toubal (2014). Common official language is dummy coded, common spoken language and common native language are the probabilities of two speakers meeting and understanding each other or having the same native language, respectively. The data set of Melitz and Toubal (2014) contains a BLX construct that comprises both Belgium and Luxemburg. As both countries are important trading partners and bordering countries for Germany, we split the construct and to duplicate common language and religion measures for both countries.

Our data on annual migrant stock in Germany is from the GENESIS database 12,521–0002 published by the Federal Statistical Office of Germany and reports residents without German citizenship by nationality. A methodological issue arises from the lack of updating migrant stocks to changes in source countries: While the borders of most countries remain stable over time, changes occur to both Sudan and the former Yugoslavia in the observed 2007–2012 period. Upon consultation with the Federal Statistical Office, there exists no possibility to disentangle migrant stocks for Sudan/South Sudan and Serbia/Montenegro/Kosovo for the years prior to their transformations so we drop these countries from the analysis.

Table 4.3 and Table 4.4 summarize our data.

Table 4.3 Variable summary for the gravity model at the national level

Variable	Coding	Source
Treatments	Treatment count	German hospital statistics
Geographic distance	ln(Distance)	CEPII
Common border	0/1	CEPII
Common native language	0-1	Melitz and Toubal (2014)
Common spoken language	0-1	Melitz and Toubal (2014)
Common legal system	0/1	Melitz and Toubal (2014)
Common religion	0-1	Melitz and Toubal (2014)
EU membership	0/1	–
GDP	ln(GDP/1,000,000)	WDI
Migrant stock	ln(Migrants)	DESTATIS
Internet penetration	0-1	ITU
Public health expenditure share of total health expenditures	0-1	WDI
Population	ln(Pop/1000,000)	WDI
Infant mortality	0-1000	WDI

Table 4.4 Correlation matrix for the gravity model at the national level

	Dist	Border	CNL	CSL	CLeg	CRel	EU	GDP	MigStock	IntPen	Pop	InfMort
Dist	1.00											
Border	−0.60	1.00										
CNL	−0.24	0.45	1.00									
CSL	−0.50	0.49	0.35	1.00								
CLeg	−0.38	0.27	0.13	0.09	1.00							
CRel	0.03	0.20	0.08	0.35	0.22	1.00						
EU	−0.72	0.48	0.13	0.57	0.36	0.21	1.00					
GDP	−0.32	0.26	0.13	0.16	0.25	−0.01	0.32	1.00				
MigStock	−0.55	0.27	0.16	0.11	0.38	−0.16	0.40	0.73	1.00			
IntPen	−0.52	0.40	0.18	0.65	0.27	0.20	0.55	0.52	0.33	1.00		
Pop	−0.04	0.03	0.01	−0.29	0.09	−0.19	−0.01	0.74	0.66	−0.09	1.00	
InfMort	0.32	−0.22	−0.11	−0.41	−0.31	−0.17	−0.38	−0.42	−0.26	−0.73	0.14	1.00

4.4 Estimation

To estimate Eq. (4.38), we need to address a variety of estimation issues: excess zeros, unobserved heterogeneity, overdispersion, dynamics, non-stationarity and cross-country correlation. We will discuss them in turn.

Zero trade flows are a common feature of trade flow data and were commonly addressed by omission due to the infeasible logarithmic transformation of zeros. Count data models are an obvious option to represent non-negative observations with a large probability mass at zero. Santos Silva and Tenreyro (2006) propose a Poisson Pseudo-ML estimator primarily to deal with heteroscedastic error terms that are introduced by the log-transformation of (4.8) which turns out to perform well even in the presence of excess zeros (Santos Silva and Tenreyro 2011) and to be more robust to misspecification than a Heckman selection model (Helpman et al. 2008). For this reason we employ a Poisson Panel model with fixed effects as our benchmark model. The Poisson Pseudo-ML with country dummies yields the same consistent results, does not suffer from incidental parameter bias (Nickell 1981) and does not require Poisson distributed data. However, the large number of dummies, our lack of interest therein specifically, and the availability of only unidirectional trade flow data lead us to employ a standard conditional likelihood Poisson panel estimator to account for fixed effects. This is also the estimator that Baldwin and Taglioni (2007) suggest as a second-best solution for multilateral trade flow data. We forgo the investigation of zero-inflated and other two-stage models as there is no theoretical foundation to hypothesize multiple data-generating processes at this point.

Our benchmark FE estimator with clustered standard errors is appropriate to control for multilateral resistance and other forms of unobserved heterogeneity and robust to misspecification (Cameron and Trivedi 2009) but it rules out time-invariant variables in which we are also interested. RE specifications allow the inclusion of time-invariant variables but they assume zero correlation between covariates and unobserved heterogeneity. We adopt the CCR effects approach proposed by Mundlak (1978) to consistently estimate within effects as in in the FE specification but note that between effects may suffer from country-level confounding.

A potentially more efficient and more flexible approach to modeling overdispersion in our data is the use of a Negative Binomial distribution. These specifications are susceptible to scale-dependence of the dependent variable (Bosquet and Boulhol 2014), which requires corrections unless we measure trade in natural units—which we do. Unfortunately, conditional ML does not yield a consistent FE Negative Binomial estimator as is available for FE Poisson. The FE Negative Binomial estimator proposed by Hausman et al. (1984) is improper in that it does not actually correspond to a FE model (Allison and Waterman 2002), produces coefficient estimates for time-invariant variables in our data set and we thus discard it. We thus turn to RE Poisson specification whose extensions are designed to deal with overdispersion or unobserved heterogeneity. Extensions differ in computability and interpretability: Poisson models are parameterized by $\lambda_{it} = \exp(X_{it}\beta)$ which yields equidispersion. If we enhance the formulation by $\lambda_{it} = \exp(X_{it}\beta + u_{i/t} + \epsilon_{i/t})$, i.e. two random effects that can vary over units *i* and/or time *t*, we obtain most of the overdispersion models commonly used. They are commonly written in multiplicative form by factoring out $\ln(u_{i/t})$. Specifically, $u_i \sim log\Gamma$ yields the RE Gamma Poisson, $u_i \sim \mathcal{N}$ yields the RE Normal Poisson, $u_{it} \sim log\Gamma$ yields the Negative Binomial, $u_{it} \sim log\Gamma, \epsilon_i \sim \Gamma$ yields the RE Gamma Negative Binomial and $u_{it} \sim log\Gamma, \epsilon_i \sim \mathcal{N}$ yields the RE Normal Negative Binomial. Greene (2005) further proposes an identified RE Normal Negative Binomial model with $u_{it} \sim \mathcal{N}, \epsilon_{it} \sim \mathcal{N}$. In these models, the *u* term produces the Negative Binomial kernel while the additive ϵ term captures the unobserved heterogeneity of the panel units. The former allows for a very flexible model in terms of fit but ignores the panel structure while the latter is flexible across units but less so across time. The choice of error distributions is often driven by mathematical convenience rather than by theory. The main offender is the RE Gamma Negative Binomial model whose random effects collapse into one parameter that captures both overdispersion and unobserved heterogeneity (Rabe-Hesketh and Skrondal 2012). This parameter is drawn from a Beta distribution whose two defining parameters can neither be disentangled into parameters of the constituent Gamma distributions nor do they lend themselves to interpretation. Ex ante, the theoretically most appealing specification employs normally-distributed heterogeneity across units along with Gamma-distributed heterogeneity to fit additional overdispersion. It allows the distinction between two sources of overdispersion and avoids the somewhat implausible Gamma distribution of unobserved heterogeneity. To test the robustness of our parameter estimates with regard to the error distributions and to assess the magnitude of both variance components in our data set, we specify four models: RE Gamma Poisson, RE Gamma Normal, RE Gamma Negative Binomial and RE Normal Negative Binomial. We estimate these models with CCR effects, i.e. time-averaged exogenous variables.

In addition to zeros, unobserved heterogeneity and overdispersion, our data set contains two other features that somewhat restrict the methodological approach. On the one hand, our data set resembles a macro panel in that cross-correlation between countries cannot be ruled out, as would be the case for a typical random sample of micro data (Baltagi 2013). On the other hand, our data set does not exhibit the long time dimension that is typical for macro panels. A long time dimension in macro panels leads to the development of extensive methods such as heterogeneous panels or, more broadly, the CCE framework. Such methods rely on $T \to \infty$, however, and invite additional complications in non-stationarity and cointegration, which are ignored in short panels and most gravity modeling. Baltagi (2013) provides a discussion of the mixed performance of heterogeneous panel estimators and Fidrmuc (2009) finds the FE estimator appropriate to deal with cointegrated trade and GDP series, so we are confident to rely on short panel techniques and forgo time series diagnostics.

In our panel with $t = 6$, we encounter the initial condition problem for our dynamic specification which refers to biased parameter estimates as the lagged dependent variable is mistakenly taken as exogenous when it truly depends on unobserved heterogeneity. This is unproblematic for *T* and *N* approaching infinity as the bias in the overestimated parameter of the lagged variable fades out (Skrondal and Rabe-Hesketh 2014) but this does not apply to $t = 6$. To deal with the initial condition problem, we follow Wooldridge (2005) who proposes a multiplicative and Gamma-distributed individual heterogeneity term that is uncorrelated with the covariates. We can conveniently estimate the model by augmenting the set of covariates with the response in t and individual-specific averages of time-varying variables for each period t. A constraint Wooldridge solution saves degrees of freedom but potentially introduces serious bias (Rabe-Hesketh and Skrondal 2013); we thus follow their suggestion to use within-means of time-varying covariates and their levels of the initial time period, the initial endogenous variable and all time-invariant covariates to model the unobserved heterogeneity. Skrondal and Rabe-Hesketh (2014) find that joint specifications allow consistent estimation of time-invariant covariates but only in the absence of country-level heterogeneity. As there exists no Hausman and Taylor (1981) type estimator for dynamic count models in joint specifications, we restrict our focus to time-variant variables here and go with a conditional specification.

Finally, cross-correlation between countries is an econometric concern. Spatial correlation can be modeled to follow a specific process but we have little theoretical justification for any particular process. Such processes are typically designed to capture spillover effects but we are hard-pressed to think of omitted variables that transmit across borders and expect such effects to be minor in the context of medical tourism. Some word-of-mouth may spread across borders or patients may be driven to seek access to foreign care in neighboring countries when armed conflicts occur, but we assume the former to be negligible and the latter is unproblematic as we do not use medical visas or nationalities in our analysis but rely on the actual places of residence. Spatial models—with error correlation or lag processes—are further virtually unavailable for our complex nonlinear models. An alternative that has been employed with nonlinear models by Griffith (2002), for example, is the eigenvector variant of semi-parametric spatial filters but it suffers from its own deficiencies: First, the spatial weights matrix is based entirely on discretionary spatial weights such as contiguity measures, distance measures or k-nearest neighbors. Second, eigenvector filtering is based on Moran's I to identify spatial correlation (Griffith 2000). This indicator makes distributional assumptions about the variable of interest across regions. Addressing these assumptions by data requires further assumptions, which renders the spatial correction procedure discretionary at two steps. Only recently did Holmberg and Lundevaller (2015) suggest an alternative that also works well for nonlinear models. Third, the resulting synthetic map patterns are difficult to interpret as either omitted variables or spatial interactions (Wang et al. 2013).

From a theoretical point of view, gravity models explicitly model spatial interactions. We directly model distance, local information, include second-round effects via dynamics and control for unobserved heterogeneity. While the inclusion of other discretionary distance measures may increase model fit, we consider it second-round exploratory analysis whose results potentially allow new hypotheses and require ex-post theorizing. We leave such exploration to future research.

4.5 Results

Column 1 in Table 4.5 reports the results of our benchmark FE Poisson specification. The model passes the RESET test and yields consistent estimates of within effects denoted by _w suffixes. As expected, GDP of the source country and migrant stock in Germany have positive effects on treatments in Germany. The structure of health expenditures at home has a significant negative effect as measured by the public health expenditure share. Our measures of internet penetration, population size and infant mortality in the source country remain insignificant.

Columns 2–7 depict the RE Gamma Poisson specifications that allow the identification of our time-invariant variables of interest. Between effects are denoted by _b suffixes. As expected, the full model in column 7 produces the same consistent within effects of column 1. In addition, we find significant positive between effects for common border, GDP, common native language and migrant stock and significant negative effects for distance, common religion and common spoken language. While the positive effects are well in line with theory, two negative effects are somewhat unexpected. A common spoken language allows easier access to information about German providers and easier communication with physicians in Germany—both lower the costs of distance. Melitz and Toubal (2014) note that CSL is potentially endogenous as more trade may induce a language to be spoken more but we find this highly unlikely for medical treatments, which represent a very short term and individual engagement in trade relations that is hardly preceded by individual efforts to learn a language. On the supply side, we have a very small facilitator industry with an atomic structure so we do not expect any endogeneity in our aggregate language measure. We have no explanation to theorize this result at this point but note that the transaction cost channel of CSL does not appear to apply to medical travel. On the other hand, a negative effect of common religion may point to privacy concerns as a reason for treatments abroad or to failed efforts at establishing trusted facilities at home that offer the specific variety of medicine practiced in Germany. Given the descriptive spatial statistics in Sect. 2.2, this result is quite robust to the type of religion as inpatient flows draw from a number of regions that differ fundamentally in their religious imprints. We will return to both common spoken language and common spoken religion in our specifications below.

An overdispersion test based on Cameron and Trivedi (2009) indicates overdispersion after accounting for the panel structure so we jointly test within and between effects for equality (Rabe-Hesketh and Skrondal 2012). The approach is asymptotically equivalent to a Hausman test and we reject endogeneity of the variables that appear in both the FE and the final RE specification. However, this conclusion does not extend to variables that appear only in the RE specification even if their estimated effects are remarkably stable across all models.

Our most serious concern is treatment aggregation, which may introduce unknown and differing shares of incidental treatments to the panel units. Table 2.5 in chapter 2 displayed the dominant differences in treatment shares between two and three clusters, respectively. A multivariate regression identified a significant influence of

Table 4.5 Results of the static specifications

	All treatments						
	All countries						
	FE poisson	RE gamma poisson					
	(1)	(2)	(3)	(4)	(5)	(6)	(7)
Distance		−0.975***	−0.846***	−0.607***	−0.590***	−0.581***	−0.601***
		(0.157)	(0.167)	(0.173)	(0.178)	(0.167)	(0.170)
Common border		0.420	0.532	0.662*	0.664*	0.810**	0.828**
		(0.441)	(0.371)	(0.347)	(0.349)	(0.322)	(0.321)
Common native language		1.604***	1.564***	1.866***	1.800***	1.555***	1.539***
		(0.576)	(0.502)	(0.459)	(0.454)	(0.441)	(0.437)
Common spoken language		−0.505	−0.561	−1.848**	−1.699**	−1.715**	−1.584**
		(0.566)	(0.542)	(0.723)	(0.706)	(0.741)	(0.768)
Common legislation		−0.0414	−0.202	−0.188	−0.171	−0.242	−0.279
		(0.219)	(0.242)	(0.229)	(0.227)	(0.221)	(0.208)
Common religion		−2.609***	−2.403***	−2.456***	−2.665***	−2.446***	−2.437***
		(0.901)	(0.846)	(0.835)	(0.798)	(0.832)	(0.832)
EU		0.516*	0.514**	0.387	0.356	0.349	0.334
		(0.264)	(0.241)	(0.271)	(0.269)	(0.248)	(0.245)
GDP_w[a]	0.330*	0.514**	0.449**	0.309**	0.330**	0.350**	0.330*
	(0.183)	(0.210)	(0.226)	(0.154)	(0.149)	(0.163)	(0.183)
GDP_b[a]		0.592***	0.533***	0.326***	0.334***	0.583***	0.534***
		(0.057)	(0.070)	(0.086)	(0.083)	(0.150)	(0.150)
Migrant stock_w	0.486***		0.478***	0.452***	0.473***	0.491***	0.486***
	(0.106)		(0.129)	(0.127)	(0.111)	(0.115)	(0.106)
Migrant stock_b			0.138**	0.278***	0.282***	0.333***	0.315***
			(0.068)	(0.075)	(0.074)	(0.073)	(0.077)

(continued)

Table 4.5 (continued)

	All treatments						
	All countries						
	FE poisson	RE gamma poisson					
	(1)	(2)	(3)	(4)	(5)	(6)	(7)
Internet penetration_w	0.497			0.725	0.515	0.522	0.497
	(0.409)			(0.528)	(0.411)	(0.406)	(0.409)
Internet penetration_b				2.700***	2.454***	1.145	0.982
				(0.750)	(0.800)	(1.067)	(1.106)
Public health expenditure_w	−1.586**				−1.689**	−1.588**	−1.586**
	(0.620)				(0.665)	(0.620)	(0.620)
Public health expenditure_b					0.480	−0.230	−0.267
					(0.637)	(0.657)	(0.664)
Population_w	−0.164					−0.195	−0.164
	(0.675)					(0.674)	(0.675)
Population_b						−0.336**	−0.268
						(0.158)	(0.172)
Infant mortality_w	−0.007						−0.007
	(0.015)						(0.015)
Infant mortality_b							−0.006
							(0.006)
Year dummies	Yes	Yes	Yes	Yes	Yes	Yes	Yes
Observations	865	968	968	968	968	968	968
Countries	145	163	163	163	163	163	163
LL	−6423	−8326	−7896	−7746	−7544	−7537	−7534
BIC	12,921	16,762	15,915	15,629	15,239	15,240	15,246
Hausman	–	0.71	0.01	0.10	0.00	0.15	0.20

Significant at 0.1*, 0.05**, 0.01***

[a]The suffixes _w and _b denote within and between effects. See CCR in Sect. 4.4

cluster membership in the two-cluster model on ICD 1, 2, 3, 5, 10, 11, 15, 17, 18 and 19 treatment shares at the 5% level. The two clusters are associated with ICD chapters 1, 5, 10, 11, 15, 18 and 19 and 2, 3 and 17, respectively.

We pursue three strategies to deal with this heterogeneity. First, we add our cluster indicator from Sect. 2.2.2 as a measure of treatment type composition to the model. A homogenous process with a cluster-specific mean effect implies that treatment composition demanded by patients from a given country determines average patient flows to Germany while the impact of other drivers remains identical across all source countries. The implied assumption is that countries have a specific incidence of medical conditions or an otherwise exogenous demand portfolio for treatments and that Germany caters to certain demand portfolios more than to others.

Second, we model cluster-specific processes that relax the assumption of a homogenous process across clusters and allow for cluster-specific coefficients. This allows countries with predominantly incidental and elective treatments to follow their own economic decision-making processes. Note that cluster membership depends on treatment shares as opposed to treatment counts and clustering does not split our sample into high and low demand countries.

Third, we model a homogenous process across countries at a more disaggregated treatment level. A homogenous process at a disaggregated product level is in the spirit of the gravity theory but suffers from data restrictions, i.e. we cannot obtain data disaggregated by country, year and treatment groups at the same time. This lack of data often forces gravity modeling to a level of aggregation that leaves it open to criticism of product subgroup heterogeneity and in our case disaggregation may be critical if some treatment categories are only marginally governed by economic decision-making processes or by-products of tourism which puts them beyond the reach of our theory. We thus filter all treatments as outlined in Sect. 4.3 and run our model on only elective and ICD 2 treatments. This step removes the potential distortion introduced by incidental treatments.

The introduction of a cluster indicator for membership in cluster 2 of our two-cluster solution in Sect. 2.2.2, to stick with the notation in chapter 2, reduces the sample to 544 observations and 92 countries and column 1 in Table 4.6 reports the results of our pooled specification in column 5 of Table 4.5 with a cluster dummy. The results are very similar qualitatively and the cluster indicator enhances the explanatory power of the model substantially but we cannot reject potential cluster-level confounding based on the Hausman test. There appears to be more heterogeneity involved, i.e. different processes may govern our clusters.

Columns 2 and 3 display the results of two separately modeled processes for both clusters which split the sample into 60 countries with 357 observations and 32 countries with 187 observations, respectively. First, we note that the effect of a common border is unidentifiable in cluster 2 and that its smaller number of observations generally leads to less precise estimates. Second, inspection of both processes suggests that our measures of cultural proximity govern both clusters quite differently. The effects of common religion, CNL and CSL are driven by cluster 2 countries while the effect of migrant stock is substantially larger for cluster 0 countries. The significant within effect of internet penetration in cluster 0 is initially

Table 4.6 Results of the static specifications, by treatment group and country cluster

	All treatments		Electives		ICD 2	
	All countries	Cluster 0	Cluster 2	All countries	All countries	All countries
	Gamma poisson					
	(1)	(2)	(3)	(4)	(5)	(6)
Distance	−0.494***	−0.368***	−0.096	−0.417***	−0.633***	−0.474**
	(0.146)	(0.134)	(0.693)	(0.144)	(0.173)	(0.185)
Common border	1.052***	1.115***		1.114***	0.901**	1.104***
	(0.324)	(0.315)		(0.321)	(0.364)	(0.371)
Common border/CNL				−25.783*	−55.001***	−50.143***
				(14.826)	(20.864)	(17.321)
Common native language	1.238***	0.215	57.393**	26.974*	56.522***	50.571***
	(0.436)	(0.585)	(22.762)	(14.839)	(20.838)	(17.329)
Common spoken language	−0.813	0.449	−3.614	−0.876	−1.765**	−0.501
	(0.717)	(0.882)	(2.278)	(0.742)	(0.875)	(0.852)
Common legislation	−0.116	−0.304	0.166	−0.193	−0.480**	−0.657***
	(0.248)	(0.283)	(0.476)	(0.236)	(0.219)	(0.249)
Common religion	−1.986**	−1.641	−3.258**	−1.390	−2.110**	−3.803***
	(0.919)	(1.019)	(1.615)	(0.978)	(0.960)	(0.979)
EU	0.500**	0.671***	1.874***	0.651**	0.391	0.349
	(0.237)	(0.232)	(0.565)	(0.259)	(0.283)	(0.280)
GDP_w	0.325*	0.222	0.227	0.294	0.315*	0.437**
	(0.185)	(0.221)	(0.355)	(0.184)	(0.175)	(0.207)
GDP_b	0.641***	0.950***	0.164	0.589***	0.583***	0.651***
	(0.171)	(0.254)	(0.347)	(0.162)	(0.159)	(0.157)
Migrant stock_w	0.481***	0.675***	0.177	0.512***	0.427***	0.357**
	(0.104)	(0.106)	(0.131)	(0.100)	(0.116)	(0.160)
Migrant stock_b	0.138*	0.242***	0.071	0.154**	0.299***	0.280***
	(0.075)	(0.078)	(0.155)	(0.076)	(0.080)	(0.089)

Internet penetration_w	0.467	−0.842*	0.556	1.753***	1.716**	0.889
	(0.418)	(0.432)	(0.490)	(0.631)	(0.750)	(1.106)
Internet penetration_b	−0.442	−2.904**	2.049	−0.917	0.227	−0.085
	(0.997)	(1.189)	(1.740)	(1.884)	(2.197)	(2.343)
Internet penetration^2_w				−1.373**	−1.017	−0.163
				(0.629)	(0.782)	(1.082)
Internet penetration^2_b				0.777	0.187	−1.274
				(1.832)	(2.064)	(2.224)
Public health expenditure_w	−1.612**	−0.897	−1.415**	−1.556**	−1.359**	−1.439**
	(0.641)	(0.875)	(0.651)	(0.614)	(0.639)	(0.579)
Public health expenditure_b	0.220	−0.577	0.652	0.145	−0.809	−0.586
	(0.806)	(1.250)	(1.038)	(0.807)	(0.718)	(0.805)
Population_w	−0.134	−0.690	0.317	0.048	−0.061	−0.356
	(0.678)	(0.777)	(0.628)	(0.679)	(0.728)	(0.798)
Population_b	−0.291	−0.793***	0.160	−0.289	−0.408**	−0.561***
	(0.203)	(0.302)	(0.497)	(0.189)	(0.180)	(0.181)
Infant mortality_w	−0.012	0.003	−0.002	0.021	0.003	−0.006
	(0.017)	(0.017)	(0.030)	(0.021)	(0.024)	(0.037)
Infant mortality_b	−0.005	−0.005	−0.001	−0.005	−0.008	−0.019**
	(0.007)	(0.007)	(0.021)	(0.006)	(0.006)	(0.008)
Cluster dummy	0.423*			0.327		
	(0.240)			(0.242)		
Year dummies	Yes	Yes	Yes	Yes	Yes	Yes
Observations	544	357	187	544	944	824
Countries	92	60	32	92	159	139
LL	−6375	−3467	−2530	−6286	−5552	−3864
BIC	12,919	7087	5190	12,761	11,289	7909
Hausman	0.04	0.00	0.55	0.01	0.89	0.60

Significant at 0.1*, 0.05**, 0.01***

implausible but consistent across various specifications. This hints to internet penetration as imperfect measure of autonomous information, i.e. we suspect that internet penetration captures technological development and possibly broader economic development in addition to available information channels. Developed countries with higher internet penetration percentages may thus produce fewer patients who seek care in Germany while the improvement of internet penetration percentages at lower levels may coincide with both higher demand capacity and access to information about treatments abroad. We thus include a squared effect of internet penetration in subsequent models to investigate if there are countries whose technological and economic development spurs medical travel before they attain the ability to provide suitable services at home.

Closer inspection of the stark difference in CNL parameter estimates further leads us to believe that the issue may be related to emigrant stock for which no data is available but which is likely correlated with CNL. There is no reliable data set that captures emigrant stock abroad but DESTATIS (2012) shows that emigration occurs to a great deal to countries with a common border. We suspect that CNL measures in bordering countries are distorted by emigrant stock and thus include a CNL-border interaction effect.

The resulting model in column 4 confirms the moderating effect of a common border on CNL, which was disguised in the clustering solution as one cluster included no bordering countries at all. The common border effect remains positive as expected and we conclude that the role of emigrants as both facilitators and consumers of medical travel is quite limited whereas trust as measured by CNL after controlling for emigrants plays an important role. This conclusion about the role of emigrants is in line with our results in chapter 6 where we find little evidence for facilitating activities by or demand from emigrants. We also find weak evidence for a squared internet penetration effect, which suggests a technological/economic sweet spot that allows for information channels and the economic means to consume medical treatments abroad while domestic alternatives do not have yet fully developed. Our cluster solution had apparently split the sample into a cluster 0 of developed countries and a cluster 1 of developing countries which yielded two opposite effects in Table 4.6. Finally, note that that the cluster indicator turns insignificant.

In columns 5 and 6, we filter treatments and consider homogenous models over the pooled sample. Moving from all treatments in column 4 to elective and ICD 2 treatments in columns 5 and 6, we continue to find the effects of most drivers to be qualitatively similar across models. The significant positive effect of EU membership vanishes as the original sample size is restored. The larger magnitude of distance, CNL and the CNL-border interaction can be attributed partly to treatment filtering and partly to the larger sample size, so we conclude that poorer health conditions associated with elective treatments and the absence of touristic intention renders distance more inhibitive to travel. At the same time, the underlying trust in a destination as measured by CNL becomes more important.

As noted above, an overdispersion test based on Cameron and Trivedi (2009) indicates overdispersion after accounting for the panel structure and thus suggests the extra flexibility added by a Negative Binomial specification even if the FE Poisson model with clustered standard errors—and thus the within effects of the corresponding RE Gamma Poisson model—are useful benchmarks as they remain consistent in the presence of overdispersion (Cameron and Trivedi 2009). Table 4.7 and Table 4.8 present our results to highlight the effects of both Negbin and panel specifications. The first two columns of each treatment category show the Poisson and Negbin outputs for pooled models, which do not account for the panel structure of the data. All models are nested in the pooled Poisson specification and the Normal Negbin is nested in the Normal Poisson. However, Gamma Negbin is not nested in Gamma Poisson so the BIC is provided in addition to the log-likelihood.

Across treatment categories, we find that accounting for the panel structure in a Poisson specification improves model quality tremendously. A pooled Negbin specification yields even larger improvements in model fit, which is mildly surprising as it effectively corresponds to a flexible Gamma Poisson with each observation being a separate panel unit. Moving from a Poisson panel to a Negbin Panel, we find that the panel structure captures the largest share of model improvement between a pooled Poisson and a Negbin panel specification. Of the two Negbin panel specifications, Gamma Negbin produces consistently the best fit as measured by LL and model quality as measured by BIC. Unfortunately, the beta parameters preclude the interpretation of panel unit heterogeneity.

Tables 4.7 and 4.8 show that almost all parameter estimates are very robust in terms of sign and magnitude across specifications. As expected, GDP, common border and migrant stock have significant, positive effects while distance, population and public health expenditure shares have negative effects. Internet penetration has a significant positive within effect and an insignificant negative between effect in most specifications. A negative squared term turns highly significant in our best specification for electives so we continue to have some evidence for a technological/economic sweet spot, which lies at a maximizing internet penetration of approximately 49% in the Gamma Negbin model.

Unexpectedly, infant mortality takes on a negative sign in some specifications but remains largely insignificant. It is positive in the Gamma Negbin, however. We note that perceived treatment quality in a source country may not coincide with actual treatment quality. We suspected the perceived treatment quality to play an important role, i.e. a strong country-of-origin effect, and CNL as our measure of trust bears out this suspicion: The total effect of CNL is positive for countries both with and without a common border. It is much more pronounced for non-bordering countries, however, and we find no evidence for a squared effect of CNL or a CNL-distance interaction. We interpret the border-CNL interaction effect as a distortion induced by emigrants who are not expected to exhibit a strong country-of-origin effect.

CSL has a negative and—for ICD 2 treatments often insignificant—effect. It is likely endogenous for total trade as, for example, language schooling may be motivated by existing trade relations. We have argued that such endogeneity is unlikely to exist in medical travel and venture to conclude from the negative effect that learned languages do not appear to establish the trust that drives medical travel. It is a very weak connection, however, as strong trading partners with a higher CSL percentage may also be the ones that do not exhibit push factors in short supply, poor quality of supply or the wrong variety of health care supplied. We attempted to control for these factors but several dimensions of, for example, domestic health care

Table 4.7 Results of the static specifications for elective treatments, by estimator

	Electives					
	All countries					
	Poisson	Negbin	Gamma Poisson	Normal Poisson	Gamma Negbin	Normal Negbin
Distance	−0.546***	−0.698***	−0.633***	−0.801***	−0.527***	−0.811***
	(0.139)	(0.167)	(0.173)	(0.223)	(0.140)	(0.216)
Common border	0.972***	0.904***	0.901**	0.877	1.059***	0.880**
	(0.284)	(0.349)	(0.364)	(0.608)	(0.351)	(0.377)
Common border/CNL	−47.581***	−51.506**	−55.001***	−47.411**	−38.395**	−47.079**
	(9.123)	(20.173)	(20.864)	(20.666)	(15.092)	(21.835)
Common native language	48.772***	53.032***	56.522***	49.039**	39.705***	48.718**
	(9.147)	(20.159)	(20.838)	(20.621)	(15.020)	(21.843)
Common spoken language	−1.261	−1.734**	−1.765**	−1.558*	−1.725***	−1.595
	(0.934)	(0.864)	(0.875)	(0.806)	(0.537)	(1.036)
Common legislation	−0.335	−0.498**	−0.480**	−0.306	0.007	−0.318
	(0.251)	(0.221)	(0.219)	(0.240)	(0.151)	(0.250)
Common religion	−2.417**	−2.177**	−2.110**	−1.015	0.397	−0.977
	(0.997)	(0.887)	(0.960)	(1.018)	(0.640)	(0.986)
EU	0.657**	0.345	0.391	0.349	0.009	0.342
	(0.278)	(0.276)	(0.283)	(0.441)	(0.268)	(0.328)
GDP_w	0.205	0.177	0.315*	0.315***	0.518***	0.245
	(0.217)	(0.246)	(0.175)	(0.031)	(0.112)	(0.213)
GDP_b	1.135***	0.632***	0.583***	0.635***	0.781***	0.638***
	(0.178)	(0.159)	(0.159)	(0.169)	(0.107)	(0.204)
Migrant stock_w	1.101***	0.196	0.427***	0.427***	0.310***	0.180
	(0.278)	(0.182)	(0.116)	(0.026)	(0.112)	(0.185)
Migrant stock_b	0.157*	0.266***	0.299***	0.301***	0.360***	0.299***
	(0.082)	(0.079)	(0.080)	(0.087)	(0.054)	(0.096)

Internet penetration_w	2.448***	−0.325	1.716**	1.716***	1.856***	0.958
	(0.949)	(0.997)	(0.750)	(0.141)	(0.461)	(0.779)
Internet penetration_b	0.226	0.506	0.227	2.215	1.491	2.242
	(2.057)	(2.146)	(2.197)	(2.195)	(1.300)	(2.306)
Internet penetration^2_w	−1.506	−0.234	−1.017	−1.016***	−1.190**	−1.092
	(0.972)	(0.979)	(0.782)	(0.141)	(0.492)	(0.805)
Internet penetration^2_b	−1.415	−0.406	0.187	−2.456	−2.223*	−2.501
	(1.934)	(1.979)	(2.064)	(2.093)	(1.262)	(2.208)
Public health expenditure_w	−1.744**	−0.885	−1.359**	−1.359***	−1.453***	−1.014
	(0.681)	(0.989)	(0.639)	(0.123)	(0.380)	(0.696)
Public health expenditure_b	−1.730*	−0.850	−0.809	−0.811	−1.170**	−0.802
	(0.915)	(0.670)	(0.718)	(0.744)	(0.476)	(0.794)
Population_w	0.084	0.058	−0.061	−0.061	−0.580	−0.133
	(1.431)	(0.559)	(0.728)	(0.087)	(0.432)	(0.650)
Population_b	−0.842***	−0.413**	−0.408**	−0.375*	−0.743***	−0.373
	(0.197)	(0.180)	(0.180)	(0.205)	(0.131)	(0.242)
Infant mortality_w	0.001	0.001	0.003	0.003	0.024*	0.025
	(0.031)	(0.020)	(0.024)	(0.005)	(0.014)	(0.018)
Infant mortality_b	0.002	−0.009	−0.008	−0.007	0.011**	−0.007
	(0.011)	(0.006)	(0.006)	(0.007)	(0.005)	(0.008)
Year dummies	Yes					
Observations	944					
Countries	159					
LL	−38,954	−4197	−5526	−5538	−3583	−3695
BIC	78,099	8592	11,251	11,274	7372	7596

Significant at 0.1*, 0.05**, 0.01***

Table 4.8 Results of the static specifications for ICD 2 treatments, by estimator

	ICD 2					
	All countries					
	Poisson	Negbin	Gamma Poisson	Normal Poisson	Gamma Negbin	Normal Negbin
Distance	−0.461***	−0.587***	−0.474**	−0.674**	−0.649***	−0.697***
	(0.159)	(0.176)	(0.185)	(0.281)	(0.153)	(0.250)
Common border	0.815**	1.031***	1.104***	0.983	0.769*	0.989**
	(0.336)	(0.359)	(0.371)	(0.735)	(0.398)	(0.461)
Common border/CNL	−48.774***	−46.436***	−50.143***	−48.249*	−61.318***	−47.614*
	(10.952)	(17.342)	(17.321)	(25.078)	(18.676)	(24.722)
Common native language	49.467***	46.952***	50.571***	48.988*	61.623***	48.361*
	(10.906)	(17.356)	(17.329)	(25.026)	(18.649)	(24.724)
Common spoken language	−0.730	−0.682	−0.501	−0.804	−1.548**	−0.839
	(0.989)	(0.848)	(0.852)	(1.043)	(0.607)	(1.190)
Common legislation	−0.145	−0.626**	−0.657***	−0.438	−0.114	−0.454
	(0.255)	(0.248)	(0.249)	(0.308)	(0.184)	(0.295)
Common religion	−3.648***	−3.735***	−3.803***	−2.872**	0.215	−2.834**
	(0.962)	(0.942)	(0.979)	(1.331)	(0.765)	(1.168)
EU	0.742**	0.293	0.349	0.301	0.290	0.290
	(0.319)	(0.274)	(0.280)	(0.535)	(0.291)	(0.373)
GDP_w	0.281	0.724**	0.437**	0.437***	0.559***	0.552**
	(0.245)	(0.306)	(0.207)	(0.053)	(0.150)	(0.269)
GDP_b	1.114***	0.753***	0.651***	0.883***	0.855***	0.894***
	(0.191)	(0.156)	(0.157)	(0.223)	(0.130)	(0.212)
Migrant stock_w	1.083***	0.048	0.357**	0.357***	0.307*	−0.156
	(0.339)	(0.304)	(0.160)	(0.043)	(0.157)	(0.285)
Migrant stock_b	0.123	0.251***	0.280***	0.295**	0.302***	0.292**
	(0.091)	(0.086)	(0.089)	(0.115)	(0.068)	(0.125)

Internet penetration_w	1.897	−0.499	0.889	0.890***	1.544**	0.277
	(1.474)	(1.383)	(1.106)	(0.229)	(0.662)	(1.229)
Internet penetration_b	−0.744	0.058	−0.085	1.900	0.969	1.792
	(2.239)	(2.259)	(2.343)	(2.807)	(1.629)	(2.923)
Internet penetration^2_w	−0.828	0.079	−0.163	−0.163	−0.479	−0.080
	(1.409)	(1.382)	(1.082)	(0.230)	(0.682)	(1.289)
Internet penetration^2_b	−1.261	−1.678	−1.274	−3.662	−2.881*	−3.656
	(2.130)	(2.111)	(2.224)	(2.639)	(1.528)	(2.712)
Public health expenditure_w	−2.266***	−1.450*	−1.439**	−1.439***	−0.574	−0.789
	(0.625)	(0.784)	(0.579)	(0.200)	(0.513)	(0.893)
Public health expenditure_b	−2.165**	−0.874	−0.586	−0.705	−0.967	−0.708
	(1.012)	(0.777)	(0.805)	(1.008)	(0.591)	(1.047)
Population_w	−0.170	−0.319	−0.356	−0.355**	−1.306***	−0.520
	(1.449)	(0.704)	(0.798)	(0.146)	(0.500)	(0.840)
Population_b	−0.820***	−0.616***	−0.561***	−0.763***	−0.947***	−0.767***
	(0.230)	(0.185)	(0.181)	(0.276)	(0.162)	(0.271)
Infant mortality_w	−0.005	0.032	−0.006	−0.006	0.020	0.047*
	(0.045)	(0.032)	(0.037)	(0.009)	(0.021)	(0.027)
Infant mortality_b	−0.011	−0.017**	−0.019**	−0.012	0.008	−0.012
	(0.015)	(0.008)	(0.008)	(0.010)	(0.007)	(0.012)
Year dummies	Yes					
Observations	824					
Countries	139					
LL	−16,783	−3139	−3864	−3881	−2723	−2804
BIC	33,754	6472	7922	7957	5647	5809

Significant at 0.1*, 0.05**, 0.01***

quality as measured by hospital beds, physicians or nurses were unavailable for large parts of our sample so CSL may well capture some of these uncontrolled dimensions.

A curious effect arises for common religion, which has a significant negative effect in most specifications, particularly for ICD 2 treatments. Unexpectedly, this effect turns positive for both elective and ICD 2 treatments in the Gamma Negbin model even if it is highly insignificant. We have interpreted a negative effect above as the absence of a desired treatment variety that Germany may offer to patients in countries with other official religions but we do not have an explanation for the deviating common religion result in the Gamma Negbin model.

Finally, we investigate the RE Gamma Poisson model which can be extended to a dynamic specification and whose within parameters can be consistently estimated. Note that the methodology employed in our dynamic specification does not extend to Negbin models and the development of such a methodology is beyond the scope of this work, so we do not investigate overdispersion in the context of dynamic models.

The introduction of dynamics reduces our sample to 138 countries with 683 observations and Table 4.9 reports the results for elective and ICD 2 treatments. The results are quite similar to the static Poisson specification, i.e. GDP and migrant stock have the expected positive effects while distance, population and common religion have negative effects. Internet penetration displays a quadratic effect as before. Lagged treatment flows are highly significant but their introduction renders CNL, CNL-border, border, CSL and the public health expenditure share insignificant. State dependence captures so much variation that we cannot obtain precise estimates of our language-based proximity variables—whose lack of within variation does not help. We suspect that lagged treatment flows capture more aspects than word-of-mouth by returning patients such as persistent cultural and institutional ties over our short T that they preclude their precise estimation. A longer time dimension would help to investigate the role of state dependence in more detail and greatly increase the precision of our parameter estimates. More recent data is now available but cannot be accessed in the context of this study. Post-2014 data should be investigated with care as large migrant inflows were induced by conditions that also affected source countries' demand capacities. Pre-2007 data is also available but likely to be of poor quality based on our findings in Sect. 2.2.2.1.

We can embed our findings in the scarce existing literature: Lunt et al. (2014) suspect a strong role of the diaspora, historic ties and institutional ties of providers. We can confirm a strong positive effect of migrant stock in the destination country and, indirectly, a weak effect of migrant stock in the source country for Germany as a destination. We could not investigate historic ties due to data limitations but cannot reject a role of institutional ties in the form of a very strong CNL effect. On the other hand, an enhanced ability to communicate abroad—as identified by Hanefeld et al. (2015)—does not appear essential for inbound medical travel to Germany. Esiyok et al. (2017) find a negative effect of distance that decreases as medical conditions become more severe and a strong and positive effect of common religion. We find a similar effect of distance as we move from elective to ICD 2 treatments in all but the Gamma Negbin specifications. Our effect of common religion runs counter to Bookman and Bookman (2007) and Esiyok et al. (2017) but it is robust across essentially all static and dynamic specifications. We have two possible explanations for this phenomenon: First, Turkey and Germany attract treatments that differ in type, variety of medicine or desire

Table 4.9 Results of the dynamic Poisson specification, by treatment group

	Electives	ICD 2
	All countries	
	Gamma poisson	
Lagged treatments	0.0002***	0.0003***
	(0.000)	(0.000)
Distance	−0.432**	−0.282
	(0.180)	(0.190)
Common border	0.059	0.076
	(0.416)	(0.432)
Common border/CNL	−16.215	−18.169
	(24.763)	(24.338)
Common native language	17.237	17.533
	(24.654)	(24.393)
Common spoken language	−1.165	−0.297
	(0.825)	(0.834)
Common legislation	−0.401*	−0.501**
	(0.234)	(0.247)
Common religion	−2.685***	−4.112***
	(0.781)	(0.933)
EU	0.243	0.148
	(0.247)	(0.276)
GDP_w	0.268*	0.488***
	(0.150)	(0.181)
GDP_b	0.577***	0.554***
	(0.141)	(0.145)
Migrant stock_w	0.438***	0.368***
	(0.064)	(0.110)
Migrant stock_b	0.255***	0.294***
	(0.085)	(0.090)
Internet penetration_w	1.316**	0.411
	(0.660)	(1.054)
Internet penetration_b	−0.218	0.346
	(1.764)	(2.056)
Internet penetration^2_w	−1.195**	−0.262
	(0.596)	(0.927)
Internet penetration^2_b	−0.133	−1.448
	(1.796)	(2.026)
Public health expenditure_w	−0.393	−0.769
	(0.669)	(0.873)
Public health expenditure_b	−0.912	−0.862
	(0.593)	(0.734)
Population_w	0.015	−0.514
	(0.470)	(0.726)

(continued)

Table 4.9 (continued)

	Electives	ICD 2
	All countries	
	Gamma poisson	
Population_b	−0.519***	−0.579***
	(0.157)	(0.173)
Infant mortality_w	0.009	0.009
	(0.023)	(0.034)
Infant mortality_b	−0.007	−0.018**
	(0.007)	(0.007)
Year dummies	Yes	
Observations	683	
Countries	138	
LL	−4149	−3122
BIC	8494	6440

Significant at 0.1*, 0.05**, 0.01***

for privacy. Second, common religion effects for both Germany and Turkey are artifacts of single-country models, i.e. source countries are characterized by religious profiles that impede the supply of desired product varieties at home, which—coupled with strong, culturally motivated trust in other destinations—leads to excess demand abroad. The destination's religious profiles in Esiyok et al. (2017) and in our study are then coincidental. An effect of religious profiles on the establishment of an industry is not without precedent at the aggregate level and has been investigated in the economic growth literature (Fernández et al. 2001). Ultimately, this issue can only be resolved once multilateral treatment flow data becomes available and our analysis has highlighted the data requirements implied by an appropriate definition of medical travel.

Previous attempts to investigate the role of cultural ties in medical travel have struggled with a number of issues. Johnson and Garman (2015) use self-reported travel survey data which has been documented to be a poor measure of medical travel flows (Noree et al. 2016). Johnson and Garman (2015) scan a large set of country characteristics for correlations with the existence of medical travel and with their measure of medical travel volume. In multivariate regressions, the existence of medical travel is found to depend on population size, travel time and out-of-pocket health care expenditures as a share of private health care expenditures while the volume of medical travel depends on travel time, travel cost, air departures and outbound travel to the source country. Cultural proximity is measured by outbound travel from the U.S. to the source country of medical tourists, which may be a measure of expatriates visiting home but it is just as likely to represent general tourism that boosts source country GDP and thus demand for treatments abroad. Out-of-pocket health care expenditures as a share of private health care expenditures are a suboptimal measure of the expenditure structure as it may be large but negligible at the upper-tier, i.e. the share of private health care expenditures of total health care expenditures may be very small.

Esiyok et al. (2017) model patient inflows to Turkey, which the government divided into an emergency and a non-emergency care group, and use lagged GDP per capita, cultural distance based on four cultural dimensions of power (Hofstede 1980), common religion, geographic distance, tourists as share of total tourists per year and size of the source country's diaspora relative to its population as explanatory variables. They identify medical travel by nationality which is superior to Johnson and Garman (2015) but still problematic as it does not identify an act of travelling but mixes the demand from medical travelers with the demand from foreign long-term residents such as workers, retirees and students which can be substantial in numbers (Klijs et al. 2016; NaRanong and NaRanong 2011). Tourists are motivated as an indicator of word-of-mouth, which is problematic for two reasons: First, the word-of-mouth effect should be lagged if it induces planned treatments and, second, it is hard to see why tourists would produce a word-of-mouth effect for medical travel rather than for recreational travel. Returning patients, on the other hand, have been documented to recommend destinations for their treatments.

Yet there is a more fundamental problem with the inclusion of tourism: If travelers make ad-hoc decisions as in Wongkit and McKercher (2013), recreational travel flows should be modeled and recreational factors must be included. If travelers plan a combination of recreation and a medical treatment, both must be measured and modeled simultaneously. If travelers make a conscious decision to travel for a planned treatment as their main purpose, tourists will still be endogenous as medical travelers tend to travel with company of often considerable size (Musa et al. 2012; Yeoh et al. 2013). In fact, the quadratic effect of cultural distance suggests that the delineation of medical travel is crucial and that tourism is a substantial interference. As Esiyok et al. (2017) note, the quadratic effect implies that countries should be very close or very distant in terms of cultural distance, which is implausible for medical travel but highly plausible for recreational travelers who seek very familiar or very exotic destinations. If both tourism and medical treatments can be incidental to each other and medical travel is to be modeled, tourism needs to be ruled out in the decision-making process about a destination choice. To this end, we proposed and adopted a three-step approach: First, an act of traveling must occur which requires an indicator of a patient's place of residence. Second, the treatment purpose of a trip must be ensured, which we achieve by focusing on inpatient treatments. By assumption, inpatient treatments represent medical conditions that dominate any considerations of tourism. Third, inpatient treatments must be filtered to remove incidental treatments that reflect acute conditions of international visitors rather than elective procedures.

Given Greene (2005) and our results, a robustness check across multiple specifications was well advised. An open question remains the appropriate distributional assumption of country heterogeneity. Normally distributed heterogeneity appears reasonable but there is little theory to guide this decision. We found small differences for the Gamma and Normal Poisson as well as the Normal Negbin panel specifications. However, the Gamma Negbin is always preferred by both LL and BIC and produces reversed signs—if insignificant—for the common religion effect. Investigation of this behavior as well as the development of a dynamic Negbin specification also merit further research. Another interesting research avenue is the clustering of source countries. We found no strong evidence for different processes in the two countries clusters we identified. However, the clustering solution reliably identified those non-Western countries that are commonly reported and were identified in Sect. 2.2.2 to be main source countries of medical tourism to Germany. Cluster membership correlates with the share of elective treatments demanded by a given country and it would be informative to investigate if the clustering solution is driven by the difference in acute treatments, which may result from tourism, transit or temporary workers and which determine the share of elective treatments, or if there are other factors that determine incidence and demand of elective treatments. In the same vein, we started to investigate data-driven self-clustering. A finite mixture panel model is a promising alternative to the separate modeling of two hard clusters that offers soft assignment to clusters and jointly determines both the assignment and each cluster's parameter vector (Deb and Trivedi 2013). Alternatively, a full-fledged two-stage model is an option that we will return to in chapter 7.

4.6 Summary

We have surveyed the gravity modeling literature and developed a demand-side derivation that allowed us to incorporate measures of word-of-mouth, networks as approximated by migrant stock and cultural proximity in the context of medical travel. We investigated our set of variables along the treatment dimension for all, elective and ICD 2 treatments and along the country dimension for all countries and for two country clusters.

The results of our investigation were in line with the theory underlying our gravity model and further confirmed a number of hypotheses from Sect. 2.5. First, classic gravity components in geographic distance and GDP as a measure of demand capacity yield the expected signs. Our additional measures of population and domestic health expenditure structure, which dilute demand capacity and approximate the ease of reallocating health expenditures abroad, also entered with the expected signs.

Migrant stock in Germany as the key measure of networks is consistently positive and significant across all specifications so we find strong evidence for the importance of this channel. We also find strong evidence for the role of a common native language, which we interpret as a measure of trust in a destination. On the other hand, we find no positive effect for the role of a common spoken language and argued that, even if the measure is not endogenous with respect to medical travel, it may also capture domestic quantity, quality or variety of health care supply and should thus be interpreted with care. A similar concern arises for common religion with its significant negative effect across most specifications. Clearly, common religion should increase proximity so it is likely to capture another effect that we return to below. Candidates are once again domestic quantity, quality or variety of health care supply. We attempt to control for quality by infant mortality but we have no measures of quantity supplied or incidence. The growth literature has investigated the effects of religion on economic growth (Fernández et al. 2001) but it is unclear to what extent religion may influence the particular variety of health care in a country. Both common spoken language and common religion certainly merit more research.

Internet penetration turns out to measure more than the availability of an information channel for patients who seek information autonomously. We find evidence for a quadratic effect of internet penetration even after controlling for GDP so it appears to capture technology at large and potentially the sophistication of domestic health care. We find a positive effect of internet penetration in our preferred Gamma Negbin model up to about 49% of internet penetration and a declining effect on treatments in Germany thereafter. Finally, we also detect evidence for a positive effect of lagged treatment flows but their interpretation at this aggregated level may be complicated. Dynamic specifications of gravity models have been considered before: In fact, Eichengreen and Irwin (1998) suggest a dynamic formulation be indispensable for the estimation of gravity models lest they suffer from an omitted variable bias. Bun and Klaassen (2002) surmise lagged trade flows to capture habit formation and distribution networks and Campbell (2013) employs a dynamic specification to control for historic trends and omitted variables when assessing the impact of a singular event affecting a trade relationship. To our knowledge, our application is the first to embed word-of-mouth as a preference-altering information channel and to build a dynamic formulation on an established theoretical framework. However, we cannot isolate our word-of-mouth effect from other forms of habit formation, from distribution networks or broader historic trends. Still, we believe that word-of-mouth by returning patients contributes substantially to the state-dependence effect and we will expand on this issue in chapter 6.

Modeling at aggregate consumer and supplier levels provides scant insights into underlying networks that give rise to the observed cultural and social ties, i.e. we cannot identify specific networks nor can we infer the organic or induced nature of information provided by migrants. Chapter 5 will analyze the role of migrant stock at a lower level of supplier aggregation, which allows us to employ a more precise, destination-specific measure. In addition, this level allows us to investigate select provider characteristics as drivers of demand. Chapter 6 will then explore how our measures of proximity manifest themselves as information and support networks at the individual level.

References

Afman, E. R., & Maurel, M. (2010). Diplomatic relations and trade reorientation in transition countries. In P. A. G. Van Bergeijk & S. Brakman (Eds.), *The gravity model in international trade: Advances and applications* (pp. 278–295). Cambridge: Cambridge University Press.

Allison, P. D., & Waterman, R. P. (2002). Fixed-effects negative binomial regression models. *Sociological Methodology, 32*, 247–265.

Anderson, J. E. (1979). A theoretical foundation for the gravity equation. *The American Economic Review, 69*, 106–116.

Anderson, J. E. (2011). The gravity model. *Annual Review of Economics, 3*, 133–160. https://doi.org/10.1146/annurev-economics-111809-125114.

Anderson, J. E., & van Wincoop, E. (2003). Gravity with gravitas: A solution to the border puzzle. *The American Economic Review, 93*, 170–190.

Anderson, J. E., & van Wincoop, E. (2004). Trade costs. *Journal of Economic Literature, 42*, 691–751.

Anderson, J. E., & Yotov, Y. V. (2010). The changing incidence of geography. *American Economic Review, 100*, 2157–2186.

Anderson, S. P., de Palma, A., & Thisse, J.-F. (1992). *Discrete choice theory of product differentiation*. Cambridge: MIT Press.

Arkolakis, C., Costinot, A., & Rodríguez-Clare, A. (2012). New trade models, same old gains? *American Economic Review, 102*, 94–130. https://doi.org/10.1257/aer.102.1.94.
Baldwin, R., & Taglioni, D. (2007). Trade effects of the euro: A comparison of estimators. *Journal of Economic Integration, 22*, 780–818.
Balistreri, E. J., & Hillberry, R. H. (2006). Trade frictions and welfare in the gravity model: How much of the iceberg melts? *The Canadian Journal of Economics, 38*, 247–265.
Baltagi, B. H. (2013). *Econometric analysis of panel data* (5th ed.). Chichester: Wiley.
Belenkiy, M. (2008). *Robustness of the extensive margin in the Helpman, Melitz and Rubinstein (HMR) model* (MPRAPaper 17913). Munich: University Library of Munich.
Berger, H., & Nitsch, V. (2008). Zooming out: The trade effect of the euro in historical perspective. *Journal of International Money and Finance, 27*, 1244–1260. https://doi.org/10.1016/j.jimonfin.2008.07.005.
Bergstrand, J. H. (1985). The gravity equation in international trade: Some microeconomic foundations and empirical evidence. *The Review of Economics and Statistics, 67*, 474–481.
Bergstrand, J. H. (1989). The generalized gravity equation, monopolistic competition, and the factor-proportions theory in international trade. *The Review of Economics and Statistics, 71*, 143–153.
Bergstrand, J. H. (1990). The heckscher-ohlin-samuelson model, the linder hypothesis and the determinants of bilateral intra-industry trade. *The Economic Journal, 100*, 1216–1229.
Berry, S. (1994). Estimating discrete-choice models of product differentiation. *The Rand Journal of Economics, 25*, 242–262.
Berry, S., Levinsohn, J., & Pakes, A. (1995). Automobile prices in market equilibrium. *Econometrica, 63*, 841–890.
Bookman, M. Z., & Bookman, K. R. (2007). *Medical tourism in developing countries*. New York: Palgrave Macmillan.
Bosker, E. M., & Garretsen, H. (2010). Trade costs, market access, and economic geography: Why the empirical specification of trade costs matters. In P. A. G. Van Bergeijk & S. Brakman (Eds.), *The gravity model in international trade: Advances and applications* (pp. 193–223). Cambridge: Cambridge University Press.
Bosquet, C., & Boulhol, H. (2014). Applying the GLM variance assumption to overcome the scale-dependence of the negative binomial QGPML estimator. *Econometric Reviews, 33*, 772–784. https://doi.org/10.1080/07474938.2013.806102.
Bun, M. J. G., & Klaassen, F. J. G. M. (2002). The importance of dynamics in panel gravity models of trade. *SSRN Journal*. https://doi.org/10.2139/ssrn.306100.
Cameron, A. C., & Trivedi, P. K. (2009). *Microeconometrics: Methods and applications, 8. Printing*. Cambridge: Cambridge University Press.
Campbell, D. L. (2013). Estimating the impact of currency unions on trade: Solving the glick and rose puzzle. *The World Economy, 36*, 1278–1293. https://doi.org/10.1111/twec.12062.
Chaney, T. (2008). Distorted gravity: The intensive and extensive margins of international trade. *American Economic Review, 98*, 1707–1721. https://doi.org/10.1257/aer.98.4.1707.
Cheng, I.-H., & Wall, H. J. (2005). Controlling for heterogeneity in gravity models of trade and integration. *Federal Reserve Bank of St. Louis Review, 87*, 49–63.
Crone, R. K. (2008). Flat medicine? Exploring trends in the globalization of health care. *Academic Medicine, 83*, 117–121. https://doi.org/10.1097/ACM.0b013e318160965c.
Dalgin, M., Mitra, D., & Trindade, V. (2004). *Inequality, nonhomothetic preferences, and trade: A gravity approach* (NBER Working Paper Series 10800). National Bureau of Economic Research.
Deardorff, A. (1998). Determinants of bilateral trade: Does gravity work in a neoclassical world? In J. A. Frankel (Ed.), *The regionalization of the world economy* (Vol. 1, pp. 7–32). Chicago: University of Chicago Press.
Deb, P., & Trivedi, P. K. (2013). Finite mixture for panels with fixed effects. *Journal of Econometric Methods, 2*, 35–51. https://doi.org/10.1515/jem-2012-0018.
DESTATIS. (2012). Bevölkerung und Erwerbstätigkeit: Wanderungen. Fachserie 1 Reihe 1.2, Wiesbaden.
Disdier, A.-C., & Head, K. (2008). The puzzling persistence of the distance effect on bilateral trade. *The Review of Economics and Statistics, 90*, 37–48.

Dixit, A. K., & Stiglitz, J. E. (1977). Monopolistic competition and optimum product diversity. *The American Economic Review, 67*, 297–308.

Duanmu, J.-L., & Guney, Y. (2013). Heterogeneous effect of ethnic networks on international trade of Thailand: The role of family ties and ethnic diversity. *International Business Review, 22*, 126–139. https://doi.org/10.1016/j.ibusrev.2012.02.009.

Dunlevy, J. A. (2006). The influence of corruption and language on the protrade effect of immigrants: Evidence from the American states. *The Review of Economics and Statistics, 88*, 182–186.

Eichengreen, B., & Irwin, D. A. (1998). The role of history in bilateral trade flows. In J. A. Frankel (Ed.), *The regionalization of the world economy* (pp. 33–62). Chicago: University of Chicago Press.

Engel, C. (2002). Comment on borders, trade, and welfare. In S. M. Collins & D. Rodrik (Eds.), *Brookings trade forum: 2001*. Washington, DC: Brookings Institution Press.

Esiyok, B., Çakar, M., & Kurtulmuşoğlu, F. B. (2017). The effect of cultural distance on medical tourism. *Journal of Destination Marketing & Management, 6*, 66–75. https://doi.org/10.1016/j.jdmm.2016.03.001.

Felbermayr, G. J., & Toubal, F. (2010). Cultural proximity and trade. *European Economic Review, 54*, 279–293. https://doi.org/10.1016/j.euroecorev.2009.06.009.

Fernández, C., Ley, E., & Steel, M. F. J. (2001). Model uncertainty in cross-country growth regressions. *Journal of Applied Econometrics, 16*, 563–576. https://doi.org/10.1002/jae.623.

Fidrmuc, J. (2009). Gravity models in integrated panels. *Empirical Economics, 37*, 435–446. https://doi.org/10.1007/s00181-008-0239-5.

Fitzgerald, D. (2012). Trade costs, asset market frictions, and risk sharing. *American Economic Review, 102*, 2700–2733. https://doi.org/10.1257/aer.102.6.2700.

Gohin, A., & Féménia, F. (2009). Estimating price elasticities of food trade functions: How relevant is the CES-based gravity approach? *Journal of Agricultural Economics, 60*, 253–272. https://doi.org/10.1111/j.1477-9552.2009.00199.x.

Gould, D. M. (1994). Immigrant links to the home country: Empirical implications for U.S. bilateral trade flows. *The Review of Economics and Statistics, 76*, 302–316.

Greene, W. (2005). Functional form and heterogeneity in models for count data. *Foundations and Trends® in Econometrics, 1*, 113–218. https://doi.org/10.1561/0800000008.

Griffith, D. A. (2000). A linear regression solution to the spatial autocorrelation problem. *Journal of Geographical Systems, 2*, 141–156.

Griffith, D. A. (2002). A spatial filtering specification for the auto-Poisson model. *Statistics and Probability Letters, 58*, 245–251.

Guo, M. (2015). *Estimating international consumption risk sharing and financial frictions with gravity equation*. Beijing: Department of Economics, School of Economics and Management, Tsinghua University.

Hanefeld, J., Lunt, N., Smith, R., & Horsfall, D. (2015). Why do medical tourists travel to where they do? The role of networks in determining medical travel. *Social Science & Medicine, 124*, 356–363. https://doi.org/10.1016/j.socscimed.2014.05.016.

Hausman, J. A., & Taylor, W. E. (1981). Panel data and unobservable individual effects. *Econometrica, 49*, 1377–1398.

Hausman, J. A., Hall, B. H., & Grilliches, Z. (1984). Econometric models for count data with an application to the Patents-R & D relationship. *Econometrica, 52*, 909–938.

Head, K., & Mayer, T. (2010). Illusory border effects: Distance mismeasurement inflates estimates of home bias in trade. In P. A. G. Van Bergeijk & S. Brakman (Eds.), *The gravity model in international trade: Advances and applications* (pp. 165–192). Cambridge: Cambridge University Press.

Head, K., & Mayer, T. (2013). *Gravity equations: Workhorse, toolkit and cookbook* (CEPII Working Paper 27). Paris: CEPII.

Head, K., & Ries, J. (1998). Immigration and trade creation: Econometric evidence from Canada. *The Canadian Journal of Economics, 31*, 47–62.

Helpman, E., Melitz, M., & Rubinstein, Y. (2008). Estimating trade flows: Trading partners and trading volumes. *Quarterly Journal of Economics, 123*, 441–487. https://doi.org/10.1162/qjec.2008.123.2.441.

Heung, V. C. S., Kucukusta, D., & Song, H. (2010). A conceptual model of medical tourism: Implications for future research. *Journal of Travel and Tourism Marketing, 27*, 236–251.

Hofstede, G. H. (1980). *Culture's consequences: International differences in work-related values, Cross-cultural research and methodology series* (p. 5). Newbury Park: Sage.

Holmberg, H., & Lundevaller, E. H. (2015). A test for robust detection of residual spatial autocorrelation with application to mortality rates in Sweden. *Spatial Statistics, 14*, 365–381. https://doi.org/10.1016/j.spasta.2015.07.001.

Johnson, T. J., & Garman, A. N. (2015). Demand for international medical travel to the USA. *Tourism Economics, 21*, 1061–1077. https://doi.org/10.5367/te.2014.0393.

Johnston, R., Crooks, V. A., & Snyder, J. (2012). "I didn't even know what I was looking for": A qualitative study of the decision-making processes of Canadian medical tourists. *Globalization and Health, 8*, 23. https://doi.org/10.1186/1744-8603-8-23.

Jotikasthira, N. (2010). *Salient factors influencing medical tourism destination choice*. Dissertation: Southern Cross University.

Keckley, P. H., & Eselius, L. L. (2009). *2009 survey of health care consumers: Key findings, strategic implications*. Washington, DC: Deloitte Center for Health Solutions.

Klijs, J., Ormond, M., Mainil, T., Peerlings, J., & Heijman, W. (2016). A state-level analysis of the economic impacts of medical tourism in Malaysia. *Asian-Pacific Economic Literature, 30*, 3–29. https://doi.org/10.1111/apel.12132.

Klingenberger, D. (2009). Dentaltourismus und Auslandszahnersatz: Empirische Zahlungsbereitschaftsanalysen auf der Grundlage repräsentativer Stichproben im Jahre 2008. In *Materialienreihe/Institut der Deutschen Zahnärzte* (Vol. 32). Köln: Dt. Zahnärzte-Verlag.

Krautheim, S. (2007). *Gravity and information: Heterogeneous firms, exporter networks and the 'Distance Puzzle'* (EUI Working Paper ECO 2007/51). European University Institute.

Leamer, E. E., & Stern, R. M. (1970). *Quantitative international economics*. Chicago: Aldine Publishing Company.

Linnemann, H. (1966). *An econometric study of international trade flows*. Amsterdam: North-Holland Pub..

Lunt, N., Jin, K. N., Horsfall, D., & Hanefeld, J. (2014). Insights on medical tourism: Markets as networks and the role of strong ties. *Korean Social Science Journal, 41*, 19–37. https://doi.org/10.1007/s40483-014-0012-7.

McCallum, J. (1995). National borders matter. *The American Economic Review, 85*, 615–623.

Melitz, M. J. (2003). The impact of trade on intra-industry reallocations and aggregate industry productivity. *Econometrica, 71*, 1695–1725.

Melitz, J., & Toubal, F. (2014). Native language, spoken language, translation and trade. *Journal of International Economics, 93*, 351–363.

Möhlmann, J. L., Ederveen, S., de Groot, H. L. F., & Linders, G.-J. M. (2010). Intangible barriers to international trade: A sectorial approach. In P. A. G. Van Bergeijk & S. Brakman (Eds.), *The gravity model in international trade: Advances and applications* (pp. 224–251). Cambridge: Cambridge University Press.

Mundlak, Y. (1978). On the pooling of time series and cross section data. *Econometrica, 46*, 69–85.

Musa, G., Thirumoorthi, T., & Doshi, D. (2012). Travel behaviour among inbound medical tourists in Kuala Lumpur. *Current Issues in Tourism, 15*, 525–543. https://doi.org/10.1080/13683500.2011.626847.

Naranong, A., & Naranong, V. (2011). The effects of medical tourism: Thailand's experience. *Bulletin of the World Health Organization, 89*, 336–344. https://doi.org/10.2471/BLT.09.072249.

Nickell, S. (1981). Biases in dynamic models with fixed effects. *Econometrica, 49*, 1417–1426.

Noree, T., Hanefeld, J., & Smith, R. (2016). Medical tourism in Thailand: A cross-sectional study. *Bulletin of the World Health Organization, 94*, 30–36. https://doi.org/10.2471/BLT.14.152165.

Novy, D. (2013). International trade without CES: Estimating translog gravity. *Journal of International Economics, 89*, 271–282. https://doi.org/10.1016/j.jinteco.2012.08.010.

Petrin, A. (2002). Quantifying the benefits of new products: The case of the minivan. *Journal of Political Economy, 110*, 705–729.

Pöyhönen, P. (1963). A tentative model for the volume of trade between countries. *Weltwirtschaftliches Archiv, 90*, 93–100.

Rabe-Hesketh, S., & Skrondal, A. (2012). *Multilevel and longitudinal modeling using stata* (3rd ed.). College Station Tex: Stata Press publication.

Rabe-Hesketh, S., & Skrondal, A. (2013). Avoiding biased versions of Wooldridge's simple solution to the initial conditions problem. *Economics Letters, 120*, 346–349. https://doi.org/10.1016/j.econlet.2013.05.009.

Rauch, J. E. (1999). Networks versus markets in international trade. *Journal of International Economics, 48*, 7–35.

Rauch, J. E. (2001). Business and social networks in international trade. *Journal of Economic Literature, 39*, 1177–1203.

Rose, A. K. (2001). Currency unions and trade: The effect is large. *Economic Policy, 16*, 449–461. https://doi.org/10.1111/1468-0327.00082.

Rose, A. K., Lockwood, B., & Quah, B. (2000). One money, one market: The effect of common currencies on trade. *Economic Policy, 15*, 7–45.

Santos Silva, J. M. C., & Tenreyro, S. (2006). The log of gravity. *The Review of Economics and Statistics, 88*, 641–658.

Santos Silva, J. M. C., & Tenreyro, S. (2011). Further simulation evidence on the performance of the Poisson pseudo-maximum likelihood estimator. *Economics Letters, 112*, 220–222. https://doi.org/10.1016/j.econlet.2011.05.008.

Santos Silva, J. M. C., & Tenreyro, S. (2015). Trading partners and trading volumes: Implementing the Helpman-Melitz-Rubinstein model empirically. *Oxford Bulletin of Economics and Statistics, 77*, 93–105. https://doi.org/10.1111/obes.12055.

Savage, I. R., Deutsch, K. W., & Girshick, M. (1960). A statistical model of the gross analysis of transaction flows. *Econometrica, 28*, 551–572.

Sheu, G. (2014). Price, quality, and variety: Measuring the gains from trade in differentiated products. *American Economic Journal: Applied Economics, 6*, 66–89. https://doi.org/10.1257/app.6.4.66.

Skrondal, A., & Rabe-Hesketh, S. (2014). Handling initial conditions and endogenous covariates in dynamic/transition models for binary data with unobserved heterogeneity. *Journal of the Royal Statistical Society: Series C, 63*, 211–237. https://doi.org/10.1111/rssc.12023.

Straathof, B. (2008). *Gravity with gravitas: Comment* (CPB Discussion Paper 111). The Hague: CPB Netherlands Bureau for Economic Policy Analysis.

Tinbergen, J. (1962). *Shaping the world economy: Suggestions for an international economic policy*. New York: Twentieth Century Fund.

Van Bergeijk, P. A. G., & Brakman, S. (2010). Introduction: The comeback of the gravity model. In P. A. G. Van Bergeijk & S. Brakman (Eds.), *The gravity model in international trade: Advances and applications* (pp. 1–26). Cambridge: Cambridge University Press.

Veerasoontorn, R., & Beise-Zee, R. (2010). International hospital outshopping: A staged model of push and pull factors. *International Journal of Pharmaceutical and Healthcare Marketing, 4*, 247–264. https://doi.org/10.1108/17506121011076174.

Wall, H. J. (1999). Using the gravity model to estimate the costs of protection. *Federal Reserve Bank of St. Louis Review, 81*, 33–40.

Wang, Y., Kockelman, K. M., & Wang, X. (2013). Understanding spatial filtering for analysis of land use-transport data. *Journal of Transport Geography, 31*, 123–131. https://doi.org/10.1016/j.jtrangeo.2013.06.001.

Wongkit, M., & McKercher, B. (2013). Toward a typology of medical tourists: A case study of Thailand. *Tourism Management, 38*, 4–12. https://doi.org/10.1016/j.tourman.2013.02.003.

Wooldridge, J. M. (2005). Simple solutions to the initial conditions problem in dynamic, nonlinear panel data models with unobserved heterogeneity. *Journal of Applied Econometrics, 20*, 39–54. https://doi.org/10.1002/jae.770.

Yeoh, E., Othman, K., & Ahmad, H. (2013). Understanding medical tourists: Word-of-mouth and viral marketing as potent marketing tools. *Tourism Management, 34*, 196–201. https://doi.org/10.1016/j.tourman.2012.04.010.

Chapter 5
Drivers of Medical Travel at the Hospital Level

In the previous section, our analysis was restricted to aggregate flows and we did not consider different destinations within Germany. We now keep demand aggregated at the country level but consider a lower level of aggregation along the supply dimension. Our main interest at this level continues to lie with networks as captured by migrant stock. Broader measures of cultural proximity as CNL and CSL are unavailable at this level and we disregard dynamics. In addition to networks, we are interested in the effect of hospital characteristics that capture treatment quality as perceived by medical travelers.

We continue to work with the same data set on inpatients, i.e. the analysis is restricted to medical travel and recreational destination characteristics are disregarded. As the data set only captures patients who chose a destination in Germany, the results of the analysis are limited to destination choice conditional on choosing Germany. They are generalizable to comparisons with other countries only if there exist no interaction effects between characteristics at lower levels of aggregation and the country level, i.e. if, for example, hospital size in Germany is valued identically to hospital size elsewhere.

5.1 Model

Our empirical specification builds on the previous chapter, i.e. we estimate international patient volume in a gravity framework. As before, price vectors of the destinations are unavailable so we cannot calculate multilateral resistances of all locations. Once again, we can make the assumption that inpatient treatments in Germany face a rigid fee schedule and only special services such as chief physician attendance incur additional costs. We can further assume that these surcharges are strictly based on the GOÄ schedule, so the price vector remains unidentified and can be disregarded. Destination choice is then based on otherwise differentiated destination characteristics or differences in trade costs. However, we do not need to rely

K. Schmerler, *Medical Tourism in Germany*, Developments in Health Economics and Public Policy 13, https://doi.org/10.1007/978-3-030-03988-2_5

Fig. 5.1 Multilateral resistance: exports—many sources—many destinations

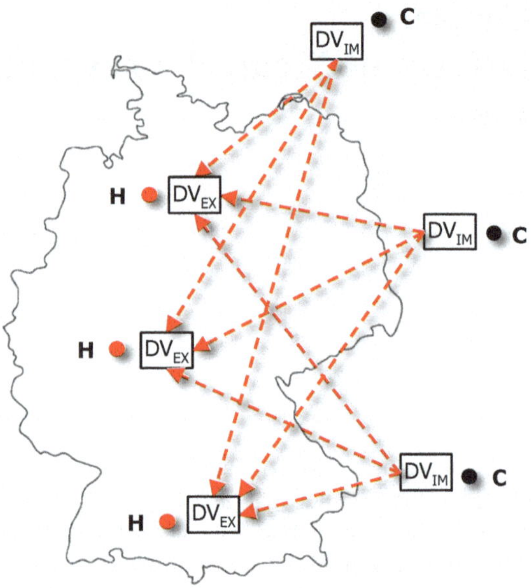

on these strong assumptions but may include the destination-specific dummy variables depicted in Fig. 5.1 as we now have variation in this dimension, i.e. across hospitals *H*.

Our dummy variables do not only capture destination-specific multilateral resistances but also any other time-invariant unobserved heterogeneity. The list of such characteristics is long, including destination-specific costs for travel and accommodation or unobserved marketing efforts at the hospital level. These dummies would also control for unobserved recreational destination characteristics even if we ruled them out as drivers of medical travel. As discussed in Chap. 2, some states such as Bavaria and Berlin pursue marketing initiatives at higher levels that can be captured by a state dummy. We further include dummies for hospitals in districts with international borders and for districts in the former Eastern and Western parts of Germany to capture historic and cultural ties.

Side issues of interest are hospital characteristics that capture the perceived treatment quality of a destination. Lutze et al. (2010) run an OLS regression of both number and share of international patients of a subset of relevant hospitals on a number of characteristics. They find a significant impact of capacity, capacity usage, large equipment, proximity to a border, and location in Western Germany on the number of non-residents treated. The private status of a hospital turns significant when regressed on the share of non-residents treated in a hospital. These results hint to the role of international patients in the utilization of equipment and hospital capacity. The private status of many providers on the other hand may either be an indicator of preferences or of unobserved marketing activities by private providers that cause them to dominate the perception of available choices. Aside from a general disjunction from demand modeling, the main problem with this estimation of hospital characteristics lies in the inappropriateness of drivers. Equipment quality, capacity usage and even capacity are likely endogenous due to reverse causality.

In the spirit of a gravity model, we control for time-invariant hospital characteristics via dummy variables. We use domestic catchment area and market power therein as measures of provider size. They are perfectly exogenous for our purpose as international patients are disregarded in their calculations. These two indices also capture expertise and reputation which both may induce farther travel. These effects are likely confounded with settlement structure which may also necessitate traveling but we control for settlement structure both explicitly and implicitly via district population density and dummy variables in a panel setting. Finally, we include private operator status and university hospital status as indicators of presumed marketing activity and high quality signaling, respectively.

In addition to accessibility and local infrastructure controls via population density and international border dummies, we enhance our specification by a number of other district variables. BIP captures the economic mass of a destination. Migrant stock captures networks originating from migrants who lower the costs of medical travel and disseminate knowledge of a foreign option. Total migrants are our broadest measure of migrant stock. In Chap. 4, we ruled out any endogeneity of migrant stock at the aggregate level: Given the small size and the atomic structure of the facilitator industry there was no reason to believe that the medical travel business draws immigrants. At the hospital level, we assume that the spatial pattern of migrant stock is exogenous and strongly affects the demand for hospitals in a given district. Finally, we neglect dynamics which translates into the assumption that recommendations refer to Germany as a country not to units of supply within.

Table 5.1 summarizes the variables that capture hospital, district, state and regional characteristics.

Table 5.1 Variables of disaggregated destination choice

	Variable	Interpretation
Hospital level	Domestic catchment area	Expertise/Size
	Market power in domestic catchment area	Expertise/Size
	Hospital dummy	Outward resistance
	Private provider	Marketing
	University hospital	Expertise
District level	Population density	Accessibility/Local infrastructure
	Border region	Accessibility
	GDP	Size
	Migrant stock	Networks
State level	State dummy	Marketing
Region level	East/West Germany	Historic ties
Source country	Country dummy	Inward resistance
	GDP	Demand capacity

5.2 Data

We use the same data set as in the previous chapter, i.e. the official German hospital statistics from 2007–2012. Of the total 459,224 treatments of international patients throughout the 6-year period, only 4 cannot be assigned to a hospital. However, the assignment of treatments to source countries is of much poorer quality than that to hospitals and varies substantially by state. Table 5.2 depicts the shares of unknown/open source countries for select states across the 2007–2012 period and highlights Schleswig-Holstein and Hamburg as states with particularly poor coding. While treatment numbers for Hamburg remain consistent across time, Schleswig-Holstein is particularly problematic with a substantial outlier in 2007 that may be due to coding errors. Consequently, the results of the subsequent data description need to be interpreted with care for these two states. The shares of unknown/open source countries for the states excluded from Table 5.2 are not displayed as they were below the reporting threshold. They lie between 1.66% and 2.81%. Finally, note that Rhineland-Palatinate and Saarland are aggregated to one state for reasons of privacy protection.

Figures 5.2, 5.3 and 5.4 display total treatments and the dynamics of treatments per state across years. First, note the aforementioned outlier of 6800 treatments in Schleswig-Holstein in 2007, which is completely out of line with the following years. Second, we find that treatments of international patients are very much concentrated in the former West Germany, which may be due to a more pronounced willingness to develop new business segments or a longer available timespan to develop such activities. Third, we find that the filtering of elective treatments does not change the overall picture qualitatively. However, the isolation of ICD 2 treatments shows that NRW and RP/SA drop in relative numbers while Hesse, Hamburg and Mecklenburg-Vorpommern rise in the ranking. This effect may be due to a number of factors at both the hospital and the state level: Both Frankfurt and Hamburg are well-connected with airports and their University hospitals and other local clinics pursue active internationalization strategies. Mecklenburg-Western Pomerania has strong exporting ties to Russia which, as we have seen in Chap. 2, is a main source country of international patients. Similarly, we have pointed out medical tourism strategies at the state level in Berlin, NRW and Bavaria which also

Table 5.2 Shares of unknown/open source countries, by state

	Shares
Schleswig Holstein	54.9%
Hamburg	56.9%
Saxony	17.7%
Saxony-Anhalt	9%
Bremen	8.4%
Brandenburg	8.4%
Baden-Württemburg	6.6%
Rhineland Palatinate/Saarland	4.8%

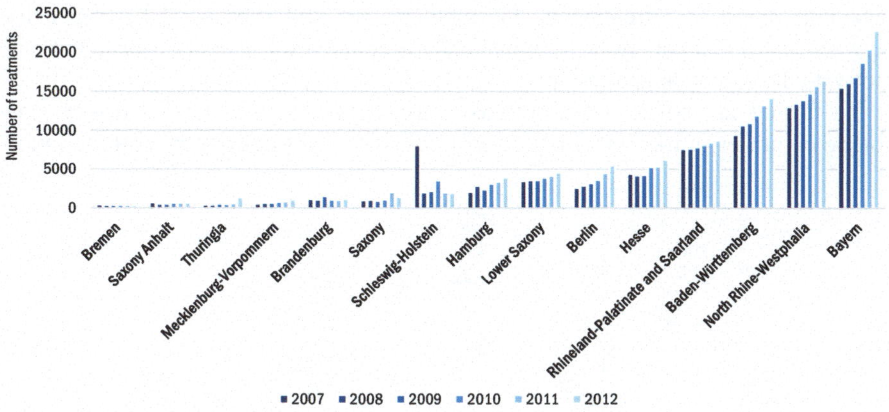

Fig. 5.2 Total treatments, by state and year

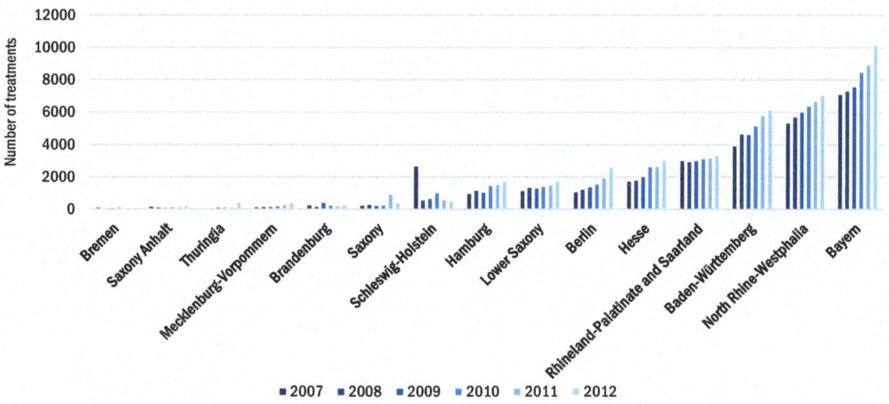

Fig. 5.3 Elective treatments, by state and year

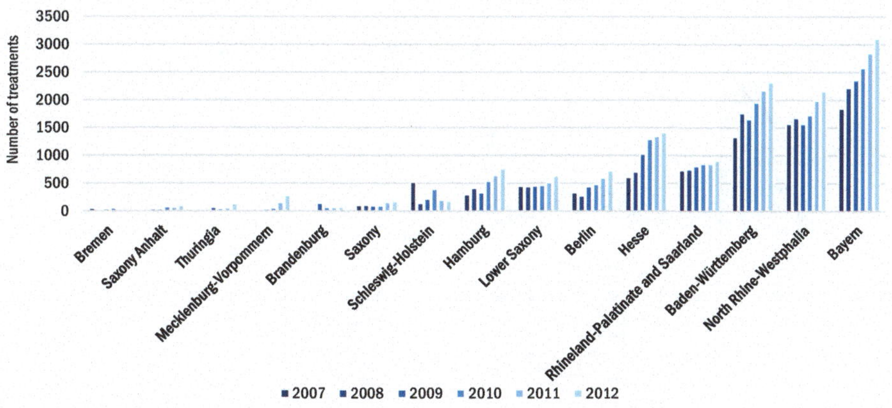

Fig. 5.4 ICD 2 treatments, by state and year

rank high for ICD 2 treatments. In summary, we find substantial heterogeneity between states that cannot be systematically accounted for in every aspect and that motivate the use of state dummies.

To further investigate state heterogeneity, Figs. 5.5, 5.6 and 5.7 display top source countries in the 2007–2012 period by state. Source country ranking omits

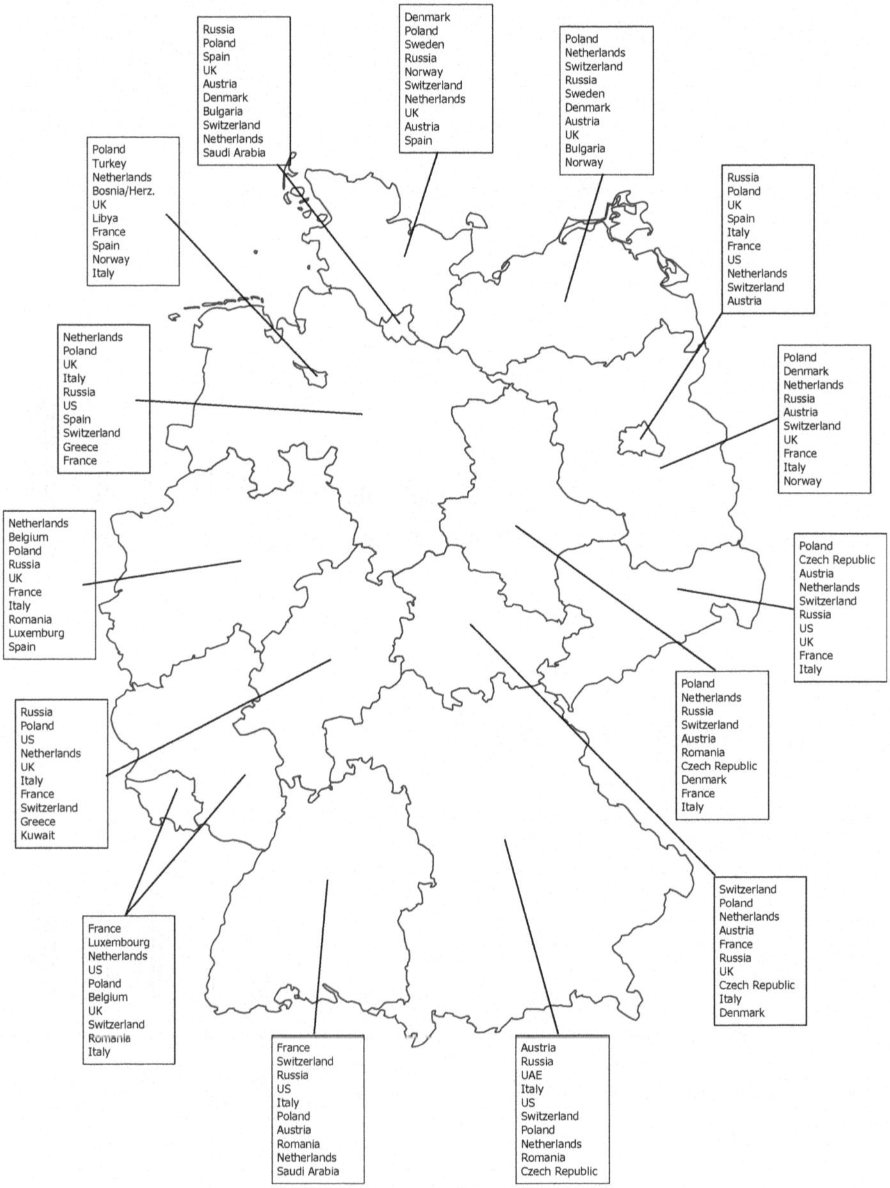

Fig. 5.5 Top source countries for all treatments from 2007–2012, by state

patients from open/unknown countries. Figure 5.5 includes all treatment types and highlights the importance of contiguity, i.e. neighboring countries often rank atop the list of source countries. In fact, the country ranking for each state with a national border is dominated by patients from one of these bordering countries: Poland, Czech Republic, Austria, France, the Netherlands, Luxemburg, and Denmark. In addition, Switzerland and Luxemburg rank second in Baden-Württemberg and RP/Saarland, respectively. Patients from Poland and the Netherlands rank high across most states which may be due to incidental treatments that occur in the course of transit. Finally, some states appear to have very specific ties that determine their top source countries. Russia is the top source country for Berlin, Hamburg and Hesse, i.e. well-connected, large cities if Hesse is taken to be represented largely by Frankfurt. Russia generally ranks among the top 10 source countries in all but two states. Bavaria shows strong ties to the Middle East, namely the United Arab Emirates; Bremen reports Turkey and Bosnia-Herzegowina as important source countries; and Thuringia appears to have strong ties to Switzerland that prevail throughout subsequent treatment disaggregation. We suspect this inflow to be a result of outbound labor migration but we do not investigate this in detail.

The filtering of elective treatments in Fig. 5.6 does not change the importance of neighboring countries but Russia moves up the rankings. The same holds for the Middle East in a number of states, i.e. Bahrain and Libya in Bremen, Kuwait in North Rhine-Westphalia, Kuwait and Saudi-Arabia in Hamburg and Hesse, Saudi-Arabia and the UAE in Baden-Württemberg, and Egypt and the UAE in Bavaria. For ICD 2 treatments only as displayed in Fig. 5.7, Russia takes the top spot in most states and Middle Eastern countries continue to move up in the ranking. Nevertheless, neighboring countries remain an important source of patients, often in first or second spot. Finally, Greece, Bulgaria and Romania now rank high in ten, six and five states, respectively. The two latter are affected by EU reimbursement schemes that entitles EU citizens to obtain medical care in other EU countries if the treatment cannot be rendered domestically in a timely fashion (Court of Justice of the European Union 2014).

In summary, there appears to be ample justification for the inclusion of both state- and country-specific dummies in addition to bilateral characteristics such as contiguity. An extra set of bilateral dummies will be forgone at both the state-country and the hospital-country level for two reasons: First, this set would be very large and second, we expect most of the heterogeneity that goes beyond the broader engagement in medical travel at the state or hospital in medical travel to be captured by our domestic measure of migrant stock. The broader engagement is absorbed by state and hospital dummies.

An increase in granularity from the state to the hospital level shows that hospitals are distributed unevenly across states and concentrated in Bavaria and Baden-Württemberg. Destination attractiveness as a measure of total treatments at the state level would thus be confounded with the number of hospitals, i.e. supply capacity. Figure 5.8 displays total treatments from 2007–2012 by state and treatment type, displaying all, elective and ICD 2 treatments from left to right. The color scheme

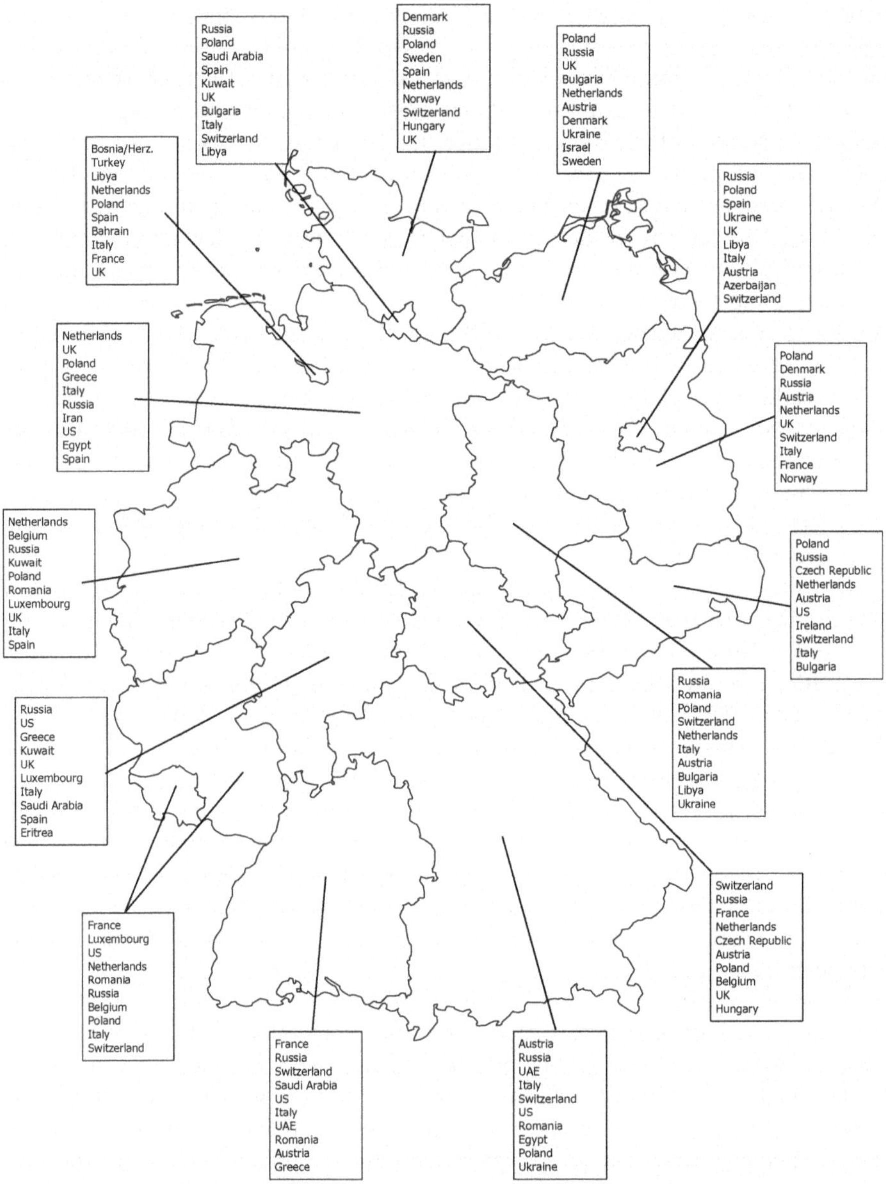

Fig. 5.6 Top source countries for elective treatments from 2007–2012, by state

represents the respective measure ranges in eight equidistant intervals. Keeping the deficient data quality of Schleswig-Holstein in mind, we find the East-West pattern discussed above for total treatments. The filtering of elective and ICD 2 treatments in columns two and three, respectively, lowers the ranking of Schleswig-Holstein

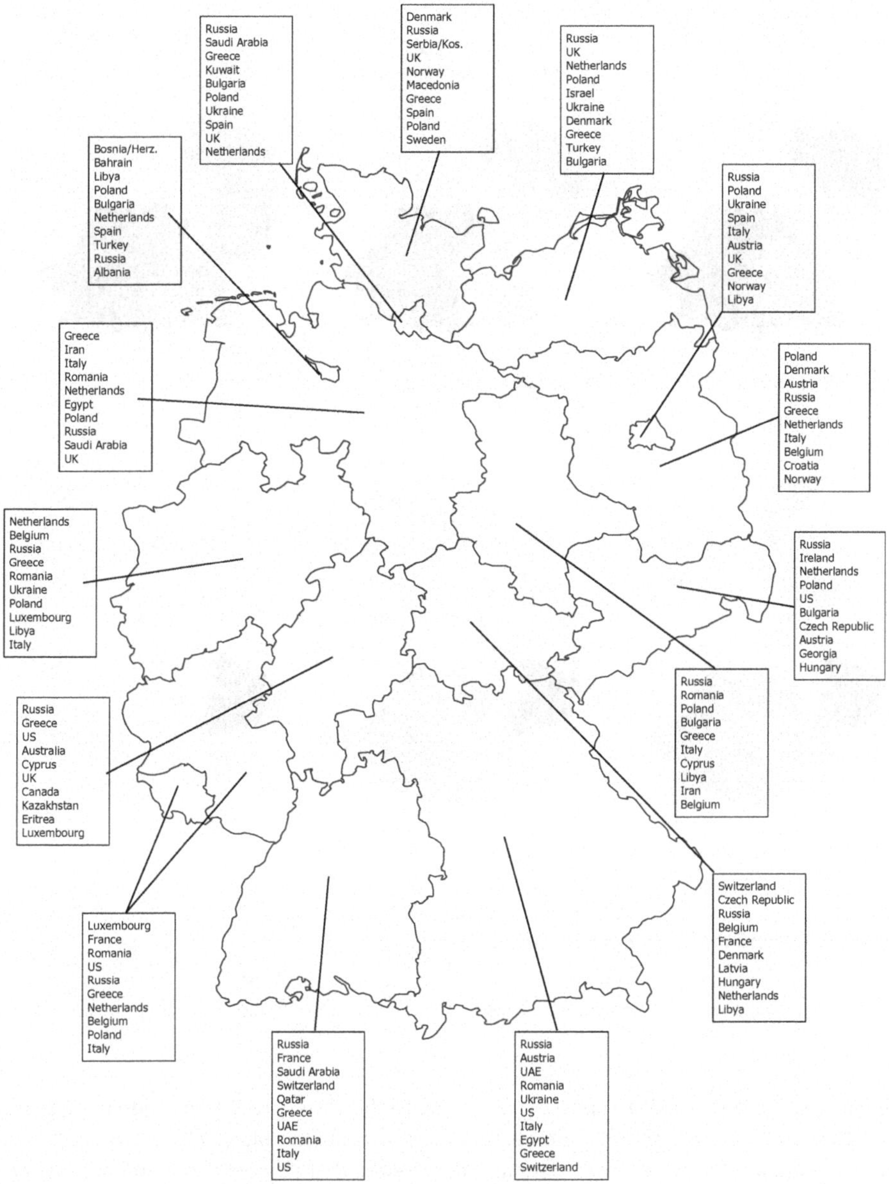

Fig. 5.7 Top source countries for ICD 2 treatments from 2007–2012, by state

and adds a more pronounced focus on Hesse and Rhineland/Saarland but it does not invoke any fundamental changes. The treatment-per-hospital measure for the 2007–2012 period in Fig. 5.9 introduces three main differences: While a general difference between the East and the West is still apparent, Mecklenburg-

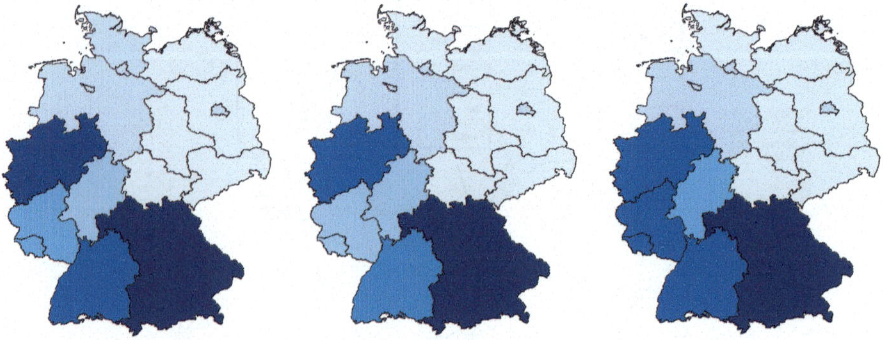

Fig. 5.8 Total treatments, by state and treatment type

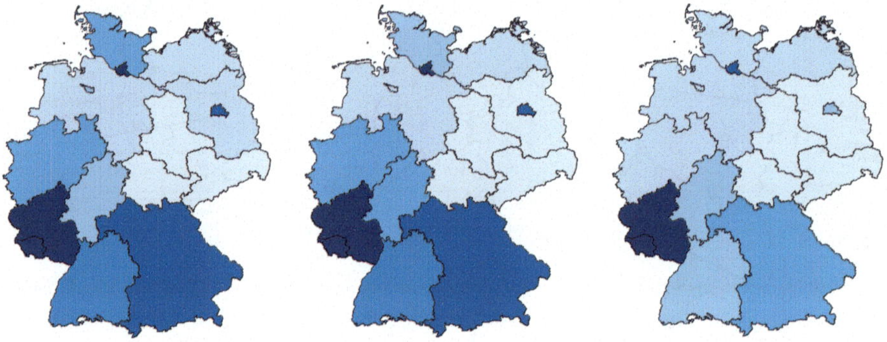

Fig. 5.9 Total treatments per hospital, by state and treatment type

Table 5.3 Number of hospitals in Germany, by year

	2007	2008	2009	2010	2011	2012
Number of hospitals	2087	2083	2084	2064	2045	2017

Vorpommern now exhibits increased activity in the East. The same holds for Berlin, which shows considerable hospital activity along with Hamburg. These two cities are underestimated by the aggregate treatment measure that neglects area and accessibility of hospitals. Finally, the Rhineland/Saarland construct ranks atop the per-hospital measure regardless of treatment filtering. This reflects an unusually pronounced cross-border activity as most treatments are rendered to residents from Luxemburg and France—who may be German citizens nevertheless.

Zooming in further to the hospital level, we find considerable heterogeneity among hospitals in terms of international patients treated, which also motivates the use of hospital dummies. Table 5.3 and Fig. 5.10 display the number of hospitals

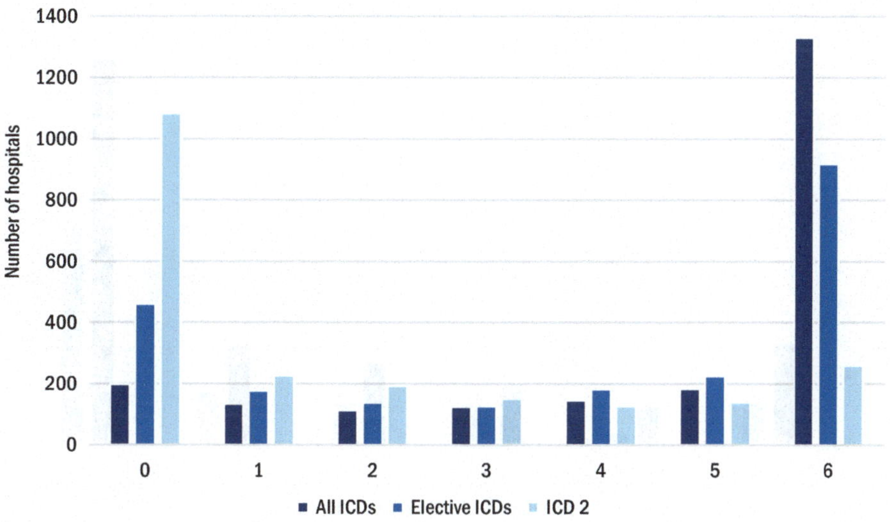

Fig. 5.10 Hospitals with treatments of international patients in 0–6 years

in Germany over time and the number of hospitals with total treatments of international patients in 0–6 years throughout the observed period. Of all hospitals, 59.6% reported treatments of international patients in every year while 8.9% reported zero years with treatments of international patients. This finding corresponds to 10,227 non-zero observations and 2154 zero observations in a hospital panel.

Treatment concentration in Fig. 5.10 is U-shaped for each treatment type. The removal of non-elective ICDs exposes an increased number of hospitals who no longer receive any international patients and a decrease of hospitals that provide services to international patients every year. This effect is even more pronounced for ICD 2 treatments which may be due to better filtering of incidental treatments that better removes the spatial distribution of patients due to tourism. It also captures the availability of specialized treatments, however. Figure 5.11 reports the average number of treatments rendered to international patients for hospitals that provided treatments to international patients in one to all 6 years of the sample. It complements Fig. 5.10 and shows that patient volume is strongly concentrated in hospitals that maintain international activities throughout the entire observation period. This result is in line with Pollard 2013 who finds that 65% of the providers in a convenience sample worldwide receive less than 100 international patients per year while 15% of the hospitals receive more than 1000 international patients per year.

Finally, Table 5.4 presents the variables, coding and sources of all covariates used in the analysis. They are complemented by East/West Germany, state and hospital dummies for destinations as well as country dummies for source countries. Table 5.5 reports the corresponding correlation matrix.

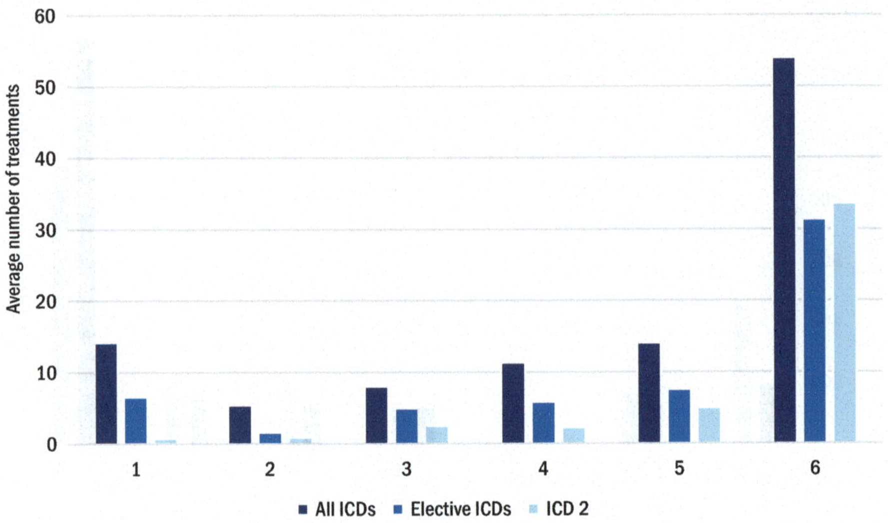

Fig. 5.11 Average number of treatments per year, by hospital group

Table 5.4 Description of variables in the regression at the hospital level

Variable	Coding	Source
GDP (destination district)	ln(1,000,000)	INKAR 2013
Population density	Persons per km^2/1000	INKAR 2013
Catchment area	Average distance between hospital and place of domestic residence/100	German hospital statistics
HHI in catchment area	Herfindahl index over patients from the catchment area. The catchment area comprises enough districts to cover a minimum of 95% of a hospital's total treatments	German hospital statistics
Migrant stock	Migrants/1000	DESTATIS table 12521-0040
University hospital	0/1	German hospital statistics
Private operator	0/1	German hospital statistics
GDP (source country)	ln(1,000,000)	WDI

5.3 Estimation and Specification

Contrary to Chap. 4 we can work within the PPML framework of Santos Silva and Tenreyro (2006), i.e. we can identify inward and outward multilateral resistances across destination hospitals and source countries and do not need to resort to a panel estimator. This estimator requires a substantial number of dummies, which is tolerable as this particular Poisson Pseudo-ML specification does not suffer from

Table 5.5 Correlation matrix for the gravity model at the hospital level

	GDP (district)	Density	HHI	Catchment	Migrant stock	University	Private	GDP source
GDP (district)	1.00							
Pop. density	0.79	1.00						
HHI	−0.31	−0.22	1.00					
Catchment	−0.09	−0.09	−0.38	1.00				
Migrant stock	0.82	0.82	−0.23	−0.06	1.00			
University	0.08	0.09	−0.04	0.00	0.04	1.00		
Private	0.05	0.05	−0.22	0.37	0.10	−0.07	1.00	
GDP (source)	0.00	0.00	0.00	0.00	0.00	0.00	0.00	1.00

incidental parameter bias (Fernández-Val and Weidner 2016). It is further desirable from a theoretical perspective due to its consistency with the assumptions of structural gravity discussed in Sect. 4.1.2 (Fally 2015).

Remaining within the gravity framework, our resulting specification resembles Eq. (4.38) without the dynamic term. Our explanatory variables include the economic masses Y for destination hospitals i at the district level k and source countries j at the national level; hospital characteristics H as listed in Table 5.1; our set of district-specific variables X_k as listed in Table 5.1; state dummies l and region dummies m as in Table 5.1, exporter and importer dummies i and j; and time dummies λ.

$$\ln q_{ij}^t = \beta_1 \ln Y_j^t + \beta_2 \ln Y_k^t + \beta_3 H_i^t + \beta_4 X_{k(j)}^t + DV_i + DV_j + DV_l + DV_m + \lambda^t. \quad (5.1)$$

Our variable set X is largely district-specific with the exception of migrant stock whose effect we investigate both as measured by total stock $Migrants_k$ and as bilateral stock $Migrants_{kj}$, i.e. as migrants from country j in destination district k.

Note that we cannot include geographic distance despite multiple origins—see Fig. 5.1. International patients are recorded only by source country so there is no variation across observations within a source country. Geographic distance thus collapses with the source-country dummies FE_j. A geographic distance parameter could only be identified a multilateral setting with additional destination countries or if international patients were recorded by their full addresses which would introduce within source country variation.

As in Sect. 4.2, we opt to estimate treatments q rather than treatment value as our export measure. Treatments in (5.1) continue to be estimated in levels due to the Poisson Pseudo-ML approach (Santos Silva and Tenreyro 2006).

5.4 Results

In a first step, we investigate the effect of treatments of patients from missing/ unknown source countries. To that end, we estimate a simple specification that models only inflows of international patients q_i to hospitals i, as opposed to source country-specific bilateral inflows q_{ij}. Clearly, this specification cannot include importer dummy variables for countries j. Column 1 of Table 5.6 presents the results of this specification excluding patients from missing source countries for all treatment types. They are very similar to the unreported results of the model including patients from missing source countries except for the estimated positive effects of population density and HHI, which are much more pronounced as unassigned patients are included. This hints to poorer coding by large hospitals in urban areas but we cannot assess whether it occurs deliberately or inadvertently due to higher patient volumes of international or German patients—both of which may underlie the missing/unknown share in question.

Excluding patients from missing/unknown source countries, column 2 displays our results for the modeling of bilateral trade flows q_{ij} with a measure of total migrant stock in district k. We find very similar positive effects of population density, HHI, and catchment area as in column 1 and an even larger positive effect for university hospitals and hospitals in the West of Germany. These effects along with the positive effect of source country GDP are well in line with our expectations. However, the effect of total migrant stock is negative and significant as in column one. This result is misleading and results from the aggregation of migrant stock across source countries, many of which have low treatment counts. Column 3 shows that the disaggregation of migrant stock to source countries produces the expected significant and positive effect on treatments.

Columns 4–6 and 7–9 repeat our analysis for elective and ICD 2 treatments, respectively. The computations for these treatment groups were difficult due to the large number of dummy variables and an increasing number of destinations with zero treatments as treatment types become more specific. We achieved convergence for elective and ICD 2 treatments but failed to produce standard errors for bilateral treatment flows of ICD 2 treatments. This problem is likely to be caused by multicollinearity but we have not been able to pinpoint the exact offenders via remote data access. Despite this unresolved issue, we choose to present the estimated parameters. For elective treatments, we find positive and significant effects of catchment area and university status on the number of international patients even if they are somewhat smaller in magnitude. For electives, there is weak evidence for a positive effect of private operator status while population density and HHI turn insignificant. As for all treatments, the parameter estimates of migrant stock are positive and significant once their bilateral nature has been accounted for.

For ICD 2 treatments, we are reluctant to give too much emphasis to our coefficient estimates in absence of their standard deviations. We only note that university status, catchment area and migrant stock display similar effects as for elective treatments while HHI and West Germany turn negative.

Table 5.6 Results at the hospital level, by treatment group

	All treatments			Electives			ICD 2		
	q_i	q_{ij}		q_i	q_{ij}		q_i	q_{ij}	
	(1)	(2)	(3)	(4)	(5)	(6)	(7)	(8)	(9)
GDP (district)	0.201	Cens.	Cens.	0.083	0.061	0.164	−0.377	−0.411	−0.410
	(0.198)	Cens.	Cens.	(0.285)	(0.244)	(0.249)	(0.510)		
Pop. density	0.445**	0.465**	0.081	0.271	0.300	0.005	−0.151	−0.079	−0.100
	(0.204)	(0.234)	(0.206)	(0.267)	(0.311)	(0.275)	(0.419)		
HHI	1.090***	1.095***	0.978***	0.394	0.418	0.301	−2.560**	−2.523	−2.509
	(0.399)	(0.322)	(0.327)	(0.703)	(0.530)	(0.535)	(1.303)		
Catchment	0.440**	0.436***	0.417***	0.392**	0.387***	0.375***	0.160	0.156	0.155
	(0.181)	(0.114)	(0.113)	(0.183)	(0.112)	(0.111)	(0.292)		
Migrant stock (total)	−0.003*	−0.003***		−0.002	−0.003*		0.000	0.000	
	(0.001)	(0.001)		(0.002)	(0.001)		(0.003)		
Migrant stock (bilateral)			0.017***			0.021***			0.025
			(0.003)			(0.004)			
University	3.219***	7.020***	4.167***	2.398***	2.425***	2.412***	2.254***	2.255	2.260
	(0.452)	(0.817)	(0.554)	(0.326)	(0.398)	(0.402)	(0.581)		
Private	0.119	0.122*	0.128*	0.199	0.202*	0.212*	0.041	0.034	0.033
	(0.126)	(0.072)	(0.074)	(0.179)	(0.118)	(0.121)	(0.337)		
GDP (source)		0.539***	0.539***		0.670***	0.669***		0.686	0.685
		(0.085)	(0.085)		(0.101)	(0.101)			
West Germany	2.303**	7.643***	4.544***	3.101**	2.118*	1.720	15.482***	−3.348	−3.341
	(0.920)	(1.450)	(1.402)	(1.323)	(1.253)	(1.239)	(2.438)		

(continued)

Table 5.6 (continued)

	All treatments			Electives			ICD 2		
	q_i	q_{ij}		q_i	q_{ij}		q_i	q_{ij}	
	(1)	(2)	(3)	(4)	(5)	(6)	(7)	(8)	(9)
Year dummies	Yes	Yes	Yes	Yes	Yes	Yes	Yes	Yes	Yes
Hospital dummies	Yes	Yes	Yes	Yes	Yes	Yes	Yes	Yes	Yes
Border dummies	Yes	Yes	Yes	Yes	Yes	Yes	Yes	Yes	Yes
State dummies	Yes	Yes	Yes	Yes	Yes	Yes	Yes	Yes	Yes
Country dummies	No	Yes	Yes	No	Yes	Yes	No	Yes	Yes
Observations	11,230	1,937,367	1,937,367	9819	1,654,510	1,654,510	6529	967,173	967,173
LL	−43,933	−695,740	−694,254	−30,242	−357,659	−356,810	−14,293	−123,045	−122,715
BIC	−60,904	−2.7e + 07	−2.7e + 07	−59,106	−2.3e + 07	−2.3e + 07	−40,652	−1.3e + 07	−1.3e + 07
R^2	0.961	0.177	0.181	0.949	0.205	0.208	0.926	0.273	0.274

Significant at 0.1*, 0.05**, 0.01***

GDP of the source country is quite consistently a positive and significant predictor of the number of international patients. GDP of the receiving district remains insignificant but two estimates were censored by the Research Data Center of the German Federal Statistical Office for undisclosed reasons.

Overall, the positive effect of university affiliation is very consistent across specifications. We interpret it as a measure of perceived quality that communicates expertise and cutting-edge treatments but it may also capture reputation and professional networks of practicing physicians who attract or acquire international patients. The visibility of a hospital and its perceived expertise are captured by both catchment area and HHI and we find a positive effect of the former. Both measures are moderately negatively correlated as shown in Table 5.5 which is reasonable as the number of competing hospitals is expected to increase as catchment area increases. It appears as if catchment area, i.e. the willingness of patients to travel farther, is a better indicator of perceived quality than HHI, which is insignificant for elective treatments and even negative for ICD 2 treatments. We expected HHI to capture a hospital's visibility to migrants who infer about its quality, but a high HHI may also result from a mere lack of alternatives. Also note that both a large catchment area and HHI could be explained by a district's settlement structure and accessibility which we controlled for by population density.

As expected, bilateral migrant stock has a positive and significant effect on treatments. This result is robust across treatment types. In absence of the standard deviation in column 9 we cannot reliably assess if the positive effect of migrant stock increases as we move from all treatments to ICD 2 treatments. The higher parameter estimate is certainly plausible, however, and points to migrants as producers of trust rather than as hosts to tourists who suffer from acute conditions. The evidence for a positive effect of our private operator dummy is fairly weak but inference here suffers from missing standard deviations in columns 8 and 9. The same problem arises for the West Germany dummy, which initially suggested a positive effect but may even be negative for ICD 2 treatments. The latter would be plausible if ICD 2 treatments can be attributed to Russian and Central Asia patients who may have stronger cultural ties to Berlin and Eastern states but this remains a weak hypothesis.

Finally, we would like to note two challenges of methodological and of theoretical nature that we encountered: First, we tacitly assume that the spatial distribution of migrants is exogenous, i.e. migrants do not relocate due to medical tourism. We consider this to be a tenable assumption but attempted to remove it employing international student stock as an instrument for migrant stock—now assuming that the location of studies in Germany is driven only by educational considerations. Similar to ICD 2 treatment flows before, our PPML-based instrumental variable estimator proposed by Windmeijer and Santos Silva (1997) runs into substantial convergence problems that were impossible to diagnose and to resolve via the restricted remote data access procedure our data set requires.

Second, there is an empirical trade-off between the disaggregation of treatments and the disaggregation of suppliers as we need to make an availability assumption of treatments that was innocuous at the national level but becomes more critical at the hospital level. Our data description and the preceding results show that the hospital level is very suitable to analyze the effect of bilateral migrant stock and that the use of higher spatial or organizational units would need to take the lower hospital level into account by controlling for hospital density, for example. A low level of aggregation along the supply dimension is thus desirable and also provides more variation. However, the assumption of treatment availability at the hospital level is much more objectionable than the treatment availability at the country level, i.e. patients may be able to choose from a set of different countries to obtain a given treatment but not from a set of hospitals as not all hospitals provide all treatments. We attempted to address this problem with our data set, which contains information about the various wards in each hospital. However, ward classifications, the multi-faceted nature of many treatments and the sheer number of medical conditions does not allow us to perform a comprehensive matching procedure between treatments and suitable wards. We aimed for an analysis including only hospitals with ICD 2–related wards—facilities for the treatment of oncological patients, hematology and internal oncology, nuclear medicine and radiotherapy—to filter out destinations that are unable to provide the treatments in question. However, ICD 2 treatments in the data set are assigned to numerous wards, ranging from oncology to internal medicine, and the latter is present in most hospitals so the availability of a treatment type is essentially impossible to gauge by available measures.

5.5 Summary

In this chapter we investigated the role of select hospital characteristics and of migrant stock at a lower level of supply. It thus extends our findings of Chap. 4.

The modeling of patient flows at the hospital level allowed the use of destination-specific dummy variables and our detailed exploration of the data set at a lower level of aggregation motivated the use of additional controls for medical tourism activities at various higher organizational and spatial levels. We also identified exogenous measures of perceived hospital quality and visibility that we investigated along with our key variable migrant stock.

We can confirm our main hypothesis that migrant stock has a positive effect on treatments of international patients. We employed multiple dummy variables and controls but our results remained very robust and thus support our findings in Chap. 4. They underlined the positive effect of bilateral migrant stock on destination choice at a far lower level of supplier aggregation with substantial variation. We interpret this measure to capture the presence of bilateral network nodes which produce trust in a destination and reduce costs via local support. It is robust across treatment types but crucially bilateral. There may be spatial spillover effects of migrant stock, i.e. migrants who disseminate information and produce trust in countries neighboring their source countries, but we suspect this effect to be small and did not investigate it in this context.

We find significant positive effects of hospital association with a university and a large catchment area in Germany on the number of treatments. Both hospital-level measures can be interpreted as perceived expertise and perceived treatment quality by international patients. University status may further capture international referral networks and data on physician staff nationality would allow the investigation of this interpretation as an avenue of future research.

On an empirical level, we encountered a trade-off between treatment disaggregation and disaggregation along the supply dimension. The inclusion of a supplier in a choice set makes the assumption that the investigated treatment type is in fact available at a given supplier which is the more reasonable the more treatment types are aggregated. This trade-off is unlikely to be overcome by better data as not even ward data allowed an informative, indirect assignment of treatment types to hospitals.

Finally, the chosen level of disaggregation invoked a substantial number of empirical estimation and convergence problems that could only be partly resolved. One barrier was the restricted access to the data which precludes the detailed investigation of estimator convergence. Another problem lies in the nature of the data that is disaggregated by treatment type, by hospital and by source country: Zero observations, the number of dummies and heavy multicollinearity eventually overwhelm the employed estimators. One possibility to handle these issues empirically is a two-stage model and we will return to this idea in Chap. 7.

References

Court of Justice of the European Union. (2014). Elena Petru v Casa Județeană de Asigurări de Sănătate Sibiu, Casa Națională de Asigurări de Sănătate. Accessed September 25, 2018, from http://curia.europa.eu/juris/document/document.jsf?text=&docid=158423&pageIndex=0&doclang=EN&mode=lst&dir=&occ=first&part=1&cid=810218

Fally, T. (2015). Structural gravity and fixed effects. *Journal of International Economics, 97*, 76–85. https://doi.org/10.1016/j.jinteco.2015.05.005.

Fernández-Val, I., & Weidner, M. (2016). Individual and time effects in nonlinear panel models with large N, T. *Journal of Econometrics, 192*, 291–312. https://doi.org/10.1016/j.jeconom.2015.12.014.

Lutze, I., Karmann, A., & Schoffer, O. (2010). Empirische Bestandsaufnahme zum Patientenimport im stationären Sektor. *Statistik in Sachsen, 1*, 30–36.

Pollard, K. (2013). *Medical tourism climate survey 2013*. London: Intuition Communication Ltd.

Santos Silva, J. M. C., & Tenreyro, S. (2006). The log of gravity. *The Review of Economics and Statistics, 88*, 641–658.

Windmeijer, F. A. G., & Santos Silva, J. M. C. (1997). Endogeneity in count data models: an application to demand for health care. *Journal of Applied Econometrics, 12*, 281–294. https://doi.org/10.1002/(SICI)1099-1255(199705)12:3<281:AID-JAE436>3.0.CO;2-1.

Chapter 6
Drivers of Medical Tourism at the Individual Level

We now broaden our perspective to medical tourism, i.e. we allow trip purposes beyond medical treatments. This third investigation explores medical tourism at the individual level and attempts to shed more light on the networks that constitute cultural ties, additional drivers of medical tourism to Germany, the role of recreational travel, real consideration sets and the relevant level of supplier aggregation. Measurement at the individual level provides a maximum of information about consumer heterogeneity but it is also most demanding in terms of data collection. Given the lack of data sets that cover our research questions, we must turn to the collection of primary data.

The sampling unit of ultimate interest is foreign patients P. As will be described below, international patients are tremendously difficult to approach due to privacy concerns and organizational barriers. In a first step, we thus investigate inbound patients with an indirect approach, i.e. interviews with three stakeholders of inbound medical tourism: German hospitals H, facilitators in Germany F_G and facilitators abroad F_A. These parties are the red nodes in Fig. 6.1 and represent relevant access points to medical treatments in Germany in that patients may visit hospitals directly, via domestic facilitators or via facilitators abroad. Our stakeholders are non-exhaustive as patients may also visit private practices or be placed by sponsors, e.g. embassies or firms. Both of these groups are of interest to us but their surveying lies beyond the means and scope of this study. However, we cover sponsors indirectly as we discuss their role in hospital interviews.

In the second part of this chapter, we directly survey international patients P who visit Germany and inquire about their networks, consideration sets, ranking of destination characteristics and individual characteristics. In addition, we elicit answers from a DCE to investigate the surmised country-of-origin effect and to shed more light on the relative importance of the different levels of supplier aggregation.

K. Schmerler, *Medical Tourism in Germany*, Developments in Health Economics and Public Policy 13, https://doi.org/10.1007/978-3-030-03988-2_6

Fig. 6.1 Network of stakeholders and gatekeepers in medical tourism

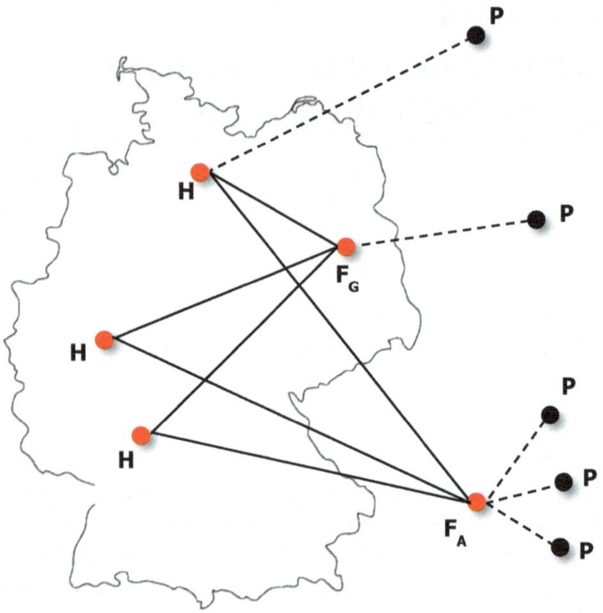

6.1 Interviews

Our interviews are structured to inquire about patient characteristics, drivers of medical tourism and the role of tourism from each of the three stakeholders. A follow-up question probes the role of supplier disaggregation, i.e. the role of physicians, providers and Germany as a country for destination choice unless the issue had already been addressed. We inquired with German providers about their patients' source countries and about the role of facilitators while facilitators were asked about their marketing channels and about destinations that they experience to be Germany's competitors. As an exhaustive coverage of facilitators is infeasible due to time and language constraints, we limit our research of and interviews with domestic and foreign facilitators to those who focus on Russian patients, i.e. the by far largest patient segment.

6.1.1 Hospitals in Germany

In the follow-up to recruit hospitals for our patient survey, we encountered seven providers who were willing to impart their substantial experiences with international patients to us. Interview partners comprised both physicians and administrative staff. Both the specific interview partners and the providers will remain undisclosed to ensure confidentiality.

Patients: Patients are consistently characterized as demanding, high-maintenance and from upper income brackets. Their treatments are reported in the fields of oncology, neurology, orthopedics and several invasive disciplines such as bariatric and thoracic surgery. One provider identifies a regional treatment particularity in congenital malformations and deformations among Middle Eastern patients but notes that they do not constitute the majority of treatments nor is an otherwise clear, regional pattern discernible. One large provider provides specific numbers on outpatient versus inpatient treatments and the former constitute 80% of total treatments to international patients.

Drivers: We asked providers to indicate the drivers that attract their patients and to indicate the unit of destination their patients seek. Most providers report the search for specialists, procedures or specific expertise, i.e. patients typically but not exclusively seek treatments in providers' flagship disciplines. Price also ranks up high in the perception of the providers. Third-party payments for up to 80% of the patients are common for specific source countries but the desire to prioritize and build up domestic capacities has led to an increasingly restrictive application and approval process in these countries, according to one provider. Other drivers mentioned include personal networks, recommendations from foreign-born physicians in or outside of Germany, maximum care offered, and poor hygiene in source countries.

Tourism: The reported role of tourism ranges from "does not matter at all" to "patients require appointments during their holiday season". The degree of tourism appears to depend on the nature of the treatment sought and is more important for patients from the Middle East with estimates of patients engaging in tourism as high as 80%.

Source countries: Well in line with the data sets previously presented, the focus of inbound patients lies on Russia, Western Asia and the Middle East. Providers generally differ in their reported focus on Middle Eastern countries with Saudi Arabia, Qatar and the United Arab Emirates but some cover the entire region. Some providers further point out source countries with armed conflicts such as Libya, Sudan and Yemen.

Competition: Although competitors are not specifically inquired, Israel and Turkey are mentioned as Germany's general competitors and Switzerland is mentioned as a competitor for patients from the Middle East. One interviewee points to increasing competition from Middle Eastern providers who employ staff with Western education. In the perception of several providers, foreign competitors lure with lower prices, common languages and marketing efforts.

Facilitation: Many providers cooperate with patient facilitators but experiences vary greatly. Billing often occurs to facilitators as opposed to patients and facilitator surcharges of up to 20% are reported. Some providers point to money inflows from Cyprus, Malta and Switzerland and perceive facilitators as criminals that they no longer cooperate with. One source describes Russians and Saudi Arabians as facilitator-based customers while other nationalities arrive via embassies but this pattern did not reemerge in other answers. This may be due to a misperception on part of the provider as another large provider noted that individuals or agencies are commonly summoned by embassies themselves to deal with organizational issues and to serve as interpreters. This provider also confirms the central role of embassies as facilitators but many providers no longer accept payment guarantees by embassies—one source cites bureaucracy and bad payment behavior as the main reason. Another source mentions the Red Cross and Red Crescent as sources of inbound patients but provides no detailed description of this channel. Finally, some countries such as Norway, Cyprus, Bosnia, Turkey, and Tunisia are reported to have contracts with providers for specialized treatments in the fields of stem cell treatment or neurosurgery, for example, to not build capacity at home. So we find some evidence of the scale effects suspected in Chap. 2.

Further issues: Our interview partners used the opportunity to point out a number of additional issues that they deemed relevant and that deserve mentioning. First, an interview partner points to a potential imperfection of official statistics as facilitators may supply their domestic addresses, which excludes the observation from entering official statistics. However, another interview partner declines this possibility as official documents are used to record their patients. Second, international patients are perceived as attractive economically but come with significant investment and risks. Many providers lament large numbers of unsuccessful quotations with one provider reporting a 4% conversion rate. Another provider points out that complex treatments are generally less predictable and often entail unforeseen extra costs that are not always covered by the patients. Related issues are the occasional unauthorized use of domestic health insurance IDs, invitations to outpatients whose health statuses escalate to serious conditions—without the personal means to cover them, and the occasional patient travelling with acute conditions that officially emerge in Germany to meet the terms of private international health insurances. However, some providers report no payment problems and even experience regular post-treatment reimbursements to patients. Third, several providers mention a growing inflow of European patients from Romania and Slovakia that travel on an S2 form, which allows patients to access providers in the European Economic Area and Switzerland while being fully or partially reimbursed domestically. These patients are reported to be as demanding as private out-of-pocket payers are but German providers may only charge DRG rates despite increased expenses for interpreters, for example. Fourth, one provider points out medical visas are a very recent bottleneck due to political turmoil in the source countries. Fifth and final, one interview partner recommends the initial isolation of international patients in general to avoid bacterial contamination.

The research of providers and facilitators in Germany led us to another expert on Russian patients in Germany who was willing to share his insights with us in order to complement our information. Peter Dehn, member of an operating company of a Proton Therapy Center in Germany and long-term expatriate in Russia, pointed out a potential mismatch between the desired level of supplier aggregation offered by facilitators and the level asked for by patients. He asserts that recommendations and word-of-mouth are the most important drivers to go abroad and that recommendations are commonly at the country level—with specific doctors coming in at a distant second. In general, Mr. Dehn notes the importance of social and cultural ties for the destination choice. Emigrants, private and business networks, and the general presence of a population that commands a patient's native language helps instill the trust required to travel for a treatment abroad. He further points out that the medical tourism business started 20 years ago when physician referrals to colleagues abroad played an important role. However, bad experiences with both agents taking cuts of up to 20% and hospitals offering exclusively high-price packages to international patients may have stifled the business. An unstructured approach and excessive pricing in medical tourism's infancy are confirmed by Braun (2014) and the drivers mentioned are quite in line with those of Shobokshi (2014) who points out word-of-mouth, physician expertise and country reputation as highly important destinations characteristics for Germany. According to Mr. Dehn, well-trained physicians and partly high-tech equipment characterize supply in Russia today but there are sometimes concerns about hygiene and distinct differences between the public and the private sector. Finally, he notes a second-round effect of tourism as it creates familiarity with and trust in a country, which allows it to enter the consideration set of a patient once the need for a treatment arises.

6.1.2 Facilitators in Germany

Our internet research identified 14 patient facilitators that are located in Germany and that focus on Russian-speaking patients. All facilitators were contacted by e-Mail and by phone and six firms ultimately agreed to answering our questionnaire either in writing or in a phone interview.

Patients: The majority of facilitators indicates a focus on middle to high-income groups. Only one facilitator reports a broader spectrum and points out poorer clients who save to send their children. This facilitator also indicates the age group of 20 or younger as its main clientele while other facilitators report age groups of 40 or older. "Young wives of wealthy men" are also mentioned but neither age nor income is specified in more detail. Three facilitators report 70:30 outpatient-to-inpatient ratios and the other facilitators note similar ratios. Inpatient treatments are generally perceived as too expensive. The most common treatment types mentioned are oncology, orthopedics and general diagnostics but other fields are also represented: gastroenterology, urology, ophthalmology, dermatology, neurosurgery and plastic surgery.

Drivers: Most facilitators perceive their clients' search for high quality treatments and high medical standards to be the main driver for treatment in Germany. Dissatisfaction with domestic health care includes high prices and poor quality, unavailability of specific treatments, a lack of specialists, and a lack of trust in both doctors and drugs at home. An important aspect of trust in German doctors comprises a basic trust in them actually performing the procedure advertised—aside from trust in the expertise of performing the procedure. Academic titles may further enhance trust. Additionally, Western Russia's proximity to Europe is pointed out as a factor in destination choice.

In terms of specific supplier disaggregation, several facilitators assert that the broader reputation of "a country's medicine" is the crucial driver of demand. The search for specific physicians is identified by two facilitators and the search for large medical centers by another facilitator. One facilitator notes that "no one looks for a country in general but for the best treatment" and goes on to note that some patients look for the best physician, but the perception thereof may well be confounded with the physician's location.

Tourism: Most facilitators ascribe a minor or negligible role to tourism in the context of medical treatments in Germany. Two facilitators describe a complementarity between treatments and subsequent travel but that is unrelated to Germany. Instead, patients continue to travel other parts of Europe. One facilitator recognizes regional attractiveness as a secondary driver of destination choice: Berlin draws patients with its reputation as a tourist destination and Munich outshines Stuttgart as a destination in terms of touristic attractiveness.

Marketing: We asked facilitators about the channels by which their clients find them and all firms list word-of-mouth among patients as the most important channel to acquire business. Trust in others' experiences implies a strong path dependence of medical tourism. Several patients also contact hospitals directly and one facilitator points out that their business model relies on a lack of international offices at various hospitals. Two firms point out a role for advertisement and one firm mentions the impact of welfare funds, websites, forums, and exhibitions on marketing efforts.

Competition: In terms of domestic competition, one firm points out the existence of between-state competition in Germany, which is in line with the marketing efforts described in Chap. 2. Another firm provides detailed information on "patient sharing" among different facilitators which implies a regional focus of most facilitators. It sometimes lives off commissions paid by providers but some large companies send their employees to Germany as part of large-scale contracts, so there is a perceived need for consolidation, which is also underlined by many small and short-lived firms. Facilitators should further grow beyond Germany's borders and include other European destinations where procedures can be performed after diagnostics were run in Germany. This cost-minimizing approach is at odds with the aforementioned search for procedures in Germany, however.

International competitors also abound: Israel is described as a lower quality but high-cost destination due to obscure calculations. Russian patients do not require a visa to enter Israel but the choice of physicians and hospitals there is limited. Clinics further tend to be smaller. Switzerland is mentioned as a very high quality and very expensive competitor. South Korea captures business from Central Asia, Siberia and Eastern Russia but it is too far from Western Russia to compete with Germany at full scale. India and China are seen as competitors with qualified physicians who were trained at Western universities and a strategy is advised to retain patients from Central Asia.

6.1.3 Facilitators in Russia

Our internet research identified 13 prominent patient facilitators that comprise eight Russian, four Israeli and one South Korean company. Most facilitators have partners in multiple countries but the focus lies on Israel and Germany, followed by Asian countries and some European countries. We contacted all facilitators by e-Mail and asked them to distribute a questionnaire among their clients. Follow-up calls revealed the facilitators' unwillingness to confront their clients with questionnaires but six Russian companies agreed to scheduled phone interviews. One facilitator further agreed to support answers with aggregated statistics wherever possible. Companies in Israel rejected any cooperation.

Patients: According to the majority of facilitators, patients are generally from high-income groups—often with their own businesses. One firm reports only 15% of high-income clients along with 80% middle-income clients who are value seekers and 5% low-income clients who seek travel with charity support. Another firm mentions charity-supported travel and the middle-income bracket to make use of it. This incongruence may arise from differences in income bracket definitions, but the overall share of patients travelling with third-party financial support was low for all interviewees. Two facilitators report a diverse age mix while all others indicated patients of 40 or older to be the dominant age group. A common characterization is "when people start to care about their health and have the means to do so". One facilitator indicates to place mostly inpatients while two facilitators stress the dominant role of outpatient treatments in order to minimize hospitalization costs. One facilitator mentions only 1–3% of inpatient treatments for clients with strokes or orthopedic treatments, for example. The majority sees form to follow function, i.e. the type of treatment determines the type of stay.

Drivers: Most facilitators report quality to be the main driver for patients to seek health care abroad. In particular, they hint to a domestic absence of high-tech equipment or the staff's lack of expertise with it. One facilitator observes domestic efforts to improve in this domain. Another main driver is seen in domestic unavailability of treatments and waiting times. Price plays an ambivalent role for patients: Two facilitators identify price as a crucial criterion for their clients' destination choices while another facilitator assigns a minor role to price. Confidentiality, general trust in German or foreign medicine and German work ethics were also identified as drivers to go abroad. This supports our hypothesis of the country level making a unique contribution to destination utility. Finally, one facilitator reports a traditional orientation of patients in Central Russia towards Germany and Israel and traced challenges in reorienting these patients towards cheaper alternatives in East Asia back to geographic distance, i.e. long flights, despite savings of 30–50%.

Most interestingly, the reported clients' decision-making processes and relevant units of destination vary greatly between all facilitators. Two facilitators see a two-stage process which leads to a pre-selection of potential destinations by price and a subsequent decision by hospital specialization and physician. Advice and recommendations play a crucial role in this decision process. Another facilitator attributes the lion's share of destination attractiveness as perceived by the clients to the country level, with hospitals being of secondary importance. Yet another facilitator sees the clients' relevant unit of destination in physicians and presents clients with detailed physician CVs, publications and statistics. A second facilitator also has employees research suitable destinations based on physicians.

Tourism: In general, facilitators acknowledge the role of tourism depending on the treatment, i.e. a cosmetic treatment or check-up invites tourism while patients who are in search of high-quality inpatient treatments do not care about tourism. Interestingly, one facilitator places invariant importance on tourism and tourism-related costs for his clients while another reports less than 1% of clients with interest in tourism regardless of the treatment.

Marketing: Unanimously, internet searches/company websites and word-of-mouth rank atop of the channels through which clients become aware of the international treatment option via facilitators. Social media play a minor role. One firm hints to Moscow being a general hub that people visit to inform themselves about medical tourism, so location is important in this respect. Another firm discloses that online advertisement is no longer used due to a steep increase in costs.

Competition: First, firms were asked about potential treatment-country patterns among their clients, which all but two firms declined. One facilitator points to Hungary for dental treatments, South Korea for plastic surgery, and Germany for prosthetics, orthopedics and cardiology. The other facilitator points out Thailand for plastic surgery, China for extended rehabilitation and TCM, and Japan, South Korea and Singapore for high-technology, innovative medicine. Second, we inquired about countries in the consideration set of the clients. A clear pattern emerges with Switzerland serving VIP patients but losing some business to the second-most expensive option in Germany due to the crisis in Russia. An immediate and cheaper alternative to Germany is Israel, which in turn suffers from a negative image among some clients. One firm considers Israel the first stop for oncology and nursing. Turkey is another affordable alternative besides Israel that benefits from geographic proximity, visa regulations, and a low language barrier. Other cheap alternatives mentioned are Spain and Greece. Finally, two facilitators mention Asia, which gained ground against Europe in the course of recent political crises. Here, Thailand, Singapore, South Korea and particularly India as the rising star stand out.

6.1.4 Results

The interviews with stakeholders and gatekeepers in medical tourism unearthed a number of consistent and inconsistent perspectives on medical tourists in Germany. Table 6.1 briefly summarizes the results pertaining to our main research questions, i.e. drivers of medical tourism and relevant destination characteristics, the role of supplier aggregation, real consideration sets and the role of tourism. In addition, it reports patient characteristics, which complement the picture painted in Chap. 2.

Table 6.1 Summary of stakeholder interviews

	Patients	Competition	Drivers	Level of supply	Tourism
Hospitals in Germany	High-income ~80% outpatients	Israel Switzerland Turkey	Quality Expertise Price Common language Hygiene Personal networks Recommendations	Physician Hospital	Treatment-dependent Relevance for Middle East
Facilitators in Germany	Middle/high income Age 40+ Children ~70% outpatients	Israel Switzerland China India South Korea	Quality Expertise Trust in country Distance Visa requirements Word-of-mouth Recommendations	Country Physician Hospital	Secondary role
Facilitators in Russia	Middle/high-income Middle/low-income Age 40+ Mostly outpatients	Israel Switzerland Turkey China India Singapore South Korea Thailand	Quality Expertise Equipment Price Distance Visa requirements Common language Waiting time Confidentiality Word-of-mouth Recommendations	Hospital Physician Country	Treatment-dependent

Note, however, that the results for facilitators are based on firms that operate mainly in the Russian and Central Asian markets and thus may not hold for patients from other source countries. Further, recall that the answers to our questions refer to both outpatients and inpatients so we anticipate a mismatch between these results and our previous analysis of inpatients in Chap. 2.

We find a more pronounced focus on older patients than for inpatients in Sect. 2.2.2, an outpatient share near the upper bound of our previous estimations and a focus on middle to high-income patients. At the same time, a niche for children and low-income patients appears to exist. The reported consideration sets implied by our interviews are largely consistent across stakeholders. An exception are more distant locations in Asia, which hospitals do not appear to perceive as competitors while facilitators agree on that set of countries as well.

Drivers and destination characteristics are consistent across the three stakeholders in that the quality of a treatment, i.e. the expertise in performing it, is a main criterion for destination choice. Facilitators further agree on the importance of distance and visa requirements and all stakeholders confirm the importance of networks, word-of-mouth and recommendations for the development of their business. There is mixed evidence of the role of price: Facilitators in Germany did not bring up price, which hints to a potentially price-insensitive segment of patients who are set on Germany and willing to pay for it. Interviews with Russian facilitators suggest a price threshold and two large providers confirmed a noticeable negative effect of exchange rate fluctuations. At the same time, patients from the Middle East are reportedly less susceptible to changes in economic conditions. A key difference may lie in institutionalized demand relations via embassies and countries with out-of-pocket payers. Substantial support schemes that manifest in diplomatic activities are a distinct feature of Middle Eastern countries and these schemes often cover both the patient and one extra person—even if group sizes quickly reach five or more due to the culturally ingrained concept of family nursing, according to one provider. However, this line of distinction by institutional ties is blurry as some patients from alleged self-payer countries such as Russia also receive limited financial support and as a number of patients from both the Middle East and Russia is sponsored by their employers. One large provider insists that institutionalized ties account for considerable patient volumes but that self-payers constitute the both larger and faster growing share of patients.

The role of tourism is reported to be treatment-dependent. Generally, treatment considerations appear to be the main determinant of destination choice but some patients embed their treatment in broader recreational activities. These activities are consistently reported to be more important for patients from the Middle East, which is probably due to companion group size rather than particularly tourism-compatible treatments.

Finally, we found the most glaring inconsistencies between stakeholders in their perceptions of demanded level of supply even if the answers were by no means unassertive. They pointed to physician expertise, hospitals and general trust in a destination countries' reputation. We suspect the latter to be a key contributor to destination choice as neighboring destinations such as Belgium or Czech Republic, which are commonly mentioned in the context of other source countries such as the UK, did not reappear in our context at all. However, the results are very inconclusive and probably distorted by the stakeholders' own preconceptions and business models. We thus devise a DCE in the next section and put this key question for the economic modeling of medical tourism directly to international patients.

6.2 Patient Survey

We now turn to the direct sampling of international patients, i.e. the black nodes in Fig. 6.1. Our interest still lies in the role of facilitators, the role of supplier aggregation, consideration sets, drivers of medical tourism to Germany and the role of recreational travel, and we construct a questionnaire to survey these topics. Specifically, this survey allows us to inquire about detailed information about the specific networks that patients rely on and about the relevant level of supplier aggregation on which there has been disagreement in the stakeholder interviews.

In principle, this level of consumer disaggregation allows us to estimate a comprehensive demand model that controls for consumer heterogeneity. In practice, however, our survey faces a number of limitations: First, we only sample international patients who self-select into Germany so we cannot necessarily generalize the results to patients who go elsewhere. Second, our sample is not representative of all international patients in Germany as the sampling unit spreads over a number of mutually exclusive access points. International patients may visit hospitals, small clinics or private practices focusing on specific services such as cosmetic surgery. Identification of and sampling at all relevant points are virtually infeasible and a representativeness of international patients would imply an upper-tier representativeness of sampling locations, i.e. hospitals, clinics and physicians. For logistic reasons, we had to restrict our access points to hospitals, which proved to be sufficiently cumbersome.

In fact, access to patients turned out to be as challenging as in Alsharif et al. (2010) and Musa et al. (2012): In 2014, we developed our questionnaire in English, Russian and Arabic and inquired with 57 hospitals in Saxony to cooperate in the administration of the survey. In addition, we sent hospitals a sample questionnaire in English along with the local Hospital Association's endorsement of this project. Of these 57 hospitals, 4 hospitals declined cooperation due to a lack of international patients and 1 large hospital was willing to cooperate if the survey could be made available online. We thus set up the survey via LimeSurvey which was communicated to international patients via an undisclosed channel by the hospital. No responses materialized.

In parallel to these efforts, we identified 24 large hospitals and 3 hospital networks with an online presence tailored to international patients and asked for their cooperation on this survey. 11 hospitals displayed interest, 7 agreed to interviews and 4 agreed to administering our questionnaires. Others expressed their willingness to cooperate but a general difficulty, even for hospitals with international offices, lies in the decentralized admission to wards, which greatly complicates the distribution of any material. The hospitals approached interpreters to distribute the questionnaires but interpreters hardly faced incentives to cooperate and produced few results. Eventually, one hospital distributed questionnaires independently and produced additional responses via the online version we provided; one hospital both distributed questionnaires independently and was visited for distribution; and one hospital was visited for distribution. The fourth hospital distributed questionnaires independently but eventually dropped out upon a change in personnel. In total, we obtained 42 questionnaires, so the survey remains of exploratory character. Nevertheless, it offers valuable insights into our research questions due to the broad set of topics covered. The following subsections present the structure of the questionnaire, the design of the included DCE, and the results.

6.2.1 *Questionnaire*

In line with our research questions, the main focus of our survey lies on consideration sets of patients, the role of information for destination choice and the availability of personal ties and networks at the alternatives in consideration sets. We complement this information with a comprehensive set of individual characteristics and a block on destination characteristics with a particular focus on the separation of physician, hospital and country-related characteristics.

Thematically, the questionnaire is structured as follows:

The topics and items of the survey build on our literature review in Chap. 2. Topic 1 aims to provide background information on the representativeness of patients in the sample based on the treatment types they received. Additionally, it inquires domestic availability of the received treatment, which indirectly reveals dissatisfaction with domestic health care provision.

Topics 2, 3 and 4 lie at the heart of the inquiry and attempt to reconstruct real consideration sets and to characterize alternatives therein in terms of personal pull-factors such as local support groups and recommendations. This information not only complements Chaps. 4 and 5 but can also guide the structural approach of future models. While a supply-side focus may attribute the lack of destination range to prohibitively high information costs, a demand-side focus may imply a two-stage model that predicts destination visibility based on both actionable and incidental factors in the first stage.

Topic 5 and particularly topic 6 also support model building and aim at the identification of the most appropriate level of supplier aggregation. The direct rating of physician, hospital and additional destinations characteristics is somewhat supplementary and in the spirit of Alsharif et al. (2010) and Pollard (2013). The operationalization of these characteristics draws from the aforementioned sources to ensure comparability of the results but also includes additional characteristics derived in Chap. 2:

Physician quality is reflected in reputation, specialization, track record, and communication. Reputation and track record are deliberately kept at a general level even if they may be difficult to communicate in practice via education, clinical outcome data or certifications. With respect to communication, we focus on the physician's proficiency in a common language. As discussed in Chap. 2, time spent with a physician also matters for communication but determines satisfaction rather than destinations choice as the patient can only assess it *ex-post*.

Hospital characteristics cover a broad range of criteria such as specialization, track record, medical equipment and facilities, hygiene and cleanliness, range of medical services offered, certification and a dedicated international patient service. In this context, we also inquire about the importance of nursing staff's proficiency in English. As with physician characteristics, hospital characteristics are rather broad and their breakdown for marketing purposes, e.g. hygiene into infection rates or other report card information, will not be discussed here but can be found elsewhere in the literature (Cheng 2004). The separation of these constructs into their various items is beyond our scope.

General destination characteristics capture the importance of accessibility, comfort, costs, tourist attractiveness and recommendation status of a destination. Accessibility aims at both duration and convenience via travel time and availability of a direct flight; comfort includes room, food and the catering to cultural and religious needs; and costs cover both costs of the hospital stay and accommodation costs for chaperones. Finally, tourist attractiveness and recommendation status remain at the construct level and do not distinguish between sights, landscape or shopping opportunities and facilitators, friends, family or physician recommendations, respectively.

The rating of all destination characteristics occurs on a 7-point scale. Experiences from (Alsharif et al. 2010; Pollard 2013) do not hint to indifference issues for any of our characteristics so we forgo a forced choice scale. A rich body of literature deals with the granularity of scales: Dawes (2008) find 5 and 7-point scales to be very comparable, Finstad (2010) identify interpolation problems for a 5-point scale and recommend 7 points and Leung (2011) recommends a 11-point scale for a normality assumption. We opt for a 7-point scale to allow for a sufficient degree of granularity and reject a larger scale on the grounds of excessive complexity that will reduce response rates. Based on our previous survey experiences in an international setting, we label endpoints with “not important” and “very important” as opposed to numerical labels whose ranking order is often misconstrued by individuals with different cultural backgrounds.

Topic 5 also considers the role of physician and hospital characteristics, price and country in destination choice in a DCE. We attempt to quantify the relative importance of these characteristics and to investigate their compensatory nature in a decision rule. As this question requires trade-offs, we aim to attach an order of relevance to the three aggregation levels of supply identified in Chap. 3. The country level is not explicitly included in the rating exercise and only touched on by topic 3.

Finally, topics 6 and 7 provide information on the main purpose of the trip to Germany—a crucial criterion in the definition of medical travel—and on the individual characteristics listed in Table 6.2. Aside from socio-demographics, these include the number of accompanying persons, language proficiency in German and English as a measure of cultural proximity, self-reported health, risk attitude, locus of control, degree and source of any domestic treatment cost reimbursement, and household income measured in Euros, USD and RUB.

The questionnaire, including the DCE, was pretested internally on seven persons to screen for undesired effects such as simplifying heuristics, fatigue, irrelevance, misunderstanding or room for interpretation (Johnson et al. 2013). We made small modifications to simplify the wording and found survey length appropriate with an average completion time of 8:43 min. The online survey is identical to the printed version and features a back button, as Hays et al. (2010) find no negative effect on missing data or internal inconsistency.

Table 6.2 Structure and items of the questionnaire

	Topic	Item	Question
1	Treatment information	Treatment received	1
		Inpatient/outpatient treatment	2
		Availability of treatment at home	3
2	Information channels	Treatment experience abroad	4
		Channel that raised awareness of Germany	5
3	Consideration sets	Countries considered	6
		Hospitals in Germany considered	7
4	Networks and personal ties	Support with travel arrangements	8
		Destination recommendations	9
5	Destination characteristics	Rating of physician characteristics, hospital characteristics, administration, accessibility, comfort, price, recommendations, tourist attractiveness	13
		DCE	14
6	Purpose of the trip		10
7	Individual characteristics	Nationality	15
		Country of residence	15
		Age	15
		Gender	15
		Education	15
		Number of chaperones	15
		Proficiency in English and German	16
		Self-reported health status before treatment	12
		Risk attitude	11
		Locus of control	11
		Reimbursement of treatment costs	15
		Household income	15
8	Comments		17

6.2.2 DCE

The discrete choice experiment is a central component of our questionnaire that allows us to analyze supplier aggregation in more detail and to assess the trade-off between characteristics at different supplier levels. Specifically, we are interested in the role of physicians, hospitals and countries for destination choice and opt for a DCE because it does not require explicit modeling of the cognitive process that translates preferences into choices. We will briefly discuss the experimental design, the resulting scenarios and our econometric model before we present the results of the entire survey.

6.2.2.1 Experimental Design

An appropriate experimental design is crucial for the surveying of stated preference data. As opposed to revealed preference data sets, stated preference tasks allow the researcher a controlled variation of alternative-specific covariates to ensure the identifiability and efficient estimation of anticipated effects. The goal of experimental design is an optimized test design that covers the attribute space in a way that data generated yields a maximum of information with a minimum number of profiles (Siebertz et al. 2010), i.e. a minimum number of observations needs to cover selected points, i.e. profiles, of the response surface. As the random selection of profiles is likely to lead to a poor coverage of the attribute space and a too finely grained coverage will entail a potentially infeasible number of profiles to check, a systematic approach is required to determine the test design.

The gold standard is an orthogonal array that features both orthogonality and balance. The former refers to statistical independence of attributes and minimizes multicollinearity in linear models while the latter ensures that every attribute level be used equally often which maximizes test power across attributes and allows the independent estimation of an intercept. Balance is also desirable for behavioral reasons as it avoids the dominating appearance of selected attribute levels (Kuhfeld et al. 1994). While orthogonality and balance are the key criteria generally considered to characterize optimal designs, orthogonal arrays are often unavailable for a number of restrictions: a large number of attributes, inhomogeneous attribute levels, the exclusion of infeasible or undesired attribute combinations, a non-standard number of profiles or a non-standard model with interactions or higher-order effects (Kuhfeld 1997). We restrict ourselves to a small number of attributes and employ binary coding to attributes whenever possible, but the two latter items are overly restrictive:

The research of experimental design is scattered across numerous fields and strands of literature and focuses on two very different aspects: industrial experimentation is mostly concerned with bias, i.e. aliasing of effects, while marketing research focuses more on efficiency, i.e. the precise estimation of suspected effects. Only recently have the two, somewhat isolated, strands of literature on aliasing and efficiency been merged (Jones and Nachtsheim 2011).

Full-factorial designs, i.e. all combinations of all attributes A and all attribute levels L which amount to L^A, allow the identification of and discrimination between all main effects of attributes and their interactions while fractional-factorial designs confound some of them. The idea is to alias supposedly negligible multi-way interactions between attributes A and to either eliminate their columns and lower the number of required profiles or to use their columns for screening designs by replacing interaction effects with additional attributes (Siebertz et al. 2010). The latter creates designs that become more saturated with attributes at the cost of aliasing them with various interaction effects that need to be assumed away in order to interpret the attributes' main effects.

Attribute levels L determine the design in that they reflect the estimable complexity of attri-butes. Typically, a linear effect is assumed which requires at least 2 points per attribute dimension to estimate. More complicated, higher order effects can be estimated with more sophisticated techniques such as splines or kriging but naturally require more profiles per dimension. Consequently, the resulting minimum number of profiles across dimensions with higher-order terms increases exponentially. A general methodological approach is prescribed by the surface response technique that screens for relevant attributes in a first step and then goes on to estimate higher order effects of the identified attributes in a second step. This will not be feasible in our context as it requires multiple waves of data collection. Instead, we must aim at a one-step estimation of relevant main and interaction effects.

Factorial designs are also discussed in the economic and marketing literature (Hensher et al. 2007; Louviere et al. 2007). Here, discrete choice models increase the design space to L^{AJ} as each extra alternative j may bring its own, alternative-specific set of attributes. Design concepts such as orthogonality and balance of attributes extend to an intra- and inter-alternative perspective, which requires more profiles or, rather, choices for a design of equal efficiency. Specific attribute and attribute level requirements quickly preclude the use of available standard arrays and motivate the employment of efficient designs, which minimizes the variance and covariance of the parameters to be estimated for a given functional form. Efficient designs attempt to be orthogonal and balanced but they are very unlikely to lead to the coincidental discovery of unexpected effects as they are not designed to identify them. A *ex-ante* disregard of interactions is thus problematic (Johnson et al. 2013).

Depending on the statistical model, attributes may not only represent linear, additive effects or marginal utilities of single attributes but also interactions or higher order terms thereof. Linear models often fare well even if true process is non-linear. In fact, a linear functional form in parameters is plausible if levels are not too far apart and interactions generally tend to be more important than nonlinear effects (Siebertz et al. 2010). Estimation technique also comes into play here as estimated interaction effects may partly be due to individual heterogeneity in aggregated samples, a problem that can be addressed by the use of latent classes or estimation at the individual level. At any rate, more a priori knowledge about the functional form leads to fewer required choices whereas generalized functional forms require more choices.

In addition to the differences in foci on bias (aliasing) and precision (efficiency), a fundamental difficulty lies in the non-linearity of economic decision models. In fact, non-linearity and increasing complexity of discrete choice modeling are main reasons why model estimation has leaped well ahead of experimental design. For linear models, variances and covariances for parameter estimates $\widehat{\beta}$ are given by

$$Var\left(\widehat{\beta}|X\right) = \sigma^2 (X'X)^{-1} \tag{6.1}$$

and are inversely proportional to the Fisher information matrix $X'X$. As the covariates X are the covariates whose setup is to be optimized, an optimization strategy must aim for a minimization of $(X'X)^{-1}$. Note that balance and orthogonality will lead to a diagonal variance-covariance matrix. Optimization strategies target different criteria that describe the structure of $X'X$. The most common criterion is the d-efficiency criterion that maximizes the fisher information matrix by maximizing its determinant. The maximized determined, and therefore the eigenvalues of $X'X$, can be interpreted as an indicator of minimized multicollinearity or an indicator of the size of a matrix and the subspace of the attribute space it covers (Lusk and Norwood

2005). There exist various other optimality criteria most of which deal with different characterizations of the covariance matrix (Kessels et al. 2006). More recently proposed DP- and AP criteria take the required estimation of σ^2 with a small number of replicated choices into account (Gilmour and Trinca 2012) but d-efficiency remains the standard measure.

Choice modeling is commonly done based on non-linear CL/MNL models so the above-mentioned optimality criteria do not directly carry over to non-linear models. Instead, the asymptotic variances and covariances, AVC, of the parameters β depend on the parameter values themselves (Train 2009)

$$AVC = \frac{1}{N}[-E(H)]^{-1}) = \frac{1}{N}\left[\frac{\partial^2 LL(Y, X, \beta)}{\partial \beta^2}\right]^{-1} \tag{6.2}$$

where $-E(H)$ is the negative expected Hessian or Fisher Information Matrix and the log-likelihood LL is given by

$$LL(Y, X, \beta) = \sum_{n=1}^{N}\sum_{j=1}^{J}\sum_{t=1}^{T} y_{njt} \ln P_{njt}(X, \beta) \tag{6.3}$$

where probability P depends on the model specification and N, J and T represent individuals, alternatives and choice occasions. y is a binary indicator variable that equals 1 if an alternative was chosen by an individual in a given occasion. This complication is typically disregarded in practice but has been addressed in the literature (Bliemer et al. 2009; Bliemer and Rose 2010).

Aside from aliasing, efficiency and non-linearity, a large number of design principles and constraints must be considered. First, alternatives can be labeled or unlabeled. Unlabeled alternatives focus on the role of attributes while labeled alternatives are more realistic and allow the study of a label main effect. Labeled alternatives tend to exhibit higher response rates and increased non-trading behavior (de Bekker-Grob et al. 2010) but the main danger of labeled alternatives lies in omitted variables associated with labels which violate the assumption about the error distribution (Louviere et al. 2007). This issue can be related to respondent heterogeneity and will potentially bias parameter estimates. Second, a no-choice or status quo is ideally included as an alternative in a one- or two-stage choice task (Adamowicz et al. 1998; Lancsar and Louviere 2008; Mühlbacher et al. 2016). The inclusion of a no choice is critical if actual demand share estimation is the goal but our focus lies on attribute trade-offs—whose estimation can also be adversely affected by a missing status opt-out alternative. In our context, no choice as in no treatment is no reasonable alternative for the given medical condition and it is unclear what a status quo actually means, i.e. no treatment at all, treatment at home or a treatment in another undisclosed country. An individual-specific status quo could be inquired along with its attributes but that would further complicate the task for the respondents and complexity is one culprit of a status quo effect (Boxall et al.

2009). Germany could be considered the status quo alternative as we survey international patients in Germany but we exclude an explicit status quo.

Third, there is no clear guidance to the number of alternatives *j* per occasion *t*. Pinnell (2005) suggests an increase of alternatives beyond two to improve statistical efficiency and to lower the chance of dominant alternatives through more utility balance. Fourth, there is some general guidance to the employment of repeated choices: Ryan and Gerard (2003) report an upper limit of 16 choices in common use. Rose et al. (2009) find that repeated observations can to some extent offset smaller sample sizes. The benefit of repeated choices diminishes as the sample size grows and must also be pitted against an increased burden on each individual. Lusk and Norwood (2005) note that substantial attention should be paid to design characteristics that contribute to high response rates. These include survey length, number of choices and the number of attributes (Louviere et al. 2002; Swait and Adamowicz 2001). Blocking allows the splitting of all choices of a design into groups to expose individuals to a feasible number of choices and Bunch and Batsell (1989) suggest at least six individuals per choice for an appropriate sample. On the other hand, ChoiceMetrics (2012) note that non-response removes rows and quickly destroys aspired orthogonality after blocking. Fifth and relatedly, choice orders can be randomized to avoid attention bias, learning and boredom if they survey style permits (Johnson et al. 2013).

Sixth and seventh, Huber and Zwerina (1996) suggest minimal attribute overlap as well as utility balance between alternatives within a choice. Minimal overlap is suggested as parameter estimates in multinomial logit models are based on differences in attribute levels between alternatives (Winkelmann and Boes 2009). Identical levels across alternatives thus provide no information. Similarly, utility balance between alternatives of a choice is to avoid dominant alternatives but requires priors on the attribute parameters. However, Kessels et al. (2006) find moderate levels of utility balance and overlap in their optimal designs which is plausible as perfectly utility-balanced choices lead to random alternative selection which does not provide any information.

Using NGENE, we created a D-efficient design for 10 choices in a MNL model. With Czech Republic, Germany and Switzerland as labeled alternatives we allow for both alternative-specific constants and coefficients. Hospital size, hospital quality and physician quality are dummy-coded and of presumably positive signs while alternative-specific price parameters have a negative sign for each destination country. NGENE incorporates this information to avoid dominant alternatives. We optimized our design for main effects but it provides enough free parameters to estimate all country and physician/price interactions. We did not consider Individual-specific characteristics in the design as we do not have priors on them and reason to believe that non-response to these items might be a problem.

Destination attributes or characteristics *X* comprise destination country, provider and physician characteristics as well as treatment price. Patients are requested to select a destination choice for a hypothetical hip replacement surgery that requires a 14-day inpatient stay at a hospital. They are instructed that destinations differ only in the attributes listed and that they personally have to cover the costs: there will be no

	Czech Republic	Germany	Switzerland
Hospital	Small hospital without quality certificate	Large hospital with quality certificate	Small hospital without quality certificate
Doctor	no information	reputable specialist	no information
Total Costs	6,500€	11,000€	14,000€
My Choice:	☐	☐	☐

Fig. 6.2 Example of a DCE scenario

insurance or other third-party reimbursements. Figure 6.2 depicts an exemplary choice scenario with these attributes.

Hospital and physician quality are operationalized by hospital size, accreditation and physician expertise, which allows us to investigate the prominent role of physicians (Pollard 2013) in relation to hospital characteristics. Alsharif et al. (2010) find the role of physician reputation to be less important in higher-cost destinations so we expect an interaction between physician quality and destination country. Hospital quality can be measured in a number of outcome dimensions such as infection and complication rates. However, quality report cards and quality reports are difficult to both understand and to communicate. Accreditations and certificates, on the other hand, quickly convey quality summaries and constitute very accessible marketing actions. There is mixed evidence on their role as Pollard (2013) find them to be relevant for medical travelers while Boga and Weiermair (2011) find limited relevance for health travelers. Hospital size cannot be modified by marketing but our conversations with German hospitals suggest that it may play an important role in instilling trust even if Pollard (2013) finds that 65% of the providers sampled see less than 100 international patients per year. Our previous analysis also suggests a strong role of recommendations in destination choice but we exclude this characteristic for two reasons. First, we are worried that it may dominate other characteristics, which would require us to present a substantial number of profiles to respondents to identify the effects of interest along the supply dimensions. Second, it is difficult to capture recommendations in a short DCE as they can be issued by a number of referees such as agents, friends, physicians or family members, which would add a considerable amount of attribute levels given our limited space for profiles.

Total costs span five levels with 6500€, 8000€, 11,000€, 14,000€ and 18,000€. All costs are denominated in Euros as patients are surveyed in Germany and familiarity with pricing in Euros can be expected. Each country is assigned to two levels: Czech Republic [6500; 8000], Germany [8000; 11,000] and Switzerland [14,000; 18,000]. The starting price of 6500€ for the Czech Republic was based on online price listings and includes 500€ for a flight. The upper 8000€ are based on online reports from UK citizens who reported their actual spending. Total costs for Germany start at 8000€ which includes approximately 7500€ in treatment costs as reported by the statutory health insurance in German and 500€ for a flight. The upper bound of 11,000€ was derived from online reports of approximately 10,500€ treatment costs for privately insured patients plus the flight. Finally, the upper bound on total costs for Switzerland are based on the Swiss Federal Statistical Office with 17,500€ + plus flight while the lower bound was chosen deliberately to cover the attribute space. These costs are approximate indicators and serve to highlight relative cost differences between countries. Clearly, actual total costs would also depend on comorbidities, complications and a bouquet of other variables.

6.2.2.2 Model

Discrete choice modeling builds on the well-known random-utility formulation where an individual n derives utility U from alternative j.

$$U_{nj} = V_{nj} + \varepsilon_{nj} \tag{6.4}$$

The utility of an alternative is composed of a deterministic component V that may depend on both alternative-specific characteristics X_j and individual-specific characteristics Z_n, and an unobserved error term ε. The latter can be motivated in a number of ways including unobserved preference heterogeneity at the individual level or unobserved alternative-specific or individual-specific characteristics at the aggregate level (Anderson et al. 1992). The various derivations give rise to same choice probabilities as long as the error terms follow the same distribution.

The probability that an individual chooses a specific alternative i over all other alternatives depends on the deterministic utility associated with each alternative as well as on the random errors. Specifically, the probability P_i that alternative i is chosen is

$$\begin{aligned} P_i &= \Pr\left(U_i > U_j\right) \\ &= \Pr\left(\varepsilon_j - \varepsilon_i < V_i - V_j\right) \forall j \neq i \end{aligned} \tag{6.5}$$

If we assume that the random error terms are independently and identically distributed and follow a type I extreme value distribution with scale parameter σ, the difference of two type I extreme value distributed variables follows a logistic distribution that inherits the scale parameter.

$$f(\varepsilon) = \sigma e^{-\sigma\varepsilon} e^{-e^{-\sigma\varepsilon}} \tag{6.6}$$

$$P_i = F(\varepsilon_j - \varepsilon_i) = \frac{1}{1 + e^{-(\sigma(\varepsilon_j - \varepsilon_i))}} \tag{6.7}$$

This derivation generalizes to more than two alternatives when inequality (6.5) must hold for $\forall j \neq i$ as in Maddala (2008). Individual n's resulting choice probability of alternative i is then given by

$$P_{ni} = \frac{e^{(\sigma_{ni} V_{ni})}}{\sum_J e^{(\sigma_{nj} V_{nj})}} \tag{6.8}$$

with the deterministic utility V_{ni} of each alternative depending on both alternative-specific characteristics x_{ni} and individual-specific characteristics z_n

$$V_{ni} = x'_{ni}\beta + z'_n\gamma_i \tag{6.9}$$

where x_{ni} are measured relative to one baseline alternative. As can immediately be seen from Eq. (6.8), the parameters in Eq. (6.9) are only identified up to scale, i.e. parameter estimates and the error scale σ are perfectly correlated. The basic MNL formulation assumes homoscedasticity and normalization to one, i.e. $\sigma_{ni} = \sigma_n = 1$.

We can control for observed heterogeneity in the MNL formulation in by using individual-specific characteristics Z_n and interacting them with alternative-specific characteristics but the simple MNL model still suffers from well-known shortcomings such as the IIA assumption. This problem can be alleviated by random coefficients or error components (Train 2009). Both approaches give rise to the mixed logit specification but the former are more intuitive behaviorally in that they assume preference heterogeneity that is unobserved by the researcher, i.e. preference parameters β_n are not fixed but randomly distributed across individuals N. These parameters are typically assumed to follow a multivariate normal distribution, may be correlated and can be constrained to positive values, for example, by a log-normal distribution if desired.

A second strand of literature suggests the presence of heterogeneity based on unobserved characteristics that may influence decision-making (Louviere et al. 1999, 2008). Such unobserved characteristics influence decision-making, which may scale the parameter estimates of all observed characteristics, i.e. the observed choice randomness varies across individuals n. Such randomness may also arise from different choice contexts (Louviere et al. 2002) or different decision-making rules and is captured by a varying error variance σ_n.

The generalized MNL proposed by Fiebig et al. (2010) combines preference and scale heterogeneity as can be understood from Eq. (6.10) where σ_n denotes an individual-specific scale parameter, γ a scalar typically between 0 and 1 and η_n a random vector.

$$U_{njt} = [\sigma_n \beta + (\gamma + (1 - \gamma)\sigma_n)\eta_n]x_{njt} + \varepsilon_{njt} \quad (6.10)$$

For scale parameter $\sigma_n = 1$ we obtain a mixed MNL model with $[\beta + \eta_n]$, i.e. random coefficients. On the other hand, $Var(\eta_n) = 0$ yields the S-MNL model with $[\sigma_n \beta]$, i.e. coefficients scaled by individuals. For G-MNL, two specifications arise: for $\gamma = 1$ we obtain $[\sigma_n \beta + \eta_n]$ while $\gamma = 0$ gives $[\sigma_n \beta + \sigma_n \eta_n]$ so preference heterogeneity may either depend on coefficient scaling or not.

Random coefficients capture preference heterogeneity and are always correlated across alternatives as they are individual-specific. Their identification and the estimation of a heterogeneity distribution thus benefit from a substantial number of repeated choices, which also motivates our display of 10 scenarios to each respondent. Random coefficients may also be correlated across attributes at the expense of the respective extra covariance parameters to be estimated. Random ASCs can capture residual preference heterogeneity and Fiebig et al. (2010) suggest leaving them unscaled for both conceptual and computational reasons. They find that all explanatory power may be unduly shifted to the ASCs if people make choices that disregard all other attributes. Such behavior would correspond to a destination choice that is guided solely by the country of destination.

Hess and Rose (2012) argue that the fundamental problem of separate identifiability of both scale and preference parameters is not overcome by the G-MNL specification. They demonstrate that scale and preference parameters remain correlated, which renders the interpretation of the scale parameter dubious. Hess and Train (2017) further argue that G-MNL is in fact a mixed logit with correlated preference parameters and particular constraints on that correlation. As Hess and Rose (2012), we subscribe to the notion that both preference and scale heterogeneity are important concepts and therefore investigate mixed, scaled and generalized specifications to explore individual heterogeneity. Additionally, we consider a mixed specification with correlated preference parameters. The literature offers a variety of alternative multinomial specifications including heteroscedastic models (Bhat 1995), latent class models (Greene and Hensher 2003) and augmented latent class models (Hess and Stathopoulos 2013) but they will note be investigated in this context. Furthermore, we choose to estimate our models in preference space rather than WTP space (Sonnier et al. 2007; Train and Weeks 2005) as our interest lies mainly in the estimates of the quality parameters at the three levels of supply.

The linear and additive nature of Eq. (6.9) implies a decision rule that views alternative-specific characteristics as compensatory. Louviere et al. (2007) provide examples that have found the compensation assumption to be fairly robust and recent literature has examined this issue in more detail. Hess et al. (2008) find a reference effect as suggested by prospect theory Kahnemann and Tversky (1979) and Leong and Hensher (2012) identify other heuristics in decision-making. Rose et al. (2013) consider four alternative information processing strategies among participants: non-compensatory preferences as a manifestation of extreme preferences, lexicographic preferences to simplify complexity, and inconsistent preferences due to fading attention, complex preferences or changing preferences because of learning effects. Monte Carlo simulations show that large shares of lexicographic and non-compensatory decision makers may bias parameter estimates significantly. Inconsistent decision makers are less problematic, which is in line with Hess and Rose (2009) who find that inter-respondent heterogeneity dominates intra-respondent heterogeneity. Fiebig et al. (2010) and Keane and Wasi (2012) find that G-MNL accommodates lexicographic and random choices well. Fiebig et al. (2010) furthermore find some evidence that preference heterogeneity may play a particularly important role for medical decisions while scale heterogeneity is important for complex choices, i.e. medical decisions, too. We thus expect an a priori role of both components. Finally, Louviere et al. (2007) stress the empirical importance of including interaction terms in linear decision rules and our experimental design enables us to investigate a broad set of interactions between destination characteristics and destination countries.

6.2.3 Results

Our results are based on 42 completed questionnaires from three different hospitals. 29 questionnaires were completed in Arabic, 11 in Russian and 2 in English. Nationality and place of residence coincided for nearly all patients. Figure 6.3 reports the composition of the latter shows that our sample covers the two main source regions of patients that we identified in Sect. 2.2.2, i.e. the Middle East and Eastern Europe/CIS.

The sample included 21 males and 19 females whose age composition in Fig. 6.4 differs from Fig. 2.14 in that it is skewed towards younger patients even after we take the aggregation of the two youngest age groups in Fig. 6.4 into account. 16 patients hold a high school degree or lower, 13 patients hold a Bachelor's degree and 10 patients reported a Master's degree or higher. 30 patients traveled in small groups of 2 or 3 while only one patient traveled alone and 9 patients traveled in groups of 4 or more. As expected, patients traveling in larger groups are predominantly from the Middle East.

To assess institutional ties and economic decision-making on part of the patient, we inquired about the possibility of obtaining domestic reimbursement of treatment costs. 16 patients gave a negative answer and this group included all but one patient who is not from the Middle East. 6 patients expect partial reimbursement and 14 patients report full reimbursement of their treatment costs. When asked about the source of reimbursement, 12 patients indicated public health insurance, 2 patients report a private health insurance and 10 patients report other sources of reimbursement. Based on our background interviews in Sect. 6.1, we surmise that a substantial group of other reimbursement sources are firms that send their employees. This suspicion is in line with the observation that numerous patients in the upper household income brackets in Fig. 6.5 also report eligibility for reimbursement from "other" sources.

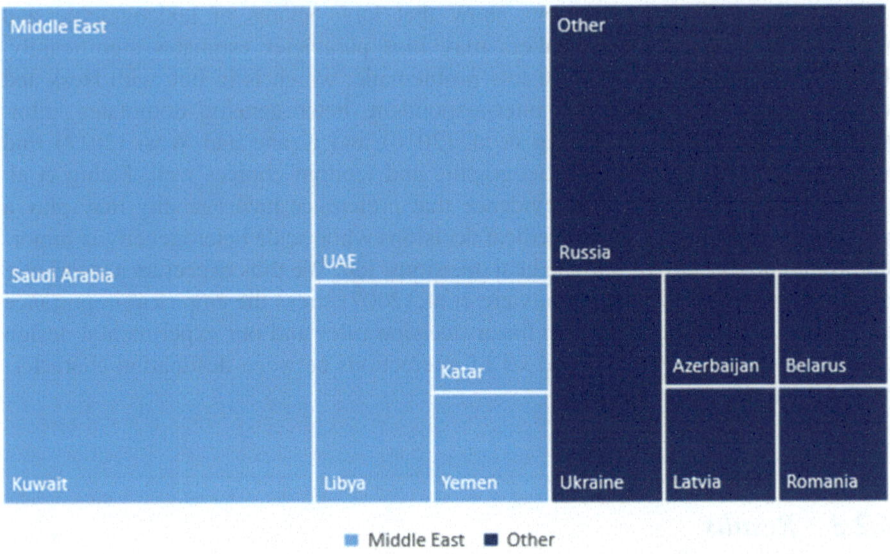

Fig. 6.3 Survey sample composition, by country of residence

We asked patients about their proficiency in English and German to gauge their importance for destination choice. In line with Chap. 4, Fig. 6.6 shows that the ability to speak German does not appear to constitute a relevant cultural tie. Note, however, that our result in Chap. 4 is based on the bilateral presence of speakers of common languages, which includes languages other than German as well. The self-reported proficiency to speak English reveals two groups with very good knowledge and little to no knowledge of English. There is no pattern discernible, which suggests a limited role of a patient's proficiency in English in the decision to receive a treatment in Germany.

Figure 6.7 reports indicators of locus of control, trust and risk attitude. We find a strong inner locus of control in line with previous studies and a large degree of trust in providers outside the country of residence in general as well as providers in Germany in particular. We did not specifically ask about domestic providers but question 4 suggests the presence of broader distrust in countries of residence rather than the presence of a home bias among respondents. Patients further exhibit a low risk awareness for treatments abroad, which may be viewed as an underestimation of risks entailed by medical tourism or as a reasonable assessment based on poor treatment quality as a domestic reference.

Patients report very diverse health statuses that precede their treatments in Germany. While 13 patients describe their health status prior to the treatment as

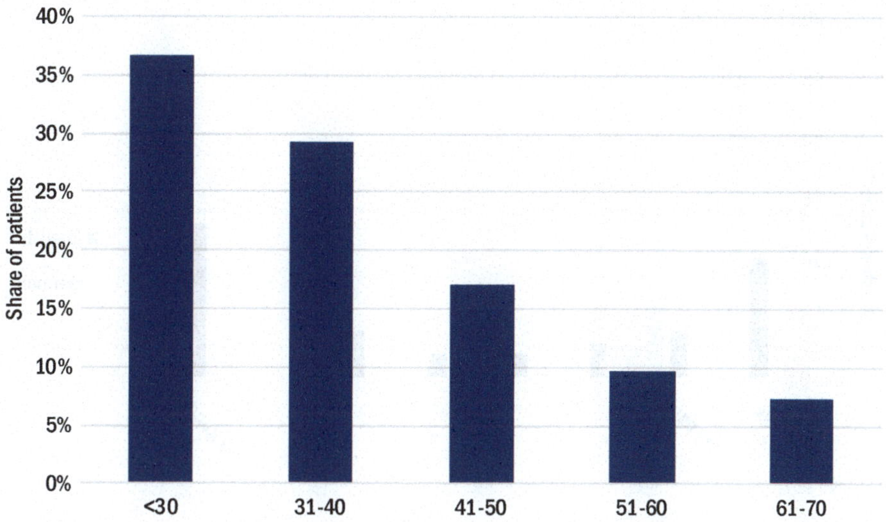

Fig. 6.4 Survey sample composition, by age

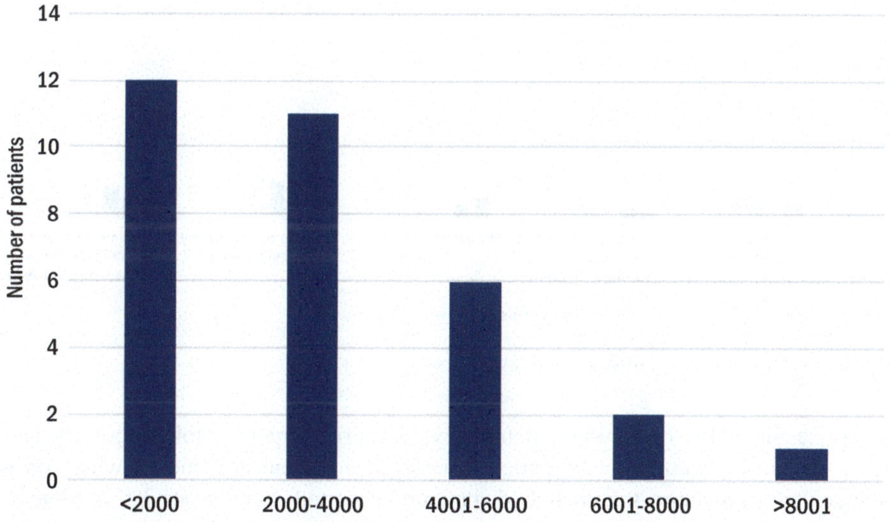

Fig. 6.5 Survey sample composition, by monthly net household income in euros

"very poor", 15 patients report their health status between "average" and "very good". We do not find a connection between health status and treatment obtained and note that a high degree of suffering does not appear to be a necessary condition to seek treatment in Germany.

Treatments received have a focus on orthopedic surgery, oncology and plastic/cosmetic surgery but cover the full range of options we provided. "Other treatments"

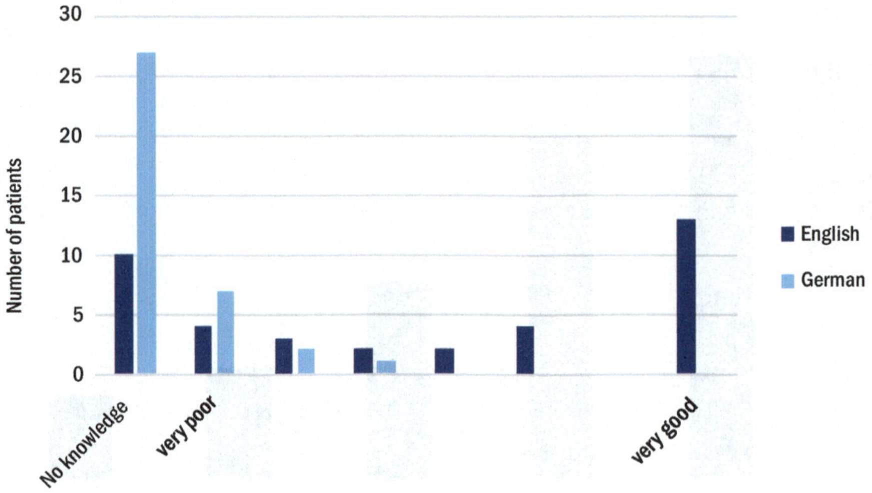

Fig. 6.6 Survey sample composition, by language proficiency

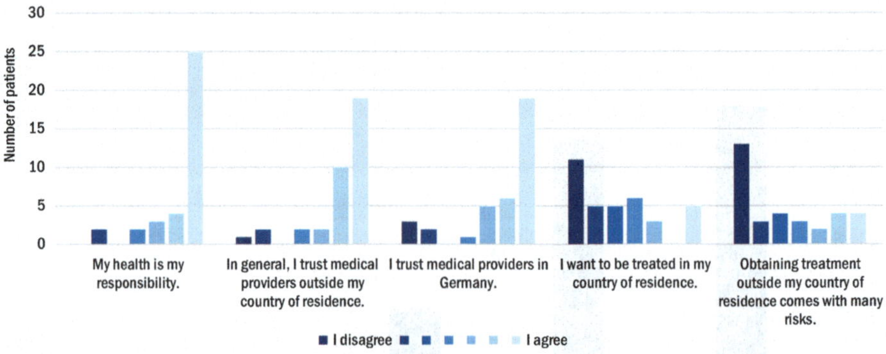

Fig. 6.7 Locus of control, trust and risk awareness

comprise the fields of urology, neurology, bariatric surgery, otolaryngology and other invasive treatments. 29 patients received inpatient treatments while only 6 received outpatient treatments. 5 patients reported both types of treatment. 31 patients said that they can also receive their treatment at home but at poorer quality and 3 patients mentioned insufficient confidentiality, waiting time and long travel as domestic barriers. 8 patients stated that they cannot receive their treatment at home but only 4 stated the reasons in the lack of a diagnosis and the treatment not being offered.

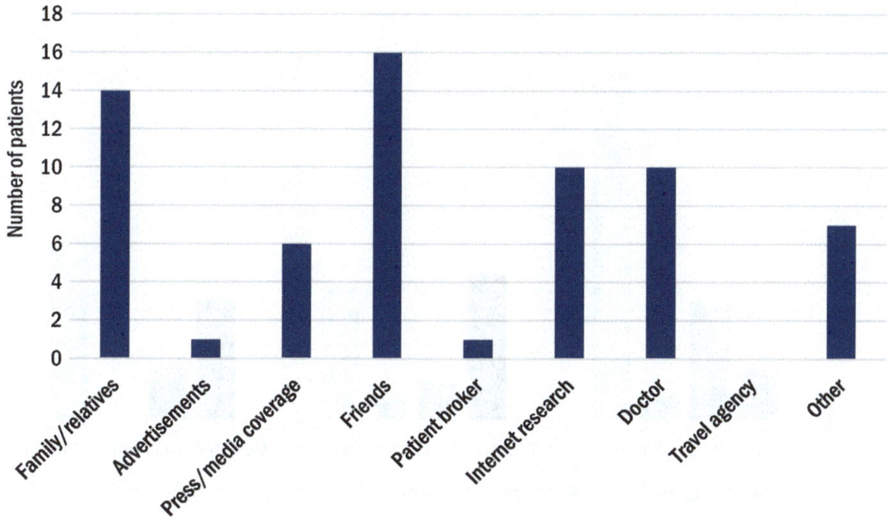

Fig. 6.8 Information channels used in destination choice

20 patients indicated own previous experiences with a treatment abroad. Previous destinations include the UK, Jordan the U.S., Turkey, France, Saudi Arabia and Czech Republic. Unfortunately, only half of the patients indicated their previous destinations so we cannot assess the number of patients returning to Germany. Figure 6.8 displays the channels that led patients to consider Germany as a destination. We find that the main sources of information were friends, family/relatives, internet research and personal doctors. 27 patients relied on only one source of information while 14 patients report multiple sources. Family/relatives, friends and doctors are reported as exclusive sources by 21 patients and only 8 patients do not report these sources at all which strongly underlines the role of informal networks and hints to a complementary role of internet research. On the other hand, a small group of patients becomes aware of Germany through autonomous information only. Other sources of information disclosed include "embassy", "foundation" and "scientific articles" which hint to institutionalized relations and a distinct treatment focus of the trip to Germany.

Consideration sets in terms of countries were very limited for the majority of patients. Only 15 patients considered other countries—the U.S., Israel, Jordan, South Korea, France, UK and Switzerland—and only 1 patient considered more than one other country. In terms of hospitals, 17 patients considered only one hospital in Germany, 21 patients considered two to three hospitals in Germany and only 1 patient considered more than five hospitals in Germany. The number of hospitals considered is similar for patients across the hospitals we sampled so there is no cluster of patients who are systematically locked-in by strong, institutionalized relations of a single hospital. Patients who considered another country also tend to consider more than one hospital but the difference to patients who focus solely on

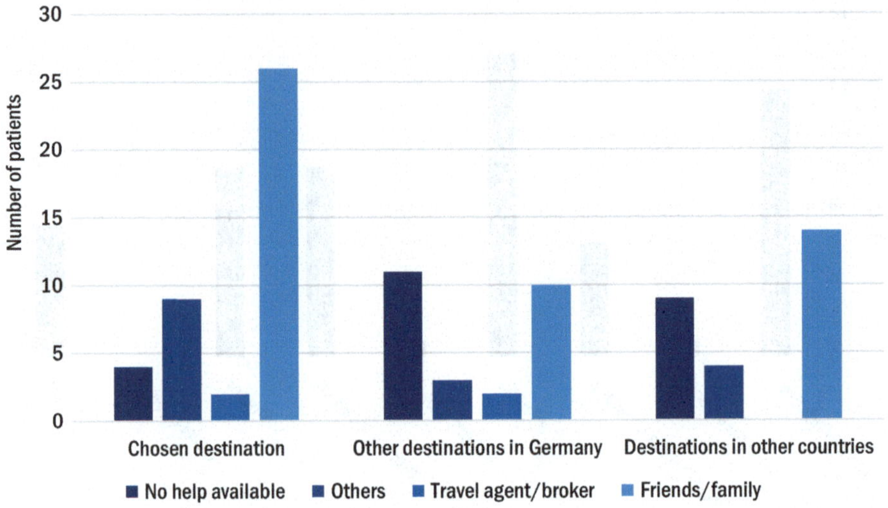

Fig. 6.9 Availability of local support at destinations

Germany is minimal. We do not find any relationship between individual characteristics such as age, education or source country and size of the reported consideration set in terms of countries or hospitals. However, we do find that patients from countries with presumably institutionalized relations to Germany were also the ones who considered other countries so there does not appear to be a lock-in effect at the country level either.

To investigate if sources of information also come to act as facilitators, we asked about existing networks and ties. Figure 6.9 shows that a majority of patients can receive help from friends or family at their chosen destination. Help at other destinations in Germany is significantly less available but slightly up again at other destinations outside Germany. Upon closer inspection of support networks, we find a number of emerging patterns: The first group of 4 patients has no supporting network at any destination. The second group of 8 patients relies on "others" and often names embassies or interpreters, i.e. institutionalized networks. The third group of 8 patients has family/friends at the chosen destination in Germany but at no other destinations in Germany, and the fourth group of 11 patients has family/friends at various destinations in Germany. 14 patients from groups three and four indicate support from family/friends at destinations abroad but they may be referring to their home countries.

In addition to information sources and support groups, we specifically inquired about recommendations received for hospitals and doctors. Figure 6.10 shows that the chosen hospital often coincides with a recommendation—particularly by friends/family. Recommendations of specific doctors are less common but also dominated by friends/family. Referrals by doctors abroad play a small but consistent role and "others" may include facilitators or embassies.

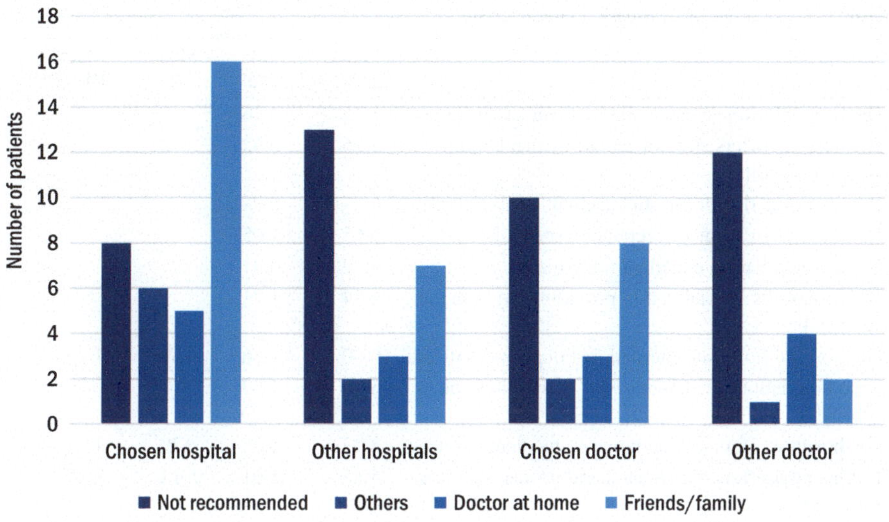

Fig. 6.10 Recommendations received for destinations

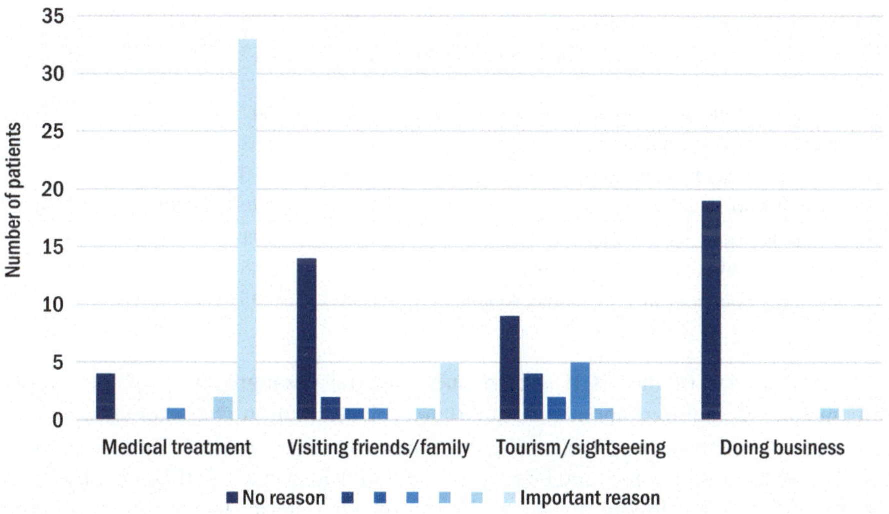

Fig. 6.11 Purposes of the trip to Germany

Due to the high number of inpatients in our sample, we expect a strong focus on medical treatments as the main purpose of a patient's trip to Germany. Our results in Fig. 6.11 are in line with this expectation. In addition, we find the visiting of friends/family and sightseeing to be complementary reasons for traveling. Doing business seems of minor importance but purposes other than "medical treatment" generally suffered from lower response rates so they should be interpreted with care.

Table 6.3 Ranking of destination characteristics

	Mean total	SD total	Mean AR	Mean RU/EN
The hospital offers a clean and hygienic environment	6.85	0.36		
The hospital offers state-of-the-art medical equipment and facilities	6.76	0.62		
The attending doctor has an excellent track record	6.73	0.98		
The attending doctor is a reputable specialist	6.65	1.05		
The hospital has an excellent track record	6.59	0.81		
The hospital is specialized in providing my specific treatment	6.54	1.21		
The hospital holds an international quality certificate	6.00	1.76	6.57	4.77
Accommodation for persons who accompany me is affordable	6.00	1.62		
The hospital offers a wide range of medical services	5.93	1.88	6.79	4.08
The hospital offers a dedicated and professional customer service	5.85	1.61	5.14	3.25
The total costs of my hospital stay are low	5.65	1.96		
The destination is recommended to me	5.53	2.10		
The patient room offers a high level of comfort	5.49	2.08	6.21	3.92
The food is catered to my preferences	5.27	2.20	6.04	3.62
The nursing staff caters to my cultural and religious needs	5.18	2.57	6.44	2.33
Travel time from my home to the destination is short	4.85	2.47		
The attending doctor is German	4.63	2.63		
The destination can be reached by a direct flight	4.58	2.60		
The nursing staff speaks English	4.07	2.70	4.89	2.31
The attending doctor speaks English	3.95	2.71	4.61	2.54
The destination offers tourist attractions	3.07	2.56	3.79	1.54
The attending doctor speaks my mother tongue	2.98	2.35		

In preparation of the DCE and in line with our disaggregation of the supply dimension, we inquired about the importance of destination characteristics associated with physicians, hospitals or the destination at large. Table 6.3 presents these results and we find that they are largely in line with Musa et al. (2012), i.e. physician quality and hospital facilities rank at the top of our criteria. In fact, the top seven items relate to anticipated treatment quality and include both items referring to physicians and hospitals. On the other hand, a common spoken language ranks low and confirms our findings in Chap. 4. Items related to institutional distance such as cultural and religious needs or food rank in the middle. Interestingly, hospital costs rank lower than affordable accommodation for company but we will shed more light on this finding below.

A number of item pairs turn out to be highly correlated as measured by Spearman's rank correlation coefficient: these include physician specialization and track record as well as hospital certificate and hospital track record. Both pairs consistently rank atop the destination criteria. Total costs of the hospital stay and an existing recommendation are also highly correlated which hints to a role of recommendations in not only finding a destination but in establishing a corresponding willingness-to-pay. Travel time and direct flight as well as physicians' and nurses' ability to communicate in English are highly correlated. For these items, we identify two groups of patients that deem either distance or the ability to communicate in English very important or not important at all. We initially suspected this difference to be due to the common use of interpreters among Arabic-speaking patients and, indeed, we can identify two heterogeneous groups based on the chosen survey language.

Columns 3 and 4 in Table 6.3 display the means that are significantly different at $\alpha = 0.5$ between patients who fill out the survey in Arabic and Russian/English, respectively. We find that the top-ranked items that refer to treatment quality do not differ but the Arabic-speaking group places greater importance on accompanying services. These include customer service, comfort of accommodation, specialized food, and accommodation of cultural and religious needs—items that are also highly correlated in the sample. These findings are in line with written comments of Arabic-speaking patients, asking for better WiFi, Arabic TV stations and Islamic food. On the other hand, such complementary services appear secondary to the treatment for Russian/English-speaking patients, which may be due to a general difference in preferences or due to the membership of many Russians in lower household income brackets. Surprisingly, the staff's ability to speak English is more important to speakers of Arabic. This result runs counter to our initial suspicion that motivated the search for clusters based on the common presence of interpreters for this group but comments indicate that patients would prefer to bypass facilitators and communicate directly with providers. Less surprisingly, the importance placed on a physician's ability to speak English correlates with the self-reported proficiency in English.

Given the self-reported size of their company, cost of accommodation for accompanying persons is plausibly and significantly more important at $\alpha = 10\%$ for Arabic-speaking patients. However, these patients also rank quality certificates and the range of medical services highly whereas these two measures are far less relevant to the other group. While a strong desire for comfort, service, catering to cultural and religious needs and membership in higher income brackets may very well distinguish Middle Eastern patients from other patients, the additional importance placed on certificates and range of services raises some concern. Potentially, these two items are lumped together with other quality-related items because of available reimbursement schemes rather than careful consideration. Finally, we note heterogeneity in the importance of the attending physician being German. We find a substantial difference in means between both groups but large variances indicate that increased trust in a German physician is independent from systematic differences captured by the chosen survey language.

Our results thus far have confirmed the importance of treatment quality as measured by various indicators for destination choice. To investigate the role of supplier aggregation, our DCE enforces a trade-off between quality indicators at the

Table 6.4 Results of the destination choice models, part I

		Model 1			Model 2	
		MXL	SMNL	GMNL	MXL	GMNL
Mean	Hospital size	0.748*	0.130	0.878*	0.871**	1.000**
		(0.404)	(0.192)	(0.457)	(0.409)	(0.458)
	Price	−0.392	0.041	−0.352	−0.435	−0.556***
		(0.304)	(0.104)	(0.326)	(0.309)	(0.205)
	Czech Republic	−5.180***	−1.848***	−5.256***	−2.971***	−5.670***
		(1.343)	(0.307)	(1.399)	(0.994)	(1.350)
	Switzerland	−2.467	−2.613***	−3.396	−3.539*	−4.685***
		(1.891)	(0.667)	(2.071)	(1.952)	(1.133)
	Physician specialization	4.739***	2.726***	5.264***	4.911***	7.157***
		(1.039)	(0.471)	(1.189)	(1.022)	(1.654)
	Hospital certificate	2.776***	1.557***	2.843***	2.808***	3.464***
		(0.642)	(0.310)	(0.667)	(0.674)	(0.807)
	Czech Republic_AR				−3.747**	−1.259
					(1.723)	(1.260)
	Switzerland_AR				1.653	3.434***
					(1.191)	(1.240)
SD	Hospital size	0.230		−0.014		
		(0.652)		(0.313)		
	Price	−0.034		0.052		
		(0.076)		(0.044)		
	Czech Republic	3.035***		−3.713***	1.025	2.921***
		(0.753)		(0.921)	(0.715)	(0.980)
	Switzerland	−2.976***		2.810***	−0.481	−2.389***
		(0.774)		(0.689)	(0.678)	(0.884)
	Physician specialization	3.438***		−2.732**	3.593***	1.835*
		(0.908)		(1.210)	(0.962)	(1.066)
	Hospital certificate	2.254***		1.667**	2.160***	0.943
		(0.618)		(0.821)	(0.537)	(0.709)
	Czech Republic_AR				4.053***	0.449
					(1.193)	(0.346)
	Switzerland_AR				2.642***	−1.131*
					(0.697)	(0.634)
	Observations	348	348	348	348	348
	AIC	380.8	448.8	380.1	365.9	368.2
	BIC	427.1	475.8	434.1	419.9	429.9
	Parameters	12	7	14	14	16
	LL	−178.4	−217.4	−176.1	−169.0	−168.1

Significant at 0.1*, 0.05**, 0.01***

physician, hospital and country level. As a first step, we investigate specifications without individual-specific characteristics. Model 1 of Table 6.4 presents the results of our basic MXL, SMNL and GMNL specifications. Note that all parameters but cost are dummy-coded so we can compare their effect sizes within a specification. Due to varying scaling parameters, they cannot be compared across specifications.

We find significant negative effects for Czech Republic and Switzerland as destination countries relative to the baseline Germany. In line with our expectations, this effect is strong for the Czech Republic but magnitude for Switzerland is surprising given the country's reputation as a high-quality destination. Apparently, other underlying factors such as cultural proximity drive Germany's country-of-origin effect. Physician quality and hospital quality as communicated by a certificate both exhibit strong positive effects on destination choice with physician quality dominating hospital quality across all specifications. Hospital size has an expected, small positive effect in the MXL and GMNL specifications and the negative cost parameter is significant only in the GMNL specification. Generally, we are not too concerned with the cost parameter as our interest lies with supplier aggregation. We thus investigate interactions between destination countries and the other destination characteristics but find no evidence of significant interaction terms. However, our parameters turn out to be very robust across all models.

As measured by AIC and BIC, the SMNL specification performs worse than MXL and GMNL across all models we investigated which strongly suggests the use of random coefficients to capture preference heterogeneity. In particular, we find evidence for random parameters on CZ, CH, physician quality and hospital certificate while hospital size and cost are well captured by fixed parameters. We therefore omit the SMNL results from the exposition for all but the first model and set cost and hospital size to fixed parameters in the following models. For a comparison of MXL and GMNL specifications, Fiebig et al. (2010) recommend the BIC and both BIC and AIC prefer MXL to GMNL for all models. Generally, both specifications produce very similar estimates and fits for our data set.

In a second step, we included individual-specific characteristics in the analysis. Given occasional non-responses, this eventually forced us to drop observations as displayed in Table 6.4. Due to a limited number of observations, we excluded a number of characteristics from the analysis including language proficiency, health status, locus of control, general risk attitude and sex. Based on our descriptive statistics, we do not expect a large role of language proficiency nor of the other variables in destination choice. However, our previous analysis suggests language of the questionnaire to be an important indicator of cultural preferences. Based on Table 6.3, we suspect this indicator to capture mainly observed preference heterogeneity as most significant differences relate to cultural items. There was also no significant difference in self-reported cost sensitivity so we do not attribute much of the questionnaire effect to the availability of reimbursement options. However, we cannot disentangle both effects as only one patient outside the Arabic speaking group affirmed any form of reimbursement.

The inclusion of the questionnaire indicator (AR) in model 2 of Table 6.4 gives rise to a robust pattern across all models and specifications: Patients with a presumably Arabic background dislike Czech Republic significantly more than other patients and other patients dislike Switzerland significantly more than AR patients—always relative to Germany. We found no such effects for the physician quality or hospital quality as measured by a quality certificate, i.e. these cultural preferences unfold only at the country level.

We find no evidence for a role of previous experience with a treatment abroad or the consideration of multiple countries in country choice. However, interactions between destination country, physician quality and hospital quality are significant after controlling for AR, which suggests that quality indicators pull different weights in Czech Republic, Switzerland and Germany. However, we do not report these results as both AIC and BIC prefer specifications with preference heterogeneity and this conclusion is supported by specifications that include additional individual characteristics.

Model 3 in Table 6.5 displays the results for income when interacted with the cost parameter. Unfortunately, these models suffers from a diminishing number of observations and even though AIC and BIC indicate better models after the inclusion of income but this result does not hold for identical samples. After all, the number of individuals in the sample does not allow for any robust conclusions with regard to income, age or education nor do these models yield significant results.

Finally, we estimate both MXL and G-MNL with correlated parameters as model 4. Following Fiebig et al. (2010), MXL is preferred to G-MNL based on the BIC and the uncorrelated model 2 is preferred to the correlated model 4 based on the AIC. However, while information criteria aim for parsimony and thus heavily penalize the additional parameters that correlated coefficients introduce, a LR test of both MXL specifications soundly rejects model 2 in favor of model 4 at $\alpha = 5\%$ with $\chi^2_{15} = 26.67$, i.e. goodness of fit is significantly improved by correlated coefficients. Closer inspection of the MXL specification of model 2 resolves this issue as it suggests fixed destination parameters. The adoption of fixed country parameters leads to our final models 5 and 6 in Table 6.5. The correlated model 6 is preferred to both its uncorrelated counterpart model 5 and to model 2 by the AIC; it rejects model 5 in a LR test at $\alpha = 5\%$ with $\chi^2_6 = 21.97$; and it is not rejected by the richer model 4 at $\alpha = 5\%$ with $\chi^2_{11} = 6.77$. We thus focus on model 6 in the subsequent analysis.

Figure 6.12 displays the distribution of individual taste parameters in our sample as estimated by the procedure proposed by Revelt and Train (2000). We find that physician specialization, hospital certificate and hospital size have the anticipated positive effects on destination attractiveness and average coefficient estimates rank in that order from right to left. There is some dispersion around both physician quality and hospital certificate but their distributions cover largely the positive domain. The fixed coefficient on hospital size is also positive but small. Estimated fixed coefficients for both Switzerland and Czech Republic are negative which is somewhat in line with our expectations: we would have anticipated Switzerland to rank ahead of Czech Republic due to its reputation as a high quality destination and even a ranking ahead of Germany would have been plausible. The bottom panel sheds more light on this issue as it displays the distributions of total estimated country coefficients for patients when answering in Arabic. Czech Republic is significantly less popular than Switzerland among these patients and covers almost exclusively the negative domain. Switzerland continues to have a negative average

Table 6.5 Results of the destination choice models, part II

		Model 3		Model 4		Model 5	Model 6
		MXL	GMNL	MXL	GMNL	MXL	MXL
Mean	Hospital size	1.229**	1.094*	1.089**	1.049*	0.860**	0.885**
		(0.616)	(0.564)	(0.507)	(0.549)	(0.410)	(0.416)
	Price	−0.102	−0.173	−0.492	−0.453*	−0.396	−0.442
		(0.420)	(0.259)	(0.338)	(0.245)	(0.300)	(0.309)
	Czech Republic	−3.053**	−3.125***	−3.231***	−3.455***	−2.721***	−2.798***
		(1.279)	(0.937)	(1.086)	(1.104)	(0.872)	(0.894)
	Switzerland	−7.034**	−6.179***	−4.719**	−5.744***	−3.960**	−3.537*
		(2.916)	(1.876)	(2.154)	(1.323)	(1.894)	(1.917)
	Physician specialization	7.529***	6.922***	6.423***	6.643***	4.832***	5.025***
		(1.906)	(1.608)	(1.543)	(2.363)	(0.920)	(1.071)
	Hospital certificate	3.356***	2.838***	3.101***	2.374***	2.895***	2.579***
		(0.929)	(0.865)	(0.819)	(0.848)	(0.671)	(0.620)
	Czech Republic_AR	−5.694***	−5.047***	−3.934***	−4.924**	−3.523***	−3.544***
		(1.884)	(1.611)	(1.336)	(2.420)	(1.138)	(1.220)
	Switzerland_AR	3.908*	3.188*	2.782**	3.191**	1.908	2.082
		(2.094)	(1.654)	(1.330)	(1.305)	(1.116)	(1.310)
	Price_income2	−0.468*	−0.325				
		(0.280)	(0.260)				
	Price_income3	−0.476	−0.409*				
		(0.297)	(0.241)				
	Price_income4	−0.690*	−0.122				
		(0.404)	(0.279)				
	Price_income5	−0.328	−0.578				
		(0.559)	(0.451)				

(continued)

Table 6.5 (continued)

		Model 3		Model 4		Model 5	Model 6
		MXL	GMNL	MXL	GMNL	MXL	MXL
SD	Czech Republic	0.702	−0.963	0.518	1.348		
		(0.592)	(0.700)	(0.779)	(1.001)		
	Switzerland	2.444**	2.134**	2.491*	1.130		
		(1.067)	(0.843)	(1.443)	(0.866)		
	Physician specialization	5.318***	1.099	3.860***	0.617	3.825***	3.203***
		(1.519)	(1.211)	(1.090)	(1.007)	(1.030)	(0.842)
	Hospital certificate	2.444***	0.794	2.812***	0.933	2.428***	2.447***
		(0.789)	(0.887)	(0.849)	(1.411)	(0.647)	(0.740)
	Czech Republic_AR	6.644***	0.678	5.155***	1.107	5.100***	4.523***
		(1.905)	(0.785)	(1.749)	(1.798)	(1.372)	(1.142)
	Switzerland_AR	−5.184***	0.688	4.943***	0.795	2.543***	3.153***
		(1.906)	(0.859)	(1.710)	(1.122)	(0.663)	(0.962)
	Observations	279	279	348	348	348	348
	AIC	301.3	306.5	369.3	373.5	364	354
	BIC	366.6	379.2	481	493	410.4	423.4
	Parameters	18	20	29	31	12	18
	LL	−132.6	−133.3	−155.6	−155.8	−170.0	−159.0

Significant at 0.1*, 0.05**, 0.01***

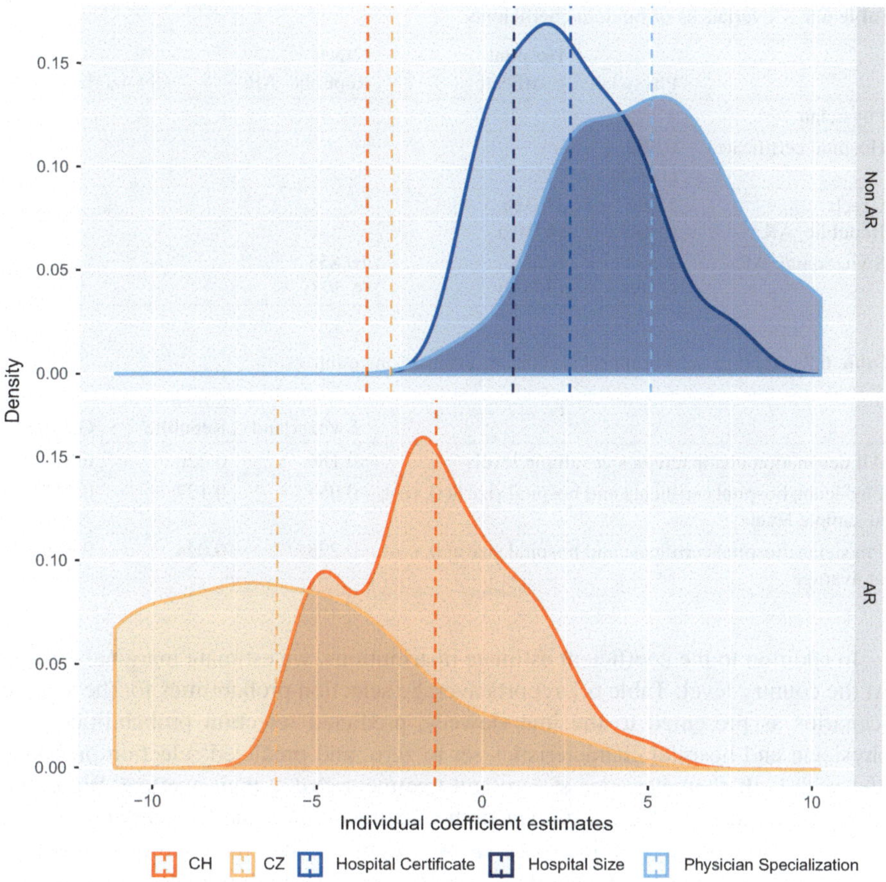

Fig. 6.12 Distributions and averages of individual coefficient estimates

coefficient estimate but there are there is some mass in the positive domain, i.e. we would expect some individuals to rank Switzerland ahead of Germany. The distinction between country effects for AR and Non-AR renders effects in the upper panel more plausible as many Non-AR patients are from Eastern European or CIS countries, which are culturally closer to Czech Republic than GCC patients are.

Figure 6.12 highlights the heterogeneity across individual, random coefficient estimates. It is more pronounced for uncorrelated coefficients but average coefficient estimates are largely identical: neither Welch nor Mann-Whitney U tests reject equal means for all estimates at $\alpha = 5\%$. Covariances for the coefficient estimates are presented in Table 6.6 and standard errors were obtained by the Delta method. We find moderate evidence for a connection between the importance placed on a hospital certificate and membership in the AR group, which is in line with the rating of destination characteristics above.

Table 6.6 Covariances of random coefficients

	Physician	Hospital certificate	Czech Republic_AR	Switzerland_AR
Physician	–			
Hospital certificate	0.562 (1.933)	–		
Czech Republic_AR	1.396 (2.485)	10.318 (5.040)	–	
Switzerland_AR	2.298 (2.494)	6.724 (3.706)	10.855 (6.507)	–

Table 6.7 Average selection probabilities of destination countries

	Switzerland	Czech Republic	Germany
All destination characteristics at sample levels	0.156	0.226	0.618
Physician, hospital certificate and hospital size at 0, cost at sample levels	0.057	0.127	0.817
Physician, hospital certificate and hospital size at 0, cost at average	0.228	0.044	0.728

In addition to the coefficient estimate distributions, we estimate marginal effects. At the country level, Table 6.7 reports average selection probabilities for the sample scenarios as presented to the interviewees, predicted selection probabilities with physician and hospital characteristics set to zero, and predicted selection probabilities with both characteristics at zero and treatment cost at their average. We find a strong preference for Germany over both Czech Republic and Switzerland in each scenario. This preference increases as we remove other moderating destination characteristics. However, Switzerland is associated with high price levels and fixing treatment costs to their average of 10,900€ across all alternatives shows that Switzerland would in fact be preferred to Czech Republic if their prices were in the same range. Unaffected by treatment costs, Germany continues to rank ahead of its competitors in predicted selection probability.

Figure 6.13 displays average marginal effects and their distributions for moderating destination features at the hospital and at the physician level in our sample. As for coefficient estimates, there is the expected horizontal pattern by which marginal effects increase in magnitude from hospital size over hospital certificate to physician specialization. We further observe a vertical pattern that suggests increasing marginal effects as we move from Switzerland over Czech Republic to Germany. Moderating destination features at the hospital and at the physician level thus pull more weight on average in destination countries that exhibit high baseline selection probabilities and may thus reinforce choices.

The distributions of the effects in Fig. 6.13 are heterogeneous, close to unimodal for Germany but often multimodal for Switzerland and Czech Republic. In particular, hospital size appears to have no effect for a number of choices while a second peak suggests a small effect for other choices. We can observe a similar but more

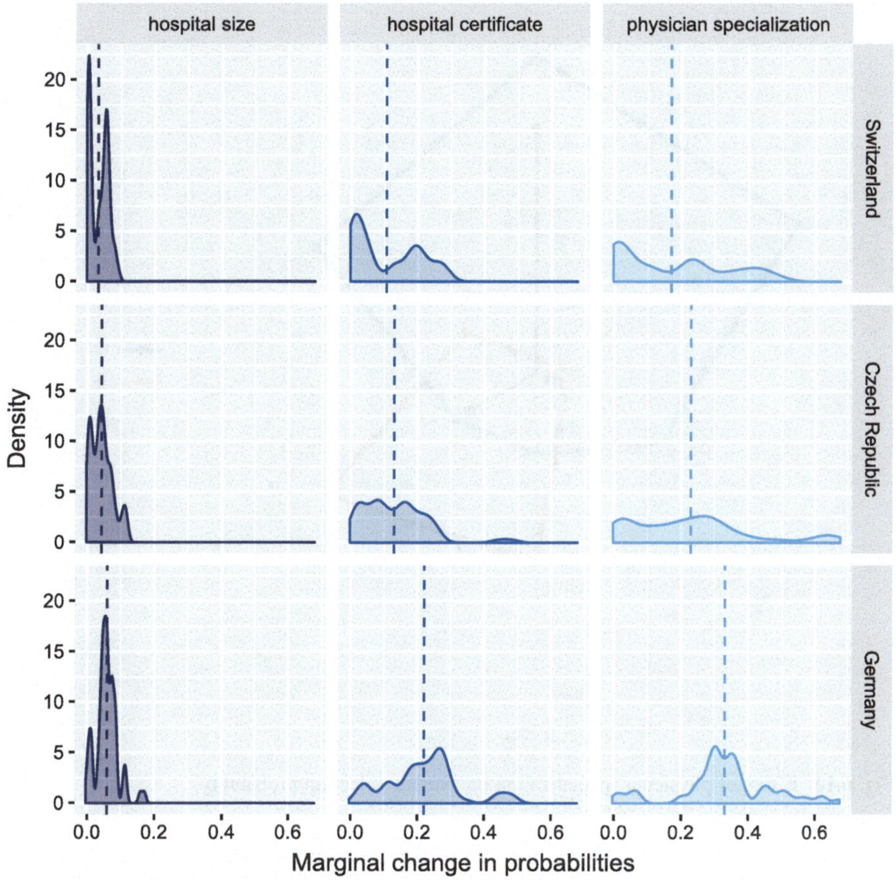

Fig. 6.13 Average marginal effects and distributions of marginal effects

pronounced effect for hospital certificate and physician specialization in Switzerland and Czech Republic: substantial mass is concentrated around the average but tails to the right indicate a more substantial impact of these features in other choice settings. On the other hand, distributions for Germany are more concentrated which means that the marginal effects of our three indicators are less context-sensitive for Germany than for both Switzerland and Czech Republic. We also compared average marginal effects for the uncorrelated and the correlated models and find that equality of average marginal effects cannot be rejected by a Welch or a Mann-Whitney U test at $\alpha = 5\%$ for any indicator and any country but for hospital certificate in Germany.

Finally, we take a closer look at physician specialization—the only effect that outweighed Germany's country-of-origin effect in model 6 of Table 6.4. Marginal effects in Fig. 6.13 were estimated with destination characteristics at sample levels as in the first row of Table 6.7. To isolate physician specialization, we now set all

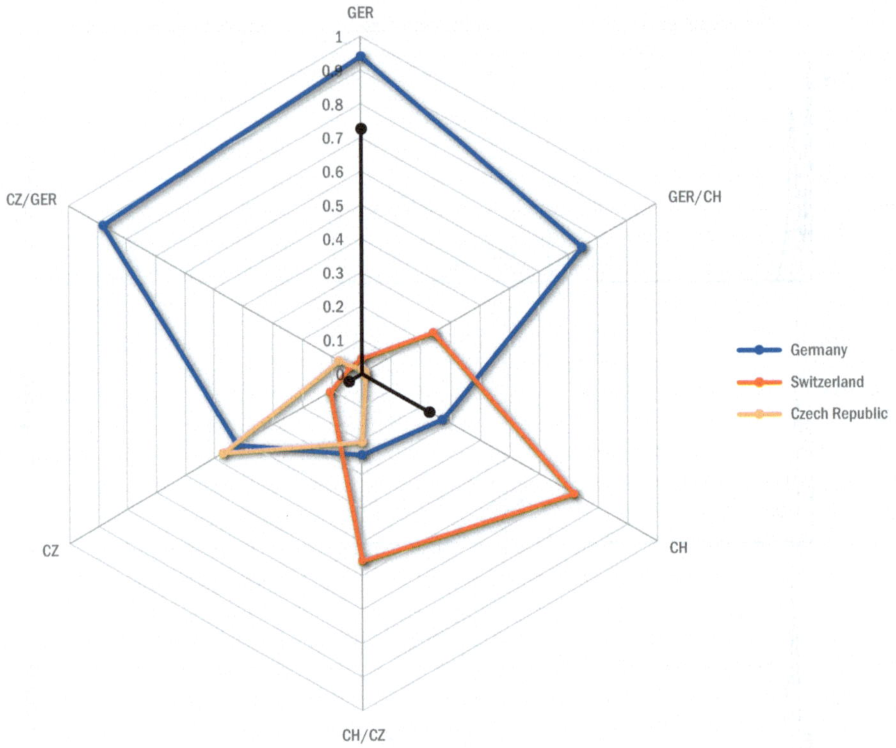

Fig. 6.14 Effect of physician specialization on average selection probability

destination characteristics to 0 and costs to their average of 10,900€ as in row 3 of Table 6.7.

Figure 6.14 shows the effect of physician specialization on the selection probability of a country as one or two destinations offer a reputable specialist. The status quo selection probabilities of Germany, Switzerland and Czech Republic from the third row of Table 6.7 are depicted in black. Here, no country has a reputable specialist. The radial axes of the diagram present the various scenarios with a specialized physician at one or multiple destinations (GER, CH, CZ). The respective selection probabilities of each country are given by the colored points and sum to 1 along each radial axis. For instance, if only Germany has a reputable specialist, it's average selection probability increases from 72.8% to 94.2% while selection probabilities of Switzerland and Czech Republic drop to 4.5% and 1.3%, respectively. Similarly, average selection probabilities of Switzerland and Czech Republic peak at 71.6% and 47% if only they have a reputable specialist. If two countries have specialists, their respective selection probabilities generally increase from the status quo. If all countries offer specialists, the status quo applies. We find that both Switzerland and Czech Republic can top selection probabilities if only they offer a specialized physician with Czech Republic only barely surpassing Germany. In fact, the selection probability of Czech Republic remains below Germany's if it shares a physician specialization with Switzerland (CH/CZ). Both Switzerland and Czech Republic benefit relatively more than Germany from physician specialization if we compare each country's selection probability to its status quo on the GER, CH and CZ axes. This result runs counter to Fig. 6.13 but all characteristics have been set to 0 and costs set to average and Switzerland benefits greatly from this equalization of treatment costs. Nevertheless, Germany's selection probability ranks far ahead of every other country if it shares a physician specialization with one or all of them.

6.3 Summary

Our interviews and our patient survey covered a large number of topics and provided invaluable insights into medical tourism in Germany. Among the vast amount of information obtained, our five main research questions stand out: First, all stakeholders point to personal networks, word-of-mouth and recommendations as important drivers of medical tourism and as sources of new customers. As suspected in Chaps. 2 and 4, the experiences of returning patients are overwhelmingly positive and we are thus confident that word-of-mouth is a substantial component of the lagged treatment flow effect in Chap. 4. We also discovered a presence of business and embassy networks in our interviews and lagged treatment flows probably capture their evolution as well. Patients confirm the role of personal networks and many of them travel to destinations recommended by their friends, families, relatives or personal doctors even if a small group of patients relies on autonomous information. A substantial number of patients can further obtain support from personal networks at their chosen destination, which may come in the form of organizational, emotional, logistic or indirect financial support by providing accommodation for accompanying persons, for example. This finding supports the results of Chap. 5 which found the spatial distribution of personal networks to determine destination choice.

Second, a number of additional drivers of medical tourism to Germany arise in both interviews and survey: our interview partners point out treatment quality as a main reason to seek treatment in Germany, which patients confirm in their ranking of both physician and hospital quality as the most important destination characteristics. This also confirms our findings in Chap. 5. The search of high-quality treatments that are sometimes unavailable at home distinguishes international patients in Germany from international patients in other countries who seek to benefit from lower prices or to circumvent waiting times at home (Pollard 2012). Facilitators point out geographic distance as an important limitation, which does not emerge in our interviews with German providers or in our patient survey. The larger growth of medical visas in more distant Russian locations in Sect. 2.2.2 supports a limited role of distance but a recent survey among Russian participants at the Moscow MedShow September 2015 finds that although 52% look for high treatment quality, 38% also care about distance and convenience of access (International Medical Travel Journal

2016). Overall, the role of geographic distance remains ambiguous but we suspect a geographic distance threshold for medical tourism that is beyond the perception of German providers and that does not show in our sample of patients who chose Germany as their destination.

We find two clusters of patients who value complementary services and comfort differently and our analysis hints to a culturally motivated appreciation of these destination characteristics. This finding is also in line with International Medical Travel Journal (2016), who report only 20% of the Russian survey participants to consider quality and range of complementary services. Unfortunately, our sample does not allow us to isolate this effect from household income or reimbursement schemes empirically but we find some evidence that patients from source regions with reimbursement schemes are not locked-in on Germany. This finding is supported by Noree et al. (2014) who report substantial numbers of Middle Eastern patients in Asia that undergo invasive procedures (NaRanong and NaRanong 2011). We thus maintain our assumption that an economic decision-making process governs destination choice. The lack of price data prevented us from explicitly investigating pricing in the two previous chapters but our interviews hint at price sensitivity with regard to exchange rates and to diminished price sensitivity among Middle Eastern patients. We suspect the latter to result from higher income levels, reimbursements or a particularly strong country-of-origin effect but our data set does not allow us to investigate the two former suspicions in more detail.

We obtain limited evidence from our interviews that the cultural imprint of a source country may have some effect on the incidence of treatment types. Our survey further indicates that a common spoken language is of little importance and thus extends our findings in Chap. 4 even if some interviews suggest otherwise. Finally, we find that approximately half of the patients have previous experiences with treatments abroad and patients have an inner locus of control, little home bias and high trust in providers outside their country of residence and in Germany in particular. These findings harden the evidence of a country-of-origin effect and a role of individual characteristics in choosing an international destination.

Third, our interviews point to a role of tourism for subgroups of outpatients who engage in post-treatment recovery or entertain their company. Unfortunately, our survey included too few outpatients so the views therein essentially reflect those of medical travelers. They are in line with our assumption in Chap. 2, i.e. treatment considerations dominate destination choice.

Fourth, stakeholders in our interviews consistently report Israel, Switzerland and Turkey as destinations in patients' real consideration sets. These destinations share a reputation of high-quality treatments and cultural proximity to source countries with Germany. In addition, facilitators also note destinations in Asia, which compete in geographic distance and price while maintaining high treatment quality. The patient survey supports these findings in terms of countries considered and adds a number of other Western destinations. However, less than half of the patients actually considered a country other than Germany and only about half of the patients considered more than one hospital in Germany even though we find no evidence of a lock-in effect due to financial support schemes. In short, there are preciously few signs of strong competition across destinations at the different levels of supply.

Fifth, our interviews produce inconsistent results with regard to the relevant level of supply in destination choice. However, the ranking exercise in our survey points to the importance of destination characteristics that capture both physician and hospital quality and the DCE carves out the strong country-of-origin effect for Germany that guides destination choice. In terms of average marginal effects, physician quality increases the selection probability of a destination more than hospital quality as measured by a quality certificate, whose average marginal effect ranks ahead of hospital size. This order of average marginal effects is remarkably robust across different destination countries and model specifications and we find no evidence of a diminished role of physician reputation in high-cost destinations (Alsharif et al. 2010). However, we do find evidence for considerable preference heterogeneity across individuals with respect to countries, physician quality and hospital quality. As a recurrent theme, cultural background explains a large share of heterogeneity. Patients from the Middle East and Eastern Europe/CIS differ substantially in their preferences for both countries and complementary services, but a strong preference for Germany is common to all patients. Our sample size precludes a more detailed investigation of income and reimbursements but we surmise that unobserved preference heterogeneity remains substantial due to the complex nature of a medical treatment (Fiebig et al. 2010). In fact, product complexity is also a compelling reason for the strong country-of-origin effect we observe, which can arise when there is little specific knowledge about a complex product (Mai 2011). The effect size of the country-of-origin effect is second only to physician quality in our DCE.

Finally, we note a number of issues that arose in this chapter and that deserve future attention: First, a larger sample is desirable to investigate the role of income and reimbursement in more detail. Second, we only investigated the stated role of provider characteristics for hospitals. Clinics or private practices would considerably enhance a future investigation as both destinations and sources of patients. Third, the DCE should be completed at destinations other than Germany or in source countries to capture the breadth of preference heterogeneity across international patients. This step also permits the estimation of country-of-origin effects for more destinations. Our investigation suffers from selection bias in that we only survey international patients who chose Germany. The results thus do not extend one-to-one to patients who selected other destinations. However, we did capture the stated preferences of real medical tourists as opposed to random individuals who are less likely to make realistic choices in a DCE. Fourth, friends and family turned out to be important providers of support at chosen destinations. They should be split into separate categories in future research and their specific support inquired. Fifth, both available support and recommendations are natural candidates to augment DCE alternatives in future research. Sixth, the signaling of treatment quality in medical tourism deserves more research. A quality certificate seems to be a natural indicator but our survey indicates that it may not be optimal. Unfortunately, no other indicator fits the bill and other measures such as complication rates or equipment quality are more difficult to communicate.

References

Adamowicz, W., Boxall, P., Williams, M., & Louviere, J. (1998). Stated preference approaches for measuring passive use values: Choice experiments and contingent valuation. *American Journal of Agricultural Economics, 80*, 64–75.

Alsharif, M. J., Labonte, R., & Lu, Z. (2010). Patients beyond borders: A study of medical tourists in four countries. *Global Social Policy, 10*, 315–335. https://doi.org/10.1177/1468018110380003.

Anderson, S. P., de Palma, A., & Thisse, J.-F. (1992). *Discrete Choice Theory of Product Differentiation*. Cambridge, MA: MIT Press.

Bhat, C. R. (1995). A heteroscedastic extreme value model of intercity travel mode choice. *Transportation Research Part B: Methodological, 29*, 471–483. https://doi.org/10.1016/0191-2615(95)00015-6.

Bliemer, M. C. J., & Rose, J. M. (2010). Construction of experimental designs for mixed logit models allowing for correlation across choice observations. *Transportation Research Part B: Methodological, 44*, 720–734. https://doi.org/10.1016/j.trb.2009.12.004.

Bliemer, M. C. J., Rose, J. M., & Hensher, D. A. (2009). Efficient stated choice experiments for estimating nested logit models. *Transportation Research Part B: Methodological, 43*, 19–35. https://doi.org/10.1016/j.trb.2008.05.008.

Boga, T. C., & Weiermair, K. (2011). Branding new services in health tourism. *Tourism Review, 66*, 90–106.

Boxall, P., Adamowicz, W. L., & Moon, A. (2009). Complexity in choice experiments: Choice of the status quo alternative and implications for welfare measurement. *Australian Journal of Agricultural and Resource Economics, 53*, 503–519. https://doi.org/10.1111/j.1467-8489.2009.00469.x.

Braun, A. (2014). How to get it – Gesundheitstourismus am Beispiel des Maximalversorgers Klinikum Stuttgart. Ravensburger Tourismustag 2014

Bunch, D. S., & Batsell, R. R. (1989). A Monte Carlo comparison of estimators for the multinomial logit model. *Journal of Marketing Research, 26*, 56–68.

Cheng, S.-H. (2004). Physician performance information and consumer choice: A survey of subjects with the freedom to choose between doctors. *Quality and Safety in Health Care, 13*, 98–101. https://doi.org/10.1136/qshc.2003.006981.

ChoiceMetrics. (2012). *Ngene user manual & reference guide*.

Dawes, J. (2008). Do data characteristics change according to the number of scale points used? *International Journal of Market Research, 50*, 61–77.

de Bekker-Grob, E. W., Hol, L., Donkers, B., van Dam, L., Habbema, J. D. F., van Leerdam, M. E., Kuipers, E. J., Essink-Bot, M.-L., & Steyerberg, E. W. (2010). Labeled versus unlabeled discrete choice experiments in health economics: An application to colorectal cancer screening. *Value Health, 13*, 315–323. https://doi.org/10.1111/j.1524-4733.2009.00670.x.

Fiebig, D. G., Keane, M. P., Louviere, J., & Wasi, N. (2010). The generalized multinomial logit model: Accounting for scale and coefficient heterogeneity. *Marketing Science, 29*, 393–421. https://doi.org/10.1287/mksc.1090.0508.

Finstad, K. A. (2010). Response interpolation and scale sensitivity: Evidence against 5-point scales. *Journal of Usability Studies, 5*, 104–110.

Gilmour, S. G., & Trinca, L. A. (2012). Optimum design of experiments for statistical inference. *Applied Statistics, 61*, 345–401.

Greene, W. H., & Hensher, D. A. (2003). A latent class model for discrete choice analysis: Contrasts with mixed logit. *Transportation Research Part B: Methodological, 37*, 681–698. https://doi.org/10.1016/S0191-2615(02)00046-2.

Hays, R. D., Bode, R., Rothrock, N., Riley, W., Cella, D., & Gershon, R. (2010). The impact of next and back buttons on time to complete and measurement reliability in computer-based surveys. *Quality of Life Research, 19*, 1181–1184. https://doi.org/10.1007/s11136-010-9682-9.

Hensher, D. A., Rose, J. M., & Greene, W. H. (2007). *Applied choice analysis: A primer* (3rd ed.). Cambridge: Cambridge University Press.

Hess, S., & Rose, J. M. (2009). Allowing for intra-respondent variations in coefficients estimated on repeated choice data. *Transportation Research Part B: Methodological, 43*, 708–719. https://doi.org/10.1016/j.trb.2009.01.007.

Hess, S., & Rose, J. M. (2012). Can scale and coefficient heterogeneity be separated in random coefficients models? *Transportation, 39*, 1225–1239. https://doi.org/10.1007/s11116-012-9394-9.

Hess, S., & Stathopoulos, A. (2013). A mixed random utility — Random regret model linking the choice of decision rule to latent character traits. *Journal of Choice Modelling, 9*, 27–38. https://doi.org/10.1016/j.jocm.2013.12.005.

Hess, S., & Train, K. (2017). Correlation and scale in mixed logit models. *Journal of Choice Modelling, 23*, 1–8. https://doi.org/10.1016/j.jocm.2017.03.001.

Hess, S., Rose, J. M., & Hensher, D. A. (2008). Asymmetric preference formation in willingness to pay estimates in discrete choice models. *Transportation Research Part E: Logistics and Transportation Review, 44*, 847–863. https://doi.org/10.1016/j.tre.2007.06.002.

Huber, J., & Zwerina, K. (1996). The Importance of utility balance in efficient choice designs. *Journal of Marketing Research, 33*, 307–317.

International Medical Travel Journal. (2016). *Medical tourism from Russia survey*. Accessed July 20, 2016, from https://www.imtj.com/news/medical-tourism-russia-survey/

Johnson, F. R., Lancsar, E., Marshall, D., Kilambi, V., Muhlbacher, A., Regier, D. A., Bresnahan, B. W., Kanninen, B., & Bridges, J. F. P. (2013). Constructing experimental designs for discrete-choice experiments: Report of the ISPOR conjoint analysis experimental design good research practices task force. *Value Health, 16*, 3–13. https://doi.org/10.1016/j.jval.2012.08.2223.

Jones, B., & Nachtsheim, C. J. (2011). Efficient designs with minimal aliasing. *Technometrics, 53*, 62–71. https://doi.org/10.1198/TECH.2010.09113.

Kahnemann, D., & Tversky, A. (1979). Prospect theory: An analysis of decision under risk. *Econometrica, 47*, 263–292.

Keane, M., & Wasi, N. (2012). Comparing alternative models of heterogeneity in consumer choice behavior. *Journal of Applied Econometrics*, 1018–1043. https://doi.org/10.1002/jae.2304.

Kessels, R., Groos, P., & Vandebroek, M. (2006). A comparison of criteria to design efficient choice experiments. *Journal of Marketing Research, 43*, 409–419.

Kuhfeld, W. F. (1997). *Efficient experimental designs using computerized searches* (Research Paper Series). Sawtooth Software.

Kuhfeld, W. F., Tobias, R. D., & Garrat, M. (1994). Efficient experimental design with marketing research applications. *Journal of Marketing Research, 31*, 545–557. https://doi.org/10.2307/3151882.

Lancsar, E., & Louviere, J. (2008). Conducting discrete choice experiments to inform healthcare decision making. *PharmacoEconomics, 26*, 661–677. https://doi.org/10.2165/00019053-200826080-00004.

Leong, W., & Hensher, D. A. (2012). Embedding multiple heuristics into choice models: An exploratory analysis. *Journal of Choice Modelling, 5*, 131–144. https://doi.org/10.1016/j.jocm.2013.03.001.

Leung, S.-O. (2011). A comparison of psychometric properties and normality in 4-, 5-, 6-, and 11-point Likert scales. *Journal of Social Service Research, 37*, 412–421. https://doi.org/10.1080/01488376.2011.580697.

Louviere, J. J., Meyer, R. J., Bunch, D. S., Carson, R., Dellaert, B., Hanemann, W. M., Hensher, D., & Irwin, J. (1999). Combining sources of preference data for modeling complex decision processes. *Marketing Letters, 10*, 205–217. https://doi.org/10.1023/A:1008050215270.

Louviere, J. J., Street, D., Carson, R., Ainslie, A., Deshazo, J. R., Cameron, T., Hensher, D., Kohn, R., & Marley, T. (2002). Dissecting the random component of utility. *Marketing Letters, 13*, 177–193.

Louviere, J. J., Hensher, D. A., Swait, J. D., & Adamowicz, W. (2007). *Stated choice methods: Analysis and applications* (5th ed.). Cambridge: Cambridge University Press.

Louviere, J. J., Street, D., Burgess, L., Wasi, N., Islam, T., & Marley, A. A. J. (2008). Modeling the choices of individual decision-makers by combining efficient choice experiment designs with extra preference information. *Journal of Choice Modelling, 1*, 128–164. https://doi.org/10.1016/S1755-5345(13)70025-3.

Lusk, J. L., & Norwood, F. B. (2005). Effect of experimental design on choice-based conjoint valuation estimates. *American Journal of Agricultural Economics, 87*, 771–785.

Maddala, G. S. (2008). *Limited-dependent and qualitative variables in econometrics. Econometric society monographs* (3rd ed.). Cambridge: Cambridge University Press.

Mai, R. (2011). Der Herkunftslandeffekt: Eine kritische Würdigung des State of the Art. *Journal Betriebswirtsch, 61*, 91–121. https://doi.org/10.1007/s11301-011-0075-0.

Mühlbacher, A. C., Zweifel, P., Kaczynski, A., & Johnson, F. R. (2016). Experimental measurement of preferences in health care using best-worst scaling (BWS): Theoretical and statistical issues. *Health Economics Review, 6*, 5. https://doi.org/10.1186/s13561-015-0077-z.

Musa, G., Doshi, D., Wong, K. M., & Thirumoorthy, T. (2012). How satisfied are inbound medical tourists in Malaysia?: A study on private hospitals in Kuala Lumpur. *Journal of Travel & Tourism Marketing, 29*, 629–646. https://doi.org/10.1080/10548408.2012.720150.

NaRanong, A., & NaRanong, V. (2011). The effects of medical tourism: Thailand's experience. *Bulletin of the World Health Organization, 89*, 336–344. https://doi.org/10.2471/BLT.09.072249.

Noree, T., Hanefeld, J., & Smith, R. (2014). UK medical tourists in Thailand: They are not who you think they are. *Global Health, 10*, 29. https://doi.org/10.1186/1744-8603-10-29.

Pinnell, J. (2005). *Comment on Huber: Practical suggestions for CBC studies* (Research Paper Series). Sawtooth Software.

Pollard, K. (2012). *The medical tourism survey 2012*. London: Intuition Communication Ltd.

Pollard, K. (2013). *Medical tourism climate survey 2013*. London: Intuition Communication Ltd.

Revelt, D., & Train, K. (2000). *Customer-specific taste parameters and mixed logit: Households' choice of electricity supplier* (Economics Working Papers). Berkeley, CA: University of California.

Rose, J. M., Hess, S., Bliemer, M. C. J., & Daly, A. (2009). *The impact of varying the number of repeated choice observations on the mixed multinomial logit model*. Noordwijkerhout: European Transport Conference.

Rose, J. M., Hess, S., & Collins, A. T. (2013). What if my model assumptions are wrong? The impact of non-standard behaviour on choice model estimation. *Journal of Transport Economics and Policy, 47*, 245–263.

Ryan, M., & Gerard, K. (2003). Using discrete choice experiments to value health care programmes: Current practice and future research reflections. *Applied Health Economics and Health Policy, 2*, 55–64.

Shobokshi, ObAM. (2014). Vortrag im Rahmen der Tagung "Gesundheitstourismus". Gesundheitstourismus, Klinikum Stuttgart, Germany

Siebertz, K., van Bebber, D., & Hochkirchen, T. (2010). *Statistische Versuchsplanung: Design of experiments (DOE), VDI-Buch* (1st ed.). Heidelberg: Springer.

Sonnier, G., Ainslie, A., & Otter, T. (2007). Heterogeneity distributions of willingness-to-pay in choice models. *Quantitative Marketing and Economics, 5*, 313–331. https://doi.org/10.1007/s11129-007-9024-6.

Swait, J., & Adamowicz, W. (2001). The influence of task complexity on consumer choice: A latent class model of decision strategy switching. *Journal of Consumer Research, 28*, 135–148. https://doi.org/10.1086/321952.

Train, K. (2009). *Discrete choice methods with simulation*. Cambridge: Cambridge University Press.

Train, K., & Weeks, M. (2005). Discrete choice models in preference space and willingness-to-pay space. In R. Scarpa & A. Alberini (Eds.), *Applications of simulation methods in environmental and resource economics* (Vol. 6, pp. 1–16). Berlin: Springer-Verlag.

Winkelmann, R., & Boes, S. (2009). *Analysis of microdata* (2nd ed.). Berlin: Springer.

Chapter 7
Connecting the Dots: Implications for Destinations and Policy Makers

We set out to conduct an empirical analysis of drivers of medical tourism to Germany with a focus on personal and informal networks. Our focus was motivated by Lunt et al. (2014a) and the notion that Germany must benefit from trust-enhancing and potentially cost-dampening channels as it attracts a substantial number of medical tourists without the low-cost strategy that is so ubiquitously offered in the medical tourism literature. In the course of the analysis, we made crucial contributions to the medical tourism research on various fronts including the development of a modeling framework and the organization of medical tourism drivers along multiple, systematically identified modeling dimensions therein; the empirical identification of true medical travelers; the empirical investigation of hypothesized key drivers in both unique and novel data sets; the identification of networks and their support functions; the investigation of supply side aggregation on destination choice; the discovery of real consideration sets; the segmentation of consumers; and a quantification of the investigated phenomena.

In Chap. 2, we defined medical tourism, discussed available data sets and surveyed the medical tourism literature to identify a large set of candidate drivers. We covered numerous fields of economic literature in large strides—medical tourism, international trade, tourism and marketing—to organize our set of candidate drivers and to assess the feasibility of empirical investigations into medical tourism given the available data in Chap. 3. We developed a modeling framework to frame our own empirical investigations in Chaps. 4, 5, 6 and 7 and to critically assess previous empirical forays into medical tourism.

In Chap. 4, we found strong evidence for the role of networks as captured by migrant stock. That role was confirmed in Chap. 5 and translated into networks of friends, family, physicians and employers in Chap. 6. Controlling for networks as measured by migrant stock, we found a strong positive effect of cultural proximity as measured by common native language at the country level in Chap. 4, which re-emerged as a country-of-origin effect in the explicit decision-making setting of Chap. 6. We also discovered a positive effect of lagged treatment flows in Chap. 4, which we could not ascribe unequivocally to the hypothesized word-of-mouth effect

K. Schmerler, *Medical Tourism in Germany*, Developments in Health Economics and Public Policy 13, https://doi.org/10.1007/978-3-030-03988-2_7

of patients returning to their source countries. However, both our interviews with facilitators and our patient survey in Chap. 6 confirmed the importance of word-of-mouth and recommendations from previous patients.

We found some evidence for a cluster of source countries that is characterized by large shares of elective treatments and that differed from Germany in religious imprints. Our analyses in Chaps. 2 and 6 showed that these source countries are heterogeneous in their specific religious affiliations and in other characteristics such as available reimbursement schemes, so our result is not religion-specific. With the opposite effect found by Esiyok et al. (2017) for similar source countries but a different destination, we surmised that the common religion effect is an artifact of unidirectional models that identifies source countries with poor domestic supply conditions for the treatments sought. Unfortunately, the lack of multilateral data precludes an in-depth analysis of religious ties.

In Chap. 4, we did not find the expected positive effect of a common spoken language on medical tourism flows. Chapter 6 revealed that interpreters are common for patients from the Middle East and that patients from Central Asia are less concerned with the medical staff's ability to speak English, so the benefits of a common spoken language appear to be rather small and this barrier to trade is quickly overcome in practice. We found moderate evidence for a squared effect of internet penetration in source countries that we suspect to capture economic and technological development rather than patients' access to and use of autonomous information. We did not expect patients who rely largely on autonomous information to contribute substantially to inbound medical travel, but our survey in Chap. 6 suggests that a moderate share of patients does fit this type. Overall, our findings explain why patients seek treatment in Germany as opposed to a culturally more distant destination, i.e. why fewer Russians travel to South Korea than one might anticipate, for example (Lunt et al. 2014b).

In addition to networks, cultural proximity and information channels, we investigated and quantified a number of other drivers of medical tourism at various levels. In Chap. 4, we found the expected effects of demand capacity, per capita dilution of demand capacity and the health expenditure structure of a source country. Chapter 5 documented the positive effect of perceived treatment quality at the hospital level as measured by a hospital's domestic catchment area and its status as a university hospital. Chapter 6 also underlined the importance of treatment quality as a driver measured at three different levels of supply: Aside from a pronounced base preference for Germany at the country level, physician quality turned out to be the strongest contributor to destination attractiveness while the impact of hospital characteristics ranked lower. In practice, both characteristics may be communicated jointly and we found, for example, a tenfold increase in medical travelers to German hospitals that signaled quality by a university association. We also found that stated preferences for some destination characteristics such as destination country and complementary services differed by individual characteristics, i.e. cultural background. We also confirmed the role of other individual characteristics such as a strong inner locus of control that characterize international patients. Unfortunately, data restrictions precluded the analysis of the full set of characteristics we inquired—including income.

What can we then learn from the German experience? We first note that Germany operates in a market for high-quality and high-cost destinations that serves international patients with and without reimbursement schemes. Perceived treatment quality thus turned out to be an unsurprisingly strong driver of destination choice but cultural proximity and networks also have a positive and significant effect on destination choice at all levels of empirical investigation. We conclude Germany's success as a destination to be difficult to emulate without similar networks and ties to designated source countries. The documented country-of-origin effect should also be difficult to reproduce and to overcome by new competitors. It is a key driver of destination choice at the country level that can overshadow and even invalidate drivers of domestic provider choice as consideration sets expand to international alternatives. A strong country-of-origin effect also has implications for an integration of health systems. It suggests that providers may struggle to overcome preconceived notions about a destination and that physician and hospital quality at a destination may be difficult to communicate. This could be offset by networks, however, which mirrored domestic catchment area as a purely domestic indicator of perceived treatment quality to international patients and thus enabled informed provider choices.

A country-of-origin effect also comes as a burden: Despite its subtle, non-intrusive nature with domestic production, foreign consumption and little public attention, inbound medical tourism faces risks from the political realm and can be very susceptible to macro-level developments. Political tensions or other industries can damage reputation at the country level and dry up inbound patient flows. Providers can increase their host countries' reputation stock as positive experiences are disseminated by networks and returning patients but they also find themselves at the mercy of domestic policy-makers. Foreign policies can be a similar threat and we have discussed how some source countries change reimbursement schemes, foster domestic competition or attempt to become medical tourism destinations of their own and invest substantial resources in centers of excellence such as Dubai Healthcare City. Several international chains, brands and teaching hospitals aim to establish themselves at these destinations and may constitute serious competition (Wright 2012). With a substantial share of Middle Eastern patients, Germany is quite susceptible to such policies even if stakeholders pointed out a majority of out-of-pocket payers. Our interviews have further shown that German providers may not be aware of all global competitors.

Our analysis was based on a high-cost and high-quality destination, but given the uncertainty surrounding the credence good that is a medical treatment, we expect our findings to hold for destinations that compete by using low-cost strategies as well, even if the magnitude of our effects may differ for these destinations. Germany's treatment portfolio is characterized by complex treatments for which trust is crucial in selecting a destination. We suspect less trust to be required for simpler treatments and thus smaller effect sizes of network ties. More generally, our empirical framework has carved out the various dimensions and potential drivers that allow countries and providers to find niches and to move to levels of disaggregation at which different drivers may become important. The product dimension, which offers a deep hierarchy of treatment types that may command different decision-making processes, lends itself to differentiation. Our distinction between inpatient and outpatient treatments is one possibility to differentiate along the product dimension. We focused on inpatients and confirmed their suspected focus on treatment-related destination characteristics but we also found that outpatients are a considerably larger group—with estimates of 40–80% based on medical visas and 70–80% based on interviews. Both inpatients and particularly outpatients thus offer ample opportunities to provide specialized treatments and that is something we do in fact observe with dental treatments in Hungary or fertility treatments in Spain. The small number of outpatients in our sample precluded a detailed investigation of their purpose of travel mix but our interviews provided at least some evidence of increased interest in recreation by outpatients that providers can cater to. We thus expect most outpatients to weigh destination characteristics differently which underlines the importance of our distinction between medical travelers and medical tourists and of our three-step approach to isolate medical travelers in Chap. 3. In fact, medical tourists may rely even more on personal networks than medical travelers despite less complex treatments as more private purposes of a trip factor into destination choice.

Our investigations suggest at least three important points to be taken into account by strategies that seek to actively develop a medical tourism destination: First, a destination's specific treatment portfolio needs to be delineated and decision-making processes corresponding to these treatments inferred. If non-medical purposes enter destination choice, these purposes must be addressed and catered to. Second, candidate source countries should be identified by multiple criteria including demand capacity (average and distribution), treatment quality, availability (waiting times, legislation) and incidence of medical conditions. Third, cultural ties with source countries should be considered and existing networks identified and tapped. The need for networks depends on the treatment portfolio and may be different for elective outpatient treatments whose destination choice is driven by cost savings. It is unlikely to be irrelevant, however.

Even if inbound medical tourism is not explicitly fostered, policies and domestic provision have indirect effects on medical tourism and public opinion: The acceptance of medical tourism is important for both source and destination countries and hinges on the domestic availability of health care services. Some incarnations of medical tourism such as transplant or circumvention tourism are typically opposed, but the public may disapprove even of legal treatments if they involve countries that trigger concerns about access of and benefits to local patients. We presented some evidence of access and equality issues in destination countries but a causal link to medical tourism is difficult to establish. Examples demonstrated that medical tourism sometimes set in after a health care system had already developed into tiers or in the aftermath of larger crises that left providers struggling for patients, so the counterfactual of medical tourism, i.e. an absence of inbound medical tourists, might only exacerbate the availability of health care in destination countries. Cohen (2011) notes that several of the feared side effects of medical tourism are within the control of governments in destination countries: Germany both requires and provides universal health care coverage and hospitals serve both the publicly and privately insured using the same facilities. Waiting times are comparatively short and there exist in fact much-lamented excess capacities for inpatient care so access and distributional concerns can be addressed in principle. Brain drain, i.e. the tapping of supply of medical staff in source countries, is another public risk that is sometimes associated with medical tourism. However, brain drain is unlikely to be initiated by medical tourism. We found of little importance the medical staff's ability to command a patient's mother tongue while receiving a treatment from a German doctor ranked substantially higher, so providers have no incentive to bring in physicians from patients' source countries to attract medical tourists specifically. This is not to deny the existence of brain drain and its associated problems but this development is unlikely to be driven by medical tourism.

Finally, public risks of outbound travel can be more difficult to control. There are multiple risks in the private domain (Hall 2011) and many of them, such as quality or continuity of care, have public counterparts. However, there has been little public ambition to act in the areas of accreditation/signaling, biosecurity, malpractice or continuity of care via record release or follow-up treatments. The same holds for consumer protection issues such as an imbalanced presentation of treatment risks and benefits, disguised commercial intentions or marketing-induced demand for unnecessary elective treatments (Lunt and Carrera 2011). Measures to foster medical tourism via insurance portability or harmonized licensing requirements are not a priority either even if the European Union has taken a first step with its EU directive (European Union 2011). Some insurers actively deal with medical tourism (Klusen et al. 2011; Rosenmöller et al. 2006) but, overall, a stronger integration of European health care systems is currently not on the agenda. Some developments in the public domain such as electronic patient records have been heralded as potential game changers (Pollard 2013) but there is no evidence of their effectiveness. Key technical challenges such as international insurance coverage and continuity-of-care remain and our research casts doubts on the possibility to compensate the trust induced by personal networks with technical features.

Despite the numerous, valuable insights we have produced and confirmed, there is substantial scope for more research: The country-of-origin effect deserves much more attention and should be tested against other concepts such as country-of-design or brand. We currently do not know the isolated effects on destination choice of the place of treatment delivery, country affiliation of a hospital and brand affiliation of a hospital, and expect their impacts to differ (Godey et al. 2012). The answer will greatly determine if the mode of delivery requires patients to travel or if reputation transfers to a foreign commercial presence and treatments can be rendered in source countries. Our exploratory patient survey should further be replicated at other destinations to obtain country-of-origin effects for patients who choose other countries with, ideally, similar treatment portfolios. This would also help assess the selection bias that any single-country survey suffers from.

Another important research avenue is trade-offs between the identified key drivers. The extent to which macro developments can be offset by treatment quality signals or network ties remains an open research question at this point. The distance-quality trade-off also remains to be quantified. While patients undoubtedly overcome geographical distance in search of treatment quality, the precise trade-off cannot be estimated with our data: In Chap. 5 we have variation in perceived treatment quality across destinations, but cannot identify the effect of geographical distance and in Chap. 4 we find a negative and significant effect of geographical distance on destination choice, but lack available measures of treatment quality in source countries. Of utmost interest is further the relative importance of the country-of-origin effect when recommendations are issued, i.e. if personal destination recommendations outweigh country reputation and quality signals as determinants of destination choice. Related to recommendations is the role of returning patients and how quickly medical tourism can be developed by relying on word-of-mouth from satisfied returning patients. Studies by Musa et al. (2012) and Manaf et al. (2015) find medical staff quality and hospital facilities to be determining factors of overall satisfaction and future intention to revisit. However, it is unclear if a focus on these factors is sufficient to induce recommendations and to overcome a potential deficit in migrant stock or reputation at the country level. The absence of cost-reducing and trust-inducing migrant stock or a weak country-of-origin effect may prevent the rapid success of medical tourism strategies at the provider level.

Another interesting development is the implementation of online platforms that seek to establish price transparency and to benefit from both direct and indirect network effects. Most platforms have not enjoyed lasting success and our research gives an indication of the reason: Personal networks produce trust which is difficult to imitate on organized exchanges. Online platforms produce awareness, contribute to price transparency and have developed schemes to communicate self-reported or certified quality but we see their key challenge in the lack of credence and accountability compared to personal recommendations. However, the comparison of personal recommendations and user reviews on online platforms is an interesting avenue for further research even if neither may be valid measures of actual physician quality (Daskivich et al. 2018). In fact, it would be informative to know if treatment quality in source countries is objectively poor or merely perceived to be of poorer quality than in Germany.

A final interesting field of research is the modeling of economic choices in medical tourism. We augmented the structural gravity model by Anderson and van Wincoop (2003), which assumed a one-stage decision-making model in Chap. 4. Upon completion of our work, we recommend the incorporation of the following insights in future modeling: There is not much evidence of competition at different levels of supply as postulated by the structural models underlying trade theory. We found evidence of some competition since main source countries for Germany also lie in the catchment area of Asian destinations—the cradle of medical tourism—but real consideration sets turned out to be much smaller than anticipated. Most patients considered very few countries and hospitals as destinations. We found some institutionalized relations at the government and employer level, i.e. institutional distortions of destination choice even at the international level, but there was no evidence of a lock-in effect and patients with access to reimbursement schemes considered destinations other than Germany and can be observed to select them (Noree et al. 2014; Whittaker 2015). In summary, patients have access to multiple destinations in principle, but consider very few.

We thus suspect some value in modeling an explicit two-stage process as opposed to the consolidated one-stage process we assumed in Sect. 4.1. A heteronomous first stage establishes consideration sets that are shaped by personal networks and returning patients, which act as sources of information. Domestic availability and quality would be additional factors that determine the propensity to engage in the research of autonomous information or may prevent such research. A second stage then determines destination choice at which a country-of-origin effect reduces uncertainty and networks provide local support, reduce costs and also reduce uncertainty. Helpman et al. (2008) offer a two-stage supply side model and Chaney (2013) developed a complex model whose central determinant is the net growth rate of a supplier network. This model is intriguing in that it acknowledges the importance of knowledge about an option or a business partner and the customer search is a passive process. A two-stage supply side process is plausible in established markets where firms actively engage in customer acquisition, however, medical tourism is far less organized and quite informal so a consumer network theory is a more appropriate basis for economic modeling. The development of a structural two-stage demand side model is thus a promising endeavor for future research. Empirical specifications that extend gravity models by a zero-inflated component, for example, have been proposed (Burger et al. 2009; Staub and Winkelmann 2012) but the underlying theoretic structure to motivate multiple processes or a specific two-stage process remains to be developed.

Finally, more data is required to obtain effect estimates that we can generalize to different contexts with more confidence. Common native language, for example, is a bilateral measure but we cannot assess the symmetry of its estimated effect in a unidirectional setting nor can we predict the magnitude of the effect in a more cost-focused setting. The availability of multilateral data is thus of utmost priority for further investigations—no small order given the requirements of suitable data set we have outlined.

References

Anderson, J. E., & van Wincoop, E. (2003). Gravity with gravitas: A solution to the border puzzle. *The American Economic Review, 93*, 170–190.

Burger, M. J., van Oort, F., & Linders, G.-J. (2009). On the specification of the gravity model of trade: Zeros, excess zeros and zero-inflated estimation. *Spatial Economic Analysis, 4*, 167–190.

Chaney, T. (2013). *The gravity equation in international trade: An explanation* (NBER Working Paper Series 19285). National Bureau of Economic Research.

Cohen, I. G. (2011). Medical tourism, access to health care, and global justice. *Virginia Journal of International Law, 52*, 1–56.

Daskivich, T. J., Houman, J., Fuller, G., Black, J. T., Kim, H. L., & Spiegel, B. (2018). Online physician ratings fail to predict actual performance on measures of quality, value, and peer

review. *Journal of the American Medical Informatics Association, 25*(4), 401–407. https://doi.org/10.1093/jamia/ocx083.
Esiyok, B., Çakar, M., & Kurtulmuşoğlu, F. B. (2017). The effect of cultural distance on medical tourism. *Journal of Destination Marketing & Management, 6*, 66–75. https://doi.org/10.1016/j.jdmm.2016.03.001.
European Union. (2011). Directive 2011/24/EU of the European Parliament and of the Council of 9 March 2011 on the application of patients' rights in cross-border healthcare.
Godey, B., Pederzoli, D., Aiello, G., Donvito, R., Chan, P., Oh, H., Singh, R., Skorobogatykh, I. I., Tsuchiya, J., & Weitz, B. (2012). Brand and country-of-origin effect on consumers' decision to purchase luxury products. *Journal of Business Research, 65*, 1461–1470. https://doi.org/10.1016/j.jbusres.2011.10.012.
Hall, C. M. (2011). Health and medical tourism: A kill or cure for global public health? *Tourism Review, 66*, 4–15. https://doi.org/10.1108/16605371111127198.
Helpman, E., Melitz, M., & Rubinstein, Y. (2008). Estimating trade flows: Trading partners and trading volumes. *Quarterly Journal of Economics, 123*, 441–487. https://doi.org/10.1162/qjec.2008.123.2.441.
Klusen, N., Verheyen, F., & Wagner, C. (Eds.). (2011). *England and Germany in Europe: What lessons can we learn from each other?* (Vol. 32, 1st ed.). European Health Care Conference 2011, Beiträge zum Gesundheitsmanagement. Baden-Baden: Nomos-Verl.-Ges.
Lunt, N., & Carrera, P. (2011). Systematic review of web sites for prospective medical tourists. *Tourism Review, 66*, 57–67.
Lunt, N., Smith, R. D., Mannion, R., Green, S. T., Exworthy, M., Hanefeld, J., Horsfall, D., Machin, L., & King, H. (2014a). Implications for the NHS of inward and outward medical tourism: A policy and economic analysis using literature review and mixed-methods approaches. *Health Services and Delivery Research, 2*. https://doi.org/10.3310/hsdr02020.
Lunt, N., Jin, K. N., Horsfall, D., & Hanefeld, J. (2014b). Insights on medical tourism: Markets as networks and the role of strong ties. *Korean Social Science Journal, 41*, 19–37. https://doi.org/10.1007/s40483-014-0012-7.
Manaf, N. H. A., Hussin, H., Kassim, P. N. J., Alavi, R., & Dahari, Z. (2015). Medical tourism service quality: Finally some empirical findings. *Total Quality Management & Business Excellence, 26*, 1017–1028. https://doi.org/10.1080/14783363.2015.1068597.
Musa, G., Doshi, D., Wong, K. M., & Thirumoorthy, T. (2012). How satisfied are inbound medical tourists in Malaysia? A study on private hospitals in Kuala Lumpur. *Journal of Travel & Tourism Marketing, 29*, 629–646. https://doi.org/10.1080/10548408.2012.720150.
Noree, T., Hanefeld, J., & Smith, R. (2014). UK medical tourists in Thailand: They are not who you think they are. *Globalization and Health, 10*, 29. https://doi.org/10.1186/1744-8603-10-29.
Pollard, K. (2013). *Medical tourism climate survey 2013*. London: Intuition Communication Ltd.
Rosenmöller, M., McKee, M., & Baeten, R. (2006). *Patient mobility in the European Union: Learning from experience*. Copenhagen: World Health Organization, Regional Office for Europe.
Staub, K. E., & Winkelmann, R. (2012). Consistent estimation of zero-inflated count models. *Health Economics, 22*, 673–686. https://doi.org/10.1002/hec.2844.
Whittaker, A. (2015). 'Outsourced' patients and their companions: Stories from forced medical travellers. *Global Public Health, 10*, 485–500. https://doi.org/10.1080/17441692.2014.998696.
Wright, O. (2012). *Global network of NHS hospitals to exploit brand: Services to be sold to the Gulf, Brazil, India and China*. Independent 2012.

The manufacturer's authorised representative in the EU is Springer Nature Customer Service Centre GmbH, Europaplatz 3, 69115 Heidelberg, Germany. If you have any concerns regarding our products, please contact ProductSafety@springernature.com

Printed and bound by CPI Group (UK) Ltd, Croydon, CR0 4YY
05/10/2026
02228146-0001